# BTEC National Early Years

Sandy Green

Published in 2002 by:
Nelson Thornes Ltd
Delta Place
27 Bath Road
CHELTENHAM
GL53 7TH
United Kingdom

02 03 04 05 06 / 10 9 8 7 6 5 4 3 2 1

A catalogue record for this book is available from the British Library.

ISBN 0 7487 6164 0

Illustrations by Jane Bottomley; Angela Lumley; Oxford Designers and
Illustrators
Typeset by Northern Phototypesetting Co. Ltd, Bolton

Printed and bound in Great Britain by Scotprint

# Contents

# Introduction

The BTec National in Early Years is a course of study involving a considerable breadth of knowledge and understanding of early years care and education. To cover all the contents of the mandatory units would involve a publication ten times the size of this book. I have therefore elected to introduce as many aspects of the course specifications as the confines of one book allow.

There are cross-references between chapters throughout the book, demonstrating how the subject areas link together. Suggestions for further reading are given in the chapters, indicated by an icon, and a more detailed bibliography and list of suggested further reading is included at the end of chapters. This additional reading is essential if you are aiming to achieve the higher grades.

At the end of each chapter is a list of key terms. These terms are printed in bold in the text on the first occasion they are used and their definitions can be found in the *Glossary*. *Test Yourself* sections are interspersed throughout to help consolidate your learning as you move through your course of study.

Chapter 1, Professional/Vocational Practice establishes the importance of professionalism and its impact on early years care and education.

# About the Author

Sandy Green qualified as a nursery nurse in the early 1970s. She has a broad knowledge and experience of early years education and care, entering teaching in the late 1980s. Sandy co-ordinated the BTec National Diploma in Early Years course and the CACHE ADCE for several years, recently leaving her post in further education to work as an early years consultant and freelance trainer. She is also an external verifier for Edexcel.

# Acknowledgements

I would like to express my thanks to my husband John for his continuous encouragement throughout the writing of this book. Also to Jeanne Smith and Caroline Trow who have patiently reviewed the book during its preparation. I would like also to acknowledge how valuable I have found the interest and support given to me by my friends and colleagues over the past year, particularly Lorna Boyd, Sally Foster and Heather Richardson.

*Sandy Green*

The author and publishers would also like to thank the following for permission to reproduce photographs and other material:
Allyn and Bacon, Coeliac UK, Harcourt Publishers Ltd, Hodder and Stoughton Ltd, Open University Press, Scholastic Publications, Sound Learning, The Stationery Office

**Photo credits**
Billy Ridgers/Team Video, p. 82, Medipics, pp. 199, 200; Digital Vision (NT), p. 240; Bob Watkins/Photovision, p. 459

Every effort has been made to contact copyright holders, and we apologise if any have been overlooked.

# 1 Professional/ Vocational Practice

This chapter covers:

- Expectations of a professional carer
- Relating in a professional manner
- The individual needs of the child
- Responding appropriately
- Stimulating learning environments
- Strategies for supporting children and their families
- Evaluating your own practice.

## Introduction

The term 'professional practice' describes the practical working life of any professional person. Being **professional** is to be competent, efficient and skilled in your work and appropriately qualified to carry it out. When you come into contact with professionals such as teachers or doctors, you probably have certain expectations of them and how they do their job that make them professional. You will be striving to gain this sense of professionalism yourself as you work towards your qualification.

Another term, **vocational**, is also regularly used in the care sector. 'Vocational' means learning through practical experience as well as theory. The BTec National Diploma in Early Years is a recognised vocational qualification for anyone working with children from birth to eight years of age. It gives what is often referred to as 'qualified status', and as the full eighteen-unit diploma it is a level 3 qualification on the UK government's National Framework. Holders of both the National Diploma (Professional Practice Unit) and the National Certificate (Vocational Practice Unit) can follow careers in education, in social services and in the health sector, including both statutory and private employment, and also with voluntary and charitable bodies. The BTec National Certificate does not, however, have qualified status in the same way.

This chapter is designed to help you achieve the core skills, attributes and competencies that are needed by everyone who works within the field of early years and which make up the professional outcomes required for Unit 6. In order to meet them, you must learn to:
- observe and **identify** the individual **needs** of children appropriate to the requirements of the setting

- respond appropriately to the needs of individual children
- promote a safe, healthy and secure childcare environment, appropriate to the individual needs of children
- promote a stimulating learning environment for children's development
- demonstrate workplace expectations of a professional carer
- explore personal effectiveness as a worker in the early years service and evaluate your own performance
- contribute to a range of methods which support parents and carers with their parenting.

The **evidence** you will need to provide will mostly be gathered from your placement experiences, building it up gradually as you progress through the course. You will present it in the form of a **professional practice log** and will include evidence of how you can:

- observe and identify the individual needs of the child, appropriate to their age and the requirements of the setting
- relate the needs of the child to their level of development and recognise influencing factors
- respond to the needs of individual children
- plan and carry out activities to promote the development of children appropriate to their needs
- respond to the importance of a safe and secure environment for children's well-being
- meet the professional requirements and expectations of the sector and the workplace
- contribute to providing a stimulating learning environment
- respond to children, parents and colleagues in a professional manner
- respect the contribution and knowledge of parents and other professionals
- review and reflect on your own practice
- prepare and maintain a personal development plan
- acknowledge parents as the primary carers and educators of their children
- recognise and value diverse parenting styles, cultures and beliefs
- support all work with reference to significant concepts, principles and theories.

The knowledge, understanding and practical application which **underpins** (supports) your professional practice will be presented both orally and in writing, and observed within practice in your placement.

Opportunities have been incorporated throughout the book for you to explore your individual development. These opportunities have been clearly signposted, using the following headings:

- *Activity*, where you can explore a practical example
- *Professional practice*, which highlights particular examples of professionalism relevant to the topic being discussed
- *Test yourself*, where you can review your progress
- *Key terms*, at the end of each chapter, which identifies all the terms you should have learned
- *Bibliography and Suggested further reading*, to broaden your understanding of the subject areas.

The assessment evidence for the professional practice outcomes makes up your professional practice log and is likely to include:

- setting out a diary, in which you record both regular and new experiences within your placement
- producing an observation file, using the range of observations techniques set out in Chapter 9, *Human Growth and Development*
- planning, implementing and recording a range of assessed tasks, set by your tutors or placement supervisor
- completing studies of children's development, of specified ages set by your tutor.

The log will link both directly and indiretly to the range of core and specialist units you undertake during your course.

## Expectations of a professional carer

Placement experience is built into all BTec National Early Years programmes, usually soon after the start of the course. Preparation for placement usually takes place during the course induction period. A diploma student needs a minimum of 800 hours of assessed placement experience, and a certificate student a minimum of 400 hours. It is important that placements are arranged well in advance to ensure that you can maximise the time available to you. Some colleges have placement officers who take on this responsibility for you, while in other colleges, you will be asked to arrange a placement for yourself. If you leave this important arrangement until the last minute, you will have less choice of suitable placements and possibly a less satisfactory placement experience.

In each placement there will usually be a member of staff allocated as the student supervisor. This person's role is to help you gain as much from your placement experience as possible. Together with other staff, your supervisor will try to make you feel comfortable in the setting, but will also expect you to be responsive and willing to learn. Most members of staff will have been students at some point in their lives and will understand the importance of a good supportive environment in which to develop your practical skills and to build on your understanding.

The student supervisor's role is to help you gain as much from your placement experience as possible

## Professionalism

Professionalism brings with it expectations. The checklists below and opposite can be used as starting points for considering what will be expected of you in each placement setting you attend.

---

**Checklist: what do you need to know?**

Before your first placement day, you will need to know:

✔ What is the address and telephone number of the setting?
✔ What time do you need to arrive and leave?
✔ Who do you report to?
✔ Who will be your placement supervisor?
✔ Are there any dress codes?
✔ Meal-time requirements: are students expected to eat with the children?
✔ Do you need to pay for meals, coffee, etc?
✔ Is there an information booklet about the setting you can read in advance?

---

These are practical, easy-to-answer questions. A visit to the setting or a telephone call before you begin your placement will enable you to arrive on your first day feeling confident. Some placement settings have special requirements and it is important that they are clarified in advance. Whenever possible, visit the placement in advance, as this demonstrates commitment and can be helpful for both you and the staff to put a face to a name. It can also give you an opportunity to discuss what will be expected of you.

**Activity**

Merryfields Day Nursery sends students the following dress code before they start their placement experience with them. Discuss it with others in your group.

---

**MERRYFIELDS DAY NURSERY**
**Staff Dress Code**

Whilst at Merryfields Day Nursery you are politely requested to comply with the following:

**Staff and students will ...**
• wear tidy trousers or skirts
• wear low heeled shoes
• wear plain rings and small earrings
• always be clean and tidy

---

- keep hair tied back
- keep nails short.

**Staff and students will not ...**
- wear jeans
- wear untidy clothes at any time
- wear heavy make up
- wear excessive jewellery
- have visible body piercings.

Thank you

1 Explain why the above requirements are both acceptable and important.
2 Do you disagree with any of them? If you do, why is this? Discuss your reservations with other students. What do they think?
3 What else would you add to the lists?

Just as you need information before starting at a new setting, it is useful for the setting to know something about you and your needs. This will help them make your induction and subsequent placement time with them as useful and enjoyable as possible.

**Checklist: what does the placement need to know?**

The setting will need the following information about you before you start the placement:

✔ your course details and placement paperwork
✔ your college address and telephone number
✔ the name of your placement tutor/course tutor
✔ your home contact number
✔ emergency contact details
✔ details of any relevant medical information (allergies, asthma, epilepsy, etc.)
✔ an outline of your previous experience (if any).

The first day in any placement can be quite daunting, and it helps if you enter with a smile. It can give you an air of confidence (even if you do not feel it) and encourages others to respond to you positively. The staff will probably remember what it was like to be very new and unsure. They will not expect you to know everything, or remember everything straightaway. The diagrams on pages 6 and 7 summarise what will be expected of you.

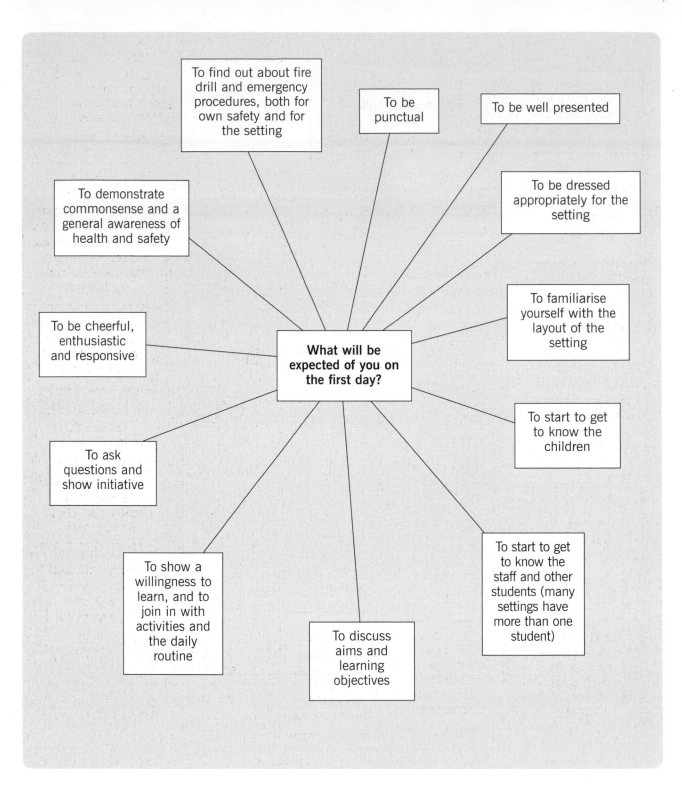

To find out about fire drill and emergency procedures, both for own safety and for the setting

To be punctual

To be well presented

To demonstrate commonsense and a general awareness of health and safety

To be dressed appropriately for the setting

To be cheerful, enthusiastic and responsive

**What will be expected of you on the first day?**

To familiarise yourself with the layout of the setting

To start to get to know the children

To ask questions and show initiative

To show a willingness to learn, and to join in with activities and the daily routine

To discuss aims and learning objectives

To start to get to know the staff and other students (many settings have more than one student)

Professional expectations: the first day of a placement

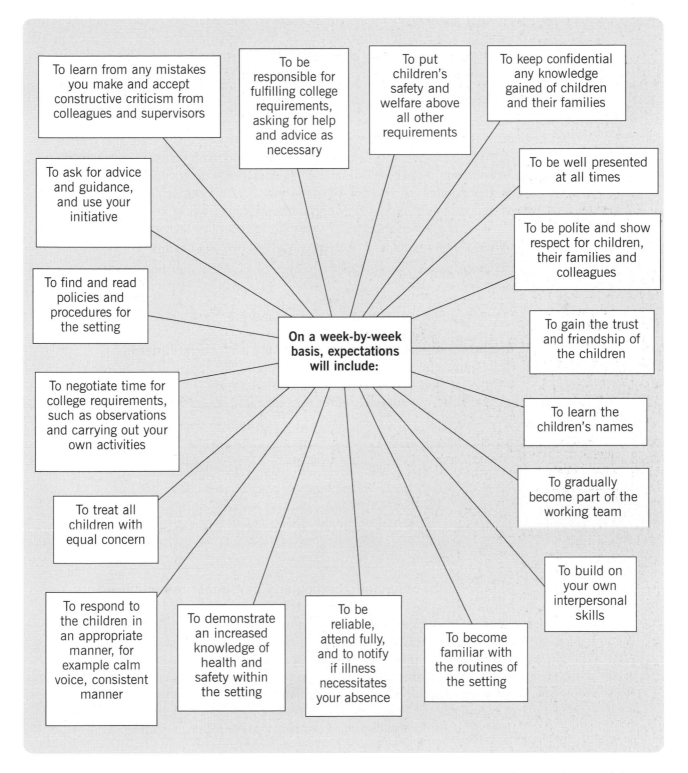

To learn from any mistakes you make and accept constructive criticism from colleagues and supervisors

To be responsible for fulfilling college requirements, asking for help and advice as necessary

To put children's safety and welfare above all other requirements

To keep confidential any knowledge gained of children and their families

To ask for advice and guidance, and use your initiative

To be well presented at all times

To find and read policies and procedures for the setting

To be polite and show respect for children, their families and colleagues

**On a week-by-week basis, expectations will include:**

To gain the trust and friendship of the children

To negotiate time for college requirements, such as observations and carrying out your own activities

To learn the children's names

To gradually become part of the working team

To treat all children with equal concern

To build on your own interpersonal skills

To respond to the children in an appropriate manner, for example calm voice, consistent manner

To demonstrate an increased knowledge of health and safety within the setting

To be reliable, attend fully, and to notify if illness necessitates your absence

To become familiar with the routines of the setting

Professional expectations: week-by-week

Follow these guidelines and ensure that you understand why each point is important. This will give you a good start in developing yourself as a professional, helping you gain, and maintain, confidence in yourself.

**Professional Practice**

To be professional is to reflect on your working practice, your level of training and the subsequent responsibility of your current role. As a professional or trainee within the field of early years you will be expected to conform to a range of expectations. These will be dependant upon your status (student, nursery nurse, deputy manager and so on) within the setting. Many of these expectations will be assessed during your training, and will continue to be refined once you have qualified. Most aspects of professionalism will directly affect your working practice, with some having a considerable impact on how you are judged by others.

Let us examine these professional expectations in more detail.

### Attendance and punctuality, reliability and commitment

Children need stability and routine in order to feel secure in their environment. A member of staff who is unreliable, or who regularly has time off work unnecessarily, can adversely affect this. It is an important point to consider.

**Activity**

1 How do you think having unreliable staff in a setting might affect the children?
2 How might it affect the working environment in general?
3 How might it affect the individual as an early years professional?
4 Discuss your thoughts with others before moving on to the next activity.

### Standards of behaviour, particularly personal presentation and hygiene

Children learn by example, and as individuals we are judged initially by what people see (their first impressions of us). Having a student or member of staff who is not well presented or who behaves inappropriately is unacceptable, and may have a detrimental effect on the working environment. This does not mean, however, that individual expression cannot be allowed, as sometimes our feelings of confidence are linked to how we feel we look, but each of us as individuals needs to consider the impact of our personal contribution to the overall setting.

**Activity**

1 Consider what you feel would be acceptable and unacceptable expressions of personality in an early years setting. Think also how behaviour impacts on working practice.

2 Why/how are children likely to be affected by inappropriate behaviour?
3 Why might negative dress or behaviour of a staff member affect the working environment in general?
4 How might they affect that individual as an early years professional?

## Maintenance of own safety

Although the managers of any setting hold overall responsibility for the safety of the working environment, staff and students have a responsibility for their own individual safety, taking into account commonsense decisions and the needs of the setting. Each individual is expected to identify and address any safety issues as they occur and is expected to work both safely and sensibly at all times. Commonsense decisions may be needed in a variety of situations, for example, if:

- an accident occurs
- the potential for an accident is identified
- health and safety precautions are lacking
- exposure to infectious material is a possibility
- you are faced with aggressive or violent behaviour
- you are being subjected to verbal abuse.

**Activity**

1 What does the term 'personal safety' mean to you?
2 Draw up a list of where you might need to be responsible for your own safety in college, in your placement and whilst travelling to and from each of them.

## Interpersonal skills

Expectations are made of you according to your role or position, but at times parents may mis-identify your role, expecting more of you than you are able to give them. The ability to interact and communicate on different levels is important and you will develop your own style of **communication**, within an ethos of courtesy, consistency and appropriateness. Your communication style will be one of the main aspects of your **interpersonal skills**. It will be part of what enables you to relate to and empathise with others. Good interpersonal skills are a crucial aspect of working with other people.

 FORWARD to Chapter 3 for a more indepth discussion of interpersonal skills.

## Confidentiality

Each setting will keep records of the children in its care. These records are private, and any information you are given, or you hear about, should be considered as strictly confidential. You will be expected to refrain from sharing anything with other people at home or in a social situation. This is all part of being professional.

At times it may feel appropriate to refer to something from your placement in a class discussion led by your tutor. This should only take place if you are certain that no individuals can be identified, or that the information you are sharing in no way contravenes the **confidentiality** of your placement setting. The same approach applies to your professional practice log. You will need to give evidence of your dealings with children, parents and staff in your professional practice log, but it should not be possible for them to be identified by the reader, even your tutor. It can be permissible to use initials, or sometimes a first name, but be aware of how much more easily some names are identified than others.

**Case Studies**

*Colleen*

Colleen has recently started a placement in a local authority nursery. A child in the nursery lives near to her home and Colleen had often thought the child looked poorly and undernourished and her own mother had commented on this too. Colleen has now discovered that the child has a place in the nursery due to her parents' difficulties with the responsibility of parenting. The child has been neglected and always eats ravenously whilst at nursery. The family are regularly visited by a family support worker.

1 If you were Colleen, would you pass this information on to your mother?
2 Would you discuss the case in college?
3 What are the confidentiality issues here?

*Briony*

Briony overhears a parent from the nursery where she is on placement gossiping in the supermarket queue about another parent's discipline methods. The parent concerned tried to draw Briony into the conversation as she checked through her shopping.

1 How should Briony respond?
2 Should Briony do anything about this afterwards?
3 What are the confidentiality issues here?

**Activity**

Are there any circumstances in which you would consider it permissible to pass on information that you have overheard or received, even by such unconventional means as Briony did? Discuss this question with other students.

**Professional Practice**  Any child protection issues that you become aware of should never be kept to yourself. If you have a concern, or you overhear comments that concern you, you should ask to speak to your supervisor, the manager of the setting, or your college tutor. If no cause for concern is found, no harm will have been done. Your supervisor (or tutor) will be pleased that you have used your initiative and discussed your concerns appropriately. If the concern is subsequently substantiated, your actions will be proof in itself of the importance of speaking up. Delays or reluctance to talk about concerns can potentially lead to further harm for a child.

▶▶  FORWARD to Chapter 6, page 222, for more about confidentiality.

# Relating in a professional manner

### Range of contacts

**Professional Practice**  In considering interpersonal skills, you will need to consider the range of people you will interact with as an early years professional. Think about the expectations and demands that are likely to be made of you.

**Activity**

1  Draw up a list of the expectations you think each of the groups listed below may have of early years professionals. Consider the contact an early years professional would usually have with each group:
   a) children
   b) parents
   c) peers
   d) other adults
   e) professionals within the immediate setting
   f) professionals outside of the immediate setting.

2  Discuss and collate your ideas within your group. Consider the questions below and compare your outcomes with those of other groups.
   a) Which do you agree with?
   b) Are there any that you do not agree with?
   c) Why is that?
   d) Justify your reasons with your peers.

### Children's expectations

Very young children are non-judgemental. They will like you for yourself. It does not matter if you cannot sing in tune, build a good model or catch a ball properly. They will simply expect you to play with them, give them your time, talk to them and be interested in what they do. Slightly older children will also enjoy having your time and attention. They may already have built up ideas about adult capabilities and may expect all adults to have the same level of skills and knowledge. At times they may expect more from you than you are able to give them.

1 How might you respond if a child demands answers or a demonstration from you that you cannot deliver?
2 How could you deal such a situation?
3 Where would you turn for advice when you feel out of your depth?
4 How difficult would you find it to acknowledge that you need help?
5 Do you think the age of the child would make any difference?

**Professional Practice**

- Patience and clear explanations are needed in these circumstances.
- There is no need to feel shame or embarrassment in admitting that you do not know something.
- Always remember that older children may be able to demonstrate a skill or introduce new knowledge to you.
- Being ready to accept and show interest in what a child can teach you may enhance your relationship with that child still further.

*Remember!* The age of the child is not the main factor here. The child's level of understanding and ability should be the main criteria in determining your responses.

### Parents' expectations

Parents put their trust in the staff at their child's nursery, pre-school or school. The staff are caring for their most precious possession, their child. Parents expect staff to have a good standard of behaviour, to adhere to equal opportunities and to be both reliable and conscientious. Parents want to see evidence that care is taken of their child in a safe and stimulating environment, and that you enjoy working with their child. They will expect to be kept informed about their child's progress and that someone will have time to discuss their child with them on a regular basis. This would usually be the child's key worker. Parents expect staff to be knowledgeable about early years issues and may from time to time ask questions about their child's health and development. Parents will not always understand the difference between the qualification levels and it is important that staff realise this and know how to respond to the situation positively, guiding the parent to someone more appropriate, whilst maintaining their faith in them as a staff member in their current role.

Parents put their trust in the staff at their child's nursery, pre-school or school

Draw up a list of staff members in your current placement.
a) Who would each staff member be most likely turn to for advice?
b) To whom would they refer a parent for general advice?
c) To whom would they refer a parent in the case of a complaint or serious concern?
d) What level of qualifications and experience has each staff member?
e) How relevant are your answers to (d) in relation to your answers to (a), (b) and (c)? Why?

### Colleagues' expectations

Colleagues within the setting will expect you to contribute to discussion and the planning of the environment. They will expect knowledge evidence appropriate to the level of your training, qualification and experience, and the ability to put it into practice. There will be an expectation that if you take on a team role, you will be able to fulfil it. Time is in short supply in early years settings and no one will be happy with a team member who does not contribute fully. It is always important that you are honest about your ability and level of understanding before taking on extra responsibilities.

1 Why is it important to be honest about your ability and level of understanding?
2 As a student, in what ways could withholding concerns about the ability to cope affect placement experience?
3 How might this affect the overall professional development of a student or newly qualified staff member?
4 What might be the effect on the placement?

**Professional Practice**

If you pretend to have knowledge and understanding when you do not, you could put children at risk, through lack of awareness, lack of supervision, or by necessitating additional staff input, taking them away from where they should be. It could also lower your self-esteem and lose you the respect of your colleagues.

### Other adults' expectations

Support staff play an important role in the running of any setting. They have a right to be treated with the same level of consideration as qualified staff and be consulted about any changes that involves their contribution to the running of the day. For example, changes to times of a meal or snacks to incorporate a specific point of interest or activity. It is important to remember that although some staff may not hold the same qualification as yourself, or have no formal training at all, they may well have years of experience. Everyone has a role to play and should be valued as part of the team.

**Activity**

1 Draw up a list of support roles that may be found within early years settings.
2 Consider the impact of not having staff specifically carrying out these roles.
3 How might your current role be affected?

### Expectations of professionals within and outside the setting

Many different professionals work within early years settings, including those who are permanently employed, some who visit occasionally and those who have a peripatetic role, visiting the setting at a specified, regular time. These include:
- health visitors
- educational psychologists
- speech therapists
- social workers
- play therapists
- physiotherapists
- music therapists
- Portage workers
- family support workers.

Each of these professionals works with specific client groups. They may be linked through the primary health care team, through the local social services departments or through the local education authority. Support may be offered on a daily or weekly basis for some children, and through regular ongoing programmes for others. Some children will be individually supported alongside the others, within the main room of the setting, while other children will be given one-to-one support in an alternative room or quiet area. The only expectation made of you by the professionals will be to support the child(ren) in continuing with any programme set by them.

**Case Studies**

Consider the following case studies. What forms of evidence do you think would have been relevant in supporting the need for professional intervention in each of them?

Exploring these case studies will help you identify how much you already know about evidence-gathering and also of the role of other professionals. You may find it helpful to refer to other chapters of this book, together with other reading sources for further information.

### Liam

Liam is almost four years old. He has cerebral palsy, affecting both his motor skills and his language skills. He currently has support from three of the professionals listed above.

1  Who do you consider Liam is most likely to receive support from? Why?
2  Compare your answer with another student.

### Katya

Katya is three. She is a very quiet child who will not interact with other children. Katya's home life includes a history of violence.

1  Who might be supporting Katya at the moment? Why?
2  Compare your answer with another student.

### Siobhan

Siobhan is five. She has a very limited concentration span and displays disruptive behaviour most days in the Reception class she attends. Siobhan has support from two of the professionals listed on page 14.

1  Who might these be? What support would they be likely to give?
2  Compare your answer with another student.

**Professional Practice**

Can you think of a child currently having professional support in your placement? Who is supporting them and why? Is this support being successful? What evidence has been used to support the need for professional intervention?

Issues of confidentiality will be relevant here (see page 10).

### Respect for knowledge and contributions of others

The breadth of staff experience, both professional and from life in general, contributes to the richness of most early years settings. Students and newly qualified staff are encouraged to observe carefully the ways of their more experienced colleagues. Different ways of doing things are not necessarily right or wrong, simply different. Your attitude to the viewpoints of others is an important part of your professionalism; it should be positive and welcoming. Diversity of opinion, language, culture and religion should be celebrated as a strength of the setting. Staff, students, children and their parents should benefit from this as it helps to broaden knowledge and understanding of people and the issues of society.

Without **equality** of opportunity for all children and their families, an early years setting will not be meeting the needs of all client groups. Equality means not simply treating everyone the same, but giving them the same opportunities, taking into account their differences and differing levels of need.

### Range of issues to be considered

All books, posters, games, puzzles, toys and similar resources should be carefully evaluated for the positive (or negative) images they portray. Those considered to offer negative images should be removed and replaced with more positive materials when funds allow. There is no benefit to having a large range of resources if they include negative images. The children will not benefit from them and may absorb the wrong messages. It is far better to have a smaller range which will enhance children's understanding of equality, be it gender, race or disability.

Toys should be evaluated for the images they convey

### Positive/negative effects of language and labelling

It is important that you use language appropriately. Take note of how colleagues address children and their parents, and value the diversity of the languages spoken within your setting. Encourage children to use their heritage language as well as the language they mostly use to communicate in the setting. Settings can demonstrate to families that their language is valued by translating notices appropriately. Asking parents to help with the translations will also demonstrate value of their involvement as well.

**Activity**

It can be useful to carry out an audit of provisions in your setting. This involves looking carefully at the materials and activities offered and making a judgement on their suitability. Ask yourself the following questions:

1 Is the range of books, toys, posters, and so on, adequate?
2 Do they cover a broad enough range?
3 Are all the activities and equipment suitable?
4 Do any of them promote unacceptable images?
5 Who you should talk to if you have identified any negativity?

FORWARD to Chapter 2, page 56 for further discussion of the importance of diversity.

For further reading on equal opportunities refer to Malik (1998) – see *Bibliography and suggested further reading*, page 54.

### Your own role within a team

In any setting, it is the staff team as a whole who make the setting successful, and this teamwork should not be underestimated. Each individual will have their own role to play, but no single person can carry the full weight of responsibility or organisation, although clearly the nursery owner and/or manager holds ultimate responsibility for the safety, smooth running and standards met within the setting. As individuals, staff and students need to consider their place within the staff team, reflecting on how well they co-operate with each other, how flexible they are willing (and able) to be, and whether they are using their skills and abilities appropriately. Clearly it does not make sense for someone who is good at carrying ideas through to completion to be involved only in the suggestions or planning stage of a project. Most settings have regular planning meetings to which staff contribute ideas and decide who will take on what responsibility. Identifying what your strengths are and where you best fit into a team will enable you to work within your capabilities and help you feel valued as a person.

Sadek and Sadek (1996) set out the characteristics of a team as follows:

'In any organisation a good team will:
• work together
• share a common aim
• co-operate with each other
• share/communicate/support between its members
• have motivation for the task in hand
• have catalytic relationships so that new ideas are extended
• be committed to the task and the team
• be comprised of members who each understand their own role in the team and are reliable in it
• complete the task.'

Some staff members work better together than others; that is human nature. There should be opportunities for internal movement of roles and responsibilities in order to ensure the greatest level of cohesive teamwork.

# The individual needs of the child

Children develop at different rates within a professionally agreed set of developmental parameters, often referred to as the developmental 'norms'. In order to understand the current stage in development of any child, you need to understand these parameters and what influences them.

▶▶▶ FORWARD to Chapter 9, page 360 for discussion of how children develop and for charts setting out the average development of children at various stages.

The underpinning knowledge and understanding set out in Chapter 9 will enable you to focus on your current role as a student and how you can support the individual needs of a child or group of children appropriately in practical everyday situations.

The term **developmentally appropriate** is a significant one. It is rare to find a child who develops according to the norms in all developmental areas. It is therefore important to accommodate the advances and delays in individual children when you plan activities or give them instructions. Taking their developmental level into account regarding the responses you expect from them is equally important.

It is important to remember that growth and development are very different.
- *Growth* refers to the measurable elements of how children change, for example their height and weight.
- *Development* refers to the stages of change in a child, recognising that although each stage may be reached at slightly different ages, they are usually reached in the same order. For example, the action of walking is mastered before the more complex actions of hopping, skipping and controlled running.

*Remember!* At times a tall, large framed child may appear older than their actual age and some people will have greater expectations of their ability and behaviour because of this. Similarly, less may be expected of a small petite child. These examples show why understanding the difference between growth and development is important.

## Observation

In order to understand the needs of the children in your care, you will use **observation skills**. These are an important aspect of your early years training. To complete BTec National courses in early years successfully, you will need to provide evidence of your ability to monitor and plan for children's individual needs through the use of observation.

There are many different ways of observing children, with some methods being more appropriate to certain situations than others. As a student you will be asked to carry out a range of appropriate observations, building up a portfolio throughout your programme of study which will be assessed by your tutors. This observation portfolio is likely to include some or all of the following observation methods:
- the written record
- target child
- baby study
- child study
- movement and flow chart
- time sampling
- checklist.

FORWARD to Chapter 9, page 405, where methods for observing children are discussed and examples of each of the above methods are provided.

# Specific needs that affect the rate of development

Before considering how best the developmental needs of children can be met, we need to look at what influences development and what early years professionals can do to enhance this.

### Factors affecting development

**Activity**

Look at the range of factors that affect development set out in the diagram below. Copy and complete the spidergram, adding any other factors you can think of. Compare your ideas with another student. You will probably find that the factors can be grouped into a few main headings

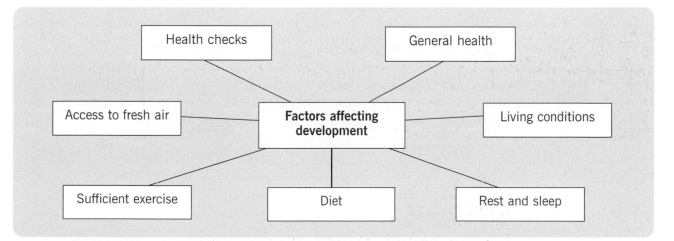

The World Health Organisation (WHO) stated in 1946 that:

'Health is the state of complete physical, mental and social well-being, not merely the absence of disease and infirmity.'

Their definition has been updated to include a more general description:

'The enjoyment of the highest attainable standard of health is one of the fundamental rights of every human being without distinction of race, religion, political belief, economic or social condition …'

**Activity**

In a group, discuss how a child might be affected if any of the factors in the spidergram on page 19 are unavailable or insufficient. How do these factors fit in with the aims of the WHO? Research health literature for examples to support your answer.

 FORWARD to Chapter 10, page 431, for further information on health.

Opportunities for healthy development are based on good health, physical care and emotional well-being. The nutritional requirements for the growth, maintenance and development of the body are found in the food that we eat, helping us maintain and repair our body tissues, and keeping muscles and organs functioning. Food helps to prevent infection and supplies the body with its energy needs too. A balanced diet contains a range of vitamins and minerals and is divided into four main food groups.

 FORWARD to Chapter 7, page 264, for information on nutrition and dietary needs.

Together with a balanced diet, children need to be in full health in order to achieve their potential. To monitor a child's health, health professionals carry out routine examinations, assessments and immunisations. Children need to feel cared for and loved unconditionally and have sufficient fresh air and opportunities for exercise, rest and activity. They need protection from harm and they need security. Without the right balance of these, a child's health and development is likely to suffer. As an early years professional, you will be one of many adults who play a role in the well-being and development of children. You will also be a role model for children, as they develop their own attitudes towards health choices.

**Activity**

1 Who else would you consider as being influential regarding children's health choices and attitudes?
2 In what ways do you consider they have influence? Discuss your thoughts with others in your group

## Identified needs

Identifying the needs of a child involves carefully considering each aspect of their current level of development. This may involve identifying where they are placed on development charts, how they interact within the setting, how they manage to communicate or what limitations they currently face in everyday activities. Once a

child's particular needs have been identified, the appropriate professional intervention and support can be arranged. This may include:
- strategies for **behaviour management**
- encouragement of physical skills, either general or specific
- emotional support
- encouragement to socially interact
- supporting cultural differences.

### Strategies for behaviour management

Managing behaviour is based upon setting clear goals and boundaries. Each setting will have statements, policies and codes of practice to ensure a consistent approach by all staff. These will cover expectations regarding behaviour, reward systems and managing the settling-in process.

 FORWARD to Chapter 7, page 281, where behaviour management is discussed.

**Professional Practice**
Before turning to Chapter 7, think about how you have managed unacceptable behaviour, or have seen it managed. How successful was this?

### Encouragement of physical skills

A child's individual physical needs will be met by evaluating their current level of development, together with their main interests. Large motor skills activities are easily supported outside in dry weather, but more initiative is needed within the confines of a small room. Fine motor skills can be developed anywhere, involving both domestic and learning activities.

**Activity**

Considering the general physical development of children aged around three years, plan three ideas to support large motor skills development indoors, and three ideas to support fine motor skills.

### Emotional support

A withdrawn or unhappy child may need additional adult support; the insecure child may need additional reassurance and sensitive settling-in, involving both the parent and the professional.

 FORWARD to Chapter 9, page 366, *Emotional development of children*.

### Encouragement to socially interact

A child who has not learned to share, to interact with others or to respond appropriately to social situations may need adult involvement to help them find their way. The role models of other children will help, along with adult encouragement and support, giving praise when acceptable socialising takes place and clear explanations when it does not.

FORWARD to Chapter 7, page 278, *Setting goals and boundaries in early years settings*, and Chapter 9, page 372, *Social development of children*.

**Professional Practice**

Have you seen an example of adult intervention in the socialising of young children?

Why was this taking place, do you think?

How helpful was the adult's involvement?

Was there an alternative approach, do you think? If yes, what might it have been?

### Supporting cultural differences

A child's culture is important to them as an individual, and important to the setting which they attend too. Enabling a child to take part in and benefit from all opportunities within the setting may on occasions mean a slight adjustment is needed to ensure that the child's cultural requirements are fully acknowledged. For example, staff need to ensure that they are not excluding individuals by assuming that all children have the same day-to-day experiences.

*Remember !*

It is important that cultural issues of diet and health care are taken into consideration as well as aspects of resources, equipment and communication.

## Codes of practice in childcare settings

Each setting will have its own codes of practice and will serve a range of client groups. As a student, it will be useful to gather information on the codes of practice, statements and policies of each setting you attend as placement experience.

**Activity**

Settings also have policies and statements covering behaviour, disability, child protection and equal opportunities. Some will of course have many more. This is an example of good professional practice.

1 Draw up a list of the main points you consider should be included in policies for each of the areas listed above.
2 Explore your ideas with another student.
3 As a pair, compare your combined ideas to real examples, obtained from your placements.
4 How well did you do?

# Responding appropriately

Part of the role of a professional early years worker is to respond to children in an appropriate manner. This includes providing appropriately stimulating activities in socially appropriate circumstances. The use of positive body language, voice intonation and eye contact is essential, to ensure that each child feels focused upon and valued.

In supporting the provision of a setting when on placement, you will be expected to plan and implement a range of stimulating activities appropriate to the needs of the children. When working with older, pre-school age groups, plans will need to be linked to the **Foundation Stage Curriculum**, set up by the Department of Education and Skills' Qualifications and Curriculum Authority (QCA) in 2000. This curriculum is divided into six areas of learning. In primary schools plans will need to work within the framework of *both* the Foundation Stage Curriculum, for children in Reception classes, and the National Curriculum for children in Years 1 and 2. The six main areas of learning that make up the Foundation Stage Curriculum (Early Learning Goals) are:
- personal, social and emotional development
- communication, language and literacy
- mathematical development
- knowledge and understanding of the world
- creative development
- physical development.

## Activity

The Department of Education and Skills has published its aims for the Foundation Stage and these are set out below. You will need to become familiar with them.

As you read the aims, make notes on how you could best support the children within your current setting, including both activities and general approaches. Use the subheadings in bold type as your prompts.

Photocopiable charts for this activity can be found in the *BTec National Early Years Tutor Resource Pack*. Your tutor will be able to tell you if these are available in your college.

When you have completed the task, discuss your notes within your group and add to your notes as necessary.

### Department of Education and Skills aims for the Foundation Stage

'The curriculum for the foundation stage should underpin all future learning by supporting, fostering, promoting and developing children's:

**Personal, social and emotional well-being:** in particular by supporting the transition to and between settings, promoting an inclusive ethos and providing opportunities for each child to become a valued member of that group and community so that a strong self-image and self-esteem are promoted;

**Positive attitudes and dispositions towards their learning:** in particular an enthusiasm for knowledge and learning and a confidence in their ability to be successful learners;

**Social skills:** in particular by providing opportunities that enable them to learn how to cooperate and work harmoniously alongside and with each other and to listen to each other;

**Language and communication:** with opportunities for all children to talk and communicate in a widening range of situations, to respond to adults and to each other, to practise and extend the range of vocabulary and communication skills they use and to listen carefully;

**Reading and writing:** with opportunities for all children to explore, enjoy, learn about and use words and text in a broad range of contexts and to experience a rich variety of books;

**Mathematics:** with opportunities for all children to develop their understanding of number, measurement, pattern, shape and space by providing a broad range of contexts in which they can explore, enjoy, learn, practise and talk about them;

**Knowledge and understanding of the world:** with opportunities for all children to solve problems, make decisions, experiment, predict, plan and question in a variety of contexts, and to explore and find out about their environment and people and places that have significance in their lives;

**Physical development:** with opportunities for all children to develop and practise their fine and gross motor skills and to increase their understanding of how their bodies work and what they need to do to be healthy and safe;

**Creative development:** with opportunities for all children to explore and share their thoughts, ideas and feelings through a variety of art, design and technology, music, movement, dance and imaginative and role play activities.'

Qualifications and Curriculum Authority (2000)

**Professional Practice**

The previous activity should have produced a considerable list of activities and situations. To consolidate your knowledge and understanding of development still further, discuss your findings in the context of SIMPLE (Social development, Intellectual development, Moral development, Physical development, Language development and Emotional development).

How do your outcomes compare with the outlines of the developmental areas as described in Chapter 9, page 360–402.

# Promoting and supporting development

### Social development

Socially, children need to develop confidence in themselves and be able to make and sustain friendships; they need to understand the ways of others and to value the differences between themselves and their peers. Within our democratic society we all need to conform to some basic rules. These too have to be learned, enabling us to respect the needs of others, to win and lose gracefully and to behave appropriately in whatever circumstances we find ourselves.

The role of the adult in helping and supporting social development is at times one of mediator, helping children to learn to share through the use of games, books and discussion, encouraging turn-taking and the apportioning of materials in play. Adults also have a responsibility to introduce new experiences, such as cultural events and religious festivals, to enhance learning and to help avoid the development of prejudice.

### Intellectual development

Intellectually, the need to achieve high academic standards is emphasised in today's society. In early years this does not mean a formal education, but rather, through:

'developing key learning skills such as listening, speaking, concentration, persistence and learning to work together and co-operate with other children.'

Hodge (2000)

All of this can be achieved through play, upholding the guidance set out by the Plowden Report in 1967, which gave 'central status' to the role of play in the education of young children.

Undoubtedly children need opportunities to explore within their play, using all of their senses. They need opportunities to conserve, to measure, to estimate, to predict. They need activities designed for understanding concepts such as volume, capacity, weight and length, but perhaps most of all children need opportunities to develop thinking skills and the power of concentration.

Opportunities for conserving, measuring and estimating occur naturally in many activities

The role of the adult in helping and supporting intellectual development can be as generalised as the setting-out of stimulating materials and activities, and as specific as noting when to intervene in the experiential process in order to enhance learning. The psychologist Lev Vygotsky (1896–1935) called this intervention the 'Zone of Proximal Development' (ZPD). As you develop your observation skills you will increasingly develop your understanding of when it is appropriate to join in with a child's play in order to enrich the learning process. This is a skill which develops over time and will be an important aspect of your professional practice.

FORWARD to Chapter 8 for a discussion of learning; more about Lev Vygotsky can be found on page 301 of that chapter.

## Activity

Joelene is aged three years and three months. She is struggling to complete a twelve-piece jigsaw puzzle. She is randomly trying to put it together.

1 At what stage would you become involved?
2 How would you approach this?
3 How might your approach differ with a child of a different age or at a different stage of development?

### Moral development

Moral development links closely with social development. A child's understanding of socially-acceptable behaviour is vital to building successful relationships. Issues of sharing and the development of understanding what is right and wrong are important, and are helped by having well-defined boundaries within the setting, together with a positive approach to addressing any problems that arise. Valuing other cultures and religions is particularly important in a multicultural society, equality needing to be both recognised and respected. Learning self-value helps us cope with peer pressure, to stand firm and maintain our beliefs and moral conduct.

The task of the professional adult in helping and supporting moral development is as a role model, and by setting clear boundaries regarding what is acceptable within the setting and what is not. It is also important that the adults within the setting are prepared to challenge unacceptable actions or discussion, both with the children and with other adults.

Careful planning is needed to ensure that all children have sufficient, and equal, access to each type of activity

## Physical development

Through play children develop physically. Powers of co-ordination are practised, with movement and games helping to extend large motor skills, and fine motor skills being enhanced by more dexterous activities. Physical exercise helps to build strength, and will add to general health. Children who live in cramped conditions, or who have little access to outside play at home, benefit in particular from opportunities to exercise their bodies through play, with spatial awareness developing through co-ordinated movement activities using large motor skills.

The role of the adult in helping and supporting physical development is often one of innovation. It can be easy to provide plenty of opportunities for large motor skills play on a fine day when there is a safe outdoor playing area, but more imagination is needed to encourage the use of these skills indoors. The use of drama, dance and exercise is important, as too are activities for encouraging the fine skills in children with limited dexterity or concentration spans. Careful planning is needed to ensure that all children have sufficient, and equal, access to each type of activity.

## Language development

Linguistically, the most important gift you can give to a child is your time. The role of the adult in helping and supporting language development is one of conversation, of supplying opportunities to use literature, and also to write using a variety of mediums. Children ideally need to be surrounded by language from birth. They need to be both spoken to and listened to. They need to be encouraged to talk, to discuss what they are doing and what they have done already. Opportunities to write can be found within imaginative play, with appropriate props being supplied to enhance the shop, cafe, and so on, that the children are enjoying. Familiar articles, pictures and objects can be labelled to help make links between spoken and written language.

Language is our main means of communication, without which it is less easy to express ourselves or make our needs known. The development of spoken language enables a child to describe and to explain, and offers opportunities to question and to clarify instructions, therefore furthering their opportunities for learning.

Children need to be surrounded by language, for example, in the role-play area, so they gain an understanding of the purpose of reading

### Emotional development

Children need opportunities to come to terms with their feelings, which may at times be confusing, upsetting or even frightening. This is all part of emotional development. They need to be reassured that it is alright to have negative feelings, such as jealousy and anger, and to be helped to learn how to manage these feelings. It is important, also, that they understand that others, adults included, have these feelings too.

A child suffering emotional stress is less likely to be as receptive to learning as one who is emotionally stable. Common family events, for example moving house, starting nursery or the arrival of a new baby, are all potentially disturbing situations. As an early years professional, you will need to offer opportunities for children to work through their concerns and problems in a safe environment.

The role of the adult in helping and supporting emotional development is one of observation and empathy, supporting the child in their anxiety and providing a range of opportunities through play, books and discussion (and at times puppets) to help them work through their feelings. Self-esteem can be closely associated with emotional stability, and you can probably think of situations where you have been made to feel unvalued. This no doubt impacted on your sense of self-worth, even if only temporarily. It can, however, potentially have an effect both in the short-term and in the long-term. Self-esteem can be boosted through the use of circle time.

**Activity**

You have been asked by your tutor to plan activities for the children in your placement. Work with a partner: one of you is currently on placement in a day nursery with the two- to three-year-olds; the other is working in a Reception class of a primary school.

Select three activities from the list below, linking them to a theme of your choice. Write plans for each activity, showing how the activities can be differentiated for the two age groups.

Activities:
Communication
Printing
Model making
Collage
Malleable play
Music activities
Interest table
Technology
Construction
Books and stories
Imaginative play
Natural play materials

A sample planning sheet can be found in the *BTec National Early Years Tutor Resource Pack*. Your tutor will be able to tell you if these are available in your college. Or you may prefer to use the planning sheet you are familiar with from your placement.

## Types of resources available

Resources available in early years settings can be described as either **human resources** or **physical resources**. It is important that consideration is given to what resources are available within the setting itself and what is available in the wider community. This will ensure that the talents and experience of the staff are fully utilised, and that the children are able to benefit from the facilities and other individuals that are available locally too.

### Human resources

The human resources within the setting itself consist of the staff, students and, possibly, parent-helpers. Jointly they are likely to have an array of experience and talent. Good teamwork will enable this talent and experience to benefit the children by encouraging individuals to share their expertise and further individual staff members' development.

From the wider community, human resources will include visitors, for example dental hygienists, police officers, road safety officers. Visits to shops or to a local farm, for example, will enable children to interact with a range of adults in their natural working environments.

**Activity**

1  What specific talent, skill or experience do you consider you bring to your current setting?
2  Do you have 'hidden talents'?
3  In what ways have you shared your skills with others?
4  Has anyone shared a new skill with you?
5  How might this be encouraged?
6  What wider community involvement have you experienced?

From the wider community visitors might include, for example, police officers

### Physical resources

The physical resources within the setting consist of the activities and equipment that are available, together with the space used for play, both indoors and outdoors. In a school, there are likely to be additional spaces that can be utilised, such as a hall, library or technology room.

In the wider community, there are a vast array of physical resources available to early years staff. As already mentioned, you could visit a shop or a farm, or you could simply go to the park, on a nature ramble, or a 'listening' walk. Each of these will open up additional avenues for exploration, discussion and learning.

**Activity**

1  How well is the physical environment in your current setting being used?
2  Are areas being under-used, or not being used in the most logical way?
3  What would you change if you had the opportunity?
4  With whom would you need to discuss this?
5  Make notes of any ideas you have for using physical resources in the wider community.

**Professional Practice**

Drawing a plan of your current setting, and adding your comments and suggestions for change could form part of your professional practice log, evidencing your understanding of responding to the needs of children and contributing to the provision of a stimulating environment.

*Remember!*  Any planning needs to take into consideration the impact on all concerned, in terms of safety, staffing, policies on permission, for example.

Physical resources in the wider community can be enjoyed simply by taking a walk

## Health and safety issues within the setting

Health and safety awareness is crucial in all settings and, in order to comply with standard requirements, it is important that all those involved are clear as to what is meant by the term 'health and safety'. Each adult working in the field of early years care and education has a responsibility to ensure that children are protected from hazards and infection whilst in their care. This applies to daily activities, visits outside of the setting, and whilst travelling with children. Every setting must have a qualified first aider present, and colleges offering BTec Nationals in Early Years include a first aid qualification as part of the course.

FORWARD to Chapter 5 for further discussion of health and safety issues.

Without the security of knowing that their child will be safe, most parents would not leave them in the care of your setting. Issues of health and safety in early years settings can be divided into three areas:
- supervision
- safe use of equipment
- procedures and policies.

Every adult working in early years care has a responsibility for the children in their care

**Activity**

1 What aspects of health and safety are relevant to your current setting?
2 Compare your setting with the settings of other members of your group. How do they differ?
3 What are the common factors between them all?
4 Copy the table below and place each health and safety issue discussed by your group into the appropriate column or columns (some may need to go in more than one).

| Supervision | Safe use of equipment | Procedures and policies |
| --- | --- | --- |
|  |  |  |

**Remember!**

Consider the following questions about each health and safety area:

- **Supervision**
  Who is responsible for watching or observing children at rest or during an activity?
- **Safe use of equipment**
  Who carries out safety checks?
  How often does this take place?
  Who sets out the equipment on a day-to-day basis?
  What negotiation is there regarding positioning and use of equipment?
- **Procedures and policies**
  Who writes them?
  What do they cover?
  Who has access to them?
  Who has 'ownership' of them?
  Where are they kept?
  How often are they updated?

**Professional Practice**

Your table for the activity above, once checked and agreed with your tutor or placement supervisor, will serve as useful reference for the future.

**Case Study**

*Donna and Marlene*

Donna and Marlene are planning a display about 'Autumn' with a group of Reception class children. They have selected a range of books and posters and have collected a variety of cones, leaves, berries and plants. Their aim is for the children to go to the park to enjoy a walk, collecting more autumn objects, and make bark rubbings from the trees to add further interest to their display.

1 What arrangements do they need to make in advance?
2 What health and safety issues can you think of related to these ideas?
3 What else could they include to extend the topic further?

*Remember !*  Remember to keep in mind the three main areas of health and safety.

What health and safety issues need to be considered when taking children outside the setting?

### The contribution of safety and security in the well-being of children

For children to reach their developmental potential, they need opportunities. Much of this will involve activities that need boundaries. For example, learning to climb needs an adult on hand to guide on limitations, and learning to cook needs adult guidance and support regarding the use of sharp implements and heat. Setting boundaries, taking into account the developmental stage of the child or children concerned, is a vital contribution to their overall safety and security, whilst enhancing their development.

### The importance of personal hygiene, cleanliness and sterilisation of equipment

Working with children involves being in constant close contact with others, both adults and children. Personal hygiene is therefore extremely important. Attention to personal hygiene procedures gives a positive role model for children to learn from, and ensures that staff smell fresh and pleasant as they carry out personal care routines where they are appropriate.

The sterilisation of equipment for babies is crucial to ensure the control of potential bacterial infection and all equipment needs to be washed regularly to prevent cross-infection. All childcare workers need to be aware of the signs of infestations, for example headlice and threadworms.

▶▶ FORWARD to Chapter 5 for a discussion of the main issues of health, safety and hygiene, and to Chapter 10, page 469 for the identification of signs and symptoms of illness and infestation.

*Remember !*    Settings should have procedures for recording when and how cleaning processes have taken place, and who was responsible for checking them. Ask to see an example of this at your placement.

**Professional Practice**

In each placement, it is important that you know the answers to the following questions. This is part of taking responsibility for your **personal safety**.

- What are the fire drill procedures for the setting?
- What is the health and safety policy?
- Who are the first aiders?
- Where is the accident book kept? Who writes in it?
- What is in the first aid box? Where is it? Who is allowed access to it?
- What is the procedure if a child becomes ill?
- When and how should equipment and furniture be cleaned? By whom?
- What happens if unplanned visitors arrive?

If you are not yet confident that you have this information in your current placement, it is important that you ask your placement supervisor.

## Routines and procedures of settings

All staff need to be aware of the routines and procedures for the setting in which they work. Changes to these need to be agreed in advance, and all staff, students and any parent-helpers need to be kept informed. Although routine is needed in order to provide security for the children and to avoid chaos or confusion, it should not be so rigid that it cannot embrace the flexibility needed for staff and children to enjoy spontaneous experience or opportunities. There needs to be a balance.

**Professional Practice**

Think about the routine in your current setting. How rigid or flexible is it? How well do you think it meets the needs of the children and the requirements of the curriculum? Does the balance need adjusting?

**Activity**

1 Make a note of the main elements of the daily/weekly routine in your placement. How does this compare to the routine of a similar setting? Discuss this with another member of your group.
2 What changes would you make if you had the opportunity?
3 How would you justify the changes you suggest?

# Stimulating learning environments

Children learn through stimulus. The verb 'to **stimulate**' means to encourage, to inspire or to act as an incentive. This refers not only to the provision of activities, but to the ways in which you interact with children, the use of body language, making eye-contact, and the giving of encouraging looks and smiles. Early years professionals need to understand the importance of ensuring that all children have an appropriate share of their time and responses. You need to recognise that some children are more demanding than others, but that the less demanding child should not lose out because of this. You need to deal with a demanding child by positively reinforcing acceptable behaviour, making it clear what your expectations are and setting clear, consistent boundaries.

FORWARD to Chapter 7, page 278. *Setting goals and boundaries in early years settings*.

However, a range of activities are needed to keep a child's interest and enhance their experience through the introduction of new ideas, by giving them the incentive to try something new and through the consolidation and extension of the familiar.

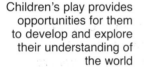

Children's play provides opportunities for them to develop and explore their understanding of the world

You will need to provide evidence of your understanding of what you consider to be stimulating activities. This evidence needs to be applied to a range of ages and stages of development during your various placement experiences. Your ability to provide stimulating activities will be evidenced through your professional practice log and also by the practical assessments you undertake in the workplace, set by either your placement supervisor or a tutor.

Various assignments set during your course will require evidence of your understanding of stages of development. This is likely to involve you making appropriately targeted books, games and activities. Most colleges will set assignments to produce items for children of a given age/stage, with the emphasis being on presentation, durability and the evaluation of the child's use and interest. The aims you set yourself will also be assessed for their relevance, and by how well they were met in the assignment.

| **Professional Practice** | What activities do you think could realistically be produced by students, that could be used and assessed as described above? Bear in mind that not all students are creatively talented and so assignment requirements need to take this into account. |
| --- | --- |
| | What specific requirements would you set, if you were the course tutor, that would produce professional-looking outcomes without relying heavily on creativity? Examples include the use of lower case lettering, word-processed text. |

The Rumbold Report 1990 identified many of the key points seen in the Foundation Stage Curriculum regarding how children learn. The Report stated (p.11, section 89):

> 'Young children learn effectively in a number of ways, including exploring, observing and listening. Playing and talking are, for young children, two principle means of bringing together a range of these activities. We believe that effective curriculum implementation requires careful attention to be given to providing fully for these.'

| **Professional Practice** | Time needs to be given to both the planning of activities, and to the children themselves. Where and when have you identified good examples of this happening? Have you seen examples where this has not happened? In what ways were the children affected? |
| --- | --- |

The Rumbold Report continued by referring to the conditions it considered as necessary for the 'potential value' of a child's play to be realised. These are:

> 'a. Sensitive, knowledgeable and informed adult involvement and intervention.
> b. Careful planning and organisation of play settings in order to provide for and extend learning.
> c. Enough time for children to develop their play.
> d. Careful observation of children's activities to facilitate assessment and planning for progression and continuity.'

This supports the need for high-quality training of teachers, nursery nurses and play workers. It also reinforces the need for the monitoring and verification of early years courses and settings. During the BTec National course, a significant amount of knowledge and understanding is externally assessed through an Integrated Vocational Assignment (IVA). Other assignments are assessed initially within the college or training centre by the teaching staff and are sampled by an external verifier. Both methods of assessment contribute to ensuring that standards are controlled and maintained (**quality assurance**).

In a nursery or school setting, inspection (by OfSTED) takes place on a regular basis. This involves taking into account the curriculum requirements of the setting, the health and safety of the children, and methods of observing, assessing and monitoring of progress, ensuring that individual children's needs are met and that differentiation and progression are planned for.

The Rumbold Report goes on to quote the HMI (Her Majesty's Inspectors) who said that:

> 'Play that is well planned and pleasurable helps children to think, to increase their understanding and to improve their language competence. It allows children to be creative, to explore and investigate materials, to experiment and to draw and test their conclusions … Such experience is important in catching and sustaining children's interests and motivating their learning as individuals and in co-operation with others.'

Therefore, the Rumbold Report of 1990 supports the ethos of learning through play. The Foundation Stage Curriculum also focuses on the value of play in education, and again it equates the quality of the play provided to the learning opportunities possible.

## Aims, practice and structure of settings

Each early years setting has its own aims, practice and structure. Many will follow the Early Learning Goals set out in the Foundation Stage Curriculum, while others will incorporate their own educational school of thought, for example, High Scope, Montessori and Steiner, each of which, despite their differences, places an emphasis on play.

▷▷ FORWARD to Chapter 8, pages 305–7 and 314–16, for more about Highscope, Montessori and Steiner.

**Professional Practice**
If you are fortunate enough to have a placement in a setting using the Highscope, Montessori or Steiner educational methods, take the opportunity to learn as much as possible about it, using this knowledge to compare and contrast differing schools of thought. This can be invaluable experience for assignment work on educational theory, and will help you to contribute usefully to classroom discussion and inform other students too.

The type of setting, and the ages of the children catered for, as well as the curriculum followed, will by necessity have an impact on the structure of the day and the scope for activity planning.

**Professional Practice**

Consider, for example, a hospital ward, with a peripatetic teacher and playworker staff. Think about how the staff would differ in their approach to activity provision compared to staff in a nursery class or primary school. Consider, also, a childminder, who may well provide a different, and possibly more limited, range of activities than a pre-school.

Why is this do you think, and what might the differences be?

**Activity**

1  In each placement you attend, note in your professional practice log the activities that are available on a daily basis.
2  Which activities can children help themselves to?
3  Which are only provided on occasions?
4  What has influenced these decisions, do you think?
5  Would you make changes if you were in a position to?
6  How would the changes you would make enhance the opportunities for the children in the setting?

## Setting up of basic and extended provision

FORWARD to Chapter 8, page 323, *identifying and promoting learning opportunities*.

## Planning, implementing and evaluating activities

It is useful to consider everyday activities, evaluating how they enhance each aspect of children's development. If you initially consider the basic opportunities each activity provides, you will move on to develop an understanding of how to extend activities further as you progress through your course of study.

FORWARD to Chapter 8, page 295, which looks at theories of play and how children learn, helping you to make links to the statements from the Rumbold Report.

**Activity**

Copy the following table and place the activities under the headings you consider to be appropriate, i.e. indicating the developmental areas you consider they would enhance. NB Some will come under several (or all) of the headings.

**Activities:**

Home corner/imaginative play
Games involving more than one child
Sand, water, clay, wood (natural materials)
Dough
Group story times
Group discussion times
Lotto games
Circle time
Activities to encourage responsibility and taking turns
Drama
Music and movement
Setting out the weather chart
Books and stories
Puzzles
Construction activities
Interest tables
Farms, car mats, dolls houses and so on (small world play)
Balls, hoops, beanbags, and so on
Bikes
Climbing frames
Threading toys
Pencil skill activities
Painting easel
Gardening

| Social development | Intellectual development | Moral development | Physical development | Language development | Emotional development |
|---|---|---|---|---|---|
|  |  |  |  |  |  |

## Supporting learning

Learning can be supported in many ways. The use of hands-on experience, together with display work and visits, can make a subject more real to children than simply hearing about it or looking at pictures, although clearly both of these mediums are valuable information sources in their own right.

Displays can involve children and their families in contributing objects and information. Parents and other family members may be able to demonstrate a skill or recount personal experience of the subject-matter.

**Activity**

Choose a topic and plan how you could introduce and extend it in as many ways as possible. Use as many different mediums as you wish.

**Professional Practice**

If, for example, the chosen topic was 'Mini beasts':
- What could be included on a display table? A wormery? Discarded snail shells? What else?
- What information books could be included?
- How many stories could be linked to the topic? *The Very Hungry Caterpillar? Odo the Snail?* Which others?
- Where could children be taken to for a visit? The park? The nursery garden? Where else?
- What creative activities could you link to the topic? Making spiders webs with wool on a pegboard? Printing with discarded (washed) snail shells? What else?

*Remember !*

Placement supervisors and staff are usually very willing for students to plan and implement activities on their own initiative. It is important, however, to agree dates for these activities in advance. Negotiation regarding display space needed, materials required and any involvement of other staff must all be discussed and clarified. Some placements will be able to supply the materials you need for an activity, but others will be either unable, or less willing. Do not assume you can use the setting's own resources and consumable materials without checking first.

If you are planning a visit, you will, of course, need to follow the setting's normal procedure for obtaining parental permission and follow the guidelines for adult:child ratios, etc.

FORWARD to Chapter 5, page 187, for information about safety issues on outings.

# Strategies for supporting children and their families

In supporting children and their families, you need to establish communication channels that are age-appropriate and understood by all concerned, and you need to be able to initiate and sustain relationships. It is important to recognise that there are different approaches to parenting (see page 45).

## Communication

Communication can be both verbal and non-verbal; it includes speech, looks and gestures. In children it is developed initially through the use of symbols. Verbal communication relies on a mutual understanding of the spoken word. It can fail if a common language is not used, or if there is no common field of experience linking the person who is speaking (the encoder) to the person who is listening (the decoder).

**Example** A course tutor of nursery nursing students who discusses the development of motor skills with the group will achieve successful communication, as the topic of conversation is both familiar and of interest to all concerned. If however, the tutor had decided to introduce the finer details of the structure of DNA (Deoxyribose nucleic acid) prior to a discussion of gene inheritance, for some students in the group (the decoders) the scientific detail may be too great. The tutor (the encoder) would therefore only achieve partial communication success.

**Professional Practice** In the example above, how could the tutor achieve a greater level of communication success in introducing the details of DNA?

FORWARD to Chapter 3, page 101–2, for a detailed explanation of the communication process.

### Communicating with babies and young children

From shortly after birth, eye-contact and turn-taking between an infant and its parent or carer is the earliest stage of pre-verbal communication. The expression of crying in order to have their needs met establishes for the infant that responses are gained by their cries. Murmurs of comfort and the verbal communication of the carer during caring routines help to build on the communication process.

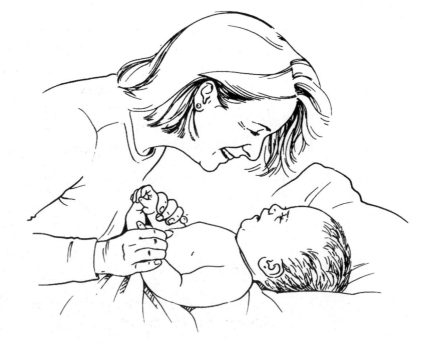

Eye-contact and turn-taking between an infant and its parent or carer is the earliest stage of pre-verbal communication

With very young children, opportunities for expression and communication need to be given through symbolic play. This allows them to learn and share meanings as they explore new ideas, and to practise and consolidate understanding by using the familiar.

**Activity**

Name three activities that involve symbolic play. How do each of these activities enhance the development of communication?

### Communication barriers

It is important to establish communication between you and the main carers of the children with whom you work. There are many barriers to communication. These include social, emotional and cultural issues.

FORWARD to Chapter 3, page 89, for more about barriers to communication.

**Professional Practice**

Using your developing observation skills, identify times when communication has not been completely successful. This may be due to confusion, wrong timing for the communication to take place or perhaps through misunderstanding.

You could use any examples which involve you as a communicator within your professional practice log, reviewing and reflecting on your own practice.

**Activity**

1  Copy the table and list as many barriers to communication as you can. An example of each has been given to get you started.

| Social barriers | Emotional barriers | Cultural barriers |
|---|---|---|
| Different first language | Shyness | Different body language |

2  How could each of the barriers you have listed be overcome? Discuss your thoughts with another student.

43

## Rights and responsibilities

The UN Convention on the Rights of the Child was adopted by the United Nations General Assembly in 1989.

FORWARD to Chapter 2, page 69, and Chapter 6, page 216, for more about children's rights.

Parents also have rights, but with rights come responsibilities. Under the Children Act 1989, the term 'parental responsibility' was introduced into legislation. It links with the term previously used in legislation, 'legal custody', and is defined as follows:

> ' "Parental responsibility" means all the rights, duties, powers, responsibilities and authority which by law a parent of a child has in relation to the child and his property.'

Allen (1996, page 13)

This definition replaced the unofficial list of parental rights and duties which, whilst not being linked to any one specific piece of legislation (they were taken from a range of legislation), were used by the courts as guidelines prior to the implementation of the 1989 Act.

## Supporting and promoting parenting

Support for parents can be a significant element of the staff–parent relationship. Early years staff can often become a stabilising part of a child's life. They offer a reliable environment at times when life at home for a child may be confusing or disrupted through life events, such as bereavement, illness or relationship difficulties between parents. Staff need to initiate and sustain good relationships to ensure the best joint care of the children. This is not always easy – conflicting views on parenting and how to deal with challenging behaviour can be a barrier.

Staff can be role models for families, demonstrating how to build up positive and caring relationships with others, both adults and children. Showing respect for and being interested in the children is a natural part of your work as a professional. It is not always instinctive in some families and at times parents may not share the ethos of the setting in which you work. This could be for a number of reasons. For example, a court order may have initiated the family's attendance at the setting, which could potentially build up an atmosphere of resentment, making communication difficult.

| | |
|---|---|
| **Professional Practice** | As an early years professional, you will need to ensure that communication continues between yourself and parents, whatever the circumstances. Forms of communication such as a warm smile or welcoming comment on arrival could be used to keep some contact, even if opportunities for conversation are currently limited. |

**Developing strategies of support**

*Jamie*
Jamie is aged three years four months. In the nursery he is always very boisterous, to the point where children are wary of him rushing past them. He is used to climbing on chairs and tables at home and continually tries to do the same in the nursery room.

1 How would you manage Jamie's boisterousness?
2 Would you refer to his opportunities to climb at home? If so, how would you approach this, ensuring that you remain supportive of his parents?

*Remember!*  It is imperative that you do not compromise parents' choices, providing of course, that these choices are not detrimental to the development, well-being or security of their child.

**Awareness of differences in parenting**

Every parent makes decisions regarding how their child is brought up. Some parents take an autocratic approach, monitoring their child's behaviour very strictly. Others are more *laissez-faire*, allowing their child much freedom of expression and little correction or guidance. The majority of parents fall somewhere between the two styles, allowing their children an element of freedom to challenge and explore, but with boundaries to incorporate safety and guidance in place. The differences in the ways families live are what gives our society its sense of richness.

Cultural practice can also mean differences between families and their lifestyles, and in how they parent their children. Terminology can be important, for example, Valerie Jackson (1996, p.51) refers to the use of the term 'beating of a child' used by a father of Caribbean background in one of her case studies. This term for many white-English people suggests a far harder punishment than the term 'smack', which it is actually referring to. Whether you agree with parents smacking their own child or not, the cultural difference in connotation is significant, and could lead to confusion and possible concern for the child's welfare.

**Professional Practice**  How do you think the policies of an early years setting contribute to the acceptance of differing parenting styles and cultural practices?

## Managing the effects of abuse

Sadly, most people who work in early years settings will, at some point, work with children who have been abused, whether it be physical, emotional, sexual or through neglect. The knowledge and understanding of development that forms such an important element of early years courses enables nursery nurses and others to identify when a child's development or behaviour strays from the 'norms'.

**Professional Practice**

Clearly there can be many reasons for a child's development or behaviour to stray from the 'norms'. Emotional disturbance, such as moving house or a burglary at the child's home, can cause changes and possible regression in development. This would usually be temporary, and with careful handling and plenty of reassurance can often be alleviated within a reasonable length of time. Other progressive signs of change in a child's behaviour or regression in development need careful consideration and observation.

FORWARD to Chapter 6, page 198, which sets out in detail the signs and symptoms that may indicate abuse. These form a useful guide. You will need to familiarise yourself with them.

### Supporting children who disclose

Young children are not able to invent stories of events that they would not usually experience. They should receive the unconditional acceptance of early years staff. All staff (and students) should know who to talk to if they have any concerns about a child. Most settings have a nominated person who is the setting contact regarding child protection issues.

**Professional Practice**

Ensure that you know the procedures and contact person for each setting you attend. If you are the person a child chooses to disclose to, you do not want to waste precious time finding out who needs to be informed.

This should also ensure that information is only shared on a 'need to know' basis.

**Remember!**

Confidentiality is paramount in child protection cases. However, an adult should never make a promise to a child that they will not tell anyone what the child has disclosed. They are legally and morally obliged to tell the appropriate person in the setting.

To make a promise to a child and then break that promise is likely to compound the child's lack of trust in others. You will have let the child down, as did the abuser. It would be considered by many to be a form of abuse too.

FORWARD to Chapter 6, page 221, *Supporting children who disclose*.

### The role of play therapy

Play therapy is one form of helping children to come to terms with what they have experienced. It is a healing process for children which encourages expression of feelings and ideas, and helps to rebuild a child's self-esteem and self-image. Play therapy is a specialised profession, which sadly, is not available to all children who might benefit from it. However, it is not a strategy that anyone can simply 'have a go at'. It takes specialist training and needs to be undertaken carefully, usually in conjunction with other professionals.

FORWARD to Chapter 6, page 224, for more about play therapy.

### Potential impact of abuse on the child and the family

Abuse not only affects the child, it can also be an extremely difficult time for family members, who are often unaware of what has been happening to the child. Sensitivity is clearly needed here. For family members who have abused, early years professionals can help by encouraging the development of new strategies for meeting children's needs and coping with challenging behaviour. Advice on group settings in their locality where they can attend with their children can be useful. Examples would be family centres, drop-in centres or a community bus that stops nearby. Phone lines, such as Crysis, for when a situation gets too much and they risk 'losing it', can be useful. These are often staffed 24 hours a day.

*To support families effectively, it is important to establish good channels of communication*

# Home visiting, co-operation with professionals and alternative forms of care

Visiting children and their families in their own homes has become more commonplace in recent years, although there has been a decrease in general home visits by health visitors. Other professionals, such as family support workers employed by social services, now undertake this role as part of the general support for both children and parents.

FORWARD to Chapter 6, page 218, for an outline of the roles of professionals who become involved in family problems such as child protection.

## Co-operation with other professionals

During your career in early years, you will be in contact with, and co-operate with, a range of other professionals. These will most likely include some or all of the following:

- social workers
- police officers
- health visitors
- nursing staff
- paediatricians
- teachers
- pre-school leaders
- psychologists
- therapists (various)
- probation workers.

**Professional Practice** Explore reasons why you might need to work in co-operation with each of the above professionals, adding more to the list if you can. You will need to consider:

- the different settings where you could be employed
- the various roles you may have within those settings.

Under the Children Act 1989, each local authority is required to set up an Area Child Protection Committee (ACPC). This committee brings together representative professionals from all the main agencies involved in caring for children to one forum, where cases of protection and dispute are considered.

FORWARD to Chapter 6, page 211, where the ACPC is discussed.

## Evaluating your own practice

**Evaluation** is a skill, and as you progress through the BTec National course you will be required to reflect upon and evaluate both your assignment work and your professional practice. This **reflection** might be through a verbal appraisal, by your tutor or supervisor, which could be either formal or informal. It could also be through written means, often included as part of the submission process for assignment work.

Your reflection should add value to the learning process. There is little benefit to stating in an evaluation that 'I could have improved upon my assignment had I started it earlier'. It would be far more useful to reflect upon your time management and how you could develop strategies for spacing your work out more appropriately.

Similarly, it is pointless to state that 'I was unable to give as much time to this assignment as I would have liked, as I also had three other assignments needing attention.' All students have the same number of assignments to complete. Tutors do not expect more from you than is reasonable. The workload does not, however, take into account unusual situations, for example, students needing or choosing to work every evening after college, or a mature student with several children to care for. This may at times seem hard, but the requirements of a full-time course assumes a full-time commitment to the course, and the workload required will have been made clear to you at the outset.

Evaluation of (or reflecting on) professional practice can form an important part of your professional practice log. You will need to consider each of the following points:
- your use of initiative and self-direction, and its importance
- your ability to meet changing needs and situations
- issues of responsiveness and adaptability
- reflecting upon own attitudes and relationships
- recognition of own knowledge, skills and contribution to team work
- how well you target-set for future development
- how well individual professional qualities have been developed, including:
  - interpersonal skills
  - verbal and non-verbal communication skills
  - professionalism
  - your knowledge base
  - level of understanding of the needs of children and families
  - knowledge of resources
  - knowledge of how to make referrals
- how well your personal management skills have developed, regarding:
  - roles and responsibilities within early years teams
  - organisational requirements
  - self-management in relation to:
    time-keeping
    dress
    personal hygiene
    punctuality
    commitment
- how effective your individual problem-solving has been, including:
  - analysis of information
  - decision-making
  - prioritisation
  - evaluation of outcomes
- issues of self-appraisal, including:
  - **self-awareness**
  - ability to review own performance in all relevant activities.

**Professional Practice** Self-awareness is needed in order to clearly reflect on your abilities and achievements.

*Remember!* Evaluation includes plans, actions and outcomes. It requires an acknowledgement of your strengths, and also the areas you need specifically to work on – your further development plan.

This last section of the chapter is set out as a series of questions linked to the following topic areas:

- use of initiative and self-direction
- the need to be adaptable
- the effects of your attitude
- the need to work within a team
- identifying your personal needs
- developing professional qualities
- developing personal management
- current self-management
- the effectiveness of your problem-solving skills.

It may seem a daunting task to consider the questions below, but you will find it helpful when building up evidence for your professional practice log if you answer them honestly, enabling you to reflect more clearly on your skills, knowledge, understanding and professionalism. As an early years student (or as a newly qualified early years professional), you would be expected to identify areas in which you feel you need to develop, so do not be concerned at making notes in these sections.

*Remember!* This ability to identify and acknowledge your own personal development needs is what makes a good professional.

### Section 1 question
*Use of initiative and self-direction*
Throughout placement experience you will increasingly be expected to use your own initiative. You should not have to be constantly guided as to what to do next. However, as a student on placement for the first time you will clearly not be expected to be as proactive as a student in the final term before qualifying. Considering where you are currently in your training and/or placement experience, answer the following:
How well do you use your initiative? Give examples.

### Section 2 questions
*Early years workers need to be adaptable to an everchanging environment.*
1  How well have you met the need for change? How flexible have you been?
2  When have you been less accommodating to the needs of the situation than you could have been?
3  Why was this?
4  Have you always been responsive? Or do you need coaxing or reminding?
5  How adaptable are you? Give examples of your adaptability.

### Section 3 questions
*Attitude can greatly affect what you do, and how you go about it.*
1  Is your attitude always positive? If not, why is this? What affects your attitude?
2  How well do you build relationships?
3  Are your relationships with others generally good? OK? Or poor? Why is this?
4  With whom do you form your best relationships? Why is this?

5  With whom do you find it hardest to form a good relationship?

6  What are the most significant factors affecting the quality of your relationships?

### Section 4 questions

*All early years workers need to be able to work within a team.*

1  How well do you contribute knowledge to **teamwork**? Give examples?

2  How well do you utilise your greatest skills? What are they?

3  How well do you consider you contribute to teamwork generally? Give examples.

### Section 5 questions

*Professional development involves identifying personal development needs (or targets).*

1  Do you usually set yourself targets for the future? If yes, give examples.

2  How useful do you find this to be?

3  If you have not set targets before, set some now. What would they be?

4  How will they benefit your professional development for the future?

### Section 6 questions

*Development of individual professional qualities is essential.*

1  How good are your interpersonal skills?

2  Give examples of where your interpersonal skills have been particularly important.

3  When communicating verbally, how successfully do you communicate with children? With parents/carers? With colleagues?

4  What messages does your body language give out? Are they always positive?

5  Give examples of good body language that you use. What effect does this have?

6  Give examples of unhelpful or negative body language you have used. What effect did this have?

7  How would you rate yourself as a professional? Support this with examples.

8  How sound is you knowledge base? Where are your strengths best evidenced? In placement? In your assignment work? In classroom discussion? Anywhere else?

9  Give examples of how your knowledge base has been evidenced.

10  How well do you understand the needs of children and families? Use examples from your placement experience to illustrate this.

11  In what ways have you demonstrated your knowledge and understanding of resources? Give examples from your placement experience and your assignment work.

12  How could you demonstrate your knowledge of making referrals?

### Section 7 questions

*Personal management skills will develop with experience.*

1  What roles and responsibilities have you had within early years teams/placements to date? List and evaluate how successful each has been.

2  How well have you been able to meet the organisational requirements of your placements? Give examples of where this has worked well and where this could have been improved?

## Section 8 questions

*Current self-management*

1  How good is your time-keeping at placement?
2  What effect does this have on you as a professional?
3  Does it have a positive or negative effect on the placement?
4  How does this affect your contribution to the placement?
5  How good is your timekeeping at college?
6  What effect does this have on you as a professional?
7  Does it have a positive or negative effect on the course and your contribution to it?
8  How good is your time keeping generally?
9  What effect does this have on your life? For example, are you always thought of as reliable? Or as late?
10  Do you usually dress appropriately? Give examples of both appropriate and inappropriate dress for placement.
11  How do you ensure your personal hygiene is always good?
12  How good is your attendance record? How does this affect what you do?
13  Are you committed to what you are doing? How is this evidenced?
14  Would college tutors describe you as committed? If not, why?
15  Would your current placement supervisor describe you as committed? If not, why?
16  Would past placement supervisors have described you as committed? If not, why was this?
17  What has changed in your level (or demonstration) of commitment?

## Section 9 questions

*Effectiveness of individual problem-solving is an important aspect of your role as an early years professional. The decisions you make can have a significant impact on the provision for the children in your care.*

1  How good is your ability to analyse information? Give examples of where a good analysis and a poor analysis has been made. What impact did these analyses have?
2  What important decisions have you had to make? In college? In placement? Give examples to illustrate.
3  What was the impact of your decisions? Have there been any negative outcomes? What were these? How could they have been avoided?
4  How do you prioritise your actions? What do you take into consideration?
5  How do you prioritise your time? What are the most important factors?
6  How good are you at evaluating the outcomes of your work?
7  How well do you plan? Can you see how your plans impact on your outcomes.
8  Give examples of how planning has affected the outcomes of your actions.
9  How self-aware are you? Are you able to identify your own limitations? Give examples from your placement experiences.
10  Do you review your own performance in all the activities, events and presentations you are involved in? Give good (and not so good) examples.

As you move through the BTec National course, you will use oral skills, written skills, information technology skills and numeracy skills. You will develop personally, academically and practically. The overall level and structure of the BTec National course will enable you to apply your newly acquired or enhanced learning to further your academic development, to take into the workplace on qualifying and to your life in general. These areas of development are linked to the Key Skills, a qualification which you will have opportunities to take alongside your main qualification. Key Skills are available at levels 1 to 4 (and to level 5 in personal skills development). They will contribute to your professional development and may be used as evidence in your professional practice log.

**Remember !**

Each student will start the course with differing levels of knowledge, skills, experience and qualifications. Your tutors will guide you to the level most appropriate to your current stage of development in each Key Skill you are taking.

Photocopiable charts which can be used as personal checklists can be found in the *BTec National Early Years Tutor Resource Pack*. Your tutor will be able to tell you if these are available in your college.

**Professional Practice**

As you read through the chapters covering the other units, your knowledge and understanding will develop further and this will impact on your practical skills.

Evaluating your professional development regularly will be a valuable process. It will enable you to see clearly how you are progressing and help you decide on your personal targets for the future.

**Test Yourself**

1 What forms might your professional practice log take?
2 What is meant by the term 'professionalism'?
3 What expectations are likely to be required of you in placement?
4 How might an unreliable staff member affect an early years setting?
5 What is meant by being responsible for your personal safety?
6 Define the term 'confidentiality'.
7 What is meant by the term 'need to know'?
8 What is important about teamwork?
9 What does 'developmentally appropriate' mean?
10 Give examples of how you can contribute to the safety of children.
11 Give a brief summary of the six areas of development.
12 What is meant by human and physical resources?
13 Name at least two alternative education programmes.
14 What barriers to communication can you think of?
15 What is meant by evaluating your own performance?

## Key terms

behaviour management
communication
confidentiality
developmentally appropriate
equality
evaluation
evidence
Foundation Stage Curriculum
human resources
identifying needs
interpersonal skills
observation skills

parents' expectations
personal safety
physical resources
professional
professional practice log
quality assurance
reflection
self-awareness
stimulate
teamwork
underpin
vocational

## Bibliography and suggested further reading

Allen, N. (1996) *Making Sense of the Children Act*, John Wiley & Sons, Chichester

Hodge, M. (2000) *Curriculum Guidance for the Foundation Stage*, QCA/DfEE, London

Jackson, V. (1996) *Racism and Child Protection*, Cassell, London

Malik, H. (1998) *A Practical Guide to Equal Opportunities*, Nelson Thornes, Cheltenham

Qualifications and Curriculum Authority (QCA) (2000) *Early Learning Goals*, DfEE, London

Sadek, E. and Sadek, J. (1996) *Good Practice in Nursery Management*, Nelson Thornes, Cheltenham

# 2 Equality, Diversity and Rights

## This chapter covers:

- ● **The importance of equality, diversity and rights**
- ● **How settings recognise and promote equality, diversity and rights**
- ● **Individual practice in promoting equality, diversity and rights.**

## Introduction

The main ethos of health, care and early years requires a thorough understanding of the diversity in society and involves all early years professionals embracing this diversity. Good practice in this context addresses all issues of prejudice, racism and discrimination and is evidenced when staff meet the needs, and promote the value of all children and families within the setting. These basic requirements ensure that the best quality of care is provided and supports the directive of the Children Act 1989, that local authorities provide day-care provision that is staffed appropriately:

> 'People working with young children should value and respect the different racial origins, religions, cultures and languages in a multi-racial society so that each child is valued as an individual without racial or gender stereotyping. Children from a very young age learn about different races and cultures including religion and languages and will be capable of assigning different values to them. The same applies to gender and making distinctions between male and female roles. It is important that people working with young children are aware of this, so that their practice enables the children to develop positive attitudes to differences of race, culture and language and differences of gender.'
>
> Children Act 1989, Guidance and Regulations, Volume 2, Section 6.10

Working to the principles of the Children Act will ensure that your professional practice is consistently good, rather than consistently adequate, and that the children you care for benefit holistically.

 Siraj-Blatchford and Clarke (2000) state that the first two foundations of learning are:
- 'The child needs to be in a state of emotional well-being and secure.'
- 'The child needs a positive self-identity and self-esteem'.

The aim of all early years staff should be to build up a child's self-identity and self-esteem by providing them with positive images of people, their lives and job roles with which they can identify. If you do not acknowledge and place value on the diversity within your working environment, you will not be fulfilling your professional role adequately and the children's sense of identity will be less positively reinforced.

 FORWARD to Chapter 9 for information on self-identity and emotional development.

This chapter explores the principle of **equity** (fairness and equal treatment) and considers how early years settings can promote **equality** (the state of being equal), diversity and rights. It will help to explore your personal values, your own practice and the practice of others, identifying examples of good practice and practice that needs to be addressed. Reviewing your own practice and identifying how you can build upon it will help you develop professionally. It is central to your professionalism and will have an impact on much of your work during your course of study.

| | |
|---|---|
| **Professional Practice** | It is important to remember that acknowledging difference is not the same as being prejudiced. It is the value that you place on difference that indicates whether prejudice exists or not. |

# The importance of equality, diversity and rights

## What do the terms mean?

The dictionary definitions of these terms are:
- *equality* – the state of being equal
- *diversity* – the state or quality of being different or varied
- *rights* – any claim … that is morally just or legally granted as allowable or due to a person.

Collins Dictionary (1991)

But what do these definitions mean in practice?

### Equality
Equality is about what is fair and what is not. It means that an individual's family or cultural background, the way they live, or their past or current state of health should not prevent them from receiving the same opportunities as anyone else in society. Intervention is needed to ensure that all children have an equal chance to achieve, to learn, to join in activities, to be parented appropriately and to live according to the cultural practices chosen by their families.

### Diversity
**Diversity** refers to the range of different levels of ability within any group of individuals, to the variety of **cultures** and religions, each with their own experiences, which make up a group or society, and to the age range of any group.

**Rights**

**Rights** are the entitlements of each individual to receive the same opportunities as others. Many rights are linked to standards of service and are protected by legislation (laws).

## Legislation

Legislation involves a range of charters and Acts of Parliament which control and monitor the treatment of individuals. Examples include:
- Children Act 1989
- Human Rights Act 1998
- UN Convention on the Rights of the Child 1989
- Disability Discrimination Act 1995.

This is the legislation most relevant to your role as an early years professional.

 FORWARD to pages 67–9 for more about this legislation.

Other legislation which it would be useful to know about includes:
- Race Relations Act 1976
- Sex Discrimination Act 1975
- Criminal Justice Act 1992
- Mental Health Act 1993
- Equal Pay Act 1970
- Equal Pay Act (Amendment) 1983
- Citizen's Charter
- Patient's Charter.

Find out what you can about these laws to build up an overall picture of the legislative rights of all people in society.

 Copies of all government legislation are available from HMSO bookshops and on UK government websites.

## Stereotyping and labelling

Children learn values and attitudes at a very young age from those of us who are their role models. When they are unsure about a new person or a new experience, children look to their role models for guidance, approval or encouragement, and therefore absorb their attitudes. These role models include their families (part of their primary socialisation) and their friends, both adults and peers, early years staff, teachers and health professionals (secondary socialisation). This also includes you!

As an early years student, you will work with a diverse range of children and families. It is therefore important that you understand **discrimination**, **stereotyping** and **prejudice**, and are clear in your mind as to what is good practice. You might find it helpful to explore how you initially formed your own views, and who or what influenced them.

**Activity**

To explore how your own views were shaped, you will need to think back to your childhood. Consider the following questions.

1 Who had most influence over you? This almost certainly included your parents, teachers and any nursery or pre-school workers.
2 Who else would you include?
3 How did each of them influence you?
4 Were the influences on you positive or negative?
5 What made them so?
6 Have you ever challenged a negative comment or action?
7 Have you ever felt you wanted to?
8 When was this and what stopped you?

Developing personal values is just the first step. Upholding them when others have different views is often hard to do, and sometimes it can seem easier to keep your views quiet and go along with the practice of others. You need to realise that this could mean that you are not working to good practice and are compromising your own values.

**Professional Practice**

If you find that your views are not free from prejudice, how might you deal with this?

If your views have been influenced by your parents, you could find yourself confronting the values of your family. This can be difficult.

Exploring your thinking, obtaining information and becoming better informed about the effects of prejudice and discrimination will help you.

## Stereotyping

Stereotyping means prejudging a group of people on the basis of one individual, or labelling an individual because they are part of a particular group. Stereotyped judgements are frequently both inappropriate and incorrect. Upholding stereotypes takes away people's individuality or personal identity. Stereotypical images can be **positive** or **negative** and, although they are sometimes built up by personal experience, they are more often due to the influences of others, including the media.

Example     An example of a stereotyped idea might be that 'all students are night clubbers'.

While many students do, of course, enjoy night club life, a great proportion do not, but students in general are a good example of a social group who are 'lumped together' for many stereotyped assumptions.

**Activity**

What other examples of stereotyping can you think of? Make a list.

## Discrimination and prejudice

To discriminate means to give favourable or unfavourable treatment to someone or something because of a specific factor. Discrimination can be:

- *institutional*, where the policies or practices of a workplace result in treating certain groups of people differently
- *individual*, where the prejudice (an opinion formed in advance) is the personal bias of one person.

Discrimination can be:

- *direct*, by telling someone that they are not allowed to do something because of their race, sex, situation or disability
- *indirect*, by excluding individuals who are unable to take part in, or do something because of their race, sex, situation or disability. For example, a school which refuses to allow hats or headgear to be worn will be indirectly discriminating against those who traditionally wear them as part of their cultural dress. This would include Jewish boys who wear a yarmulka, Sikh boys who wear a turban, Pakistani girls who wear a hijaab.

Groups of individuals can become **marginalised** by society through prejudice and discrimination, making them feel unable to initiate change or make their voices heard. This is *disempowerment* and it can have far-reaching effects. People who are disempowered see themselves as being 'less than equal' in society.

**Activity**

Consider the practice in any early years settings that you are familiar with. Can you identify any element of practice that could be classed as prejudiced or discriminatory?

*Remember!*

| Prejudice | + | Power | = | Discrimination |
|-----------|---|-------|---|----------------|
| (a pre-formed opinion) | + | (the practice of the setting) | = | (certain individuals may not receive equal opportunities) |

There are a number of groups who face discrimination in society. These include people who are the victims of prejudice on the grounds of their:

- age
- class
- disability and differing abilities
- race, culture and religion
- sexual orientation
- gender
- marital status.

**Activity**

1 Think of ways in which each group listed on page 59 faces discrimination.
2 Explain how any of these apply to early years settings. Remember to consider issues of staffing, access, communication, economics, clothing, cultural rituals and diet.

Examples   Examples of discrimination in early years settings include:

- age – teenage parents/older parents
- class – 'wrong' class from the wrong area/not good enough/too 'posh' for 'us'
- disability, differing abilities – inaccessibility/not asked to help out/avoided/limited
- race, culture, religion – only one culture catered for/devaluing or non-recognition of other cultures and religious festivals
- sexual orientation – homophobia (a dislike of homosexual people)/suspicions
- gender – fathers not encouraged/stereotyping of 'help' (men to fix toys, women to cook)
- marital status – values attached to marital status/meetings not accessible to single parents.

What else have you included?

**Professional Practice**   The points raised above indicate the need for policies. A strong equal opportunities policy is essential to monitor and maintain equality.

FORWARD to page 70, where the importance of policies and the contents of a policy are discussed.

### Effects of prejudice and discrimination

Being the target of prejudice and discrimination causes a multitude of negative feelings in an individual including hurt, devaluing of self, confusion, disempowerment and uncertainty. It is an intolerable situation which must be addressed. As an early years professional, you have an obligation to protect the rights of the children in your care by speaking up for them when they are unable to do so for themselves, and to support their value as a person.

You need to consider how you will address negativity when you come across it, because if you fail to speak out when you hear or see an act of prejudice or discrimination, you will be failing the children or families you are supposed to be supporting. To ignore an offensive comment made to one child by another will be to passively condone the comment. This passivity will compound the hurt for the child receiving the comment (as you will not have stepped in to correct the 'wrong' and to support them), and will fail to help develop more positive values in the child making the comment (sometimes children simply need guidance in how to speak and act). It is pointless having a 'correct' range of resources available to explore and promote culture and disability if negative incidents are ignored.

At times, you may feel you need support in redressing prejudice and/or discrimination. Your supervisor or tutor will be able to advise you. Alternatively, there are a variety of organisations, written materials and on-line sources that may help you.

> **Sources of help**
>
> Help and advice about prejudice or discrimination can be found through the:
> - Race Relations Act 1976
> - Commission for Racial Equality
> - Sex Discrimination Act 1985
> - Council for Equal Opportunities
> - Disability Movement.

**Activity**

What is wrong with the following statement: 'We do not have racism here. All the children are treated exactly the same.'?

Discuss this statement with others in your group.

## The origins of discriminatory practices

So where does discrimination stem from? Much discriminatory practice comes from ignorance and lack of understanding, sometimes accidental, but often intentional. As a professional in the early years sector, you need to become informed in order to avoid the accidental, and to address any personal prejudices in order to remove the intentional.

### Historical perspective of racial prejudice and discrimination

The UK has been a diverse society throughout history, beginning with the Bronze Age and the Neolithic migrants who settled in northern Europe 5,000 years ago, continuing with the invasions by the Romans, Saxons, Vikings and Normans, and many refugees, for example from France, Ireland, Russia, Uganda and Eastern Europe, fleeing war, persecution or famine in their own countries.

Significant groups of immigrants include:
- Jews, who first came at the invitation of William I (William the Conqueror) in the eleventh century. They were the founders of banking and financial services in the UK. Throughout history they have been persecuted, discriminated against and even expelled from the country at times
- from the fourteenth century, Flemish and French weavers, German mining engineers and Dutch canal builders, who brought with them new skills
- in the sixteenth and seventeen centuries, Protestant refugees from France (Huguenots), who played a major role in British society
- African slaves brought to the UK by the slave trade to work as servants (the slave trade was abolished in 1807 and slavery in 1838)

- Irish refugees, fleeing poverty and famine in the 1830s–1850s, who worked in the new industries, in the mines, docks, canals and railways.

Other significant groups of immigrants have come from Italy, China and the Indian sub-continent. In fact, according to the Commission for Racial Equality, most people in the UK today have origins somewhere else and can probably trace the immigrants in their family histories. Only about 7 per cent of the British population were not born in the UK, but immigrants have been met with hostility and resentment.

Black people, in particular, have suffered prejudice and discrimination in the UK. They were expelled by Queen Elizabeth I in 1601 and attempts were made to return them to their country of birth at various times that century. As recently as 1925, laws were passed which prevented black people from working on British ships and anti-black riots were seen in areas of the UK in 1919 and 1948.

When the UK suffered a serious shortage of labour after the Second World War, the British government encouraged immigration, first from European refugees, then from Ireland and the Commonwealth. In 1948 the first of these immigrant recruits arrived, being employed to do the low-paid, unskilled jobs that British workers had not been able to fill. However, tension arose between the ethnic minority groups and the white population, resulting in race riots. Some people claimed that the large numbers of immigrants that had relocated to the UK were causing greater economic problems for the country. In 1962 the Commonwealth Immigrants Act was introduced, with entry into the UK only allowed if certain criteria were met, for example if the applicant had a job arranged.

Since this time the UK has continued to see large numbers of black, and Asian, workers employed in lower paid and unskilled jobs, which has continued to reinforce the message of lower values for these groups of people. There are, however, greater numbers of people from ethnic minority groups than ever before achieving positions of management and power in the UK, indicating that acceptance and equality is developing. As an early years professional you will need to uphold and promote this thinking too.

 An ideal source of information about the historial perspective of racial discrimination and prejudice is Haralambos and Holborn (2000) – see *Bibliography and suggested further reading*, page 84.

| **Professional Practice** | • By exploring issues of prejudice, you come to understand the effects it can have, helping you to consider your personal values further. |
| --- | --- |
| | • Changing your viewpoint is not easy. It will only change by exploring alternative views and ideas and re-evaluating your own thoughts and feelings based on new information and understanding. |
| | • You cannot force your views on anyone, and similarly the views of others cannot be forced upon you. |

## The principle of equity

Equity is about giving an individual an equal chance, valuing and acknowledging the difficulties they face and allowing for these difficulties in your planning for, dealing with, and tolerance of, that individual.

**Case Studies**

In a small group, explore at least one of the following case studies. Consider the concept of tolerance in the context of values promoted by the early years sector.

### Ross

Ross is an extremely active five-year-old whose behaviour is often challenged by Miss Fergus, his Reception class teacher, and Mrs Stains, the classroom assistant. Mrs Stains spends a great deal of her time focusing on Ross to keep him 'on task'. At break times Ross is disruptive in the playground and recently he has been kept inside for much of the dinner break each day.

This morning Ross' mother came into school and informed staff that Ross is to be given Ritalin, a (sometimes controversial) stimulant medication used in treating Attention Deficit Hyperactivity Disorder (ADHD). After Ross' mother had gone Miss Fergus turned to Mrs Stains and said:

'Thank goodness for that. At least the medication might start to do what his mother has so far failed to do, control him. What the boy really needs is a man around to instil some discipline in him.'

1  What do you think of Miss Fergus' comment?
2  How should Mrs Stains respond?
3  What does this tell you about Miss Fergus' views generally?
4  What forms of prejudice were being displayed here?
5  What impact do you think Miss Fergus' views might have had on Ross in the past?
6  How would you have expected Miss Fergus to have responded?

### Job and Charlie

Job and Charlie have both just turned three, and have temporarily joined the pre-school where you are on placement, having moved into the area with the Gregory Brothers Touring Fair. Neither boy has been to an early years setting before but they are very confident children who are full of life and rush around excitedly exploring all the resources. They are particularly intrigued by water, favouring the water tray and anything 'messy' that will give them the opportunity to wash their hands in the bathroom.

A parent helper, Mrs Brownlow, comments that 'It is just as well they like washing their hands, as they are probably in need of a good wash, and we don't want their germs.'

1  What do you think of this comment?
2  How do you think the other pre-school staff should respond?
3  What does this tell you about Mrs Brownlow's views generally?
4  What forms of prejudice were being displayed here?
5  Why might the boys have been so fascinated by water?

## Cycle of disadvantage

Children can be disadvantaged whatever their ethnic background, religion, language, social class or gender, but for those who are members of social or cultural groups which are marginalised by society it is harder to break out of this cycle. As a child moves through life, they experience the consequences of their family's lifestyle, type of housing and employment opportunities. Some will, of course, adopt different lifestyles as they grow older, but others will not and the situation will be perpetuated for their own children.

The cycle of disadvantage

**Case Study**

*Traveller families*

A travelling group of five families were heading for an authorised traveller site near a maternity unit as two of the women were due to give birth. On arrival, the site was completely full and so they moved on to an unauthorised site which they had stopped at in the past. Whilst the first woman was giving birth in hospital that night, the five men were arrested and charged with unauthorised occupation and ordered to move on and not return to the authority. They waited until the second woman had given birth two days later, returning to her trailer almost immediately. When the community midwife went to visit the next day, both women and all the families had gone.

1  What inequalities can you identify here?
2  In what ways were these families facing disadvantage?
3  Do you consider these families to be a marginalised group?
4  What rights do you think these families were entitled to?
5  What might be the long-term health issues for these new babies?
6  What are the implications for the education of children who are moved on like this?

In the case study above, there were examples of inequality, marginalisation, disempowerment, vulnerability, potential economic disadvantage and educational disadvantage. The families were being denied equal access to services, due to the likely imprisonment of the men if the group did not move on.

Other marginalised or vulnerable groups include:
- older people
- disabled people
- other **minority ethnic groups**
- economically disadvantaged people
- educationally disadvantaged people.

**Activity**

With a partner, explore why each of these groups might be vulnerable. Include health, education and social issues such as housing, employment and leisure facilities in your discussion.

## The advantage of diversity in the UK

The UK is a pluralist society (one which consists of groups of people of distinctive ethnic origins, cultures or religions) which offers us the opportunity to explore a range of customs and distinctive elements of other ways of life. Its diversity enables us to work and socialise with people with disabilities through the increased (although still inadequate) accessibility to places of recreation, and through the greater recognition rightly given to disabled people in the workplace. There are more opportunities to interact with older people due to the population living longer, and our personal understanding is further enhanced by recognising that minority and vulnerable groups face hurdles not experienced by the rest of us and by us working to address them.

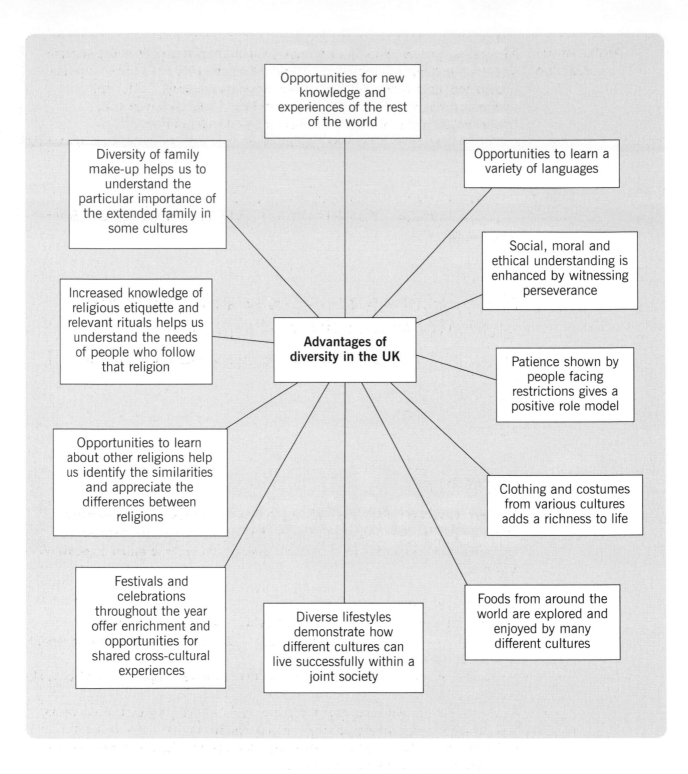

Opportunities for new knowledge and experiences of the rest of the world

Diversity of family make-up helps us to understand the particular importance of the extended family in some cultures

Opportunities to learn a variety of languages

Increased knowledge of religious etiquette and relevant rituals helps us understand the needs of people who follow that religion

Social, moral and ethical understanding is enhanced by witnessing perseverance

**Advantages of diversity in the UK**

Patience shown by people facing restrictions gives a positive role model

Opportunities to learn about other religions help us identify the similarities and appreciate the differences between religions

Clothing and costumes from various cultures adds a richness to life

Festivals and celebrations throughout the year offer enrichment and opportunities for shared cross-cultural experiences

Diverse lifestyles demonstrate how different cultures can live successfully within a joint society

Foods from around the world are explored and enjoyed by many different cultures

**Activity**

What else would you add to the spidergram, based on your personal experiences?

**Professional Practice**

It is of even greater importance to introduce diversity into early years settings where few cultures are represented. This will extend children's knowledge and understanding of alternative languages, religions and ways of life. This preparation will help them form values, and help them deal with any discrimination and prejudice they may encounter later in life.

An excellent resource for understanding discrimination, and legislation in particular, is Clements and Spinks (2000) – see *Bibliography and suggested further reading*, page 84.

# How settings recognise and promote equality, diversity and rights

The promotion of equality and rights by any organisation can be considered in terms of:
- legislation
- individuals' rights
- policies and practice.

## Legislation

The legislation most directly relevant to early years professionals is described below. This legislation may affect the children in your care either directly, regarding their own rights or needs, or indirectly, through the rights or needs of their families.

### Children Act 1989

The principles of the Children Act 1989 include the following points.
- The welfare of the child is paramount and should be safeguarded and promoted at all times by those providing services.
- Children with disabilities are children first with the same rights to services as all children.
- Parents and families are important in children's lives. Local authorities should support them in carrying out their responsibilities.
- Parents should be valued as partners with local authorities and other agencies such as health and education services.
- Children have a right to be consulted and listened to when decisions about them are being made. Their views and the views of their parents must always be taken into account.
- Health, education and social services for children with disabilities should be co-ordinated.

Dare and O'Donovan (1997)

## Individuals' rights

### Children Act 1989

Volume 2 of the Children Act specifically covers day care, and states that parents have a right to influence the quality of education that their child receives, which involves the need to make enquiries about what is available and to be able to understand the information they receive. Parents with limited use of English are disadvantaged in this and may need the help of an advocate or interpreter.

| | |
|---|---|
| **Professional Practice** | Early years settings can help parents by presenting information in languages other than English whenever possible. Visual information will help to some extent. Involving an advocate or interpreter will show that you value the family's heritage language and their need for information. |

FORWARD to Chapter 3, page 100.

Section 22(5)(c) of the Children Act states that local authorities must give consideration to the religious persuasion, racial origin, cultural and linguistic background of any child within their care. Any provider of care for children can be deregistered if these needs and rights are not properly cared for, as they would not be considered to be a 'fit' person to care for children, under the Act.

> ### Gillick Competence
>
> Although it does not form a part of the Children Act, children's rights are sometimes considered under the principle of **Gillick Competence**. This is based on a child's ability to make his or her own decisions and give informed consent. This principle was first drawn up in connection with the question of giving of medical treatment (contraception) without the agreement of parents. It is a principle that is not applied at any one particular age, as each 'child' and the relevant situation is considered individually, to ascertain whether the child is considered to be 'Gillick Competent'. The principle of Gillick Competence has been used in connection with Section 8 of the Children Act (particularly the prohibited steps order) in which a child may challenge the directive of the courts, for example in the contact they are allowed to have with a parent. A child does not have an automatic right to appeal under Section 8, and Gillick Competence is determined by health professionals, together with others relevant to the case, such as a child psychologist, to decide whether a child has sufficient understanding of all the relevant circumstances.

### Human Rights Act 1998

The Human Rights Act focuses on the individual's right to a life free from torture, loss of liberty, unfair punishment or discrimination. It also refers to respect for private and family life (Article 8), freedom of thought, conscience and religion (Article 9) and the freedom of expression (Article 10). The Act is linked to the drawing-up of no-smacking policies and is also relevant to female circumcision.

FORWARD to Chapter 6, page 207, for discussion of these issues.

### UN Convention on Children's Rights 1989

This is an international agreement on human rights which has been ratified by 191 countries. It consists of 54 articles (statements) and its four main principles are:

- *Non-discrimination* – All children have the same rights and are entitled to the same treatment.
- *Children's best interests* – The best interests of the child should be placed as highest priority when making decisions about their future.
- *Survival and development of children* – Children have the right to survive and the right to be able to develop to their full potential.
- *Rights to participation* – The views of children should be taken seriously and they should be able to take part in what is going on around them.

The Convention is important because it brings together in one document all the rights of children and adults are asked to view children as individuals with all human rights being applied to children everywhere.

*Based on a paper by Save the Children (2000)*

Examples of articles set out within the Convention have been unofficially summarised by Flekkøy and Kaufman (1997) as follows:

- *Article 2* – All rights apply to all children without exception, and the state is obliged to protect children from any form of discrimination. The state must not violate any right, and must take positive action to promote them all.
- *Article 22* – Special protection to be granted to children who are refugees or seeking refugee status, and the state's obligation to co-operate with competent organisations providing such protection and assistance.
- *Article 23* – The right of handicapped children to special care, education and training designed to help them achieve greatest possible self-reliance and to lead a full and active life in society.
- *Article 30* – The right of children of minority communities and indigenous populations to practise their own culture, their own religion and language.

### Disability Discrimination Act 1995

This Act is directly relevant to early years in that it supports the **ethos** of the Education Act 1993 of the need to provide all children who have a special need with an appropriate education at a suitable school. All settings should have a Special Educational Needs Co-ordinator (SENCO) who is responsible for ensuring that the special needs of children are met. In schools this would be a member of the teaching staff who liaises with parents and other staff and keeps records of the special educational needs within the school.

Special educational needs policies and the role of the SENCO are set out in Dare and O'Donovan (1997) – see *Bibliography and suggested further reading*, page 84.

## Policies and practice

An equal opportunities policy is a plan of how a setting will put its legal responsibilities for promoting equal opportunities into action. The policy should give clear guidelines to follow should an incident or concern arise. All staff at the setting should comply with the policy.

All early years settings must have an equal opportunities policy and many will also have statements linked to anti-**racism**, gender and the code of practice for special needs. These should be drawn up and agreed by all members of staff. When staff have been involved in drawing up a policy they are more likely to feel 'ownership' of it, understanding it fully and supporting it openly. Copies of the policy should be given to parents when they first take up a place for their child at the setting. Having a written policy that has been agreed by parents and staff provides a point of referral, if challenging a breach of the setting's policy seems difficult to face.

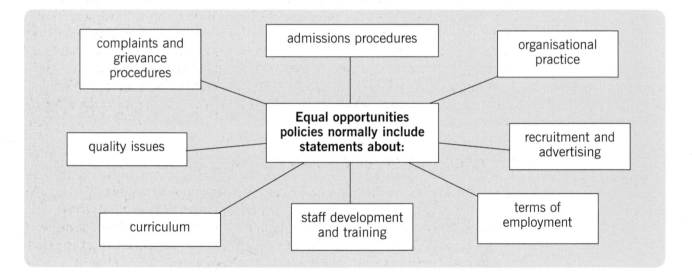

## Implementing the policy

Training is important, to ensure that the policy is fully understood. It will need to be monitored and reviewed to ensure that it meets the needs of the setting. A named person should take overall responsibility for its implementation.

### Activity

1 Ask your placement supervisor and your college's day-care setting (if there is one) for a copy of their equal opportunities policy and any accompanying statements or separate policies for anti-racism, special educational needs or sex discrimination.
2 Make a comparison of the two settings' policies, noting the similarities and differences.
3 Does either policy, or set of policies, seem more comprehensive than the other? If so, why is this, do you think?
4 Do the policies include all the statements listed in the diagram above?

For policies and equal rights legislation, refer to Sadek and Sadek (1996) – see *Bibliography and suggested further reading*, page 84.

The policy should set out clearly the grievance and complaints procedures step-by-step. The process should be available to all and people should feel able to raise a complaint or concern without anxiety or risk of harassment. The procedures should help to raise and maintain quality of provision and should be viewed as a positive aspect of the overall framework of the setting.

# Individual practice in promoting equality, diversity and rights

Staff, children and parents should promote and encourage the ethos of *all* children experiencing *all* activities. At times, a parent will be uncertain about their child enjoying particular activities, and sensitivity and encouragement will be needed. A common example is a parent's concern over his or her son ironing in the role-play area or dressing up in a nurse's uniform. It should be sufficient to explain to the anxious parent that many men share the household task of cleaning and hopefully Jeremy will too. However, where possible, obtain dressing-up clothes for both genders when they usually differ, as in nursing. This will establish the correct dress code while still promoting the role of male nurses.

## Carrying out an audit of a setting

A useful way of exploring how successfully your setting is meeting its commitment to equality is to carry out an **audit** (a type of inspection) of the various activities that are offered, looking at how many depict positive messages supporting a positive self-image, how many are simply neutral, neither particularly promoting diversity, but not causing offence or confusion either, and most importantly, considering if any depict negative messages through the images portrayed or the resources provided. If negative images are found, they should be brought to the setting manager's notice.

---

**Activity**

In a small group, draw up a checklist of points to use when carrying out an audit of an early years setting. Think about:
- policies
- staffing
- equipment
- resources
- accessibility.

When you have drawn up your checklist, discuss it with your tutor and then arrange to carry out an audit of a setting. Remember to ask permission of the setting supervisor first.

Does your setting convey positive messages?

### Tokenism

You will need to be aware of **tokenism**, a pretence at being committed to diversity and equality. Settings which have only a tokenist approach may have a few items depicting positive messages in prominent places, but when you explore the resources further, a less positive picture of equality emerges.

### The 'tourist' approach

Similarly, settings that focus on the diversity of other cultures and festivals as a 'tourist experience' may not have equality fully embedded in their practice.

| Professional Practice | Having the right resources does not in itself ensure that equality and diversity is being promoted. It needs positive language and attitudes of staff to place the correct values on the resources and activities that are provided. |
| --- | --- |

### Books and stories

Positive messages within books include:
- boys in caring roles or carrying out household tasks
- girls involved in activities or occupations involving strength or occupations of power and management
- minority ethnic groups depicted in both traditional cultural situations and occupations of power and management
- illustrations showing mixed cultural activities or the sharing of each other's festivals by a group of children or adults
- disabled people carrying out the same tasks as everyone else, and joining in activities alongside able-bodied people
- different family groupings – nuclear, extended, stepfamilies, mixed race families – to truly represent society.

Where possible, it is good to have some dual language books. These will help to involve parents who speak the languages portrayed, and give all children an opportunity to see the written word in an alternative script.

Books and stories should give positive messages about equality and diversity

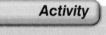

**Activity**

1 From either your current placement, or from your college library's children's section if you have one, select three books which you feel give a positive message, and share the reasons for your choice within a small group.
2 Have you found any that give a negative message?
3 Have you reported this to anyone?

**Case Study**

*Katya*

Katya is in her first term of her nursery nursing course and is currently on placement in the Reception class of the local primary school. She is enthusiastic and keen to be involved and asks the teacher, Mrs Davis if she can read to the class on her placement day next week. Mrs Davis agrees and suggests that she reads a book that she is very familiar with. Katya says she will bring a book that she reads regularly when she is baby-sitting. The following week Katya settles down to read a home-time story to the children, while Mrs Davis sorts out the paintings. Mrs Davis is horrified when she realises that Katya is reading a story about a naughty black golliwog. She lets Katya finish the story as she is unsure what to do. The children then go home.

1 What are the problems here?
2 Should Mrs Davis have checked what Katya was going to read?
3 What form of discrimination is depicted here?
4 How should Mrs Davis broach the 'error' with Katya?
5 What would you do tomorrow, if you were Mrs Davis?

> **Professional Practice**
>
> It is important that negative incidents are dealt with promptly. Mrs Davis needed to talk to both Katya and the children.

Negative messages within books include:
- boys as always physically stronger than girls, in 'macho' roles or positions of power
- girls as cute, pretty and clean, only as carers, in supportive occupations
- minority ethnic groups inappropriately or negatively characterised, depicted in manual occupations or only in traditional cultural situations
- disabled people only as wheelchair-bound, sat to the side of activities, on a different level to others in the illustration
- family groupings always of the nuclear type (two parents and two children).

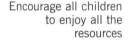

Encourage all children to enjoy all the resources

> **Professional Practice**
>
> - It is acceptable for there to be range of images, some neutral and some positive, as long as there is an overall emphasis on the positive.
> - It is never acceptable for a setting to continue to include negative images within its resources.
> - The examples of positive and negative images set out for books and stories apply to all resources and activities that involve illustrations.

### Role play

In the role-play corner, issues of gender are mostly found in the *use* of the resources rather than the resources themselves. The important aspect of gender stereotyping here is to encourage all the children to enjoy all the resources, taking different roles within their play. Culturally, an array of artefacts, clothes and foods from a range of cultures will enhance the learning of all children and positively promote the self-image of children from those cultures.

Which cultures are portrayed by the dolls in your placement? If they are all pink skinned, blonde haired and stereotypically English, they are likely to support a racist message of who is important and needs caring for.

What message do the dolls in your placement give?

*Children playing 'at home'*

A group of children are playing 'at home' when you overhear the following:

'Get the baby mummy, 'she's crying.'
'You get it.'
'No! I'm reading the paper and I've had a hard day at work.'
'I'm cooking tea.'
'So what!'

1  Would you interrupt the play?
2  Is discrimination taking place here?
3  What can be the issue with 'correcting' what some children think of as normal, as they see and hear it at home each day?

A range of resources is available to depict other cultures through role play

The range of resources illustrated on page 76 shows how depicting other cultures through role play is readily available. How well resourced is your placement? Where finances are limited, many cultural costumes can be easily made, dyeing and printing materials appropriately, and foods can be made from salt dough, copying real items or pictures.

*Remember!* Parents of children from different cultures will usually be pleased to help with improving the resources of the setting.

## Construction materials

Children often consider construction kits to be boys' toys. Encouraging both boys and girls to use construction materials will help dissipate stereotypical views, but be aware of who dominates the construction area. At times it can be appropriate to encourage girls to use construction materials without the 'help' of the boys. This will ensure that girls have the opportunity to plan, predict, experiment and achieve on their own.

▶▶ FORWARD to Chapter 9, page 377. Carry out the gender activity recommended there. What results did you get when you carried out the activity in your placement?

**Professional Practice** How gender specific are pictures on the boxes of the construction kits in your placement? This is an easy aspect to change. Simply remove the construction material from its original box and place in a more suitable container.

Encourage both boys and girls to use construction materials to help to dissipate stereotypical views

## Creativity

This is an area where children can experiment and be involved in a non-competitive way, as you cannot paint a 'wrong' picture. Opportunities for creative expression involve the use of a range of mediums and a range of utensils.

Brushes or alternatives need to be suitable for all hands. A child with limited manipulative dexterity will benefit from chunky brush handles (light-weight wallpaper brushes can be useful), and all children will enjoy the experience of painting with (thoroughly cleaned) roll-on deodorant containers (plastic) or large sponge rollers.

For children with skin problems such as eczema, it can exacerbate the irritation if they have direct contact with paint and other 'messy' mediums. *Supervised* activities such as finger painting under a length of clingfilm can keep them involved without risking infection or further discomfort. Using large bubble-wrap as an alternative can add to the sensory experience.

The range of festivals throughout the year, representative of many different cultures, offer enormous scope for creative activity. Examples include:
- *Diwali*, the Hindu festival of light
  - Rangoli patterns – a decoration laid at the entrance to the home to welcome the Goddess of fortune, Lakshi
  - Diwali cards – a popular design would be to use a hand shape and decorate it in the traditional mehndi patterns.

A mehndi hand pattern

- *Chinese New Year*, the first day of the lunar calendar each year
  - Teng Chieh, the lantern festival, denotes the end of the new year celebrations – decorated sheets of paper are cut and made into lanterns
  - Money envelopes (*lai see*) – It is traditional for children to receive money in red envelopes decorated with gold writing
  - Dragons, one of the twelve animals in the Chinese animal years – making a huge dragon can be a super whole-group activity, culminating in the 'dance of the dragon'. Activities such as this allow every child to contribute, working together towards a joint goal.

Lanterns used in the celebration of the Chinese New Year

**Professional Practice**  A range of skin-tone colours in both paints and crayons will enable all children to represent themselves and their families accurately in their pictures.

## Puzzles

Puzzles can be for table or floor use, and can have both large and small pieces. Consider differentiation of manipulative control – the use of large pieces will help the less-able child, as will puzzles with sturdy knobs to lift and replace pieces. Issues of positive images apply in the same way as with books and stories.

*Remember!*  Just because a child needs large pieces to meet their physical need does not necessarily mean that they cannot enjoy a challenging picture. Physical and cognitive needs are not always parallel with each other.

## Music, movement and singing

It is very easy to include diversity in this area of the curriculum. There is an abundance of musical instruments available from a vast array of cultures and to suit most physical needs. A musical instrument box should not simply hold tambourines, drums and cymbals as this is limiting for expression and restricts opportunities to explore the multitude of other options available.

Dance is also an important part of many cultures. It can encourage children to explore and communicate through a range of expressions and movements. It can be combined with the use of instruments, encouraging children to accompany each other, building up co-operation and appreciation of each other as equal partners in a joint activity.

Electronic musical activities, and those involving vibration, are particularly useful for children with severe hearing loss, as they offer a multiple-sensory experience.

It is very easy to include diversity in music activities

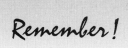

**Remember !**    Tapes and CDs of world music can be borrowed from music libraries. Children can enjoy a range of songs from around the globe, enjoying learning to sing in different languages, placing emphasis on rhythm and dance, linked to appropriate cultures.

**Activity**

What songs and music have you heard in your placement? Are any from cultures other than British? Make a list.

Examples    'Kookaburra sits in an old gum tree' – Australia
'Frère Jacques' – France

What other examples can you think of?

**Professional Practice**
- It is important to look at the content of traditional nursery rhymes and songs too. For example, 'Taffy was a Welshman, Taffy was a thief' is not a good example for promoting cultures and raising self-esteem.
- Inviting musicians into the setting allows children to hear a variety of instruments for real. Musicians from various cultures can explain how the instruments link with festivals and special occasions.

Hand and body signs for musical notes can be used with older children. The Addison body notation and Curwen hand signs are two examples.

Addison body notation

Curwen hand signs are similar to Addison body notation but do not involve the whole body (as their name suggests).

## Cooking activities

What food-related activities have you seen, and what are planned for the future at your placement? Ask your supervisor to let you see the plans for the full academic year, as this will enable you to gain a more accurate picture.

The customs and diets of all children need to be taken into account when planning activities with food, including practical, medical and cultural needs. Examples of medical dietary considerations include children with:

- diabetes
- coeliac disease
- cystic fibrosis
- food allergies, particularly those who have an anaphylactic response.

FORWARD to Chapter 10, page 469, *Common childhood illnesses*.

Practical and cultural needs would include children who are:
- vegetarian
- from cultures where certain foods, or combinations of foods, are not allowed.

FORWARD to Chapter 7, page 271, for a table setting out the cultural requirements for diet.

Festivals lend themselves to a range of cooking activities, for example:
- *Baisakhi*, the Sikh festival to celebrate the start of Guru Nanak's travels – people provide vegetarian foods, such as dahl and chappattis, both of which can be made with children
- *Lent*, the Christian period of 40 days leading up to Easter which Christ spent in the Wilderness – pancakes are traditionally made on Shrove Tuesday, the day before the start of Lent
- *Raksha Bandhan*, the Hindu festival of protection and care between siblings and close friends – a traditional offering is coconut barfi, similar to coconut ice, which needs no cooking so is an ideal cooking activity.

### Activity

What other festivals can you think of that would provide opportunities for cooking activities? Make a list.

### Case Study

*Pete and Sammy*

Pete is making pancakes with small groups, as part of the exploration of the Christian festivals of Lent and Easter. The children join him eagerly and clamour to be next. Pete chooses his next helpers, and turns to Sammy, saying 'You can make them Sammy, but you won't be able to eat them, as they have wheat in them.' Sammy, who has coeliac disease looks disappointed, but joins in anyway.

1  How would you deal with this situation?
2  What form of discrimination is described here?
3  Are there any problems with Sammy cooking with a wheat-based flour?
4  What could Pete have done to enable Sammy to be fully involved in the activity?

### Professional Practice

Parents are the ideal people to involve in cooking recipes from other cultures.

### Persona dolls

Promoting self-esteem is an important element of a child feeling valued. **Persona dolls** can be used to help to promote self-esteem. The dolls represent children from various cultures and with a range of disabilities. A persona doll can be provided for any individual need and can be an ideal way of encouraging children to accept difference and pave the way for a child to settle and integrate easily into the group or class.

When using a persona doll, the adult explains the doll's background and tells a special story which can lead to a discussion with the children, exploring difficulties that can be faced by an individual, bias that can be experienced and the hurt that can be felt.

*Persona dolls encourage children to accept difference*

Billy Ridgers, Team video

 For information on using persona dolls, refer to Brown (2001) – see *Bibliography and suggested further reading*, page 84.

Self-esteem can also be promoted during circle time, which gives each child an opportunity to speak and be listened to.

**Improving your own practice**

To improve your understanding of equality and therefore your professional practice, it can be helpful to explore a range of scenarios. This last section is designed to help you think and reflect on your ability to work to good practice. Try the following activities.

1 a) What would concern you about the following statements?
    i) Nursery nurse: 'We can't ask Mrs Jones to help because she's got five kids.'
    ii) Nursery nurse: 'Mr Daniels will be useful to have around as there'll be plenty of heavy lifting.'
    iii) Nursery manager: 'I've put Darren on bathroom duty, but always with another member of staff.'

iv) Parent: 'Is it true you've accepted a child with HIV? If it is, I'll take my Michael away, you know.'

v) Parent: 'I don't want my Jess to have Darren as a key worker. He's a man, it's not natural.'

vi) Child: 'My dad says I can't play with Ephram anymore. He's black.'

vii) Child: 'I don't want Jenny to help me, her arm's all funny.'

b) What assumptions are being made?

c) What forms of discrimination are seen here?

d) How would you challenge each of these statements?

e) What do the children's comments tell you?

f) Will you follow up any of these comments?

g) How will an equal opportunities policy help you?

h) Share your answers with a partner. Were you both in agreement?

**Professional Practice**

As an early years professional, you will at times have access to information that should be kept confidential. You will need to take this responsibility seriously. Confidentiality is linked directly to rights.

FORWARD to Chapter 6, pages 222 and 233, for information on record-keeping and confidentiality.

2 a) Which of the comments below (or similar) have you heard being used?
  • The girls are sitting lovely and quiet as always!
  • Would a strong lad come and help me with the construction box please?
  • Which of you girls will look after the new children?
  • Whose dad has got an electric drill?
  • Can you all ask your mummies if they would have time to help us sew the costumes for the play, please?

b) What stereotypes were being reinforced here?

c) Rephrase each comment more appropriately.

3 a) Which of the following statements will be most likely to ensure equality of opportunity in an early years setting?
  • All staff are entitled to staff development training.
  • All staff are entitled to equal amounts of staff development training.

b) Explain the reason for your answer.

c) What might be the implications in the long-term for each statement?

**Professional Practice**

• Working positively will encourage the promotion of equality in others – colleagues, parents and children.

• Being a role model for children is a privilege and should be taken seriously.

• You should always remember that your actions and words could have a lasting impact on the development of the values and self-esteem of the children in your care.

**Test Yourself**

1 Give an example of tokenism.
2 Define 'institutional discrimination'.
3 What is prejudice?
4 Why is it not enough just to have a range of resources giving positive messages?
5 Explain one way of helping a child with a medical dietary need to be involved in cooking.
6 Which religion celebrates Diwali?
7 How could a deaf child's enjoyment of music be enhanced?
8 What is a persona doll?

## Key terms

**You should now understand the following words and phrases. If you do not, read through the chapter again and review them.**

audit

culture

cycle of disadvantage

discrimination

diversity

equality

equity

ethos

Gillick Competence

institutional discrimination

marginalise

minority ethnic group

persona dolls

positive and negative images

prejudice

racism

rights

stereotyping

tokenism

tourist approach

## Bibliography and suggested further reading

Breuilly, E. and Palmer, M. (1993) *Religions of the World*, Harper Collins

Brown, B. (1998) *Unlearning Discrimination in the Early Years*, Trentham Books

Brown, B. (2001) *Persona Dolls in Action: Combating Discrimination*, Trentham Books

Clements, P. and Spinks, T. (2000) *The Equal Opportunities Handbook*, 3rd edition, Kogan Page, London

Dare, A. and O'Donovan. M. (1997) *Good Practice in Caring for Young Children with Special Needs*, Nelson Thornes, Cheltenham

DfEE (1994) *Code of Practice on the Identification and Assessment of Special Educational Needs*, HMSO, London

Flekkøy, M.G. and Kaufman, N.H. (1997) *Rights and Responsibilities in Family and Society*, Jessica Kingsley Publishers, London

Haralambos, M. and Holborn, M.(2000) *Sociology: Themes and Perspectives*, Collins, London

Lindon, J. (1999) *Understanding World Religions in Early Years Practice*, Hodder & Stoughton, London

Malik, H. (1998) *A Practical Guide to Equal Opportunities*, Nelson Thornes, Cheltenham

Mukherji, P. and O'Dea, T. (2000) *Understanding Children's Language and Literacy*, Nelson Thornes, Cheltenham

Nursery World (1999) *All About Celebration: Activity Handbook*, TES

Pre-School Learning Alliance (1996) *Equal Chances: Eliminating Discrimination and Ensuring Equality in Pre-schools*, Revised edition, PLA, London

Sadek, S. and Sadek, J. (1996) *Good Practice in Nursery Management*, Nelson Thornes, Cheltenham

Siraj-Blatchford, I. and Clarke, P. (2000) *Supporting Identity, Diversity and Language in the Early Years*, Open University Press, Buckingham

# 3 Communication and Supportive Skills

**This chapter covers:**

- Interpersonal interaction and communication
- Supportive skills
- Communication
- Supportive skills with distressed individuals.

## Introduction

The ability to communicate and get on with others is an extremely important aspect of most people's lives, both personally and professionally. Communication and interpersonal interactions, both verbal and non-verbal, are the means of giving and receiving information, and letting others know how you are feeling.

Effective communicate is central to the good working practice of all early years professionals, and relationships with children and families may be impaired without it, reducing the effectiveness of your working in partnership with parents. The way you communicate sends a message about you as a person – your attitude, the way you talk, how well you listen and your approach to various situations.

Communication involves a successful exchange between two people. Sometimes your work as an early years practitioner and team member will be judged on your ability to communicate appropriately. It is important to remember that individuals with good **interpersonal skills** identify when communication has not been effective by noting the responses of others, and are both willing and able to adjust their approach accordingly. As you read this chapter, there will be opportunities for you to reflect on your personal ability to communicate and interact, enabling you to review your current practice and build on it for the future.

▶▶ FORWARD to page 101 for an explanation of the communication process, known as the Communication Cycle.

## Key skills

This unit of study will also be of significance in the gathering of evidence for Key Skills, particularly in Communication. The ways in which you contribute to discussions, and invite the contributions of others in discussion and conversation, together with writing reports, giving oral presentations and interpreting information will all be relevant. You should be able to draw evidence from all aspects of your course – classroom discussion, placement experience and through your professional practice portfolio.

# Interpersonal interaction and communication

Communication can be verbal, written, visual, textual or aural, involving the written word, music, drama or creativity. When you begin a communication you need to consider how the other individual involved communicates best, and whether there are any barriers to them communicating successfully with you.

Early years workers need to be able to respond appropriately to children from a variety of backgrounds

## Different family structures

You will work with children from a variety of family situations and structures, including children from:
- nuclear families
- extended families
- lone-parent families
- stepfamilies
- economically challenged families

and children with:
- gay and lesbian parents
- a range of cultural influences.

It is your responsibility as a professional early years worker to communicate with, and respond appropriately and equally to, all families. You should be aware of any personal bias or preconceived ideas you may have about any social groups. Your responsibility is to welcome all families and respect their rights, ensuring that both your attitude and your language is appropriate.

BACK to Chapter 2, *Equality, Diversity and Rights*.

*Remember !* A diverse community is a rich community, and the opportunities to share and explore elements of each other's lives will enhance the learning of all.

**Activity**

Think of the ways in which you communicate with others in a range of settings, including college, home, your placement, social situations, in shops and so on.

a) How does your communication differ between the age groups/social groups you interact with. Include babies, young and older children, your peer group, your parents and your grandparents generations in your thinking.

How is your communication different in the groups you interact with?

b) Consider how you use your voice (verbal communication). Think about:
   - volume
   - tone
   - speed
   - the language used
   - the emphasis you place on words.

c) What about your body language (your non-verbal communication)? Consider:
   - posture
   - gestures
   - eye contact
   - physical contact
   - spatial awareness.

d) Think of a conversation you have had where the communication felt unsuccessful to you? Why was this, do you think? What could you have done to have improved it?

e) When has communication felt particularly successful? What made it so?

# Barriers to effective communication and interactions

A barrier can be anything that causes an obstruction or prevents progress. **Barriers to communication** can include any of the points in the diagram below.

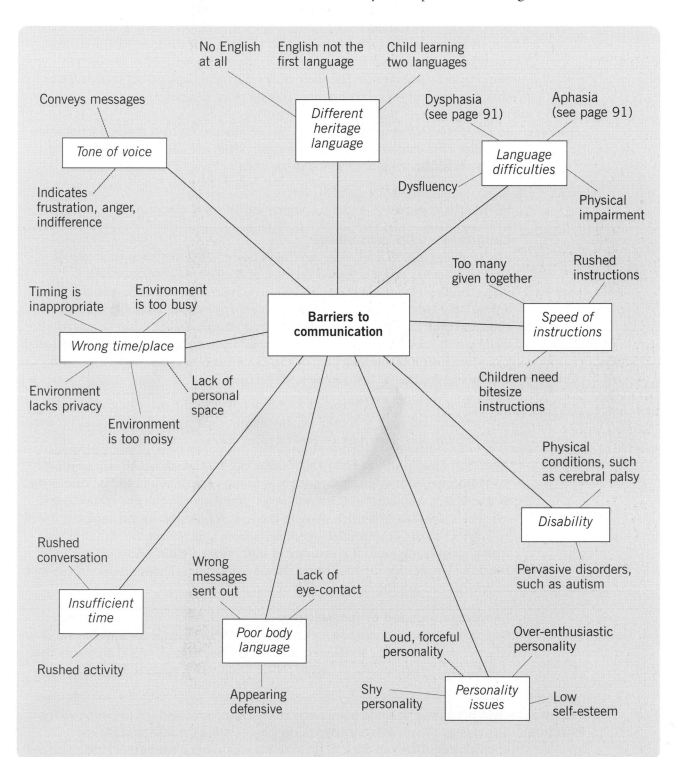

Let's look at some of these in more detail.

### Tone of voice

The tone of your voice can convey many things. It can indicate frustration, anger and irritation as well as pleasure, encouragement and praise. We all respond better to positive tones and are hurt or confused by the negative. Young children may not always understand what is being said to them, but the tone of voice used conveys a message, which at times may be the wrong one. Also, the use of inappropriate language for the stage of development or depth of knowledge a child has can prevent communication taking place successfully.

**Example**    To ask a child 'What are you doing?' can be interpreted by a child as a negative question if the emphasis is placed wrongly: '**What** are you doing?' This could convey frustration and annoyance to the child.

 FORWARD to page 101 and the communication cycle diagram.

### Language – different culture

The language usually spoken in the child's home is referred to as their *first* or *heritage language* and it is passed on from generation to generation. An understanding of cultural practices, child-rearing, religious beliefs and elements of a child's heritage language will help you build appropriate communication with a child and their family. It is important that you communicate within context (i.e. using words relevant to what is happening at a particular moment) and show that you value their heritage language by using it whenever you can, perhaps with a welcoming greeting at the door as a starting point.

Children will often quickly absorb a small amount of the main language used by children and staff in their school or nursery, but their parents may not as yet have acquired this. It is important to explore other ways of communicating.

Asking a non-English speaking child if they need to use the toilet will be more easily understood if you accompany them to the bathroom and use gesture as well as vocabulary, emphasising the word 'toilet'. Similarly, if you need to find out whether a child has had chickenpox (if there is an outbreak in the nursery), it will be helpful to show non-English speaking parents a picture of the rash, together with a questioning look. If a member of staff speaks a child's heritage language, it is usually sensible for them to be the child's key worker. However, all staff should be encouraged to communicate with all families.

### Language – speed of instructions

Giving instructions or guidance in bitesize pieces and talking steadily is a more effective way of helping someone who is struggling to understand an instruction than listing the process they need to follow and leaving them to it.

**Professional Practice**    Each of us have at some point been given instructions and left to get on with it. This neither fills us with confidence nor ensures that the task is achieved appropriately. Can you think of an example when you have been in this position? How did it make you feel?

**Case Study**

*Colleen*

Reception class teacher, Mrs Jackson, asks her nursery nursing student, Colleen, to organise the children for playtime. Colleen gets the children's attention and gives them the following instructions:

'It is playtime. Those of you who have finished your milk, get your coats on. Those of you who have not, please finish your milk, putting your straws and cartons in the bin and then get your coats.

If you need the toilet, go now.

If you have a hat or scarf, put them on please.'

1 How did Colleen do?
2 How many different instructions were there?
3 Do you think all the children will have done all they needed to? If not, why not?
4 How could you have improved upon this?

**Professional Practice**

Children will focus on what ever grabs their attention most – playtime! It is unlikely that they will have taken in all of the student's instructions. Colleen needed to break down her instructions and give them one at a time: 'Who has not yet finished their milk? Please finish it before doing anything else' and so on.

It is important to give clear, 'bite-size' instructions

### Language – difficulties

Problems with speech can hold back the flow of communication and interaction. Such difficulties include:

- **aphasia** – describes a child who is *unable* to express thought in words
- **dysphasia** – dysphasia refers to a child who has *difficulty* in expressing their thoughts in words

- stammering (dysfluency)
- language impairment – which can be part of a condition, such as cerebral palsy, or an impairment in its own right.

 FORWARD to Chapter 9, page 398, where dysfluency is discussed.

*Remember !*  When talking to children, it is often the adult who initiates the development of conversation and, for some children, school or nursery is the only time of day when they have the full attention of an interested adult. It is particularly important for these children that you enrich their language as much as possible by extending and encouraging their use of new terms.

### Personality issues

Sometimes people are loud and forceful in their approach to others which can be off-putting to many individuals. This can be particularly so for young children.

**Activity**

Imagine you are two years old and quietly sitting in your stroller, when suddenly a large face appears beaming at you, exclaiming loudly and poking at your cheeks.

a) How might you feel?
b) What response would you expect from a child in this situation?

## Other forms of communication

There are various non-verbal types of communication, including signing, Braille and art. They each serve a purpose and are favoured for different reasons.

Signing is used by deaf people, those with impaired hearing, people with certain forms of disability and by many people communicating with them. **Signed language** does not only involve hand signs, but uses the whole face and body to communicate. Signed languages are languages in their own right, they are not simply a direct interpretation of a spoken language.

Mukherji and O'Dea (2000, page 152) define a range of non-verbal communication forms as follows:

- *Signed language*
  'The manual and gestural system of communication used by people who are deaf; the sign languages used in different countries are languages in their own right, and not manual means of communicating the spoken languages of those countries.'

The standard manual alphabet: each of the letters is represented by different hand positions

- *Bliss symbols*
  'A universal language of pictographic symbols which is used by people with reading and writing disabilities.'

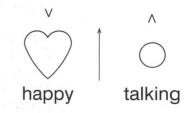

happy    talking

Bliss symbols: each child using this system has their own chart of the symbols they wish to use

**93**

- *Makaton*
  'A basic signing system using signs borrowed from British sign language, used by people who have severe learning difficulties.'

Makaton signs: a system used by many children and adults who have communication difficulties

**boy**
Brush right index pointing left across chin

**rabbit**
Palm forward 'N' hands, held at either side of head, bend several times to indicate ears

**fish**
Right flat hand waggles forward like a fish swimming

**bird**
Index finger and thumb open and close in front of mouth like a beak

- *Braille*
  'A touch-based reading and writing system used by people who are blind.'

Braille is a system of letters made from raised dots

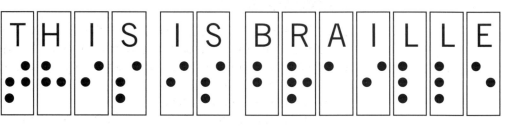

- *Cued speech*
  'A system of eight handshapes made in four locations near the face to assist children (or adults) who are deaf, in lip-reading.'

 FORWARD to page 104 for more about non-verbal communication.

---

**Review your own performance**

Think about the range of communication and interpersonal interactions you have had during your placement experiences and which have been most successful. Which, on reflection, could have been improved upon?

Copy the table and add at least five examples from your practice. An example has been given to get you started.

| Type of communication | With whom? | Any potential barriers identified in advance? | Evaluation of the success of the communication process |
|---|---|---|---|
| Informing parent about headlice in the nursery | Father of a child | Father speaks very little English | Information was successfully passed on through the use of a leaflet and gestures showing how headlice jump from head to head |

**Test Yourself**

✓

1  Name three aspects of verbal communication.
2  Name three aspects of non-verbal communication.
3  What does the term 'barrier to communication' mean? Give an example.
4  What is the difference between dysphasia and aphasia?
5  What is a heritage language?
6  How many alternative forms of communication can you name?

# Supportive skills

Good communication skills enable you to support others. This may be by developing your listening skills, having good written skills and being able to clearly present information in a visual format. Support involves understanding the need for individuals to feel valued, building up their self-esteem, knowing when help is needed from additional sources and what options that help might include. As a good listener, you will develop a better understanding of the children in your care, and their families.

## Listening skills

Listening involves taking in a range of different sorts of information. It is not the same as hearing (as when listening to music), as you need to *take in* the information and often act upon it. In an early years setting you will listen to:

- children telling you their news
- children asking for your help
- children sharing their experiences of activities with you
- children explaining their problems
- parents giving you important information about feeds, diet, health, and so on
- parents confiding in you about family issues that may affect their child
- colleagues explaining changes to the daily routine
- colleagues passing on useful hints and ideas
- colleagues updating you through the cascading of information
- outside professionals (for example, a Portage worker) giving you guidance.

Each of these 'speakers' needs your attention to enable you to meet the needs of the children in your care adequately. Listening carefully is a skill which is well worth practising. Think about when you listen best and what affects your listening. Is it noise? Other people? Or the level of activity going on around you? Do you consider that you always give people your full attention?

**Activity**

1  Talk to a partner for three minutes on any subject you choose. When the time is up, your partner should repeat what you have said. What did they leave out? Change roles and repeat the exercise.
2  How hard was it to keep focused?
3  Which are you best at, speaking or listening? Why is this?

4 What did your partner's body language tell you? Did they appear interested in what you were saying? Or did they appear bored?
5 How did their body language affect you?
6 Think about what effect a 'listener's' body language might have on a 'speaker'.

**Professional Practice**

It can be useful to study the communication processes in a range of early years settings, noting the effects of the staff's responses on the children.

**Case Study**

*Hopes and Dreams Day Nursery*

Hopes and Dreams Day Nursery is your new placement, and your supervisor has suggested that you take a couple of days to observe how the nursery day is structured and how the staff work with the children. You settle with a notebook and observe the following:

**Observation 1**

Tom is crying as someone has scribbled on his picture. Sarah (nursery nurse) stops what she is doing (clearing a table for snacktime) and sits down with Tom to listen to what he is saying. At first he is very distressed, but begins to calm down with her full attention and is able to explain to her what happened more clearly. Eventually, when he is completely calm and ready to go back to the activities, she finds a special piece of paper for him to draw another picture.

**Observation 2**

Sophie runs to Stella (nursery nurse) telling her that her model has been knocked down *again* by James. Stella is more focused on a conversation between two members of staff about the changes to the rota. Stella tells Sophie 'never mind, make another one'. Stella returns to the construction area and kicks the construction materials and then sits down in a corner and does nothing.

1 What was the main difference between these two observations?
2 How should Stella have responded to Sophie?
3 What does this tell you about the importance of listening?

**Professional Practice**

Consider what you find most difficult about listening:
• Think about when you have really listened to another person.
• Have you ever avoided listening to someone for any reason?
• Can you remember when someone has listened carefully to you?
• When have you not been listened to as carefully as you would have liked?

How did you feel about each of these situations?

*Remember!*

It is important to:
• show that you are listening by focusing on the speaker
• make eye-contact and use encouraging smiles and gestures
• try not to interrupt, let their speech flow, particularly if they are upset or agitated.

### Active listening

#### Paraphrasing

**Paraphrasing** involves summarising what has been said and is an easy means of checking that you have understood what you have heard. Your response would start with statements such as:

- 'So what you are telling me is …'
- 'Would I be right in thinking that …'.

This checks that you have understood what has been said to you and also shows the speaker that you value them and have been listening carefully to them.

#### Reflective listening

**Reflective listening** is more about showing that you understand what people are feeling, rather than the details of what they are saying. Your responses to them focus firstly on their feelings and emotions. These can be positive emotions, such as excitement or elation, or less positive emotions, such as anger, worry or sadness.

Reflective listening at any age involves understanding the feelings of others

**Review your own performance**

Copy the table and complete it to review your own performance in listening reflectively to children. An example has been included to get you started.

| When | Where | Child's initials | Incident if known | Emotion being communicated | Response by you |
|------|-------|------------------|-------------------|----------------------------|-----------------|
| Mon a.m. | Nursery | BH | Broken toy | Worry | Reassurance |

## Written skills

In early years you will at some point need to write reports, observations, letters of application and draw up a CV (*curriculum vitae*). Writing effectively involves taking the appropriate approach and using the correct level of language. You will need to pay attention to both your spelling and your use of grammar as your material will lack credibility if poorly written.

A written report may be required, for example, to record the progress of a child, to contribute to a child protection enquiry or to record an accident or an incident within the setting.

FORWARD to Chapter 5, page 191, and Chapter 6, page 233, for information about writing these types of report.

> **Checklist for writing reports**
>
> ✔ Ensure that you cover all the required details.
> ✔ Make clear what are facts and what are opinions.
> ✔ Set your report out clearly, with an introduction, a middle and a conclusion.
> ✔ Avoid the use of abbreviations.
> ✔ If you are writing a report as a student, make sure it is countersigned by your placement supervisor.
> ✔ Ensure that black ink is used if your report is to be photocopied.
> ✔ Add recommendations if requested.
> ✔ Ensure the level of English used is appropriate for the target 'audience' (readership).
> ✔ Where appropriate, send the report to a named person, not simply to an office.

Information on writing CVs can be found in Brumfitt *et al.* (2001) – see *Bibliography and suggested further reading*, page 115.

## Visual forms of information

Working in partnership with parents is a strong emphasis of most providers of early years care and education and it is important to keep parents well informed. You need to pass on information through mediums which parents can readily access, and more than one medium may be needed to meet everyone's needs. Options include:

Newsletters

Home/setting books

Noticeboards

Posters

Photographs

Displays of children's creativity

### Newsletters
A regular newsletter set out clearly, with an outline of what has been happening and plans for the future, is ideal. Where possible, translate it into the heritage

languages of the families involved. Illustrations will help non-readers and non-English-speaking parents to understand. For example, a sketch of a coach and a lunchbox with dates alongside will help indicate a forthcoming trip.

# HOPES & DREAMS NURSERY
# NEWSLETTER
June 2002

## News
The final topic for this term is 'farms' to coincide with our end-of-term trip. Any relevant items for display will be appreciated, particularly photographs of real farms and farm animals.

## Diary Dates
The end of year photograph of those children moving on to school will be taken on 28 June at 11.30 a.m.

**3 July Trip to City Farm**
Coach leaves the Nursery at 10.00 a.m.

Please bring lunch boxes.

## Home/setting books
This simple idea involves an exercise book, usually kept in a plastic wallet, in which staff and parents can exchange comments and information about the child. They are particularly useful for children who are escorted to and from the setting via local authority transport, where contact with parents is minimal.

## Noticeboards and posters
Bright, visual posters will attract attention and can be a particularly important means of conveying health and safety guidelines, such as skin protection in the sun and the hazards of toxocaria in animal faeces. Their visual emphasis reduces the need to read the accompanying wording, extending accessibility.

A noticeboard that is updated regularly will be more likely to encourage parents to look at it than one which has the same material displayed for weeks on end.

## Photographs
A montage of photographs showing what the children have been doing recently is a lovely way of keeping parents informed of their child's activities, particularly for parents who work full-time and have not been able to attend picnics, sports days and similar events.

## Displays of children's creativity
Wall and table displays, which are changed regularly, will encourage parents to look around more frequently, appreciating the creations of their own child and those of others. Labelling items with children's names and mounting displays tidily are an important indication that you value what the children have been doing.

Displaying work encourages children's interest

 *Remember!*

- It is important that all children are represented in displayed material.
- Parents should be actively encouraged to show interest in their child's activities.
- Photographs of children should not be displayed outside the setting without parents' permission.

FORWARD to Chapter 6, page 235, *Case Study: Abigail.*

## The support of advocates, interpreters and translators

**Advocacy** means speaking on behalf of another individual and representing their interests, and the person taking on this role is referred to as an advocate. Advocates are involved if parents are unable to access the services they need due to a lack of sufficient spoken English, to ensure that they are understood or if they are unfamiliar with which services may be available to them and their children. An advocate may also be brought in if parents feel that a child's needs are not being recognised by the professionals currently involved.

The role of the advocate is to listen and interpret for the parent, following this with liaison and negotiation regarding the outcomes of the meeting or consultation. Advocates are usually known to the family through their role as health visitor, social worker or representative from an organisation to which they belong. They can be particularly useful to parents with a child who has a special need, ensuring the rights of the child to suitable education provision are met.

Child Advocacy is referred to in Sections 3.11 and 4.67 of the Code of Practice (1994). They are referred to here as a 'Named Person' who can:

> '... give the parents information and advice about their child's special educational needs, supporting them in their discussion ...' 3.11

'... LEAs should inform parents that they may be accompanied by friends, relatives, or their Named Person, at any meetings.' 4.67

**Test Yourself**

1  List at least five different sorts of information you will listen to as an early years worker.
2  What is paraphrasing?
3  Give an example of reflective listening.
4  When is visual information particularly important?
5  What does the role of an advocate involve?

# Communication

For **communication** to be successful it needs to meet the needs of both speakers. Any breakdown in this will result in a lack of communication taking place.

## The communication cycle

The diagram below shows how communication can be explained as a cycle, in which we each in turn take the part of the 'encoder' (the person who sends the message) and the 'decoder' (the person who deciphers, and therefore understands, the message). During conversation we continually swop roles from encoder to decoder and as the diagram demonstrates, the *common field of experience* is where the message is initially decoded. Without a common field, the message is likely to get lost or distorted and can be likened to conversing with another person when there is no shared language between you.

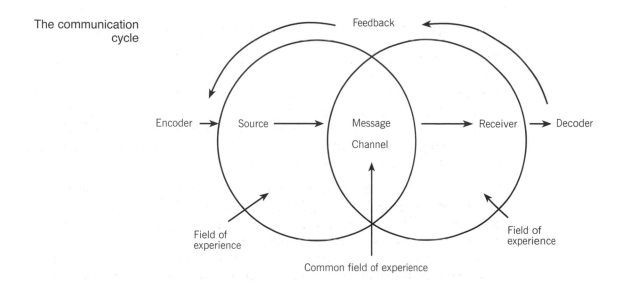

The communication cycle

For communication to work successfully, the message channel needs to be a common field of experience for both the encoder (the speaker) and the decoder (the listener).

Communication can fail because of:
* lack of vocabulary
* nability to speak, see or hear
* lack of listening skills
* inability to concentrate
* lack of knowledge
* lack of interest
* misinterpretation
* wrong (or confusing) body language/facial expressions
* surrounding noises
* wrong timing/place/person.

Failing to communicate may make us feel:
* frustrated
* hurt
* angry
* misunderstood
* inadequate.

## The importance of a common field of experience

A 'language' which is understood by both early years workers and parents is important to the building and maintaining of relationships. Without it, communication will break down quickly and hinder the sharing of information about the child's progress or needs and the setting's ability to work in partnership with parents.

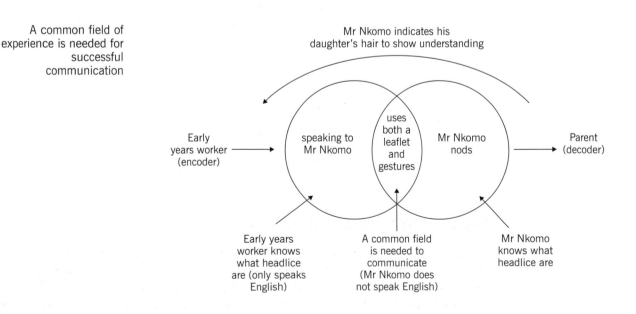

A common field of experience is needed for successful communication

*Henry*

Henry's key worker, Sue, is talking to his mother when she comes to collect him. She asks her if she has noticed an increase in Henry's spatial awareness. Henry's mother looks slightly embarrassed and shrugs her shoulders. Sue goes on to say that there has been a great improvement noticed by the staff in the nursery and Henry is pleased with his newly acquired skills.

Sue was assuming Henry's mum's shared knowledge of the developmental term 'spatial awareness'. Henry's mum went away without understanding what skill he was developing.

1  How else might Sue have phrased the question?
2  What affect might the embarrassment have had on Henry's mum?
3  Should Sue have noticed Henry's mother's discomfort?
4  What does this tell you about parent–staff relationships?

**Activity**

It would have been far better for Sue to ask Henry's mum if she had noticed how Henry can now steer round obstacles or find a suitable space in which to carry out his roly-polys without knocking others over. This would have maintained a more positive form of communication, and Henry's mum would have understood what he had achieved.

Put this into a communication cycle like the one below.

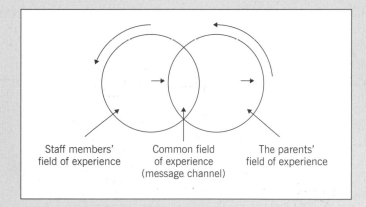

Staff members' field of experience    Common field of experience (message channel)    The parents' field of experience

## Open and closed questions

Another aspect of conversation involves asking questions. The way in which questions are phrased makes a difference to the answers (feedback) you receive. Questions can be useful to clarify something you are unsure of and can indicate to the other person that you are interested in what they have to say, by extending the conversation further. An **open question** offers the opportunity for a wide-ranging answer, whereas a **closed question** restricts the answer to one word, such as 'yes' or 'no', or a limited statement. Think carefully about the type of question you are asking.

Example    'Did you enjoy your lunch?' is a closed question. 'Yes' or 'No' are the likely answers, whereas 'What do you prefer to eat at lunch time?' offers the opportunity for a range of answers and therefore extends conversation.

*Remember !*    You will only receive the information you are looking for if you ask the right questions in the appropriate way.

**Activity**

1 Decide whether the following questions are open or closed.
   a) Does Sangita have any allergies?
   b) Did you enjoy going on an aeroplane?
   c) Where did you go on your holiday?
   d) Do you enjoy listening to stories?
   e) Which is your favourite book?
   f) How did Mollie react to the new baby?
   g) What can you remember seeing when we went to the farm?

2 How could you alter the closed questions to make them more open?

## Non-verbal communication

Non-verbal expressions can tell us a great deal about how people are feeling. However, it is important to remember that different cultures have differing cultural practices. As an early years worker, you should, whenever possible, research the cultural customs and practices of the children in your care, recognising that a cultural 'norm' will not be followed by all families of that particular culture. This will help you to avoid causing offence or embarrassment.

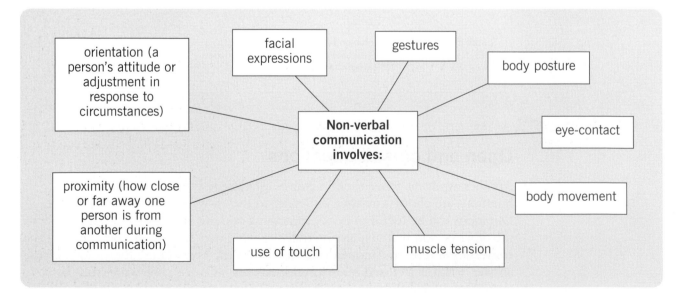

At times we need to interpret what children are trying to say to us through their actions and **body language** (their **non-verbal communication**), which can be displayed either consciously or subconsciously. This can be particularly important if they have been hurt or abused and the observation skills and level of understanding you develop will enable you to be alert to such non-verbal signs.

## Activity

Copy the table. Consider the non-verbal forms of communication listed and make notes about the messages you may observe for each of the emotions listed.

| Non-verbal forms of communication | Sad | Anxious | Scared | Happy | Shy |
|---|---|---|---|---|---|
| Eye-contact<br>Tone of voice<br>Body posture<br>Voice level<br>Facial expression<br>Level of activity<br>Gestures | | | | | |

 FORWARD to Chapter 6, pages 198–202. *Indicators of abuse*.

## Professional Practice

A smile gives encouragement and a gesture can indicate how to approach an activity. To help to gain the confidence of a shy or anxious child, you can set up a favourite activity and do it with the child.

## Touch

How we make contact with others can say a great deal about us. Each of us makes contact with other people everyday, at times this is just verbally, but at others it is more tactile. You need to consider how closely others wish to be in contact with you, and in what circumstances, asking yourself whether you ever 'invade the space' of anyone, and what signs they have given you to indicate this. How do you feel if another person sits or stands too close to you? What indication of this do you display?

**Activity**

Think about the contact you have with other people.

a) Which circumstances involve physical contact?

b) What determines whether you initiate touch?

c) When do others initiate touch with you?

d) Has physical contact ever felt inappropriate or unnecessary? If so, why was this?

Sometimes, as an early years worker it is inadvisable to touch a child, especially if there is a danger of your touch being misinterpreted. You need to be aware of what forms of touch are appropriate and what are not. You also need to consider the issues of consent.

FORWARD to Chapter 6, page 234, for more about this important area of your professionalism.

### Eye-contact

**Eye-contact** can keep a conversation going. When no eye-contact is made, it is likely that the conversation will trail away. When individuals are feeling nervous, embarrassed, shy or guilty, it is a natural response to avoid eye-contact.

Eye-contact is a connection between the speaker and the listener. It makes them feel accepted by one another.

### Body language

Your body language is part of your personality. Some people are more physically demonstrative than others. Gestures and positioning of the body can suggest a range of feelings, including submission, aggression, defensiveness and assertiveness. They can also demonstrate a welcome, humour, warmth and openness.

BACK to page 93 for information on other forms of non-verbal communication – signed language, Bliss symbols, Makaton, Braille and cued speech.

***Review your own performance***    Think about how well you communicate with others. Copy and complete the table (based on Burnard, 1992).

| Person I am communicating with | How do I find communication with them? | | | |
|---|---|---|---|---|
| | Easy? | Difficult? | Unsure? | OK? |
| Child under 5<br>Child 5–10<br>Young person<br>Teenagers<br>Adults socially<br>Adults in placement<br>Parents in placement<br>A complete stranger<br>Non-English speakers<br>Child with a special need<br>Adult with a special need | | | | |

## Oral presentations

Communication skills are needed when presenting information orally to others. This may be during your course of study, as you present a piece of research to a group or, once qualified, through giving a short presentation to groups of parents. Your tone of voice, use of body language and facial expression will contribute to how well you keep the attention of those you are speaking to. Making eye-contact will again be important, as this involves others in what you are saying, and indicates that you are speaking to them personally. When you give a presentation you may wish to use visual aids, such as overhead projector transparencies, video recordings or give a handout. These need to be prepared carefully, so they add something to your presentation and do not detract from it.

You may feel apprehensive before a presentation, particularly if it is a new experience. This is quite normal and it can be useful to focus on the fact that everyone will be doing the same and will share your concerns.

*Remember !*    A slightly short, but clear, presentation, which is interesting and demonstrates preparation, will be assessed more highly than a long-winded presentation which demonstrates little preparation or forethought.

A useful source which has a section on preparing for an oral presentation is Green (2000) – see *Bibliography and suggested further reading*, page 115.

**Test Yourself**

1 Explain the communication cycle.
2 What is the difference between open and closed questions?
3 What examples can you give of non-verbal communication?

# Supportive skills with distressed individuals

This section looks at how communication and interpersonal skills can help to support others in a range of situations. Professionally this can involve children, their parents and the colleagues you work with, but socially and at home the same skills apply. At times, we understand how others are feeling (we have *empathy*), perhaps due to previous experiences of our own, but at other times we cannot really imagine how an individual feels, or why they are so distressed about something. This is where your interpersonal skills will really help you to succeed. You will use these skills in respecting the views, feelings and needs of others and in finding an appropriate means of supporting them.

Distressed behaviour can include:
• anger
• aggression
• being withdrawn
• uncontrollable crying.

## Reasons for distressed behaviour

The main reasons for distressed behaviour are shown in the diagram below.

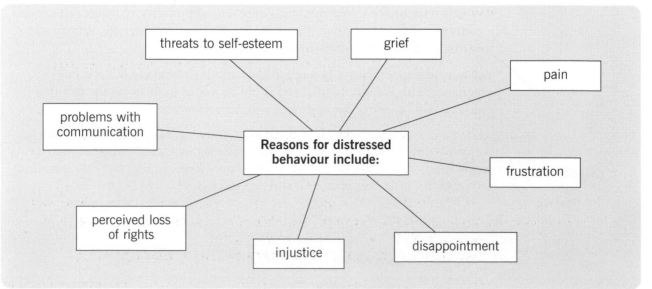

Any of these are difficult for an individual to cope with, but imagine how much harder it might be if you did not have the skills or the language to express yourself and ask for the help you need. Who would *you* turn to in these circumstances? It is worth exploring who you would turn to and why – what do you feel makes them approachable? Is it their calm nature, their practical approach, or what? How do you think you might feel if someone confided in you or sought your advice on a serious matter?

**Activity**

What feelings do you think you (or others) might feel if a distressed person turns to you? Might you feel:
- scared that you might 'get it wrong'?
- pleased that they felt able to turn to you?
- out of your depth?
- unready for this level of responsibility?

What else?
Dealing with distress sometimes necessitates the helper (you) also being helped. This is the same for trained counsellors who are counselling clients regularly and have considerable experience. They have a mentor who they can turn to when necessary, together with regular 'supervision' sessions, as taking on the stresses of another person can be stressful for you and, being bound by confidentiality much of the time, the lack of opportunity to 'off-load' stressful issues can be hard to cope with.

## Strategies of support

The following strategies for supporting distressed individuals are a useful starting point in considering how to prepare for any future situations you may find yourself in:
- Remain calm.
- Allow the distressed person time to sit quietly.
- Let them release their emotions through crying if that seems to be needed.
- Offer practical support, drink, tissues, and so on.
- Use reflective listening.
- Paraphrase when appropriate.
- Be aware that often you will only be able to start the helping process, not complete it.

**Professional Practice**
- There are cultural differences in the mourning process following death, and developing a knowledge of these differences will ensure that you respond appropriately to the families within your care.
- Dealing with disclosure of abuse needs particularly careful handling.

FORWARD to Chapter 6, page 221, for important guidelines on dealing with disclosure.

Your interpersonal skills will help you to support distressed individuals

As an early years worker, once you have gained experience and (in a day nursery) have been made a key worker or room supervisor, it is likely that parents will turn to you for advice. It can be useful to have previously researched and drawn up a list of useful contact addresses that can be passed on if appropriate. These might include helplines such as Cry-sis (if an infant's crying becomes too much) or Cruise (bereavement support). What others can you think of?

### Activity

With a partner, research a range of useful addresses and telephone numbers and put them together in a pack or on an information sheet. Keep this in your professional practice portfolio for future reference.

## Dealing with confrontation

You will no doubt have to use your interpersonal skills at some point to deal with confrontation. You may be faced with an angry parent or an awkward member of staff, and the approach you take will make a difference to whether you achieve a successful outcome.

The word 'assertive' can sometimes be confused with 'aggressive', so it is worth exploring the difference between them.

* An **assertive** person is one who can remain calm during an incident of confrontation or disagreement, clearly outlining what they wish to say, and repeating their point if necessary without becoming over-excited or angry. They remain in control of themselves and stay within appropriate boundaries.

- An **aggressive** person is one who often talks loudly and excitedly, displaying agitated and angry body language, and may make personal comments unrelated to the conflict or disagreement. They are not therefore fully in control of themselves or the situation.

Assertive skills are useful when you need to stand up for something, for example, when:
- justifying a course of action you have taken
- challenging a request to take on a greater workload when you are already overstretched
- declining to accept having to change your plans when you know that it will cause considerable stress at home for you to do so, and others are available
- asking for an individual's views to be listened to by your headteacher or manager
- requesting an increased level of support to enable you to achieve something specific.

Burnard (1992) describes three approaches to coping with confrontation, which are summarised below.

> **Three possible approaches to confrontation**
> - *Submissive approach* (pussyfooting) – the person avoids conflict and confrontation by avoiding the topic in hand
> - *Assertive approach* – the person is clear, calm and prepared to repeat what they have to say
> - *Aggressive approach* (sledgehammering) – the person is heavy-handed and makes a personal attack of the issue

Burnard clarifies this further by describing the body language of each approach as follows:
- *Submissive approach*
    - hunched or rounded shoulders
    - failure to face the other person directly
    - eye-contact averted
    - nervous smile
    - fiddling with hands
    - nervous gestures
    - voice low-pitched and apologetic
- *Assertive approach*
    - face-to-face with the other person
    - 'comfortable' eye-contact
    - facial expression that is 'congruent' with what is being said
    - voice clear and calm
- *Aggressive approach*
    - hands on hips or arms folded
    - very direct eye-contact
    - angry expression
    - loud voice
    - voice threatening or angry
    - threatening or provocative hand gestures.

In reflecting on your own practice, ask yourself:
- Where do I see myself in the above three descriptions?
- Who can I identify as using each type of approach?
- What am I learning about my responsibilities as an early years professional?
- How well am I currently able to deal with aggression in a situation of conflict?

**Case Study**

*Shabana*

Shabana has just started work as a nursery nurse. Her working day is shared between two Reception classes of a primary school. She is unhappy with her list of duties for the coming term, as the majority of her time will be taken up with preparing materials for the class teachers and supervising domestic tasks, such as children undressing for PE and toilet duties. Shabana understands that her role is as a support to the teaching staff, but feels that the knowledge, understanding and practical experience she has of young children through her qualification, and the two years of study taken to achieve it, is being underused and undervalued.

Shabana wishes to have her duties reviewed.

1  How would you put your case across to the teaching staff if you were Shabana?
2  Share your ideas with another student.
3  Where would your planned approach fit in with the thinking of Burnard?
4  What changes would you need to consider?

## Legislation and confidentiality

Confidentiality is directly linked to communication and will be a vital aspect of your professional role in the early years sector. You may find that parents will talk to you about their child, and sometimes about matters that worry them too. As your relationship builds up, you may be trusted with personal or family problems that are private to them. You should feel privileged that someone has trusted you sufficiently to speak to you in confidence – that trust should not be abused.

At other times you may have information passed on to you that is of concern to you. You will need to decide when it is appropriate to pass information on and when it is not.

Throughout this book you will find reference to the term 'need to know'. This means exactly what it says, the information you are given only needs to be shared with those who *need to know* about it.

**Activity**

In each of the following cases, who, if anyone, is the person who needs to know this information? How much do they need to be told?

a) David has a urine infection and needs to go to the toilet regularly (and urgently) throughout the day. He cannot 'hang on' for five minutes until breaktime.
b) Jessica's father has left the family home suddenly after a violent row with his wife. Jessica is very upset and unusually quiet.
c) Selina's mother is depressed and takes anti-depressants regularly.
d) Paula's mother leaves her alone for three hours each evening to work at the local store. There is a coal fire in the sitting room, which does not always have a fire-guard.
e) Jerome's dad (who helps out regularly in your pre-school) was placed on list 99 when he left his teaching post.
f) Earl's mother is a stripper in a night club and he is cared for by his older sister much of the time.

FORWARD to Chapter 6, page 235, for an explanation of list 99.

**Professional Practice**

- Information should only be passed on to people to enable them to care for a child more appropriately or to maintain safety: of the child, or of the setting.
- Prejudging a situation based on 'hearsay' or 'gossip' can be dangerous.
- At times you will have to break a confidence for the safety and well-being of a child. Whenever possible, the person who has given you information initially should be told if you have felt the need to pass it on.

FORWARD to Chapter 6, page 222, for further discussion of confidentiality.

Confidentiality is protected through various Acts of Parliament, including:
- Data Protection Act (1998)
- Access to Personal Files Act (1987)
- Access to Medical Reports Act (1988)
- Access to Health Records Act (1990).

Legislation is important because it helps to ensure that personal details are recorded appropriately and that unauthorised access to them is prevented. It directs what may and what may not be kept on records, and what information can be kept manually and through technological means. Legislation states the rights of individuals to see their personal records, although in certain cases there are exceptions to this, for example if having access to medical records would be detrimental to a person's well-being. Legislation sets out that each person should know who has access to their files and that records held in respect of any enquiry should hold only facts and not personal opinions.

It would be useful to familiarise yourself with each of the Acts listed above. They are available from HMSO publishers and on the Internet.

*Review your own performance*  Having read the chapter and reflected on your communication skills, copy and complete the table as an evaluation of how well you communicate.

**An evaluation of your current communication skills**

| Current strengths | Areas for particular focus |
|---|---|
| 1<br>2<br>3<br>4<br>5 | 1<br>2<br>3<br>4<br>5 |

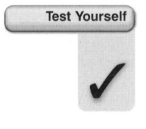

**Test Yourself**

1 What can be the cause of distressed behaviour?
2 Why do counsellors need a mentor?
3 What strategies of support can you think of?
4 What is the difference between being submissive, assertive and aggressive?
5 Why is eye-contact important to successful communication?
6 Why is legislation important in the context of confidentiality?

# Key terms

**You should now understand the following words and phrases. If you do not, read through the chapter again and review them.**

active listening
advocacy
aggressive
aphasia
assertive
barriers to communication
body language
closed questions
communication
communication cycle

dysphasia
eye-contact
interpersonal skills
non-verbal communication
open questions
paraphrasing
reflective listening
signed language
submissive

## Bibliography and suggested further reading

Brumfitt *et al.* (2001) *Human Resources*, Vocational Business series 4, Nelson Thornes, Cheltenham

Burnard, P. (1992) *Communicate! A Communication Skills Guide for Health Care Workers*, Edward Arnold

Burnard, P. (1995) *Learning Human Skills: An Experiential and Reflective Guide for Nurses*, 3rd edition, Butterworth and Heinemann, London

Green, S. (2000) *Research Methods in Health, Social and Early Years Care*, Nelson Thornes, Cheltenham

Mukherji, P. and O'Dea, T. (2000) *Understanding Children's Language and Literacy*, Nelson Thornes, Cheltenham

Porritt, L. (1990) *Interaction Strategies: An Introduction for Health Professionals*, 2nd edition, Churchill Livingstone, London

# 4 Research

---

**This chapter covers:**

- Research methods
- Statistical research information
- The purpose and role of research
- Ethical issues
- Using research skills.

---

## Introduction

Research skills are important to all courses of study, particularly at level 3 and above. To achieve a BTec National in Early Years your research skills will need to be well developed, as each unit you study will require an element of personal enquiry, with many units demanding considerable levels of independent research and study. Your college tutors will arrange an induction into the college library and resource centre, with introductions to the staff who are available to give you advice and guidance.

Personal research involves the exploration of both technological and non-technological sources. You will need to know how to access both.

As you progress through the course, you will need to make reference to how thinking and practice in the field of early years has been improved due to the impact of research outcomes. An example of how research has contributed to the improvement of practice in early years is the study of the care of children in hospital. During the 1950s and 1960s, James and Joyce Robertson (both child psychiatrists) observed and filmed children during separation from their primary carer (usually their mothers) during hospital stays and residential care. They identified a pattern of distress which raised concern about the long-term effects such separations could have on the children. In 1959 the Platt Report (initiated by the UK government) set out the welfare needs of children in hospital and as a result the National Association for the Welfare of Children in Hospital (NAWCH) was established (now known as Action for Sick Children, ASC). The outcomes of the Robertson research, together with the Platt Report, resulted in parents being encouraged to accompany their children when receiving hospital treatment.

This chapter will help you to understand the research process, by enabling you to gain the practical, written and analytical skills that are required, and by helping you to understand how research has an impact on professional practice (the purpose and role of research).

You will need to be able to:
- describe and evaluate a range of relevant research methods
- use and present statistics
- understand the purpose and role of research
- understand the implications of ethical issues in the research process.

## Key skills

Research projects offer ideal opportunities for you to gain the key skills of:
- Communication
- Application of number
- Information technology.

If you are gathering evidence for the wider key skills:
- Working with others
- Improving own learning and performance
- Problem-solving
- Personal skills development,

you will also find that the activities you carry out, and the decisions you make, will contribute to your portfolio of evidence.

# Research methods

Research is the systematic investigation of a topic for a purpose, using orderly and scientific methods. An analysis of the outcomes of research can lead to the development of new ideas and improved practice.

Methods of research vary considerably and you need to choose the method most suitable for your current assignment task or personal enquiry (for example if you undertake Unit 15 *Project*). Research methods can be divided into two types – **primary research** and **secondary research**.

## Primary and secondary research

The significant difference between primary and secondary research is that:
- primary research is research you have carried out yourself
- secondary research is the use of material researched and presented by others.

In general assignment work, you will almost always use more secondary sources than primary sources, as you explore material produced by others to support your written work, interpreting (clarifying and explaining) your findings and analysing (evaluating) their relevance. Primary research is needed, and is a mandatory requirement, in Unit 15 (*Project*) and in specified assignment briefs. For example, a practical activity that could be linked to Unit 13 (*Developmental Psychology*) may ask you to replicate Piaget's conservation experiments within your current placement, presenting and evaluating the outcomes with reference to Piaget and his subsequent critics.

FORWARD to Chapter 9, page 382, for an explanation of Piaget's conservation experiments.

**Examples of primary and secondary research methods**

| Primary | Secondary |
|---|---|
| Interviews | Literature searches |
| Questionnaires | Media analysis |
| Action research | Technology based research |
| Observation | Case studies |
| Case studies | Statistical analysis |
| Experiments | |

## Quantitative and qualitative research

Research can be either **quantitative** or **qualitative**:
- Quantitative research produces results which can be expressed using numbers or statistics, exploring the extent to which something happens.
- Qualitative research explores individual viewpoints which are not so easily measured. In contrast to quantitative research, qualitative researchers wish to gain an understanding of their topic rather than make an analysis of statistics.

At times a piece of research can involve both approaches.

In all research, the quality of the information you receive is directly linked to the questions you ask. It is important that your questions are well thought out for your resulting data to be of any use to you. The wording of questions needs to be carefully thought through.

FORWARD to page 124 for more about questions in research.

## Longitudinal, cross-sectional and cross-cultural studies

Research can include longitudinal, cross-sectional or cross-cultural studies:
- A longitudinal study is a study carried out over a given length of time, following the progress of something or someone (for example, a child's development).
- A cross-sectional study takes a 'slice' (a cross-section) of its target group and its overall findings are assumed to be typical of the whole group.
- In a cross-cultural piece of research, the researcher would decide on the main focus of their research and then apply it to a range of cultures. This could be confined to a single community or could be applied across a range of communities.

Explore a range of research studies, either past or contemporary (current).

a)  Make notes on what each study was about.
b)  Place them under the headings of longitudinal, cross-sectional and cross-cultural studies.
c)  What was the main purpose of each study?
d)  Do you think the type of study used was the best option for the purpose?
e)  Would an alternative approach have been possible?

FORWARD to page 149 and read the section *The purpose and role of research* before you do this activity.

## Bias and objectivity

In all research, **objectivity** (an impartial viewpoint) is important. Personal opinion, bias or prejudice can influence both the process of research and the interpretation of the results. Maintaining objectivity will ensure that your research is 'value-free'. This is not always easy. The results of research will not always be what you expect, and it is important that you accept the outcomes of research. Carrying out an honest analysis of the outcomes and producing an accurate report ensures that your research is as objective as possible. **Subjective** research outcomes (a viewpoint influenced by your own opinions) will be of little value to either yourself or anyone else.

## Forming a hypothesis, an issue or research question

In any piece of research, the overall aim needs to be made clear. This will usually be in the form of:
• a research issue – a statement of fact or a concern that could be explored by the researcher
• a research question – when the researcher wishes to find out a specific answer
• a hypothesis – a statement which the researcher sets out either to prove or disprove.

Forming a hypothesis is a requirement of Unit 15 (*Project*). Your hypothesis will need to be both achievable and identifiable.

### A hypothesis
A hypothesis can be either:
• *single-ended* – for example 'Girls read more than boys' is a single-ended hypothesis because it suggests which way the outcome of the enquiry is likely to be and it can be proven either right or wrong
• *open-ended* – for example 'Day care affects children's social skills' is an open-ended hypothesis because it does not predict an outcome, but simply infers that one factor (day care) will affect another (children's social skills).

A research question or issue can sometimes give a clearer aim for you to work towards, but setting a hypothesis is often more interesting and thought-provoking.

The research process can be summarised as follows:
• Research has a purpose: to inform and improve practice.
• Research enables society to develop new ideas based on enquiry.
• Research may involve a new line of enquiry (primary research method).
• A previous piece of research may be referred to (secondary research method).
• The results of research may be measurable (quantitative research).
• Research may simply give insight into a subject (qualitative research).
• Research can be used to compare, to explore a theory or to identify change.
• Research needs a specific focus, in the form of a hypothesis, an issue or a question.

**Activity**

Explore the outcomes of a piece of research carried out during your lifetime.

a) What was its purpose?
b) What primary research methods were used?
c) What secondary sources were referred to?
d) Was the research quantitative or qualitative?
e) What was the hypothesis?
f) Was it proved or disproved?
g) In what ways was objectivity on the part of the research team important?

FORWARD to page 149, and read the section *The purpose and role of research* before you do this activity.

## Primary sources of data collection

Primary research involves carrying out a new line of enquiry. The interview is a common primary research method.

### Interviews

Interviews can be either structured or unstructured, or they can be a combination of both. They are particularly useful if you are trying to find out people's individual opinions or experiences (a qualitative approach), although quantitative research can also be carried out in this way. Most interviews are planned in advance, but on occasions an interview can be carried out 'on the spot'. The level of structure to an interview can be drawn as a continuum (a line upon which we can mark differing positions):

•——————————————————————————————•

*Structured interviews*                    *Unstructured interviews*

The interview is a common primary research method

### Structured interviews

The level of structure in the interview can usually be equated with its level of formality. The more formal approach usually follows a rigid course of pre-set questions which every participant is asked. These answers are controlled by forming questions which do not allow for expansion of the topic area. They are known as closed questions and can be particularly useful in quantitative research.

### Advantages and disadvantages of structured interviews

| Advantages | Disadvantages |
|---|---|
| The questions are firmly set in advance. All participants are asked the same questions. The structure and outcomes can be narrowly focused. The outcomes are easy to collate. Time management can be carefully controlled by the researcher. | There is no flexibility. The additional information a participant may have available will be missed |

### Unstructured interviews

In an unstructured interview, each participant is asked the same set of questions, but time is allowed for questions to be developed further. It is often considered to be a far more relaxed process.

### Advantages and disadvantages of unstructured interviews

| Advantages | Disadvantages |
|---|---|
| The questions set in advance are asked exactly the simply as a guide or prompt | Not all participants are used same questions |
| Flexibility is offered to explore if appropriate | Questions about the points further reliability of the outcomes may be raised |
| The structure and outcomes either not so easily narrowly or broadly focused | Time management is can be controlled by the researcher |
| | The interview can become simply a 'chat' if not carefully contained |

### A combined approach

A combined approach usually involves a list of specified questions but the interviewer allows expansion where it is felt appropriate. This enables a degree of control to remain while allowing flexibility within the interview. This would place the interview nearer the middle of the continuum:

•_____•_____•_____•

*Structured interview*    *Combined approach*    *Unstructured interview*

### Length of interviews

Interviews should not be overly long, and it is usual for the researcher to impose a time limit. A structured interview would normally take less time than an unstructured interview due to the pre-set process involved. Your proposed time limit should be stated in advance. Consider how much time *you* would be willing to give up for someone else's research before you ask others to agree to your request.

You need to make note of participants' responses throughout the interview, and so the ability to use shorthand would be an advantage. It is important to be systematic, using the same approach to each set of interview notes to make it easier to compare participants' responses at the analysis stage.

Recording an interview on tape or video recorder is an alternative approach. It can be useful if you need to record answers verbatim (word-for-word). A video recording also enables you to look at participants' body language, but transcribing tapes is time-consuming and so these methods should be selected with caution. It is imperative that participants have agreed to the recording in advance and have had a genuine opportunity for refusal. It is completely inappropriate to covertly (secretly) record an interview and you should always remember that **confidentiality** is of the utmost importance, as is the security of any recorded tapes.

Selection of participants needs to be made carefully. You should consider if it really is convenient for them. If, for example, you choose to interview other students within your college, do not make them late for their classes.

Pick an appropriate time to carry out your interview

## Surveys and questionnaires

Another primary method is the survey, usually carried out using a questionnaire. It tends to be a popular method with students. However, questionnaires are not as easy to produce as they may at first look. It is worth considering the following issues:

- the reason for using a questionnaire
- when to use a questionnaire
- how many questions to ask
- the order of questions
- writing open and closed questions
- piloting the questionnaire
- distribution and collection of questionnaires.

It is important that you are able to justify why and how a survey will enhance the outcomes of your work. Ask yourself:

- What extra information will it enable me to gather?
- Is the information available from another source? If yes, from where?
- How deficient would my project be without it?
- Will including a survey add quality to my work or just quantity?

Questionnaires can be an ideal method of gathering primary data if you are seeking the views of many people. If the subject area is sensitive, it can offer anonymity which may encourage participants to share information they might otherwise have kept back. Time restrictions may mean that carrying out interviews, which would normally be an ideal method for your chosen topic area, would be impractical, whereas questionnaires can be distributed and collected later, limiting the amount of time needed.

Questionnaires can be distributed by hand or they can be posted. Postal surveys often have a poor return rate and can be costly for the researcher to administer.

Postal surveys can be costly to administer and have a poor return rate

### Questions

The questions you ask in a questionnaire must be relevant. They should flow into each other, following a logical sequence, and not jump from one topic to the next. Questions need to be carefully thought through. They should not offend or pry into a participant's privacy. Your tutor will be able to offer advice as to whether any questions drawn up are inappropriate, and the piloting process will provide a check on the questions before the questionnaire is distributed.

FORWARD to page 125, *Piloting your questionnaire*.

*Remember!*

- The wording of questions must be clear.
- It is important to avoid ambiguities (double meanings).
- Keep your questionnaire as short as possible – a lengthy questionnaire can be very off-putting to your participants.

Which type of question should you use? Questions can be open or closed:
- An open question offers opportunity for an individual answer.
- A closed question restricts the participants' answer to one word or statement.

A combination of both types may well be appropriate for your questionnaire if you use one. This would give you control over some aspects of the questionnaire (the closed questions gaining some 'core' information), more flexibility would then be possible by using open questions to allow participants to express their views more freely. Always ask yourself whether the questions being asked will get the information you are looking for. If you are unsure, rethink your questions or ask your tutor for advice.

The language level used in questionnaires should be appropriate for the target group – participants may become indignant if your questions indicate they have limited understanding, or can be confused if your questions are inappropriately academic.

**Activity**

1 Collect examples of questionnaires. These can be found in magazines, newspapers (results of opinion polls) or in books on research methodology (for example, Green, 2000).
2 Consider each of the questionnaires you have found and answer these questions:
   a) How would you feel if asked to complete them?
   b) How easy or complex did their completion appear?
   c) Did they make sense?
   d) Did you identify any ambiguities or irrelevant questions?
   e) Was it made clear how you should record your answers?
   f) Which would you be most happy to complete? Why is this?
   g) Which would you be least happy to complete? Why is this?
   h) How appropriate were the numbers of questions asked on each?
   i) Did the questionnaire include open or closed questions, or both? Did this seem appropriate?
   j) What influenced the above decisions?

### Piloting your questionnaire

Piloting a questionnaire helps to identify any ambiguities in its layout before it is distributed to your target group. It involves getting a small number of 'similar' participants to complete the questionnaire and asking them to comment on the layout, the instructions for its completion and the clarity of the questions. You need to allocate time for the pilot to be completed, returned and analysed, as well as any necessary alteration made prior to the main distribution. This should be built into your time plan for the research process.

### Categories of response

You need to think carefully about how the questions will be answered. Instructions for this should be given at the beginning of the questionnaire and they should be very clear to the participants. Questions can be answered in a number of ways, including by:
• ticking a box
• writing in the space provided
• circling the chosen answer.

Responses should be kept as consistent as possible. There would not usually be more than two styles of response on any one questionnaire. Responses can be:
• scaled – participants are given a choice of responses on a scale
• ranked – participants put a list of qualities in rank order according to importance
• by category – participants choose their answer from a range of given categories.

Examples  **Scaled responses**

Q1    How important is it for young children to see positive gender images?
Vital _____ Very important _____ Important _____ Quite important _____
Not important _____

Q2  Training in providing positive images is very important for all day-nursery staff.
Strongly agree _____ Agree _____ Disagree _____ Strongly disagree _____

**Q3** Circle the number on the scale below which represents how important you feel it is for day nursery staff to have had training in equal opportunities, 1 being the lowest and 10 being the highest importance.

1    2    3    4    5    6    7    8    9    10

### A ranked response

**Q4** Which of the activities listed below do you consider to be most important in the development of fine motor skills? Place them in order of importance, 1 to 5.

> Threading activities
> Opportunities for mark-making
> Construction materials
> Small world play
> Jigsaw puzzles

Which number did you think should be used to indicate the greatest importance – 1 or 5? It is important that you always make this clear to the participant. It is better to say:

Place them in order of importance 1 to 5, with 1 indicating the greatest level of importance.

This will avoid any confusion. You have indicated to the participant in which order your scale is set out.

### A category response

**Q5** How long is it since your last first aid training update?
0–3 years \_\_\_\_\_ 4–8 years \_\_\_\_\_ 9–12 years \_\_\_\_\_ 13–16 years \_\_\_\_\_ No training at all \_\_\_\_\_ Other (please specify) \_\_\_\_\_

This can enable a researcher to consider links between the responses made to other questions and how long it is since the person making a particular response qualified.

*Remember !* Always ensure that categories do not overlap (0–3, 3–8, 8–12, and so on) as participants will be unsure where to place their responses. It also makes it difficult to collate and present the findings, and the accuracy of the outcomes may be in question. Clear categories would be 0–3, 4–8, 9–12.

### Target group checklist

It is important to ensure that the intended target group is appropriate for your survey. It would be of limited benefit, for example, to ask for opinions from motor vehicle students about a range of books for two-year-olds. Similarly, early years students are unlikely to be the ideal participants in a survey on a range of car engine components. Ask yourself:

- Do your participants need to have a working knowledge of your chosen subject?
- Do they need to be from a particular:
  - age range?
  - type of employment?

– culture?

– sex?

– geographical area?

and so on.

*Remember!*

- Questionnaires can take many forms.
- Be clear what you are trying to achieve.
- Match your questions to your target group.
- Always pilot your questionnaire.
- Make your instructions clear.
- Avoid ambiguity.
- Keep your questionnaire simple – you will have to analyse the outcomes.

## Advantages and disadvantages of surveys

| Advantages | Disadvantages |
|---|---|
| Questionnaires can offer anonymity to participants which is not possible during an interview.<br>The same questions are answered by all participants.<br>The researcher's time can be used effectively.<br>Participants are able to complete the questionnaire without time pressure.<br>A good return rate is possible but not always achieved. | Return rates for postal surveys are often low (below 35 per cent).<br>Postal surveys can be costly.<br>Collection and distribution of questionnaires can be time-consuming.<br>If questions remain unanswered on some questionnaires, it can affect the outcomes.<br>Unless carefully set out, questions can be misunderstood.<br>Preparation time should not be under-estimated. Careful planning is important.<br>Piloting of questionnaires is vital, but adds to the time allocation needed. |

### Observation

Observation is rarely chosen as a research method by inexperienced researchers. However, when it is selected, observation is useful – while a participant may *tell* you that they would respond as X, during observation you may note that in practice they really respond as Y, thus obtaining a truer overall result.

The aim of observational research is to see 'what really happens'. It is important to carry it out unobtrusively, as any interruption to normal events could change (and therefore invalidate) the outcomes of the research.

### Direct and indirect observation

- Researchers using direct (participant) observation obtain their findings by joining in with the situation they are observing.
- Researchers using indirect (non-participant observation) obtain information by observing from a distance.

Observation can be an important tool in research in childcare settings where it is already used as a routine part of early years care and education.

Observation can be direct (participant)

... or indirect (non-participant)

## Advantages and disadvantages of observation

| Advantages | Disadvantages |
|---|---|
| Behaviour is seen in a natural environment. The process of social situations can be observed – what preceded a certain factor or what resulted from it. Observation can either be direct (participant) or indirect (non-participant). | Observation is time-consuming. It is not always considered to be a reliable method as it can be subjective. The presence of the researcher can affect what is being observed. |

Direct observation can sometimes be difficult

> **Professional Practice**
>
> Make a note of three situations that could be researched through observation. What would be most appropriate, a direct or indirect approach?
> How could you ensure that no interruption to the usual routine occurs?

### Action research

Action research is an excellent example of how the outcomes of research can have an impact on praxis (the practice involved in an area of study, for example early years). It involves you, as the researcher, studying an aspect of your own working environment. It could, for example, involve exploring how well staff in your pre-school or nursery utilise certain equipment or resources. Alternatively, it could include analysing how well the parents are involved with the setting.

You need to consider carefully whether to use action research or not, as you will have to carry on working within the setting after the research has been completed. There is always the possibility of outcomes from this type of research raising discontent in other staff. The possibility of both positive and negative outcomes needs to be thought through at the planning stage. This is not a method usually used by students at level 3.

---

**Professional Practice**

Consider the following research ideas. Would they all be suitable for a piece of action research?

a) An exploration of the encouragement given by staff to both girls and boys in the use of construction materials in your nursery

b) The promotion of home–school links in your primary school

c) The value placed on exploring cultural events and festivals by staff in your pre-school.

Make a note of as many potential positive and negative outcomes you can think of.

---

## Case studies

The study of a situation, an individual, a group or a family, in which the researcher looks at a range of factors as the basis for discussion, is often referred to as a case study. As the researcher you would make an in-depth analysis of your findings, possibly making comparisons to other cases or examples.

This method is particularly useful in social research, and case studies are often used in academic texts to illustrate particular points. In using this method, it is unlikely that you will be able to claim that your outcomes are representative of society at large, but they may produce interesting ideas and thought-provoking material that can be explored further. In a research project at level 3, it can be useful to include a case study to illustrate a particular point you are trying to get across (as a secondary source). If you are unsure how best to do this, your tutor will be able to help you.

---

**Activity**

Sonia has chosen to look at examples of emotional disturbance commonly found in children's lives and intends to use the following case study as part of her discussion. Read through the case study and consider the questions that follow it.

Janine is seven and her brother, Alan, is five. They have recently moved from a two-bedroom house, the only home they have known, into bed and breakfast accommodation, following the family's financial difficulties and eviction for mortgage arrears. Alan is behaving unacceptably both at home and in school. Janine has begun to wet her bed at night, which is causing her a great deal of distress, and significant laundry problems for her parents. She has become very quiet and withdrawn. Their mother is tearful a lot of the time and their father is short-tempered with everyone.

a) How might Janine and Alan be feeling?
b) How might their parents be feeling?
c) What help might be available to the children?
d) What might the role of a classroom support assistant be in this situation?
e) How useful do you consider this case study to be to Sonia's research project?

### Experiments

Polit and Hungler (1991) define experimental research as:

'a research study in which the investigator controls or manipulates the independent variable and randomly assigns subjects to different conditions.'

Experimental research usually involves two groups of people – the experiment group and the control group:
- The control group is a group of similar people/subjects controlled by the researcher, treated alike (the constant variable) and used as a comparison to the results found during the experiment process.
- The experiment group are randomly subjected to other conditions (independent variables).

It is important that the two groups are as alike as possible at the outset to enable a greater level of comparison and subsequent outcomes from the experiment.

The control group and experiment group should be as alike as possible

Experimental research is usually associated with laboratory testing rather than the more people/behaviour/opinion-orientated focus of social research. It is unlikely that experimental research would be undertaken as a level 3 early years course research project, although as mentioned earlier, the **replication** of experiments of pioneers such as Piaget may be undertaken.

Many experiments have been considered controversial, and ethical issues often arise.

Find three examples of experimental research. If possible, include one linked to the subject of your chosen research project.

a) Was there a clear independent variable?
b) Were there any controversial aspects to the experiment?
c) What ethical issues needed to be taken into account?

▶▶ FORWARD to page 151 for a discussion of ethics .

## Secondary sources of data collection

Secondary research is the use or presentation of material which has been researched or written by someone else. It will support your chosen topic area and your primary research findings (or data collection) for Unit 15 (*Project*). Secondary research data will be used in most assignments during your course of study.

### Forming a literature base

Every researcher needs to read around their subject area in order to broaden the scope for their research and to form a solid literature base. This base will include both technological and non-technological sources.

It is important to set yourself clear parameters. If your research becomes too wide, it may result in a thinly covered topic area with limited value. A narrower, but more deeply considered, approach may give a greater insight into your chosen topic area, producing outcomes of a higher value. The subject being explored will sometimes indicate natural parameters, but at other times you, as researcher, will need to set them for yourself.

Deciding how widely to research can be difficult. It is useful to set clear boundaries, for example by asking yourself:

- How far back shall I research – to 2000, to 1990, to 1980, to 1950? You need to decide how much your decision will impact on your outcomes. Will it be a mistake to limit your research to just the past year, rather than the past decade? Will you miss out on important historically relevant data by only focusing on recent years?
- Should I restrict my work geographically? Will focusing on the UK be appropriate? Would you benefit from including USA statistics, or would a comparison with Europe be relevant? Perhaps focusing on your own local area is sufficient. Tutors will be able to offer guidance on these questions.

Should I restrict
my work
geographically?

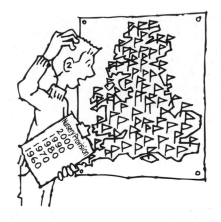

### Finding information

An initial literature search helps to establish where the most significant amount of material for a subject area is to be found, and should help set the research parameters. You will need to consider local sources of material too. For example, if the subject to be researched is health-related, you should be asking yourself what sources are available locally. There may be a health promotion office at your local hospital or surgery.

Ideally you should start by considering what is the general subject area appropriate to your chosen research topic. Is it:
• health?
• childcare?
• education?
• community provision?
• special needs?
What else?

The clearer the definition of the subject area, the easier it will be to establish sources of secondary data. In the field of early years there is a wealth of sources to explore. These include:
• public libraries
• academic libraries (college and university)
• health promotion offices
• resource centres
• government offices
• support groups
• organisations
• GP surgeries, dentists, pharmacies
• bookshops
• the Internet.

### Published sources

Published (written) sources include:
• books
• magazines
• specialist journals

- newspapers
- information sheets and pamphlets
- government documents
- Hansard (transcripts from parliamentary debate)
- Internet material
- CD-ROM material.

For more information about sources of information and guidance on how to refer to published sources in your writing, refer to Green (2000) – see *Bibliography and suggested further reading*, page 159.

**Activity**

1  What other sources can you think of?
2  Where could you access them?

*Remember!*  Many early years professionals write media articles, sharing their expertise and indicating current thinking. Their viewpoints can be particularly useful in discussing subject areas involving current policy or practice.

### Media sources

Media sources includes television, radio, newspapers, journals and magazines. Each offer current information on a vast array of subjects, and can be useful in discussing your subject area. However, it is important to remember that many media sources portray bias (a prejudice). Exploring the alternatives to points raised in articles is important to obtain a balance of views. Television and radio programmes offer topical discussions, current affairs and documentaries. If any of these is to be referred to in a piece of research, the reference details should be set out as described in Green (2000).

Newspapers and journals also cover current affairs and topical issues. They often include articles on controversial subjects and can also portray bias. Being aware of the source or author can establish whether objectivity can be assumed. For example, an article on the benefits of disposable nappies written by an 'expert' working for a leading manufacturer of disposable nappies is unlikely to be completely objective. It would be likely that any reference to ecological or economic factors would be marginalised in comparison to the emphasis on convenience factors and benefits over rival products.

It is important to remember that many media sources portray bias

### Technological sources

Researchers today have the benefit of a range of technological resources, for example:

- *CD-ROMs*, which are usually held in college libraries, offering the opportunity to explore many avenues of enquiry quickly. Many national newspapers produce CD-ROMs of past articles, producing updates at regular intervals. There are also many specialist subject areas on CD-ROM too, for example, menu planning for young children. These are often interactive, extending learning by exploration

- *the Internet*, which provides on-line libraries and encyclopaedias. From the Internet public library you can access a collection of texts which can also be downloaded. Always check for copyright status – some are copyright-free, but others are not. Be sure that you do not break copyright laws. Details of these laws are displayed in all libraries, often beside the photocopier.

  Search engines guide you through the mass of information on the Internet. Two popular search engines are Yahoo and Ask Jeeves (see below). Most college libraries provide these. Staff will help you if you are unsure.

  National newspapers are often on-line too. Their Internet website addresses can be found printed in each edition of the newspaper. Transcripts from parliamentary debate (known as Hansard) can also be accessed in this way. This would be particularly useful if your subject area is policy-led.

  Nelson Thornes (publishers of this book) has a website and you may find it useful to explore what it offers: www.nelsonthornes.com

- *microfiche*, a database on film, used in many libraries, to store newspapers, books and other data

- the *Educational Resources Information Centre (ERIC)*, usually found in libraries in colleges of higher and further education. It is a facility that searches for information from key words, to produce titles of books and articles. ERIC is only of use if you have access to the titles it suggests.

Examples    **Using search engines**

Search engines such as Yahoo refine the material with each subsequent search, while search engines such as Ask Jeeves offer the opportunity to ask further questions, but they are not refined (or categorised) in any way.

In Yahoo:

1 Type in the category you are studying, for example, Rashes. A large index will appear of relevant options.
2 Select another category from this index. A further index will appear.
3 Continue to select and re-select until you have the information you are looking for.

In Ask Jeeves:

1 Ask the computer a question. It will give you a list of possibilities.
2 From this list, ask another question, narrowing down the field of answers.
3 Continue until you find what you were looking for.

Researchers today have the benefit of a range of technological resources, such as CD-Roms and the Internet

### Case studies

Case studies published by a previous researcher can be used as a secondary source of data. You can use them in more than one way:

- as a point of discussion, analysing the main components of the case and discussing each part, making reference to your own primary research findings or other outcomes from your literature base
- to identify differences and discuss comparisons in a number of case studies.

### Statistical reports and sources

Statistics can make an important contribution to research. They may show how a trend has developed relevant to a topic area, for example, the number of babies born to teenagers in the year 2000. It is important to use the most recent statistics you can find – there is little point in discussing a current issue and using statistics from 1995 as an example. Using past statistics can be relevant, however, if a comparison is to be made, for example, comparing the numbers of babies born to teenagers in 1970 and in 2000. The subsequent discussion would usually explore what changes have occurred, and how and why they have occurred.

A good source for social statistics (both national and regional) is the government publication, *Social Trends*, which is published annually by The Stationery Office. Most libraries hold copies.

*Remember!*

- Research involves both primary and secondary sources of information.
- You will usually be expected to incorporate both research methods.
- Length and breadth of interviews can be controlled through questions and structure.
- Questionnaires need to be clear, piloted and targeted appropriately.
- Avoid using leading questions.

- Observation, both direct and indirect, must be as objective and unobtrusive as possible.
- The long-term impact of action research needs careful consideration.
- Secondary sources used to support research should be carefully selected.
- Issues of bias must be considered in all that you read and also in all that you write.

# Statistical research information

A great deal of information is produced during a research project. Much of it will be in a numerical form and is known as your **raw data**.

There are many ways in which raw data can be presented. Tables and graphs are common, and in some subjects it can be appropriate to use a pictorial method. You need to become familiar with the different types of presentation and their uses, so you can understand findings published by other researchers and know how to present the findings from your own research.

Raw data are the result of primary research – questionnaires, interview notes, observations, and so on. They need to be kept in a logical order so they can be understood and explained if a query is raised. It is particularly important that raw data are kept safe until after a piece of work has been read and graded by your tutors. They may be needed as evidence of your research process.

*Remember !* Keep your data safe – you may need them as evidence of your research.

## Methods of presentation

Numerical data can be presented as:
- tables
- bar charts
- line graphs
- pie charts
- sociograms
- pictographs.

Very often you will find that you can use several of these methods to present your data and your decision about which to use will be a matter of personal choice.

### Tables
A **table** is one of the most basic methods of presenting information, both numerical and written. It offers versatility in that it can include a great deal of raw data and can also be used to present sub-sets of information.

**Parental responses to child behaviour**

| Type of behaviour | % Positive response | | % Negative response | |
|---|---|---|---|---|
| | Boys | Girls | Boys | Girls |
| Playing with blocks | 36 | 0 | 0 | 0 |
| Manipulating objects | 46 | 46 | 2 | 26 |
| Transportation toys | 61 | 57 | 0 | 2 |
| Rough/tumble toys | 91 | 84 | 3 | 2 |
| Aggression | 23 | 18 | 50 | 53 |
| Climbing | 39 | 43 | 12 | 24 |
| Playing with dolls | 39 | 63 | 14 | 4 |
| Dancing | 0 | 50 | 0 | 0 |
| Asking for help | 72 | 87 | 13 | 6 |
| Dressing-up play | 50 | 71 | 50 | 6 |

adapted from B. Fagot (1978), 'The influence of sex of child on parental reactions to toddler children', cited in Cullis *et al.* (1999)

Presenting information numerically

**Comparison of three learning systems**

| | High Scope | Montessori | Steiner |
|---|---|---|---|
| Specific staff qualification | No | Yes | No |
| Specific training needed | Yes | Yes | Yes |
| Specific equipment needed | No | Yes | No |
| Particular daily routine | Yes | No | Yes |
| Particular teaching methods | Yes | Yes | Yes |
| Own terminology | Yes | Yes | Yes |
| Particular method of grouping children | Yes | No | No |
| Particular room layout | Yes | No | No |

from Jameson and Watson (1998)

A factual table, offering an 'at a glance' comparison of a range of learning systems

## Bar charts

**Bar charts** are particularly useful for showing comparisons between sets of information. The length of each bar is clearly seen in relation to its neighbours.

A bar chart

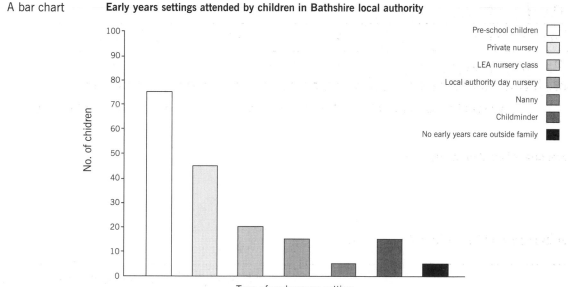

Early years settings attended by children in Bathshire local authority

Pre-school children
Private nursery
LEA nursery class
Local authority day nursery
Nanny
Childminder
No early years care outside family

No. of children

Type of early years setting

## Line graphs

**Line graphs** give clear 'at a glance' understanding for the reader. They show trends or changes in quantity and are particularly useful for displaying information over a period of time. The horizontal axis indicates the continuously variable aspect of the data being presented.

A line graph

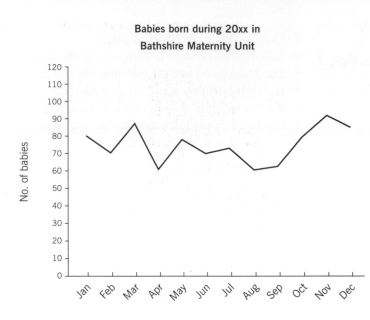

Babies born during 20xx in
Bathshire Maternity Unit

**Remember!**

- A line graph should have a clear and informative title.
- The horizontal axis needs to be a continuously variable quantity, such as age, time or temperature (i.e. it should not be discrete or descriptive categories).
- Both axes should be clearly labelled.
- The units of measurement should be clearly indicated.
- You cannot plot a line graph unless you have quite a lot of data. Trying to join just a few points plotted from sketchy data may give an unreliable impression.

### Pie charts

A **pie chart** is a circular graph, with the 'portions' of the 'pie' showing clearly the relative proportions of different categories. It is a visual chart which is easily understood by the reader.

The portions of a pie chart can be coloured or shaded to make the data clear, but it also needs to be clearly labelled, either with simple descriptive labels for each category or, for more accuracy, labels giving the percentage share of the whole for each category.

To draw a pie chart, the angle at the centre of the circle (360°) is shared between the different categories in proportion to their size using a mathematical calculation. It is worth learning how to draw a pie chart, although software programs are available which can do this for you.

A pie chart

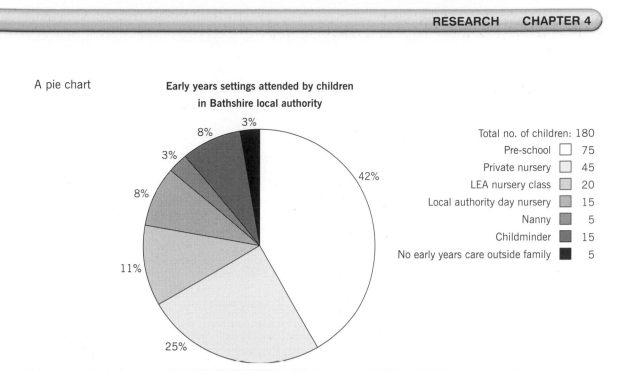

**Early years settings attended by children in Bathshire local authority**

42%

25%

11%

8%

3%

8%

3%

Total no. of children: 180
Pre-school ☐ 75
Private nursery ☐ 45
LEA nursery class ☐ 20
Local authority day nursery ☐ 15
Nanny ☐ 5
Childminder ☐ 15
No early years care outside family ■ 5

*Remember!*

- The advantage of pie charts is that they are especially useful for showing, at a glance, the relative proportions of different categories.
- Their disadvantage is that they are quite difficult to draw.
- The more categories you are trying to represent, the more difficult it is to draw the chart.
- The pie chart should have a clear and informative title.
- Each slice or segment should be shaded or coloured to distinguish it from the others.
- Each segment should be labelled to indicate which category it represents, or a key should be provided.

### Sociograms

The term 'socio' means 'denoting social or society'. A **sociogram** presents data describing relationships between members of social groups.

Sociograms can depict the social relationships of either one person, or of a complete group of people. The sociogram on page 142 shows the inter-relationships of a group of children.

A sociogram

**Number of times each child in a class was a quoted as being the best friend of another child in the class**

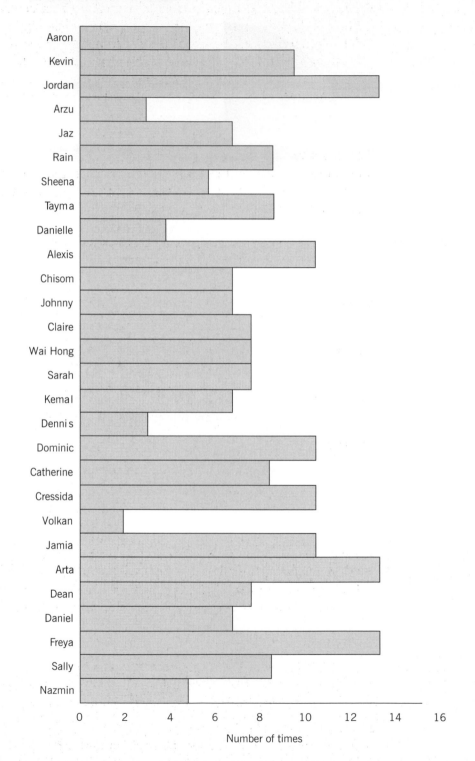

Number of times

from Hobart and Frankel (1999), pages 83–4

**Remember!**
- A sociogram should have a clear and meaningful title.
- The different group members should be clearly identified on the sociogram.
- The axis depicting frequency of contact should be clearly labelled.
- A sociogram is an excellent way of depicting the social structure of a group.
- It can be a useful way of identifying popular children, and also those who may need some help settling into the group.
- It can be misleading, and should be treated with some caution.

## Pictographs

A **pictograph** works in the same way as a bar chart, but pictures are used instead of bars to represent the data. This is a very visual graph and may have a greater impact on the reader than a bar chart.

A pictograph

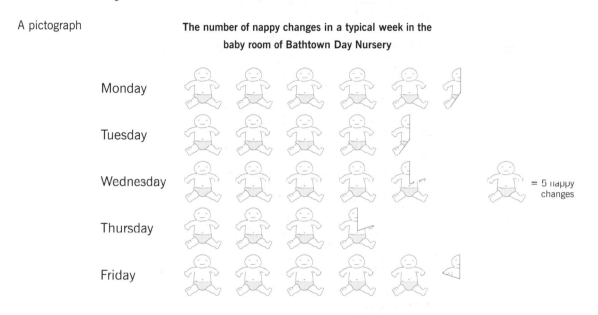

The number of nappy changes in a typical week in the baby room of Bathtown Day Nursery

Monday

Tuesday

Wednesday

Thursday

Friday

= 5 nappy changes

**Remember!**
- A pictograph should have a clear and informative title.
- The symbols used should be consistent.
- A key should show the quantities represented by each picture.
- The symbols used should be clearly labelled to indicate what they represent.

**Activity**

Look again at each of the examples of data presentation.

a) Is the data clear in each one?
b) Are you able to easily identify the main outcomes?
c) Which type of graphic presentation do you prefer? Why?
d) Are the labels helpful?

**Professional Practice**

Select a set of statistics from any source of your choice. Present the information in as many different ways as you can.

a) How successful was this?

b) Which type of graph was easiest to produce? In what way?

c) Which type of graph was most appropriate for the statistics you used? Why?

*Remember!*

- Data can be presented in a variety of ways.
- It is important that method of presentation is appropriate for your data and your purpose.
- The reader needs to be able to evaluate the outcomes of your research easily.
- Provide clear explanations.
- Carefully label all diagrams, tables, charts and graphs.
- Always cite the source of your information.
- Include a key where appropriate.

## Some basic statistical tools

When you collect numerical data, you will usually need to manipulate or describe them in some way. Statistics is the area which deals specifically with the description and manipulation of numerical data. For the purposes of level 3 research, you need to understand the following terms:

- the **mean**, **median** or **mode** – three different kinds of statistical averages
- the **range** – the difference between the smallest and largest result in each collection of data
- **standard deviation** – how widely the results in a collection of data are distributed, taking the mean as a point of reference.

### The mean

The mean is the score which is normally recognised as being the average. It is worked out by adding up all the scores that are being dealt with and then dividing it by the number of those scores.

Example

In Oak class at Country Primary school, there are 24 children. Their reading ages are as follows:

- two have a reading age of 6
- three have a reading age of 7
- fourteen have a reading age of 9
- four have a reading age of 12
- one has a reading age of 14.

If these reading ages are added together, it makes 221:

6 + 6 + 7 + 7 + 7 + 9 + 9 + 9 + 9 + 9 + 9 + 9 + 9 + 9 + 9 + 9 + 9 + 9 + 9 + 12 + 12 + 12 + 12 + 14 = 221

To obtain the mean, 221 is divided by 24 (the number of children):

221 ÷ 24 = 9.2

The mean reading average of Oak class is therefore 9.2 years.

### The median

The median reading age is the point in the sequence of reading ages that divides the lower half from the higher half.

Example    In Oak class:

    6 6 7 7 7 9 9 9 9 9 9 9    9 9 9 9 9 9 9 12 12 12 12 14

The median reading age is therefore 9 years.

### The mode

The mode score is the score (or reading age) that is the most common in the data.

Example    As there are fourteen children in Oak class with a reading age of 9, the mode will also be 9 years:

    6 6 7 7 7 9 9 9 9 9 9 9 9 9 9 9 9 9 9 9 12 12 12 12 14

It is important to be aware of the effect of statistics on prospective parents (see page 146)

### Range and standard deviation

The range of numerical data gathered can sometimes be shown on a chart as standard deviation. This gives a curved illustration of all the data, or scores, gathered.

#### Range

The range is the difference between the lowest and the highest result taken from your research. You would calculate the range by subtracting the lowest result from the highest.

Example    In Oak class, as the highest reading age is 14 and the lowest is 6, the 6 needs to be subtracted from the 14:

    $14 - 6 = 8$

Therefore, the range is 8.

#### Standard deviation

The standard deviation is indicated by how widely the results are distributed. If you take the mean as your point of central focus, you need to consider how far either side the range of results spreads. A small standard deviation would see all the results in a narrow band towards the middle of the grid. A large standard deviation would see the results spread over a broad band on the grid.

A standard
deviation graph

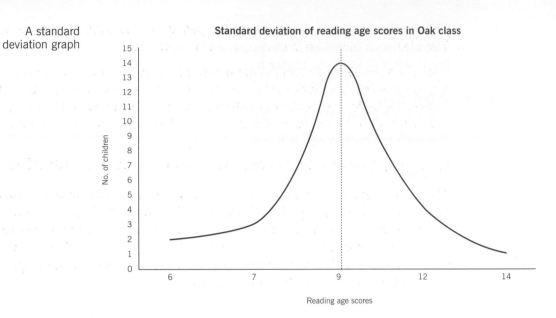

**Standard deviation of reading age scores in Oak class**

No. of children

Reading age scores

## Misuse of statistics

At times statistics can be misleading. They can be manipulated to show one thing, when the raw data really suggest something else. School achievement tables are a good example of this.

Example

**A-level results, showing pupils with three grades A–C**

| School | 1998 | 1999 | 2000 |
|--------|------|------|------|
| School A | 80% | 82% | 80% |
| School B | 61% | 63% | 63% |
| School C | 35% | 38% | 42% |
| School D | 58% | 63% | 62% |
| School E | 49% | 51% | 48% |

To someone who is not familiar with the schools included in this table, it would seem clear that School A is the better school because the results are far better at A-level (80 per cent gain at least three passes at A–C) than those of any other school. This figure is a consistent achievement by the school and they should be commended for it accordingly. However, to someone who is familiar with the school's policy of selective entry at both Year 7 and again to enter the sixth form (only pupils with five GCSEs at A–C are admitted), it would seem logical that its results are the best.

No other school in the table has selective entry at any stage, and School C (with 42 per cent of pupils gaining at least three passes at A–C) has increased its achievement levels consistently over the past three years (35 to 38 to 42 per cent). This clearly indicates an improving academic record.

Statistics such as these can therefore mislead prospective parents who are looking to select a school for their child. The improving school (School C) may well be the better choice for the child concerned, as it is clearly improving the overall standard of results of pupils of 'across the board' academic ability.

## Using technology to analyse and present statistics

There is a range of software packages available to help you analyse and present your data. One popular package is the SPSS (Statistical Package for Social Sciences). It is likely to be available in your college library or resource centre. Your tutors or resource centre staff will be able to help you install and use it. Another popular package is Excel. Both packages will enable you to produce graphs and tables which are clear and look professional.

## Validity

**Validity** refers to how accurately a subject has been researched. Can it be said to be both genuine and soundly based? Something is valid if we know it to be true, that it is authentic and that it measures what it claims to measure. If a piece of research is valid, it is unlikely to be disputed. In research terms, validity is giving a true representation of what has been researched. It addresses what it says it addresses and therefore it can be said that the evidence it presents is correct. It is important that researchers are as sure as they can be that their participants have told them the truth.

### Reliability

Validity is linked to **reliability**. Any identified change to practice needs to be supported by evidence – it needs to be reliable. This applies equally to the field of early years, and an outcome will not be considered as valid evidence if it is only applicable to one research project, or to one sample group of participants. It is important to establish that another similar research enquiry would achieve the same results. Validity can therefore be linked to what is considered to be true, reliable and retestable.

### Retestability

Retestability is directly linked to reliability. In research terms, it often refers to the research methods used. Was an appropriate research method used? Researchers should ask themselves:
• Was the method reliable?
• Was it the best method for the subject being studied?
• What were the alternatives?
• Would the outcomes have been different if another method had been used?

And the important question:
• Would the same results be achieved if the enquiry was replicated (carried out again)?

Successful replication of research is the only way to demonstrate reliability.

For most research on a level 3 early years course this will not be practical. It is therefore important to be able to justify your choice of research method by careful selection of participants and careful preparation of questions, observations, and so on.

### Representative groups

Reliable results can only be achieved if participants (the target group) are genuinely representative. Targeting research appropriately is vital.

Example    It would be of limited value to ask a retired nursery nurse how successful he or she considers the introduction of the Foundation Stage to be from a practitioner's point of view. To get a genuinely useful response, the researcher would need to ask a practitioner who has worked both prior to and with the Foundation Stage guidelines.

### Triangulation

Validity can be augmented through **triangulation** (supporting your findings from research in more than one way).

Example    Both questionnaires and interviews could be used to obtain parents' views regarding safety aspects of the local park. These responses could then be supported by observations made by the researcher after spending time at the park in question. If the three methods support each other, it will enhance the validity and reliability of the overall research project.

---

**Activity**

Consider the research projects below. Which do you consider would be likely to achieve reliable and valid outcomes? Which would you be less certain about? Which would be replicable?

- Parents' views on the day-care option they have chosen for their children
- Teachers' views on the introduction of the Foundation Stage Curriculum
- Parents' evaluation of their own behaviour management strategies
- Library services for young children in a rural community
- Gender stereotyping of young children

a) What are the main points you have raised?

b) Would objectivity concern you?

c) How would issues of objectivity affect the validity and reliability of the above projects?

d) Do you think the type of research method used would have made any difference?

---

*Remember!*

- Validity refers to the accuracy of the research – does it address what it claims to address?
- Reliability is linked to the ability to replicate the research.
- Careful selection of participants is needed. They must always be representative.
- Mutually supportive research methods (triangulation) enhances the validity and reliability of research.

# The purpose and role of research

Research plays an important part in the development of early years standards and provision. It enables comparisons to be made and needs to be identified. In considering the purpose of research in its more general sense, it is useful to think of research that has been undertaken in recent years, and then more specifically, in the field of early years health, care and education. Identifying research and evaluating its aims, its relevance and its outcomes will help you to focus on its necessity.

Research can be used for many purposes, including to:
- identify need
- highlight gaps in provision
- obtain feedback on standards
- see what is happening currently
- find out why something is happening
- plan for future development.

Its role can be said to be to:
- confirm policy or practice
- extend knowledge
- improve practice
- allow progress to be monitored
- examine topics of contemporary research.

### Activity

What examples of research can you think of? Copy the table below and list as many as you can. Examples have been given to get you started.

| Child health | Early years care | Education | Behaviour |
|---|---|---|---|
| Immunisation Genetics | Sudden Infant Death syndrome | Head Start EEL project | Relationships Attachment |

## Evaluating a piece of research

### Activity

Carefully read through at least one piece of research, and answer the questions.
a) What was the main aim of the research? Was the aim met?
b) Who was carrying out the research? Was this significant?
c) Did the research outcomes identify a need or a gap in current practice or provision?
d) Did it identify what was currently happening? Why?

e) Have the research outcomes enabled feedback on a current situation?

f) Will the research be likely to impact on future planning?

g) Did the research involve policy-making?

h) Will the research outcomes extend knowledge? If yes, for who?

i) Will the research outcomes improve practice?

j) Is the research of a contemporary nature?

When considering the aim of a piece of research, the question 'Has it been achieved?' should be considered. If a hypothesis was explored, was it proved or not? Was the hypothesis single- or open-ended?

Regarding who was responsible for the research, issues of objectivity need to be considered. For example, the managing director of a chain of day nurseries may not be the ideal person to carry out an objective research of provision offered within the nursery chain. How do you think objectivity could be assured?

If research outcomes had identified a need, or noted a gap in what is happening or being provided at the time of the research, consider whether the outcomes are likely to lead to the need being met, or the gap being filled.

Have any questions raised through the research been answered? For example:
• Who was responsible for ...?
• Why was ...?
• When should ...?
• What is the purpose of ...?

Has feedback to (or from) the participants or setting(s) included in the research been incorporated? How relevant was this?

In what ways would the research be likely to impact on future planning? For example:
• Did the outcomes identify the need for immediate improvements?
• Were any long-term improvements or projects identified? Think back to the reference made earlier in this chapter to the impact of research on children in hospital.

In what way was any policy involvement relevant to the research outcomes? Did policies need rewriting? Did 'ownership' of policies need to be reviewed? How widely were the policies distributed?

Other questions to ask yourself might include:
• Who will benefit from the research?
• Will they benefit through extended knowledge?
• Will they benefit by an improved service or provision?
• How will the research outcomes link in with contemporary issues and opinion?

| **Professional Practice** | If you take a more evaluative approach to reading the summary or outcomes of a piece of research, you will understand the research more fully. |

# Ethical issues

Ethics are the principles or moral codes used as guidelines for the behaviour standards common to all people within a group or profession. Ethics determine what is right and wrong; they help to maintain standards.

Individual definitions of the term 'ethics' may vary slightly, but most people will agree that in general, ethics act as guidelines for the decisions we each have to make and the consequences that may arise from any course of action we take. They are directly linked to the values and morals of both individuals and society as a whole. Ethics, therefore, are about doing what is right according to the majority, linking personal values, standards of behaviour and conscience to actions.

Research ethics are the rules governing good and bad practice in the field of research. To behave unethically during the research process is to behave badly when dealing with the views and contributions of any of your participants. In research, ethics include consideration of the participants' rights, the importance of confidentiality and issues around preserving **anonymity**.

| **Professional Practice** | Various organisations and professions produce their own codes of ethics. Examples include:<br>• health districts – they each have an ethics committee<br>• British Medical Association<br>• British Psychological Association<br>• social workers. |
| --- | --- |

**Activity**

Using your college library or the Internet, find a code of ethics for a relevant profession. Read its main points and consider how the ethical principles for that profession might apply to your role as an early years professional.

Research ethics involves responsibility. As a researcher you will have a responsibility to all your participants to ensure that their privacy is not invaded unnecessarily, or without their permission. Participants are doing you a favour by participating in your research. At times you may ask for responses on subjects that may be sensitive to them. They should be respected for this and treated accordingly.

It is unethical to carry out research without the subjects of the research knowing it is taking place (i.e. covert observation). This is particularly important if you are carrying out research in your workplace. Covert observation breaks the trust of colleagues if, for example, information given in conversation is used in a subsequent piece of research. It also includes observing and recording the actions and/or conversations of colleagues without their knowledge.

The research methods chosen for any project will have an impact on the way the findings of research are presented. At the outset of a piece of research, the proposed methods should be fully considered, ensuring that they will allow a true representation of participants' contributions to be presented.

There are occasions when ethical considerations may not be as necessary. This could occur if you were carrying out observations in a public place, for example, watching students socialise around the college campus or children playing in a park.

**Activity**

1 Why might ethical considerations not be necessary when carrying out observations in a public place? Note your reasons and discuss them with another student.
2 Think of a range of topic areas that could be suitable for exploring as a research project, linked to the subject units studied during the BTec National in Early Years.
   a) Which of them might be classified as sensitive? Why is this, do you think?
   b) How might participants be adversely affected by research in these areas?
   c) What restrictions do you think you might find as a researcher studying these topics?

   Discuss the outcomes in your group.

**Professional Practice**
- You need to be aware that sensitive subjects may also affect you as the researcher. The responses you receive and the material you read in the literature may at times be distressing.
- It is important for all researchers to have supervision. Supervision helps you with the process and practical application of your project. It also helps you deal with stress and concerns. Professional researchers are supervised, as well as student researchers. Your tutor will usually supervise your research project.

## Benefits of the research to the researcher

As a first-time research student carrying out a small-scale project, it is unlikely that the outcomes of your research will benefit anyone other than yourself. Any risks that might be taken during the research process need to be balanced against the benefits the outcomes of the research will bring (this is sometimes known as the costs:benefits ratio). When this is a personal piece of work undertaken as part of a course, you need to be absolutely sure that the benefits (primarily to yourself) justify the costs (primarily borne by others). In a larger scale piece of research, any potential risks should be identified at the onset, and the benefits of the research should be clearly set out by the researcher.

## Access to information

It is important that you obtain any appropriate permission before carrying out your research. If participants are young (school age or younger), you will need to obtain the permission of their parents or guardians. The research may be considered to be completely non-threatening and non-intrusive (for example, asking children questions about favourite toys or television programmes), but the general principle of obtaining permission from the adult with responsibility for the children concerned is still important.

In a school or similar setting, the headteacher or manager will need to give their written consent. They are held *in loco parentis* while children are in their care. This permission needs to be arranged well in advance, so time management and planning need to take this into account. A letter of support from a course tutor will usually be sufficient proof of the authenticity of the project. The following details may also be required:
- your name
- a contact telephone number
- your college's telephone number (plus your tutor's name)
- dates of planned involvement by the setting, for example:
  - letters to parents (if needed)
  - interviews (How many? Who will be interviewed?)
  - distribution plans for any surveys
  - collecting arrangements for surveys
- the time plan for your research
- the availability of the research findings to the participants, or their parents/guardians
- details of who else will have access to the research findings
- issues of identification or confidentiality within the research:
  - What guarantees have been given?
  - If guaranteed, how will anonymity be assured?

## Confidentiality

Participants who agree to help in the research process are putting their trust in you as the researcher. You therefore have a responsibility to set clear guidelines as to how, when and where the outcomes of research are to be published. An individual participant will also need to know if they will be identified within the findings. If it is agreed that they will not, then it is imperative that this is adhered to.

You need to clarify the different ways in which a participant can be identified in research, other than by name. If, for example, in a piece of research about changes facing primary school teachers, reference is made to the difference in written planning required by teachers during their probationary teaching year, it will be very obvious whose responses are being referred to if one teacher in the participating school has been teaching for twenty years and the others are newly qualified. Therefore the individual participant will be identified quite easily. Similarly, using initials will easily identify participants with more unusual names.

Full permission from participants, and from any organisation they may be considered to represent, is needed prior to the commencement of any research. This applies equally to any research carried out internally in your own placement or work setting.

> **Remember!**
>
> Every participant in a research project has rights. These include:
> * guaranteed privacy
> * observation of their right to withdraw at any point
> * anonymity
> * confidentiality
> * respect at all times
> * trust that their contribution will be portrayed fairly and accurately.

## Data protection and human rights legislation

The privacy of, and rights of access to material relating to, any individual are covered by legislation.

**Activity**

In a small group, locate copies of the relevant legislation in your college library or from the Internet.
a)  Read through the main aspects of each piece of legislation.
b)  Note which elements might be relevant to your research project.
c)  Note which elements are relevant to research in general.
d)  How important do you consider the legislation to be?

## Vulnerability of client groups

People who are unable to understand fully the possible consequences of being involved in research and cannot therefore give informed consent can be described as being vulnerable. In these situations, those responsible for them, or for guiding and/or supporting them in their decision-making, need to be fully informed and consulted by the researcher.

## The ethical issues of different research methods

Ethical issues occur in all forms of primary research. Below are brief summaries of the most pertinent aspects in the most commonly used primary research methods.

### Interviews
* Interviews put the researcher (you) in a position of power.
* You should not use your control of the situation to your own advantage.
* Leading questions can be a problem, with personal bias making the approach subjective rather than objective.
* Sensitivity is needed, as is an awareness of how the outcomes of interviews are to be used.
* It is important that you take into consideration how the interview may affect the participants.

### Surveys

- Using a survey (or questionnaire) approach will also raise issues of confidentiality, anonymity and the sensitivity of the subject-matter.
- Leading questions can be a problem here too.

### Case studies

- Case studies involve discussion of a real situation and respect for the people portrayed in the case study is needed.
- It would not usually be appropriate to identify the individuals involved.
- It is important to consider how the outcomes of the research will be used and who will have access to it.
- Awareness of personal bias is important.

### Observations

Appropriate permission is particularly important if observing indirectly, or when observing individuals who are unable to give permission for themselves.

## Examination of contemporary research

As part of the Btec National in Early Years, you will need to evaluate pieces of published research. You will be asked to comment on various aspects, including the ethical issues.

Look again at the examples of ethical codes of practice you found for the activity on page 151. These will help you to consolidate your understanding of the codes of practice and charters that many professionals adhere to in their working professional practice.

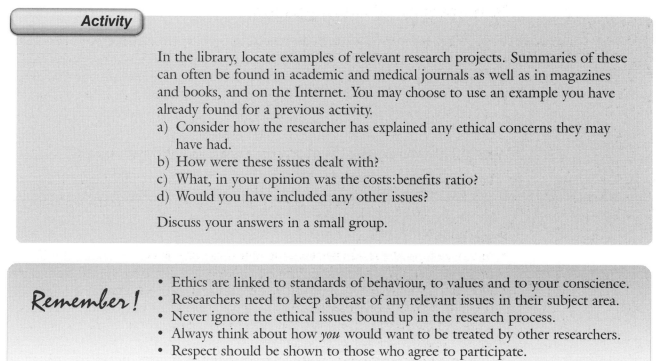

**Activity**

In the library, locate examples of relevant research projects. Summaries of these can often be found in academic and medical journals as well as in magazines and books, and on the Internet. You may choose to use an example you have already found for a previous activity.

a) Consider how the researcher has explained any ethical concerns they may have had.

b) How were these issues dealt with?

c) What, in your opinion was the costs:benefits ratio?

d) Would you have included any other issues?

Discuss your answers in a small group.

*Remember !*
- Ethics are linked to standards of behaviour, to values and to your conscience.
- Researchers need to keep abreast of any relevant issues in their subject area.
- Never ignore the ethical issues bound up in the research process.
- Always think about how *you* would want to be treated by other researchers.
- Respect should be shown to those who agree to participate.
- Participants in research have rights. These must be acknowledged and respected.

**Test Yourself**

1  Why is research important?
2  What is the difference between primary and secondary research?
3  Define the terms 'qualitative' and 'quantitative'.
4  What is meant by objectivity?
5  What is a hypothesis?
6  What are the advantages and disadvantages of interviews?
7  List at least five important points to remember when planning a questionnaire.
8  What is action research?
9  Give an example of how case studies can be used.
10  What is the purpose of the control group in an experiment?
11  List as many secondary sources of information as you can.
12  List as many ways as can you think of to present statistical data.
13  What is the difference between mean, median and mode?
14  Explain validity and reliability.
15  Give an example of research affecting practice.
16  What do research ethics involve?

# Using research skills

You should by now have identified how the general principles of research methodology are relevant to the whole process of your training. Throughout your studies, you will need to locate printed and non-printed (technological) sources of information and each time you do this you are carrying out a form of research.

Each assignment you prepare will need:
• planning
• a literature search
• decisions about scope and parameters
• validity
• referencing
• clear presentation.

Each of these are part of the research process.

In your interactions with others, both in college and in placement, you will need to show respect and consideration, treating others as you would wish to be treated yourself. You will also need to respect their rights and privacy.

The new thinking and practice that is introduced into the settings that you attend will most likely be based on research of some description and will enable you to witness firsthand how the practical application of the research process impacts on standards, achievement and professionalism.

The research project (Unit 15 *Project*) will enable you (if you are taking this as one of your specialist option units) to bring together the knowledge gained from this *Research* unit. Applying this knowledge practically will consolidate your understanding and enhance your personal development. It is an opportunity for you to explore an area of particular interest to you, and it can help you to formulate a career plan, by enhancing or dispelling potential aspects of early years care or education as career opportunities. This final section summarises the main points that you will need to consider.

For a useful guide in planning, presenting and evaluating your project, and in developing your personal research skills, look at Green (2000) on which the following summaries are based (see *Bibliography and suggested further reading*, page 159).

To achieve the *Project* unit you will need to:
- identify a suitable topic and produce a plan for a research proposal
- conduct the research
- analyse and present the findings of the research
- identify and evaluate your own learning from the process.

You will need to produce a research project which shows:
- a relevant hypothesis for the research
- a range of primary and secondary sources
- your analysed and presented findings
- discussion of your findings which relate back to the hypothesis
- your planning and progress throughout the research
- your own research skills and how these could be further developed.

## Planning a research project

To produce a successful research project, it needs to be planned and taken in stages. This involves:
- choosing the subject area
- writing the aims and objectives
- setting out a hypothesis
- setting parameters
- selecting an appropriate approach to the research
- identifying ethical considerations
- managing time
- keeping records
- tutorial support
- avoiding common pitfalls.

## Presentation

Presentation of the research is likely to include both written and oral presentation skills. The written presentation would usually include the following:
- abstract
- introduction
- methodology
- presentation of data
- main text (discussion)
- conclusions and any recommendations
- evaluation
- bibliography
- appendices.

An oral presentation would usually include the use of some or all of the following:
- overhead projector transparencies
- audio-visual resources (tape recorders, videos, slides)

- tables, charts, graphs
- handouts
- questions from the 'audience'.

Each of these is described in Green (2000).

## Evaluating the learning process

When evaluating your learning from the research process, the following points should be considered:

- oral skills
- written skills
- information technology skills
- numeracy skills
- personal development
- academic achievement
- practical skills
- applying new skills to other situations.

# Key terms

**You should now understand the following words and phrases. If you do not, read through the chapter again and review them.**

| | |
|---|---|
| anonymity | quantitative |
| bar chart | range |
| confidentiality | raw data |
| line graph | reliability |
| mean | replication |
| median | secondary research |
| mode | sociogram |
| objectivity | standard deviation |
| pictograph | subjectivity |
| pie chart | table |
| primary research | triangulation |
| qualitative | validity |

# Bibliography and suggested further reading

Bell, J. (1998) *Doing Your Research Project*, 2nd edition, Open University Press, Buckingham

Cullis, T., Dolan, L. and Groves, D. (1999) *Psychology for You*, Nelson Thornes, Cheltenham

Green, S. (2000) *Research Methods in Health, Social and Early Years Care*, Nelson Thornes, Cheltenham

Hobart, C. and Frankel, J. (1999) *A Practical Guide to Child Observation and Assessment*, 2nd edition, Nelson Thornes, Cheltenham.

Jameson, H. and Watson, M. (1998) *Starting and Running a Nursery*, Nelson Thornes, Cheltenham

McNeill, P. (1990) *Research Methods*, 2nd edition, Routledge, London

Ogier, M. (1998) *Reading Research: How to Make Research More Approachable*, 2nd edition, Baillière-Tindall, London

Polit, D.F. and Hungler, B.P. (1991) *Nursing Research: Principles and Methods*, 4th edition, J.P. Lipincott, Philadelphia

# Safe Environments

This chapter covers:

- Safety and emergency procedures
- Maintaining a safe and secure environment
- Applying health and safety procedures.

## Introduction

This chapter provides the knowledge and understanding of many health and safety issues, acknowledging the fact that accidents and incidents within early years settings are inevitable, helping you to learn the relevant health and safety requirements and raising your awareness of the need for training in first aid. The chapter gives appropriate guidance on preventing cross-infection, preparing a first aid box and the requirements regarding emergency first aid procedures. It does not provide detailed instructions for each first aid procedure — you will get these from your practical sessions on first aid instruction.

Procedures for storage, administration and recording of medications are discussed, along with the reporting of accidents, recording of incidents and safe practice for all staff and students, according to guidelines set down by the statutory authorities.

## Safety and emergency procedures

### First aid procedures

Knowledge of **first aid** is essential in early years settings – the initial actions carried out following an accident or incident, before the arrival of the emergency services, can have a significant impact on the eventual outcome. First aid is about limiting the effects of an accident or incident and taking action to aid the recovery of the person concerned.

Every early years setting is required to have at least one person on duty at all times who is qualified in emergency first aid procedures. This person should be named and all staff should know who they are and where they can be found. All first aiders need to be regularly updated and assessed externally, and they are required to renew their qualification every three years to ensure that they remain up-to-date with current thinking and show that they can still remember and carry out basic procedures. Nannies and childminders need to take responsibility for updating their first aid qualification for themselves.

Each college offering the BTec National in Early Years will arrange first aid training for its students, but the timing of this will vary from college to college, as there is different thinking on where it is best placed within a programme of study.

- In some colleges, it will take place near to the beginning of the course, the thinking being to maximise your understanding of emergency procedures whilst you are on placement experience (although a student should never be considered to be the qualified first aider for the setting).
- In other colleges, it will be placed near to the end of the course, the thinking here being that you will have gained in confidence and that first aid training at this point will build on your all-round knowledge and understanding of children. It also enables you to qualify with three years of first aid 'currency' ahead of you.

Some colleges will focus purely on first aid for young children, whereas others will incorporate the full first-aid-at-work training into their programme, usually with a specific section on first aid for young children alongside it.

As an early years worker, you will need to know how to:
- check for signs and symptoms
- prioritise treatment
- deal with an unconscious casualty
- use the **ABC procedure**
- deal with allergies and anaphylaxis
- treat minor and major injuries:
  - bleeding
  - burns and scalds
  - fractures
  - poisoning
  - choking and breathing difficulties
  - foreign bodies
  - seizures.

An introduction to the treatment of each of the above can be found in Dare and O'Donovan (2000) – see *Bibliography and suggested further reading*, page 192.

First aid manuals are provided by recognised bodies such as the Red Cross and the St John's Ambulance. Your college will tell you which you will need to obtain. It is important that you refer to the most up-to-date edition, as procedures change from time to time, based on new understanding.

## Dealing with an emergency

As children's bodies are still developing, it is not always appropriate to use the same techniques for emergency first aid as you would use on an adult, to avoid injuring the child unnecessarily. In some cases, techniques designed for adults can be extremely dangerous to a young child. For example, tilting the head of a young infant back too far may actually occlude (block) the airway, rather than open it. Similarly, if too much pressure is placed on the soft tissue under the jaw when opening the airway, this may block it.

### Emergency procedures for babies and young children: a summary

#### Stage 1
- Review the situation, assessing as far as is possible what has happened.
- Decide what are your immediate priorities.
- Stay calm.
- Consider if there is anyone else who could help you.
- Professional help should be sought unless only a minor injury has occurred (if on your own, **shout for help**!).
- Whenever possible, any other children present should be reassured and led away.

#### Stage 2
Remove any dangers. You will be of little use to the casualty if you become injured yourself. Ask yourself: Is it safe to proceed with first aid? For example:
- Is the fire out?
- Is the electricity turned off?

*Remember!* You should not put yourself in unnecessary danger too.

#### Stage 3
- Assess the casualty for any response. Remember that during the pre-verbal stage, the inability to speak will not automatically mean they are unconscious. Consider:
  - Is the child moving?
  - Have they opened their eyes?
  - Have they given a verbal response – a cry, moan or any other vocalisation?
- If no response is obtained, it is likely that they are unconscious.
- You will need to begin the ABC procedure.

## The ABC of resuscitation

### A stands for *airway*

The airway needs to be kept clear. If it becomes blocked and the child stops breathing, they will soon become unconscious. This will eventually lead to the heart slowing down and stopping due to the lack of oxygen.

Remove any obvious obstructions from the child's mouth, but be aware that a 'blind-sweep' may block the child's airway further! Ask yourself:

- Is the child's chest rising and falling?
- Is the tongue well forward?
- Can you hear breathing sounds when your ear is close to the mouth?
- Can you feel the child's breath on your cheek?

If not you will need to open the airway for the child.

### To open a baby's airway
- Place the baby on his back tilting with the head back slightly.
- Use one finger under the chin to move it forwards (imagine the baby is sniffing a flower and position him accordingly).
- Look, listen and feel again for breathing.
- If there is no change, you will need to try **artificial ventilation** (see **B** below).

Opening a baby's airway

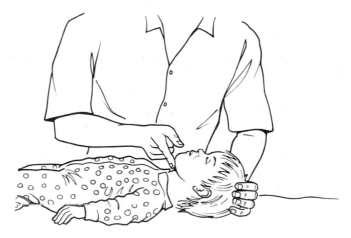

### To open an older child's airway
- Place the child on her back.
- Place two fingers under the chin.
- Place a hand on the forehead and tilt the head backwards, again ensuring not to tip it too far!
- Look, listen and feel again for breathing.
- If there is no change, you will need to try artificial ventilation (see **B** below).

Opening a child's airway

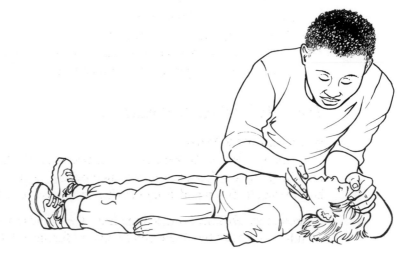

### *B* stands for *breathing*

Have a look at the casualty's tummy. Can you see it moving? If breathing has stopped, you may need to do this for them. Whenever possible, send someone to call for an ambulance. If you are on your own, perform the following procedure for 1 minute and then go and call an ambulance yourself. If the casualty is a young baby, you may be able to take them with you and continue the breathing procedure for them.

**To carry out artificial ventilation for a baby**
- Open the airway as in **A**.
- Place your lips around the baby's mouth and nose.
- Give five 'rescue' breaths (breaths which are hard enough to make the chest move as though the casualty had taken a deep breath for themselves).
- Continue to blow, very gently at a rate of 20 breaths per minute.
- After each breath, remove your mouth and watch for the chest to fall as the air expires.
- If, after five rescue breaths, you have not been able to establish effective breathing, recheck their mouth and head position and try again.

Artificial ventilation for a baby

**To carry out artificial ventilation for an older child**
- Open the airway as in **A**.
- Pinch the child's nostrils together.
- Place your lips firmly over the child's mouth.
- As with a baby, give five rescue breaths, then …
- Blow gently in to the mouth at a rate of 20 breaths per minute.
- Again, as with a baby, remove your mouth after each breath and watch the chest fall as the air expires.

Artificial ventilation for a child

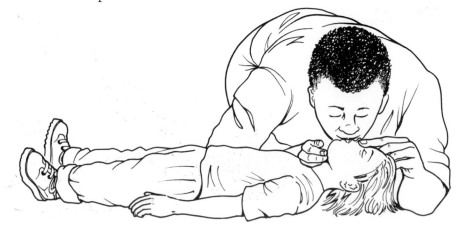

The updated UK Resuscitation Council guidelines state that only professionally trained health workers should check the pulse during resuscitation attempts.

### C stands for *circulation*

The circulation is the beating of the heart which keeps the blood flowing through the body. The usual signs of circulation are breathing, coughing or movement. If you cannot see signs of circulation, you will need to start the procedure known as **chest compression**.

### Chest compression for a baby

- Place the tips of your fingers one finger's width below the baby's nipple line.
- Press down sharply to between one third and one half of the depth of the chest.
- Give five compressions per one breath, 100 compressions per minute if working alone.

Chest compression for a baby

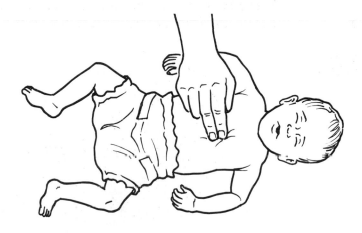

### Chest compression for a child

- Use the heel of your hand rather than your fingers.
- Press down sharply to between one third and one half of the depth of the child's chest.
- Work in cycles of fifteen compressions per two breaths, 100 compressions per minute if working alone.

Chest compression for a child

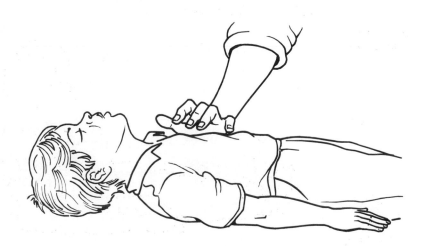

## The recovery position

Once a child has begun to breath for themselves, they need to be placed in the **recovery position**.

### The recovery position for a baby
Hold the baby in your arms with their head tilted downwards to help keep the airway open.

The recovery position for a baby

### The recovery position for a child
1 Ensure that the airway is open.
2 Bend the arm nearest to you at a right angle. Bring the child's furthest arm across his chest and cushion his cheek with the back of his hand.

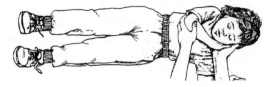

3  Roll the child towards you. Keep his hand pressed against his cheek. Bend his outside knee, grasp him under the thigh and, keeping his near leg straight, pull him towards you.

4  Bend the child's top leg at a right angle to his body to keep him on his side and to prevent him from rolling onto his front. Tilt his head back to ensure his airway remains open. Check his head is still cushioned by his hand.

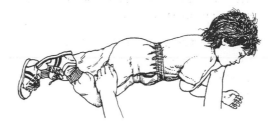

Once the child has been made comfortable in the recovery position, he should be closely monitored and reassured as necessary until professional help arrives.

**Test Yourself** ✔

1  How many qualified first aiders should be on duty in an early years setting?
2  How regularly should first aid training be updated and reassessed?
3  How many types of injury can you think of that you may need to deal with?
4  What does the A stand for in the ABC procedure?
5  What does the B stand for in the ABC procedure?
6  What does the C stand for in the ABC procedure?
7  How many compressions and ventilations should you give per minute?
8  To what depth should the chest be compressed?
9  Why is it important to put the injured person into the recovery position?
10  How does the recovery position differ between a young baby and a child?

## First aid boxes

Every setting needs to have a first aid box. It is a legal requirement of all employers under the Health and Safety (First Aid) Regulations, 1981.

The container should be both airtight and waterproof and it should be easily recognised – the most usual design is green with a white cross. The box should always include a guidance sheet on emergency first aid. Every setting will have different requirements according to the numbers and needs of its children and staff. The first aid box should be checked regularly and kept in good order by a specified person.

Some of the contents of a first aid box

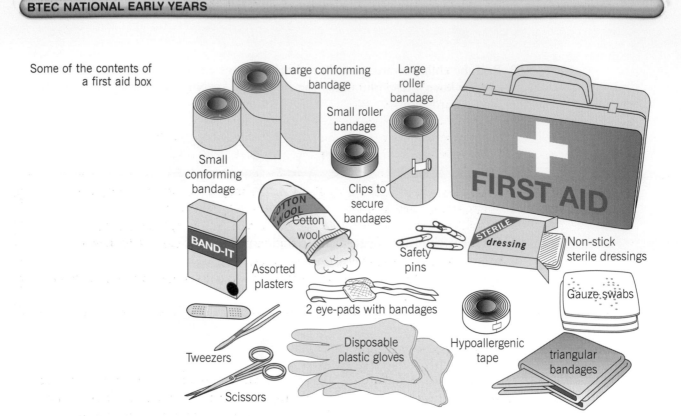

Large conforming bandage

Large roller bandage

Small roller bandage

Small conforming bandage

Clips to secure bandages

Cotton wool

BAND-IT

Assorted plasters

Safety pins

STERILE dressing

Non-stick sterile dressings

Gauze swabs

2 eye-pads with bandages

Tweezers

Disposable plastic gloves

Hypoallergenic tape

triangular bandages

Scissors

FIRST AID

### Local policy
Some local authorities recommend settings not to use certain items, such as plasters and lotions, because of the risk of allergy in some children. Each setting needs to ensure that its first aid box is drawn up in accordance with local policy.

### Parental consent forms
Written consent is needed regarding emergency treatment for a child. Some parents have cultural or religious beliefs that will mean they withhold permission for some forms of treatment.

### Contents of a first aid box
An employer with ten or more staff is required by law to include the following in the first aid box:
- twenty individually wrapped sterile adhesive dressings (various sizes)
- two sterile pads
- four triangular bandages (ideally sterile)
- six safety pins
- individually wrapped unmedicated wound dressings, six 12 × 12 cm; two 18 × 18 cm
- one pair of disposable gloves
- one first aid guidance leaflet.

### Additional items
An early years setting will also need to include additional items such as:
- scissors (kept only for first aid use)
- tweezers
- several pairs of disposable gloves

- non-allergic tape
- non-allergic plasters (if used)
- bandages in various sizes
- sterile gauze
- digital thermometer (never a glass or mercury thermometer)
- checking sheet for the contents.

| Professional Practice | • A specified person (or persons) should be responsible for checking and replenishing the first aid box regularly, and after every use. <br> • A checklist of the minimum requirements should be kept in the box. <br> • A form should be kept in the box, and be signed and dated after every check and each time the box has been cleaned. <br> • All staff should be aware of parents' wishes in the event of emergency treatment for their child. |
| --- | --- |

## Emergencies

There are many emergencies other than accidents that early years workers need to know how to react to, including fire, suspected or actual gas leaks, flooding and bomb scares. Each setting should have a clear procedure for evacuating the building, with all staff knowing who and what they are responsible for and where they are to congregate following the evacuation. An agreed procedure for ensuring that the emergency services have been called must be established. This is likely to be the responsibility of the manager, but settings need to consider what happens if it is the manager who has had the accident!

As a student you should not be given any responsibility for evacuating children from the setting during an emergency procedure, but it is important that you are fully aware of what the procedure involves and where you should go, remaining calm and helping to reassure the children.

### Emergency exits
Emergency exits should be signposted with appropriate symbols, like those below.

Emergency exit signs

Emergency exits should be kept clear at all times. Tables, cupboards, activities and temporary displays should not be placed as an obstruction. Each exit should be unlocked (though childproof) and be easily opened from inside.

### Evacuation procedures

There should be clear instructions setting out the emergency **evacuation procedure** on display in the setting at all times. Copies should be placed near the main entrance and in all the rooms that are used. All staff, students and parents should be referred to these and asked to familiarise themselves with the instructions. Where more than one language is spoken in the setting, copies of the procedure should be translated accordingly.

### Activity

Find out the emergency procedures for your current work placement.
a) Ask to see the relevant policies.
b) Read the evacuation procedure carefully. It should be on display.
c) Note which members of staff have particular responsibilities during an emergency.
d) Look at where the assembly point is situated, and consider why this site has been chosen.
e) Following a practice evacuation, evaluate the success of the setting's procedure, considering timing, reactions of the children and staff, and the taking of the register at the assembly point.

### Fire alarms and evacuation practice

An obvious fire alarm of some kind is needed, together with smoke detectors in suitable places. (The kitchen itself is not suitable, unless it is spacious, as steam from cooking may set it off regularly, causing unnecessary anguish. By the kitchen doorway is more usual.) Alarms that automatically trigger lights when they are activated are ideal as they allow better vision in a smoky atmosphere.

Practising an evacuation (often called *fire practice*) should be a regular activity, and all new staff should be trained as to what their responsibility is to be. These practices should occasionally include having to take a different route, pretending that the straightforward route is unpassable. This will help staff think through the procedure more thoroughly.

### Professional Practice

Times and days of practice evacuations should be varied so all children who attend the setting experience the procedure.

**Case Study**

*Top of the World Nursery*

Top of the World Nursery is based in the centre of a small town. It is held in the first floor hall of a large community centre on a triangular 'island' of buildings. The emergency exit, which is approved by the registering authority for the nursery, involves taking the children down an outside staircase onto a narrow pavement below, which is the assembly point. The nursery staff are keen to have regular practices at evacuating the children, as some children are reluctant to walk down the outside staircase and staff worry about having to cajole them down it in a real emergency. The nursery currently has a fire practice every two weeks.

A new parent has questioned the wisdom of this, pointing out that the children are potentially in greater danger from being led onto a narrow pavement on such a regular basis. This has worried the staff further.

1  What are the benefits of both arguments?
2  What are the drawbacks of both arguments?
3  How could the nursery reach a compromise on this, while still practising regularly?

**Professional Practice**

- A member of staff should have responsibility for taking the register with them to the assembly site.
- Children need to be taught to respond to emergencies, which is why practising is important.
- Children need to be familiar with holding hands, grouping together and standing still when required (for a head count).
- Early years staff need to promote the importance of fire practices without raising undue alarm in children.

**Case Study**

*Safe as Houses Nursery*

Safe as Houses Nursery looks after twenty children each day, predominantly for full day care, due to its proximity to a large local business.

Most of the children arrive between 8.00 and 8.30 a.m. each morning, with only three arriving later, usually just after 9.15. All the children gather together in one large group for news, weather and the register at 9.30, having played freely in the largest room until this point. The children then divide into their keyworker groups and move to preplanned activity areas.

1  Is there any problem with this practice, do you think?
2  Would you change anything, if you were able?
3  What might be the problem if a fire broke out at around 9.00 a.m?
4  How could Safe as Houses Nursery be made safer without altering its daily structure?

### Information for parents following an emergency

If an early years setting has had to relocate mid-session due to an emergency, there needs to be clear, informative and reassuring information left for parents in a central and obvious place. To leave a message reading:

will no doubt cause panic among parents and carers and much undue distress, thinking that children have been injured. Whereas to leave one reading:

will help to dispel any initial panic in parents and carers regarding their children's well-being.

*Remember!*

In an emergency, children may be scared to move, or frightened by what they see. This is understandable as they will be feeling insecure. It is important that you:
- remain calm
- give them clear instructions
- remove them from the scene if possible
- comfort them and offer reassurance
- be as honest as you can without adding to their fears.

After the event, children often refer back constantly to the incident. It is important to recognise that children sometimes need to talk about incidents in order to 'sort events out' in their minds. Reassuring books and stories, together with plenty of active play will eventually move most children on. On occasions, however, some children may need professional help to see them through the aftermath of a crisis or emergency.

**Professional Practice**

- Early years staff need to consider the feelings and views of the parents as well as the children.
- As an early years worker, you have responsibility for a parent's most precious possession – their child.

**Test Yourself** ✓

1 Why is it necessary to have a specific person responsible for the first aid box?
2 Give three important points regarding emergency exits.
3 Where should emergency evacuation procedures be displayed?
4 When should children's attendance be registered?
5 Why might children refuse to move or to co-operate in an emergency?

# Maintaining a safe and secure environment

Each early years setting must be registered with its local authority and has to meet certain criteria in order to retain its registration. This involves adhering to a range of regulations, Acts, guidelines and care standards regarding the setting up and maintenance of safe and healthy practice in all provisions, including those in the diagram below. The regulations are overseen by statutory authorities such as Social Services Inspection and Registration Units (joined with OfSTED from September 2001), environmental health officers, local education authorities and the Health and Safety Executive.

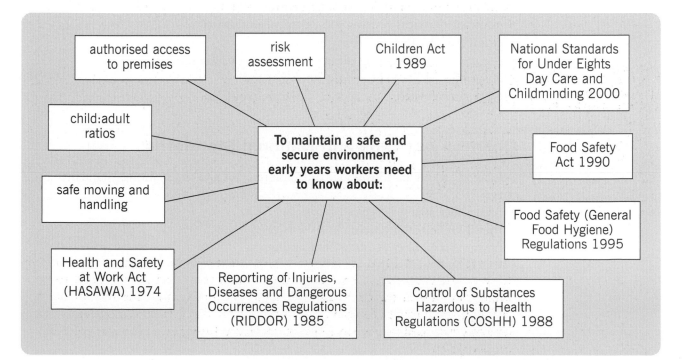

authorised access to premises

risk assessment

Children Act 1989

National Standards for Under Eights Day Care and Childminding 2000

child:adult ratios

To maintain a safe and secure environment, early years workers need to know about:

Food Safety Act 1990

safe moving and handling

Food Safety (General Food Hygiene) Regulations 1995

Health and Safety at Work Act (HASAWA) 1974

Reporting of Injuries, Diseases and Dangerous Occurrences Regulations (RIDDOR) 1985

Control of Substances Hazardous to Health Regulations (COSHH) 1988

The Children Act 1989 includes statements on the safety of premises. To read these in detail, see Annex D of Volume 2, *Family Support, Day Care and Educational Provision for Young Children*.

The publication *Guidance to the National Standards For Under Eights Care* (2000) also sets out guidelines for safety, including fire safety (reference criterion 6.9–6.11). The guidelines cover the following five types of setting and each can be downloaded from the Ofsted website (www.ofsted.gov.uk):

- full day care
- sessional day care
- childminding
- creches
- out of school care.

Settings should refer to the most appropriate *Guidance* document for the provision they are registered as. The main standards from the *Guidance* linked to safety are standards 5, 6, 7 and 8. It will be useful to compare the difference between each type of provision. They each follow the same order for subject referencing.

Under the Fire Precautions Act 1971 some, but not all, premises require a fire certificate. This does not as yet automatically apply to day-care provision. However, advice from the fire services is available on request by a local authority or an individual provider, particularly when setting up a new facility, and fire safety information is usually available. In general, the main points of concern regarding fire safety in day-care settings, including childminders' homes, are:

- accessibilty of the register
- the presence of smoke alarms in suitable places
- the means of escape from the building
- the heating and any fire/heating guards used
- safety of electrical systems and electrical equipment
- storage of any flammable materials
- the means of preventing unsupervised access to the kitchen
- ensuring that fire exits remain unobstructed
- who is responsible for checking fire exits regularly.

## Children Act 1989 and National Standards

Guidance and regulations under the Children Act and the National Standards also cover:

- adult:child ratios
- minimum space requirements
- maximum number of places in a setting
- toilets and handbasins.

## Adult:child ratios

**Standard recommended staff:child ratios for the under fives in day care and education settings**

| Type of setting/Age range | Ratio | Comments |
| --- | --- | --- |
| Under 5 years' full day care<br>0 to 2 years<br>2 to 3 years<br>3 to 5 years | <br>1:3<br>1:4<br>1:8 | Because of management and administration duties, managers or officers-in-charge should not be included in these ratios where more than 20 children are being cared for |
| Nursery schools and nursery classes | 2:20<br>(minimum) | One adult should be a qualified teacher and one a qualified nursery assistant |
| Reception classes in primary schools | | Where 4-year-olds are attending Reception classes in primary schools, the staffing levels should be determined by the schools and local education authorities |
| Childminding<br>Under 5 years<br>5 to 7 years<br>Under 8 (no more than three being under 5) years | <br>1:3<br>1:6<br>1:6 | All these ratios include the childminder's own children and apply to nannies employed by more than two sets of parents to look after their children |
| Day care services for school age children<br>Where 5- and 7-year-olds are cared for on a daily or sessional basis (i.e. care at the end of the school day and full care in school holidays)<br>Where facilities are used by children aged over 8 years as well as under 8 years | <br>1:8 | A higher ratio may be necessary if children with special needs are being cared for. A lower ratio may be appropriate for some short sessional facilities not lasting the full day<br><br><br>Providers should ensure that there are sufficient staff in total to maintain the 1:8 ratio for the under eights. |

reproduced by kind permission of The Stationery Office, from The Children Act 1989, *Guidance and Regulations Volume 2*, Seventh Impression, 1998

A higher ratio of staff to children will be required if staff are not all qualified or trained to the required level. The inclusion of children with a special need may also necessitate a higher staff ratio, depending on the children's level of individual need.

### Minimum space requirements

**Minimum space requirements in an early years setting**

| Age of child | Square feet | Square metres |
| --- | --- | --- |
| 0–2 years | 37.7 | 3.5 |
| 2 years | 26.9 | 2.5 |
| 3–7 years | 24.8 | 2.3 |

### Maximum numbers of places

No setting is allowed to place more than 26 children in one room except for special occasions. This is regardless of the size of the room. A separate room is always needed for babies and toddlers, adjacent to changing and food preparation facilities.

### Toilets and handbasins

- Hot and cold running water should be available.
- Water temperatures in children's hand basins should not exceed 39°C (102°F).
- There should be a minimum of one toilet and one hand basin for every ten children in the setting.
- Staff should have separate toilet and hand washing facilities

 FORWARD to page181, *Physical environment*, and page 185, *Potential hazards*.

## Food Safety Act 1990 and Food Safety (General Food Hygiene) Regulations 1995

This legislation includes guidelines on both personal and general kitchen hygiene. It can be summarised as follows.

### Personal hygiene

This involves:

- regular hand washing throughout the day
- washing hands before all food preparation
- washing hands after any activity with the potential for bacteria:
  - nappy changing
  - using the toilet
  - coughing
  - sneezing
  - nose blowing
- use of antibacterial soaps
- nails kept clean and short
- cuts and sores covered
- use of disposable gloves.

Also:

- Hair should be kept tied back to reduce the risk of infestation, **cross-infection** and general untidiness.
- Clean clothing and overalls should be worn at all times, changing as necessary for food preparation and cooking activities.
- Covering the nose and mouth when coughing and sneezing should be automatic, and needs to be encouraged in all children too.

### Kitchen hygiene

This involves:

- keeping surfaces cleaned and free from bacteria
- ensuring all surfaces used are unblemished and unchipped
- using separate boards for cooked and uncooked foods
- using separate knives for cooked and uncooked foods
- keeping floors cleaned thoroughly
- washing up as dirty utensils occur to eliminate additional bacteria growth (where possible use a dishwasher as this is the most effective method)
- all waste being wrapped securely and bins emptied regularly
- regular cleaning and defrosting of refrigerators and freezers
- ensuring the temperature of a refrigerator is kept at 4–5°C (39–41°F)
- storing cooked foods at the top of the refrigerator, raw foods below
- minimal handling of all foods
- keeping food well covered
- ensuring use-by dates are adhered to
- any reheated food being served piping hot
- not keeping food warm for more than a few minutes.

### Activity

1 Check the temperature of the refrigerator at your home (if it has a thermometer).
2 Is the food in the refrigerator stored properly? Are all raw meats stored at the bottom?
3 Is there anything 'lurking' at the back? If yes, check its use-by date and discard if necessary.
4 Ask at your placement how often the refrigerator and freezer are defrosted and who is responsible. These procedures should be recorded.
5 How often and who checks the temperature of the refrigerator at your placement?
6 Is the food in the refrigerator at your placement stored properly?

**Professional Practice**
- Some colleges include a certificated Food Hygiene course in their training for early years students.
- An opportunity to obtain this additional certificate will enable you to consolidate and evidence your knowledge and understanding of food hygiene issues.
- Obtaining the certificate during your training may help you in gaining future employment.

## Control of Substances Hazardous to Health Regulations (COSHH) 1988

Health problems such as skin irritation and asthma can occur due to the presence certain chemicals in some substances. The symbols drawn up by COSHH have been devised to warn people in advance of **potential hazards**. Most of these substances covered by the regulations will not be used in early years settings. However, bleach and some other common cleaning products are used and can cause irritation and respiratory reactions.

In schools, chemicals may be used within the context of design technology or art. Although many products are now 'safe', potentially harmful substances include some marbelling inks and spirits for cleaning, and some spray paints and glues. These would usually only be handled by adults, but children may be present during their use.

**Professional Practice**
- Always read instructions for the use and dilution of any product, and the importance of ventilation when using them.
- A risk assessment is a systematic check of any potential 'risks' in a setting. An assessment should be carried out by all settings and any potentially hazardous products identified. Relevant information on the storage, use and treatment following spills should be noted.
- Cleaning products should not *at any time* be left where they can be reached by children.

**Activity**

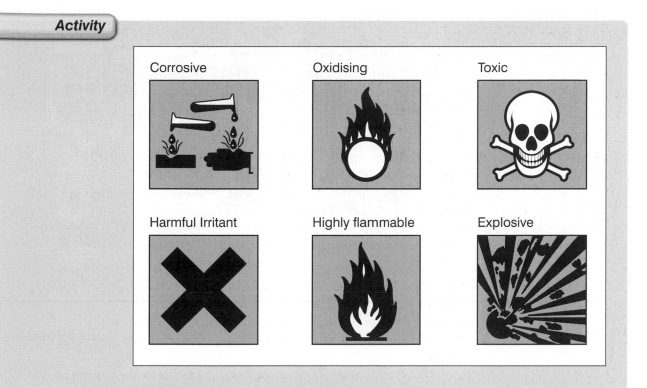

1  Match each symbol above to the appropriate hazard it is used for, from this list:
   a) Corrosive
   b) Explosive
   c) Flammable
   d) Harmful
   e) Irritant
   f) Toxic.
2  Ask permission to look around your current work placement to identify how many potentially hazardous substances there are. Make a note of what you find.
3  Were they all stored appropriately?
4  Were they all recorded on the register following the setting's risk assessment?
5  Have a look around your home. How many potentially hazardous substances can you find there?
6  Are they stored out of reach of children and pets?
7  How well do family members read instructions before use?
8  If you wanted to work as a childminder from your home, would you need to alter anything regarding the storage of these substances?

## Reporting of Injuries, Diseases and Dangerous Occurrences Regulations (RIDDOR) 1985

These regulations require a setting to report by telephone to the local authority all deaths, and any serious injuries that result in a child, a parent, a visitor or a member of staff being taken to hospital from the setting.

If a member of staff is injured (but not seriously) or becomes ill due to their work, the local authority should be informed in writing, using a specified form.

There are regulations concerning the reporting of serious injuries

**Professional Practice**

All settings should have an accident book in which they report all accidents and incidents, both large and small.

## Health and Safety at Work Act (HASAWA) 1974

This Act protects employees and anyone else who could be affected by the procedures of a setting. It requires settings to have a safety policy and to assess, and reduce accordingly, the risk of accident or injury.

There should be a written health and safety policy and a named person with responsibility for health and safety in any setting which employs more than five people.

Local authorities can (under the Children Act 1989) ask early years settings to produce health and safety policies irrespective of how many people are employed by the setting.

**Activity**

What would you include in a health and safety policy? Draw up a list of ideas.

**Professional Practice**

It is good practice to have a health and safety policy, whether or not it is required.
* All staff and students should be asked to read the health and safety policy.
* The policy should be available for parents to read if they so wish.
* Ask to read the policy at your work placement if you have not seen it already.
* Make a note of all areas of safety and health that it covers. How does it compare with your own ideas?

Examples of health and safety policies can be found in Dare and O'Donovan (2000) and in Sadek and Sadek (1996) – see *Bibiography and suggested further reading*, page 192.

# Physical environment

Ensuring that the **physical environment** of an early years setting is safe and secure includes giving consideration to the:

- layout of the setting
- space available
- furniture and fixtures and their positioning
- mobility of the children, taking into account any specific physical needs
- safety of all toys, activities and equipment.

It also means considering the heating, lighting, ventilation and ease of cleaning of the equipment and the setting itself.

FORWARD to Chapter 6, page 227, for information about securing access to the premises.

## Layout and space

The design of every setting is different, determined by practicalities and the personal choice of the staff and management. The shape of rooms, levels of equipment and furnishings, and whether the setting has sole use of the building will all have an impact on how it is arranged and how flexible the arrangements can be.

The layout of the setting needs to allow sufficient space for:

- children to play in groups
- children to use the floor
- differentiated use of the rooms for quiet activities, messy activities, active play, and so on
- displaying children's creativity, both two-dimensional and three-dimensional
- storing equipment and activities, allowing access to some items by the children
- moving safely between activities
- safe evacuation of the building in an emergency
- rearranging activities and equipment without undue disruption to the setting
- staff to oversee activities in general whilst involved in other areas of the room.

## Furniture and fixtures

- All cupboards, shelving and any other permanent storage must be securely held in place, and any doors should close firmly and remain closed when not in use.
- Access to storage should not interrupt play or be hazardous to children playing.
- Mobile storage needs to be stocked carefully, avoiding overloading or the risk of items falling.
- Furniture should be child-sized.
- Ideally tables that can combine to extend or alter shape should be used.
- Furniture should be sturdy and be kept in good condition.
- Wooden chairs should be checked regularly for splinters and plastic moulded chairs examined for cracks.
- All surfaces used by the children should be hygienic and in good condition.

### Cleaning the environment

This includes both the setting itself and the equipment and furnishings within it.

- Cleaning should take place at the end of each session, or day, and as necessary throughout the day.
- Carpeted floor surfaces should be easily cleaned with a vacuum cleaner and washable non-slip surfaces with a mop (disinfected daily).
- Suitable anti-bacterial products should be used regularly to clean all surfaces.
- Toys and activities should be cleaned with anti-bacterial products regularly.

| **Professional Practice** | • It is particularly important to clean surfaces before any food preparation, cooking activities and before snack time.<br>• If early years staff are responsible for cleaning the setting, there should be a rota to ensure that it is kept clean and hygienic at all times.<br>• Staff should not carry out cleaning duties while still responsible for supervising children. |
| --- | --- |

#### Cleaning messy-play materials

- Sand should be sieved daily to remove any bits and cleaned regularly. Any sand that has been spilt on the floor should be sieved and cleaned before returning to the sand tray or discarded.
- Outdoor sand pits should be kept securely covered when not in use to prevent fouling by animals, and to prevent rubbish and garden debris settling there.
- Water should be replenished daily, and water trays cleaned and disinfected regularly.
- Any pets should be kept scrupulously clean, following normal petcare routines
- Dough should be renewed regularly and stored in a refrigerator.
- Dough should be discarded and replaced following any infectious illness in the setting to avoid cross-infection.

Pets should be kept scrupulously clean

### Mobility of children

- The layout of a setting needs to take into account the mobility needs of the children it caters for. Baby rooms will need a significant area of floor space to encourage mobility and floor play with staff.
- A child with a physical disability may benefit from a more spacious layout, enabling easier access between activities, particularly if they use a wheelchair or walking frame, or need support from an adult.
- If a setting is supporting a child who is blind or has significant vision impairment, keeping a familiar layout will allow the child a degree of autonomy and independence.

### Safety of toys, activities and equipment

All equipment used in early years settings should be made to a recognised safety standard. A range of **safety marks** are used by manufacturers as required by legislation and these are shown on page 184. These are changed and updated from time to time, and it is worth checking for the most recent recommendations.

### Safety of outdoors surfaces

Outdoors, concrete, gravel and similar surfaces are not suitable because they do not absorb impacts. This can result in serious injury if a child should fall on them. A more suitable surface for general play is grass, but in dry summer months, this will also become hard and unyielding.

It is particularly important that surfaces under and around play equipment from which a child may fall a distance of 60 cm (2 feet) or more should be able to absorb some of the impact of the fall, reducing the risk of serious injury. **Impact-absorbing playground surfaces (IAPS)** include:
- loose-fill substances such as tree bark or sand (at least 30 cm [1 foot] deep)
- 'wet pour' rubber which sets to form a spongy surface
- thick rubber tiles.

Surfaces should meet the BSEN 1177 safety standard. They should be kept in good condition, repairing any damage and regularly raking tree bark or sand for debris and animal excrement.

### Heating, lighting and ventilation

#### Heating
- Room temperatures must be 18–20°C (65–68°F).
- A wall thermometer should be on display and checked regularly.
- Whenever possible, radiators should be controlled by individual thermostats.
- Fire guards or heater guards should be fitted where necessary.

#### Lighting
- Natural light is important to avoid headaches and eye strain.
- Lighting must be adequate for safe working practice.
- Accidents are more likely to occur in poorly lit settings.

#### Ventilation
- Children and staff work best within a well-ventilated environment.
- Good ventilation reduces the risk of cross-infection.
- Ventilation points need to be kept clean, as they can easily attract dirt and a build-up of bacteria.

## Safety marks

| Mark | Name | Meaning |
| --- | --- | --- |
| | BSI Kitemark | Indicates a product has met a British safety standard and has been independently tested |
| | Lion Mark | Indicates adherence to the British Toy and Hobby Association Code of Practice and ensures a product is safe and conforms to all relevant safety information |
| | Age Warning | Indicates: 'Warning – do not give the toy to children less than 3 years, nor allow them to play with it Details of the hazard, e.g. small parts, will be near the symbol or with the instructions |
| | BEAB Mark of the British Electrotechnical Approvals Board | Indicates that electrical appliances carrying this mark meet a national safety standard |
| | BSI Safety Mark on gas appliances, light fittings and power tools | Indicates the product has been made and tested to a specific safety standard in accordance with the British Standards Institute |
| | Safety Mark on upholstered furniture | Indicates upholstery materials and fillings have passed the furniture cigarette and match tests – a lighted cigarette or match applied to the material will not cause the article to burst into flames |
| | Low Flammability labels | Children's pyjamas, bathrobes made from 100% Terry towelling and clothes for babies up to 3 months old must carry a label showing whether or not the garment has passed the Low Flammability Test. Either of these two labels is acceptable. Always look for these labels when choosing such garments. |
| | Keep Away From Fire label | Indicates the garment is not slow burning and has probably not passed the Low Flammability Test. Great care must be taken anywhere near a fire or flame |

## Potential hazards

There are many potential hazards for young children in the average home, with some also present in early years settings, and you will need to think about these carefully. As a student, you are likely to spend placement time in a family setting at some point, and may go on to choose to work in the field of nannying or as a childminder when you have qualified.

### Potential hazards in the home

Kitchens, bathrooms and gardens are the obvious places of concern when considering dangers, but think also about the hazards of glass front doors, sofas beneath window-sills (ideal for climbing on and reaching window catches), electric leads from televisions, video recorders and computers, and so on.

---

**Activity**

1  Draw a diagram of a house and garden like the one below. List as many hazards as you can think of that could be present in each (average) room, then do the same for the garden, including the shed.
2  Compare your 'house of hazards' with a partner's.
3  What safety arrangement would need to be put in place if you wanted to care for children in that particular house?

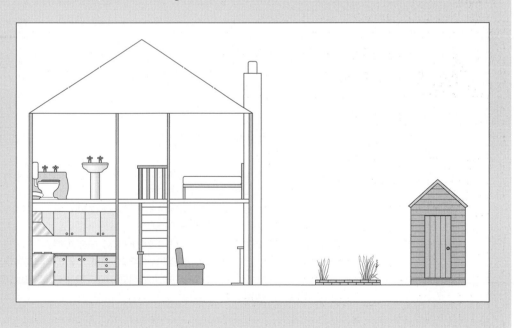

---

### Potential hazards in early years settings

As in the home, kitchens and bathrooms are obvious places of potential hazard, but what else can you think of?

**Activity**

Look at the picture below. How many good safety points can you identify here? What would you change if you were in a position to?

**Professional Practice**

- Children must be registered on arrival.
- Good adult supervision is needed at all times.
- Emergency evacuation procedures must be on display.
- Emergency exits should be clearly identified.
- Equipment must be stored safely.
- Safety glass should be used in any low level windows, dividing panels or glazed doors.
- Window locks must be fitted to any windows accessible to children.
- Fire or heating guards must be fitted.
- Electrical sockets must be covered, and ideally should not be within children's reach.
- Electrical appliances need to be checked regularly.
- Small parts should not be accessible to babies and toddlers.
- A safe area should be available for storing the personal belongings of staff, students and visitors.

**Activity**

1 Empty out the contents of the bag you usually take to your placement.
2 How many potential hazards for a child have you found?

This activity should have emphasised why your personal belongings could be a hazard if accessible to a young child.

### Safety issues on outings

- Ensure that the destination is suitable, for example, no open water that will completely restrict the children's freedom.
- Appropriate adult:child ratios for outings must be adhered to:

  0–2 years    1:1
  2–5 years    1:2
  5–8 years    1:5

- Ensure that an accurate register is with you at all times.
- Ensure that the register is checked regularly throughout the day.
- Parental consent forms must be signed and returned before the outing takes place.
- All adults should know which children they are responsible for.
- All adults should understand their role and responsibilities for the day.
- Identification badges for children are a useful 'extra' precaution, but do not include their name or personal details on this. Just the name of your school, nursery or group.
- Ensure that you take a small emergency first aid kit with you.
- Identify in advance how you will call for emergency services if needed.
- Check that any transport used meets safety requirements regarding seat belts.

Always check that the coach meets the required safety standards

**Test Yourself**

1  In what year were the National Standards for Under Eights Day Care and Childminding introduced?
2  What does COSHH stand for?
3  What does RIDDOR stand for?
4  What is the purpose of a risk assessment?
5  What are the required adult:child ratios for different types of provision?
6  What is the maximum number of children allowed in one room?
7  What is the maximum temperature for water accessed by children?
8  List as many points as you can about personal hygiene.
9  List as many points as you can about kitchen hygiene.
10  List at least ten safety issues regarding the physical environment of a setting.
11  Why is concrete not a suitable surface under a climbing frame?
12  List at least five safety precautions that should be considered when taking children on an outing.

# Applying health and safety procedures

In order to prevent cross-infection, every setting needs to plan how its staff should deal with any potentially infective material, including all body fluids (urine, faeces, blood and vomit) and associated waste materials. This is important when caring for children with any infectious condition, particularly HIV, Aids or hepatitis.

## Handling and disposal of body fluids

Policies and procedures need to be set out regarding both the handling and the disposal of infective material and staff should assume the need for a high standard of protection and prevention of cross-infection at *all* times, including when:

- changing nappies
- clearing up after accidents, nose bleeds and vomiting
- storing and disposing of waste materials.

**Professional Practice**

- You will not always know whether a child is potentially infectious, so sensible precautions at all times will protect both yourself and others.
- Having a standard policy for potential infection will prevent the labelling of any one child, where a known potential hazard such as HIV has been disclosed to the setting.

**Activity**

Ask to see the policy for your setting if you have not already been shown it. If anything is unclear, ask for clarification.

### General points for dealing with body fluids

- Disposable latex gloves and aprons should be worn during nappy changing and when clearing up any body fluids.
- Gloves and aprons should only ever be used once.
- For staff with an allergy to latex, alternative disposable gloves must be provided.
- After use, gloves and aprons should be placed in sealed disposal bags along with the disposable nappy or other waste material, and disposed of safely.
- Blood soaked items should be immersed in cold water to release the staining before washing in the normal way.
- Sluice facilities should be used to rinse off vomit, or solid matter from towelling nappies. These should be securely bagged (two layers) and labelled with the child's name if not being washed in the setting.
- Wet or soiled nappies should never be left around the setting.
- Following accidents or vomiting, the affected area should be cleaned thoroughly with disinfectant or bleach (diluted according to directions on container).
- Soft furnishings should be cleaned with hot soapy water (bleach will discolour them).

# Cross-infection

Cross-infection is the passing of infection from one person to another. It can happen very quickly and can be an on-going headache for early years settings, as parents do not always put their child's needs first due to pressures from work. Most settings and schools have experienced an obviously ill child arriving for the day with a parent reassuring them that the child is just 'a bit off-colour' but still wanted to come. Others will claim that their child was 'sick in the night, but fine now'. Clearly this is unacceptable and is an example of how infections spread around the classroom or setting.

Policies to deal with this are necessary, and most settings refuse to take a child who has been sick or had diarrhoea, asking for them to be clear from their symptoms for 48 hours before attending again.

The most common infectious conditions that affect early years settings on a regular basis are:

- diarrhoea and/or vomiting – children should be kept away from the setting for at least 48 hours after suffering these symptoms
- conjunctivitis – this condition is highly infectious and parents should be asked to get appropriate treatment and keep their child away until the infection has passed
- threadworm, scabies and headlice.

FORWARD to Chapter 10, page 456–7, for information about conjunctivitis, thread-worm, scabies and headlice.

Staff, students and parents should all be informed about the occurrence of these infections in the setting, so that they can be alert to signs or symptoms in themselves, their child or other children and get appropriate treatment. Most settings do not exclude children with these conditions.

# Administration and recording of medication

Although children who are ill will not normally be attending school or an early years setting, there are occasions where a child has a chronic (on-going) condition which allows them to attend as usual, but may need medication to be administered at certain times during the day. When this occurs, it is important that the following guidelines are adhered to.

---

**Guidelines for administering medication in early years settings**

- Parents' consent to give the medication should be in writing, and signed by them.
- Parents should give exact doses, timings and any other information for administering the medication, again in writing.
- If more than one medication is to be given, check with a pharmacist that the proposed items are safe to be given together.
- A trained member of staff must take responsibility for administering the child's medication.

---

- A second member of staff should check that the dose given is correct, and administered to the correct child.
- Medication should be administered quietly and without drawing undue attention to the child.
- Written records of when medication has been given must be kept by the setting.
- Parents should be informed of any reluctance or failure to administer the medication, and the incidence should be recorded.

**Professional Practice**

- Children should *never* be given medication that is not their own.
- Hands should be thoroughly washed before handling medicines.
- An explanation should be given to the child as to what will take place, for example, that you will lay them back to administer eye drops, or lay them to one side to administer ear drops, and so on.
- Rewarding the child with a small treat if they have been reluctant or very 'brave' can be appropriate.
- Recording the time and the dose or medication administered should take place immediately afterwards.
- Hands should be washed afterwards.
- Medicines should not be dissolved into food or drinks.

## Sharing health and safety information with parents

**Case Study**

*Learn Through Play Nursery*

When a parent takes up a place for their child at the Learn Through Play Nursery, they are given a contract setting out all the general aspects of nursery administration and nursery–parent agreements, together with a range of health and safety points. These points are as follows.

- An emergency telephone contact number is required for all parents.
- Parents have a responsibility to notify staff of alternative numbers in advance.
- A health record and details of GP are needed for each child.
- A list should be given to parents of exclusion periods following communicable or common illnesses.
- Details regarding the administering of medicines, including consent forms, are given.
- A statement regarding the handling of body fluids and washing responsibilities should be made.
- Notification of the whereabouts of evacuation procedure details and the assembly point should be given.
- Attention should be drawn to the nursery noticeboard where general health and safety information is placed.

1 How comprehensive do you consider these points to be?
2 How else could the nursery keep parents up-to-date on relevant health issues?
3 Consider the following scenario: a child at the Learn Through Play Nursery has contracted meningitis. The nursery staff have been contacted and have informed all other parents in writing of the incident. What else could they do to dispel the fears of parents?

## Appropriate reporting procedures

Whenever possible, parents should be informed immediately that their child has had an accident, although in emergency situations you will dial 999 for an ambulance in the first instance. The parent consent form regarding emergency treatment should always go with the child to hospital to ensure that the wishes of the parents are acknowledged.

Every setting must have an accident book, in which the details of all accidents and incidents, however large or small, must be recorded. It is never sufficient to simply tell a parent or carer what has happened. A written account must be made, which must include:
- the child's name
- the date and time the accident occurred
- where the accident occurred
- a description of what happened
- any injuries sustained by the child (however slight)
- what first aid treatment was administered and by whom
- any further relevant information, for example:
  – Was it necessary to get outside help?
  – Were the child's parents contacted, and at what time?

Following a serious accident, a written account of what happened should be drawn up, giving as much detail as possible, as soon as is practicable. This should then be signed, and then countersigned by another member of staff. Most settings give copies of accident records to the parent or carer of the child and keep a copy filed with the child's records.

▷▷ FORWARD to Chapter 6, page 214, *Case Study: Kieron* for an example of how the accident book can also help safeguard both children and staff in a setting.

**Test Yourself**

1 Why is it important that all staff in a setting follow the same procedure when handling body fluids?
2 How does a settings policy contribute to a child's right to confidentiality?
3 What is meant by cross-infection?
4 How can settings insist that children are kept away until clear of infectious symptoms?
5 What is needed before a setting can give medication to a child in its care?
6 What approach should you take before administering medication to a child?
7 What should be recorded following an accident?
8 At what point should parents be informed?
9 Why should a child be closely monitored following an accident?

## Key terms

You should now understand the following words and phrases. If you do not, read through the chapter again and review them.

ABC procedures

artificial ventilation

chest compressions

COSHH

cross-infection

evacuation procedures

first aid

HASAWA

IAPS

physical environment

potential hazard

recovery position

RIDDOR

safety marks

## Bibliography and suggested further reading

Dare, A. and O'Donovan, M. (2000) *Good Practice in Child Safety*, Nelson Thornes, Cheltenham

Sadek, E. and Sadek, J. (1996) *Good Practice in Nursery Management*, Nelson Thornes, Cheltenham

# Protecting Children

## Introduction

Child protection is one of the most difficult and sensitive areas of work for early years professionals and at some point in your career you are likely to be involved with a child who has been abused or is in danger of being abused. It is therefore important that you have an understanding of child protection procedures and the range of different types of child abuse, and that you learn how to support the children in your care. This chapter introduces and defines the term 'abuse' and discusses how those working with children should respond to incidents of abuse or suspected abuse. It also discusses the support available to parents and carers of abused or at-risk children, both within the local community and through the legal system. Issues of safety within individual childcare settings are explored and opportunities are given for evaluation.

*Remember!* Responsibility for the protection of children is an essential requirement of any professional in this field and so this unit of study is particularly important.

## Identifying and responding to the range of child abuse

Historically children have suffered a great deal of abuse, partly due to a general lack of understanding and acceptance that children should have rights and protection as individuals. Social attitudes have thankfully moved on, although the process has been slow and haphazard, progressing from the seventeenth-century thinking that 'children's inherent [natural] badness needed disciplining' (Reder *et al.*, 1993), moving through phases in which childhood was essentially denied and children were considered to be extensions of their parents rather than individuals in their own right, and leading eventually to the current **paramountcy principle** of the Children Act 1989.

The Children Act 1989 has encompassed the development of society's attitudes, together with a multitude of parliamentary Acts, producing one of the most important pieces of legislation ever for children in the UK.

## The paramountcy principle

The paramountcy principle gives priority to the welfare, safety and protection of children; any decision taken about children must be in their best interests. It demonstrates that children are at last being considered as people in their own right, who can contribute to decisions about their own futures.

The Children Act 1989 will be referred to many times during this chapter. A copy of the Act or volumes drawn from it are usually available in college libraries; it is also available from Stationery Office bookshops.

## Historical perspective of abuse

The table below sets out the historical developments in the UK, outlining changes in thinking from medieval times through to the implementation of the 1989 Children Act in 1991.

**The evolution of 'child abuse' and child protection**

| Year/s | Transitional event | Prevalent social attitude | Professional involvement |
| --- | --- | --- | --- |
| Medieval | Poor Law Act | Childhood denied; caring problems caused by moral failings; communality of life | |
| 17th century | | Children's inherent badness needed disciplining | |
| 18th century | | Family life more private | |
| 19th century | | Influence of private philanthropists | Child maltreatment observed but denied |
| 1833 | Factory Act | Children's need for protection recognised | |
| 1834 | Poor Law Reform Act | Family's moral failings needed correction | |
| 1872 | Infant Life Protection Act | Children recognised as individuals | |

| 1880 | Education Act | Children's developmental needs recognised | |
| 1889 | Prevention of Cruelty to and Protection of Children Act | Child cruelty considered a crime | Emphasis on prosecution of perpetrators |
| 1889 | Poor Law (Children) Act | | Poor Law Guardians for children introduced |
| 1890 | | | NSPCC established |
| 1904 | Prevention of Cruelty to Children Act | | Local authority empowered to remove child from their family |
| 1908 | Children Act | | Special courts for juveniles |
| 1920s | | | Child's emotional life acknowledged; child guidance clinics established |
| 1933 | Children and Young Persons Act | Welfare of the child emphasised | Care proceedings introduced |
| 1940s | | | Child abuse 'rediscovered' |
| 1945 | Denis O'Neill inquiry | | |
| 1948 | Children Act | Children's best interest paramount | Attempts to keep families intact |
| 1950s | | Sanctity of the biological family | Attachment theory elaborated |
| 1963 | Guardianship of Infants Act | | Local authorities to undertake preventative work to keep families intact |
| 1969 | Children and Young Persons Act | | Local authorities given clear powers to remove children from their families |

| Year/s | Transitional event | Prevalent social attitude | Professional involvement |
|---|---|---|---|
| 1970 | | | At Risk Registers and Area Review Committees introduced |
| 1974 | Maria Colwell inquiry | Blood-tie re-evaluated; media interest in child abuse | |
| 1975 | Children Act | | Permanency policy |
| 1980s | | | Child sexual abuse 'rediscovered' |
| 1985 | Jasmine Beckford inquiry | | |
| 1987 | Kimberley Carlile inquiry | | |
| 1988 | Cleveland inquiry | Media interest in child sexual abuse | |
| 1989 | Children Act | Parental responsibility emphasised; ambivalence to family vs state | |

from Reder *et al.* (1993) pages 8–9

---

**Activity**

Having read the information in the table above, you might find it useful to read further about past attitudes and legislation that you are not familiar with.
This will help you build a fuller understanding of the historical development of child protection.

---

Copies of government Acts and legislation are available through Stationery Office bookshops and many can be found on the Internet. Alternatively:
- Chapter 3 of Carver (1980) is an accessible text about past legislation, although you should bear in mind that it was published before the Children Act came into being
- Department of Health (1991a) provides a summary of some of the most high profile cases during the 1980s.

See *Bibliography and suggested further reading* on page 237.

## Defining abuse

Across society (and indeed across the world), there are varying definitions of what constitutes discipline and what constitutes abuse. Some people consider that smacking a child is a harmless and effective form of managing unwanted behaviour, but to others smacking is considered an offence. In most parts of the UK, however, parents are still able, by law, to smack their own child with a bare hand, but are not allowed to use any kind of implement. This continues to be a controversial issue. In Scotland, recent legislation has now declared it an offence to hit any child under the age of three, and any child of any age around the head. This is seen by many childcare organisations as a starting point towards greater legal protection of young children.

Most professionals in early years consider smacking to be both unacceptable and ineffective, and early years trainers promote the use of a range of alternative strategies in the management of children's behaviour and promote the establishment of clear boundaries. In day-care settings, physical punishment of children is not allowed in any form, but controversially, the National Standards for under-eights care for childminders (reference criterion 11.4–11.6) allow children to be smacked by a childminder with the written agreement of parents. This has caused considerable disquiet in the field of early years.

| | |
|---|---|
| **Professional Practice** | Consider why the field of early years is so unhappy with the smacking criterion for childminders. Most childminders are equally unhappy. Why do you think this might be? |

---

**Activity**

The organisation **EPOCH** campaigns for changes to be made to the law regarding the physical punishment of children.

a) Find out what EPOCH stands for and what its aims are.
b) Do you agree with the ethos of EPOCH?
c) Were you smacked as a child?
d) If so, what do you remember about being smacked?
e) What is your view of smacking?

---

If asked to define the term 'abuse', you will most likely respond by referring to the four main categories – **physical abuse**, **neglect**, **sexual abuse** and **emotional abuse**. As a general summary, it can be said that abuse of a child occurs when any avoidable act, or avoidable failure to act, adversely affects the physical, mental or emotional well-being of a child.

You should be aware that abuse can be both deliberate and non-deliberate. The physical effects on the child are the same, but at times the intentions and understanding, or limitations in understanding, of the parent/abuser will be taken into account when a situation is investigated.

Cultural practices need to be understood and taken into consideration, particularly regarding the terminology used within some cultures.

 FORWARD to page 207 for a discussion of cultural practices.

C.H. Kempe (1992) defined the four main categories of abuse. His definitions are useful, although each local authority will have its own definition set out in the literature given to each early years provider; you may also find it useful to refer to these. Kempe's definitions are:

- physical abuse
  'Physical abuse implies physically harmful action directed against a child; it is usually defined by any inflicted injury such as bruises, burns, head injuries, fractures, abdominal injuries, or poisoning.'

- neglect
  'Neglect can be a very insidious form of maltreatment, which can go on for a long time. It implies the failure of the parents to act properly in safe-guarding the health, safety and well-being of the child. It includes nutritional neglect, failure to provide care or to protect a child from physical and social danger.'

- sexual abuse
  'Sexual abuse is defined as the involvement of dependent, developmentally immature children and adolescents in sexual activities they do not truly comprehend, to which they are unable to give informed consent, or that violate the social taboos of family roles.'

- emotional abuse
  'Emotional abuse includes a child being continually terrorised, berated, or rejected.'

**Professional Practice** Researching the definitions drawn up by the authority in which you work or study will help you consolidate your understanding.

## Indicators of abuse

This section sets out a range of indicators that could alert professionals that a child *may* be suffering abuse or *may* be at risk of being abused. It is important that the indicators are not used in isolation – they need to be noted carefully and any concerns considered, together with recent observations of the child and discussions with management or senior staff, with decisions for further investigation being made where applicable. Naturally, there can be times when one specific sign or injury is considered to be significant on its own, in which case immediate action will need to be taken.

### Accidental injuries

It is important to remember that all children injure themselves from time to time, and it is common to see toddlers with blackened eyes or bruised foreheads as they tend to fall over or run into furniture such as coffee tables. Older children learn to ride bikes and climb trees and fences, tumbling in the process, and scraping knees, grazing legs and arms, and on occasions suffering from more serious injuries, such as concussion and bone fractures. It is important that you consider the age and stage of development of the child concerned when you make a judgement on whether an injury is considered to be of concern, and take into account the circumstances of the injury.

Although children regularly have physical marks following accidental falls, the *site* of the injury can be the easiest indicator of the need for concern.

### Possible indicators of physical abuse

- *Bruises* on the soft areas of the body (inner arms, thighs, buttocks)
- *Bald patches*
- *Unexplained injuries*, including bruises, burns, bone fractures
- *Bite marks* – remember that a dog bite will look very different to a human bite and that an adult bite mark is considerably larger than that of a child's
- *Finger-tip bruising* on the face – this could be caused by forced bottle feeding of a baby or young toddler
- *Unusual shaped bruises* – consider how a child might show non-accidental bruising other than by being hit with an implement such as a stick or a lash

How do you think this bruise was caused?

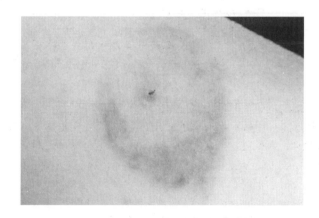

- *Thumb and finger-tip bruises* each side of the torso which can indicate that a child has been shaken or held forcefully
- *Pin-point haemorrhage* in the ears which can be caused by shaking
- *Scald and burn marks* – an accidental scald (if, for example a child pulls over a kettle of boiling water) will have different signs from a scald caused, say, by a cup of tea deliberately thrown. The photographs over the page show very severe scalding on the leg and foot of a baby, and a burn inflicted by a cigarette butt.

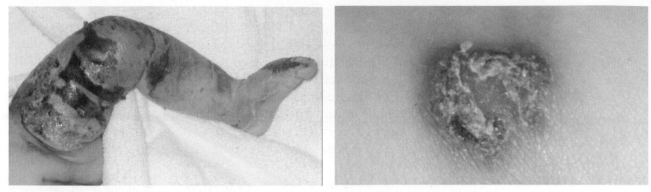

Severe scalding on a baby (l) and a cigarette burn (r)

- *Evenly spaced scald marks* which can indicate the deliberate placing of hands or feet in hot water – these will often have the appearance of socks or glove marks
- *Repeated black eyes* or injuries which should start to raise alarm bells.

| **Professional Practice** | At times innocent injuries can be misinterpreted. Examples include:<br>• the condition impetigo which can be mistaken for cigarette burns<br>• the 'hidden' condition osteogenesis imperfecta (brittle bone disease or Lobstein's syndrome) which can be mistaken for non-accidental fractures. |
| --- | --- |

### Behaviour

Physically abused children may display a change in behaviour, which can vary considerably from child to child. One child may become withdrawn and quiet, while another may become aggressive towards others. Children may show reluctance to go home, or be with particular adults, parents or carers. They may show physical signs of discomfort such as difficulty in movements when dressing, changing or during physical activity.

As children grow older, their bodies are less often seen by the adults who care for them. Be aware of a child who wishes to remain covered up or who always arrives at the setting in long-sleeved tops and long trousers, whatever the weather.

### Bruises

Bruises are damaged blood vessels where the skin has not been broken. They develop through stages, initially appearing purple or blue shortly after the injury has occurred. Gradually they become yellow, and usually disappear within ten to twelve days. Therefore, a yellowing bruise has not 'just appeared'. Similarly, a dark blue bruise is unlikely to have been there for more than a couple of days.

*Remember!*
- The explanation of how and when a bruise occurred can at times be important.
- Bruises often appear darker on dark-skinned children.

### Possible indicators of neglect

Neglect can stem from ignorance and a lack of practical childcare skills, and is not always intentional. This does not, however, lessen the physical effects for a child. A neglected child may:

- be *under weight*, possibly emaciated
- be *hungry,* and may scavenge for food or wolf food down at mealtimes
- be *dirty and unkempt*, with poor personal hygiene
- suffer *frequent minor injuries*
- appear to have *no regular bedtime pattern* – the child may indicate watching late, and unsuitable, television programmes
- suffer from *frequent minor infections*, such as colds and coughs, due to inappropriate nutrition and subsequently becoming run-down
- have a *lack of experience of common childhood activities* such as looking at books and using creative materials
- be *left unsupervised* on a regular basis – the child may indicate this in conversation
- *lack parental interest* in their progress in school or at nursery
- display *self-comforting behaviours*, such as rocking and head banging.

### Behaviour

Neglected children often seem constantly tired due to going to bed when they choose, and not having a time set by their parent. They may display a lack of concentration, and lack of attention (due to tiredness). Stealing of food is common (hunger), as is frequent and excessive masturbation (self-comfort). Neglected children frequently display low self-esteem and low self-confidence. They are likely to be fearful of new situations and can at times be over-friendly to any adult available, indicating their need for attention.

## Possible indicators of sexual abuse

Sexual abuse often goes undetected and research has shown that two-thirds of all children who are sexually abused do not tell anyone about their experiences. These children may suffer long-term physical harm affecting them medically in adulthood, depending on the nature of the abuse suffered, as well as having the mental scars that abuse brings generally. The child's behaviour more often raises concerns than the actual physical signs.

Sexual abuse includes:
- the use of pornographic material, by showing it to children or involving children in the making of it
- **incest** – an incestuous relationship is one which involves sexual activity between family members who are too closely related to be able to marry, for example between father and daughter or brother and sister.

Physical signs of sexual abuse include:
- *bruises* on areas such as the inner thighs and genital areas
- *soreness* in anal or vaginal areas, or in the throat
- *vaginal discharge* in girls
- *swollen penis* or discharge in boys
- *sexually transmitted diseases and urine infections*, sometimes found if medical examination takes place
- *distress when having nappy changed* (babies and toddlers)
- *difficulty or reluctance to pass urine or faeces*, often resulting in constipation
- *difficulty in walking*, and in standing up or sitting down
- *pain on movement* generally
- *poor personal hygiene*

- *obsession with sexual matters*
- the child having *unexplained sums of money* on a regular basis (older children).

### Behaviour

A sexually-abused child may cling on to a parent or trusted carer and they may avoid individuals or show distress at being left with certain adults. Their development may regress, for example, starting to bedwet again when they were previously dry at night. They may become withdrawn and appear saddened, and concentration may suffer leading to poor progress at school.

Some children display sexually-inappropriate behaviour towards adults. Their drawings may also include explicit body parts, for example, an erect penis, which does not fit in with the developmentally normal drawing process of 'a person'.

As children get older, they may want to talk about their 'friend's' problems and hint at secrets. Abused children regularly isolate themselves from their peers and do not form relationships which would involve inviting friends home. Eating disorders such as anorexia or bulimia are common, as is frequently running away from home. Poor hygiene and obsessive cleanliness can both be present.

| Professional Practice | It is important to remember that not all cases of anorexia or bulimia are linked to abuse. Such cases do however need to be investigated and the appropriate support offered. |
|---|---|

## Possible indicators of emotional abuse

Emotional abuse accompanies all other experiences of abuse. Children quite understandably become bewildered and confused when a person they love or trust begins to abuse them. Emotional abuse is rarely cited as the main type of abuse in official reports, the term only being used if it is clearly defined as the only form of abuse suffered by the child concerned. This would perhaps occur if a child was cared for physically but was denied love and constantly rejected, or put down and ridiculed, by the abuser.

These children may:
- have *low self-esteem* and *lack confidence*
- have a *poor concentration span*
- show *developmental delay*
- be *fearful of new situations*
- be *concerned about their parents being contacted*
- *respond inappropriately* to situations
- have *speech disorders*
- find it *hard to build social relationships* with their peers
- use *self-mutilating behaviours*, such as head-banging and pulling out their hair.

### Behaviour

Emotionally-abused children learn from their abuser that they are not of value, and their feelings of self-worth can disappear. One child Helen, in Doyle (1990), felt that her mother only liked the children that she supported through her charity work, who were emaciated and deprived, and so Helen began to dress in her oldest clothes to become more desirable to her mother and gain her love.

### Predisposing factors to abuse

It is not easy to predict when a child may be at risk of abuse, but research has suggested that some factors may predispose individuals to abuse. These can be related to the past and current experiences of parents and to the child or children in a family unit.

#### Predisposing factors in relation to the parents

**Predisposing factors** might include:

* *parents who have not had good role models to follow themselves*
  - this may affect their parenting practices and ability to manage their children's behaviour in a positive manner
  - they may have lowered self-esteem and a poor image of themselves
  - they may also have been abused themselves as a child
* *very young or immature parents*
  - they may not have as yet developed the skills to cope with difficult circumstances
  - they may have unrealistic expectations of their child's rate of development
* *separation at birth through maternal illness*, which can result in disruption of the bonding process
* *lack of support*
  - from a partner resulting in lone parenting
  - from extended family
  - through discord within a reconstituted family
* *illness*
  - of either parent or child
  - parental illness may result in inability to care for the child appropriately
  - illness in the child may cause resentment in the parent
* *bereavement* – any form of stress can lessen a person's ability to cope, particularly bereavement
* *learning difficulties* – parents whose understanding is limited may make inappropriate decisions and cause suffering unintentionally
* *social problems* – unemployment, poverty and housing problems can cause high levels of stress.

#### Predisposing factors in relation to the child

* *Prematurity*
  - Caring for such a vulnerable child increases a new parent's anxiety.
  - Premature and low birth-weight babies are more difficult for parents to learn to care for.
  - Sometimes a child is born before the parents have fully prepared themselves.
  - Separation at birth may affect the bonding process.

* *Disability*
  - Difficulty in feeding and general caring routines can cause resentment.
  - At times, parents feel they have lost the child they thought they would have and need help in learning how to care for, and enjoy their disabled child.

| **Professional Practice** | It is important to note that the cycle of abuse is not automatic – many people who have been abused as children become caring and loving adults and parents. |

### The young abuser

From time to time we hear reports in the media of abuse or murder which have been carried out on a child by another child, and this is met with shock and horror by society. A high proportion of these children have been abused themselves, or have had 'less than ideal' parenting and need help in addressing their behaviour. Children abuse sexually, physically and by bullying. Many people find it hard to believe that sexual abuse can take place between children, but as with all other aspects of development, children learn by example.

Cases of children abusing and/or murdering other children include the Mary Bell case in Newcastle in 1968, and the Robert Thompson and Jon Venables case in Liverpool in the 1990s. Both are well documented cases and raise serious questions about how children are both supported and failed within society.

Sereny (1999) charts the 'terribly damaged life' of Mary Bell and follows her years of trial, detention and imprisonment. The book raises serious questions about the roles of some adults and of society in supporting children. See *Bibliography and suggested further reading*, page 237.

**Test Yourself**

1 What is your personal definition of abuse?
2 Explain the four main types of abuse.
3 What should indicators of abuse be considered in conjunction with?
4 Give at least five examples of indicators of physical abuse.
5 Give at least five examples of indicators of neglect.
6 Give at least five examples of indicators of sexual abuse.
7 Give at least five examples of indicators of emotional abuse.
8 What is meant by the term 'predisposing factor'?
9 What examples of predisposing factors can you think of relating to parents?
10 What examples of predisposing factors can you think of relating to a child?

## Theories/models of abuse

The experience of one or both parents can influence the way in which their children are treated. The family's circumstances, both financial and environmental, and any medical complications can also have an effect.

The reasons why people abuse can be categorised according to four main models (or theories) of abuse:
- the **medical model**
- the **sociological model**
- the **psychological model**
- the **feminist model**.

### The medical model of abuse

The medical model sees the abuse as an underlying physiological condition, i.e. it is an illness which needs a cure. With regard to sexual abuse, there are medical treatments to reduce arousal which are sometimes successful if used together with more generalised behavioural approaches.

## The sociological model of abuse

The sociological model links abuse to the social environment, the support structures that are either available or absent and the family make-up (extended, reconstituted, and so on).

## The psychological model of abuse

The psychological model links abuse to the abuser's previous experience. It includes the abuser's own upbringing, the role models they had, the effects of the bonding process with both their parents and now with their children, and any problems regarding attachment to their own main carer. It also involves the ability of the abuser to understand the care needs of an individual child.

## The feminist model of abuse

The feminist model looks at the role of women and how they have always been perceived as carers, and in particular as the main carer of their family. The model focuses on how women and children are offended against, and ignores the offences that are perpetrated by some women, both alone and in conjunction with men. Many people find it inconceivable that a woman, for whom maternal instincts are seen as inherent, could harm a child, but this is a dangerous misconception. As long as this view is held, society will continue to deny the full potential of women to injure, damage and exploit the children they give birth to or care for.

Useful further sources of information on the models of abuse can be found in Elliott (1993) and Waterhouse (1993) – see *Bibliography and suggested further reading* on page 237.

### Munchausen Syndrome by Proxy (MSBP)

Munchausen Syndrome by Proxy is relatively uncommon, but is an example of abuse that is mostly carried out by women. It is often referred to as 'factitious illness by proxy'. MSBP involves parents (most often mothers) fabricating illness in their child and seeking repetitive medical investigations, often moving from doctor to doctor. This can result in children being subjected to unnecessary medical intervention and prolonged periods of monitoring and/or hospitalisation. On rare occasions, children have been deliberately made ill (or more seriously ill) by a nurse on the ward in which they are already being treated.

The adult perpetrator of MSBP abuse (usually a parent) tries to mirror in the child the symptoms of various conditions. The abuser often has a degree of knowledge of medical matters. Examples of falsely creating symptoms include:
- altering temperature charts or warming up thermometers
- giving a child laxatives to instigate diarrhoea
- adding blood (often their own) to a child's urine sample
- inducing vomiting by giving the child salt or an emetic (vomit-causing) drug
- simulating apnoea attacks (temporary inability to breathe) by partial suffocation.

The syndrome is a psychological condition in which the adult seeks attention themselves, or wants to be seen as a good, caring parent. It can be very difficult to detect, and the child usually suffers for a considerable length of time before a diagnosis is reached. In many cases, other children in the family will have suffered abuse of some kind too.

A well-documented case illustrating MSBP by a medical professional is the investigation and subsequent conviction of Beverley Allitt, a nurse on a children's ward. Research the reports on this case. This will consolidate your understanding of how subtle the approach of such perpetrators can be.

## Variations in family functioning

Families are a central force in society and for most of us they are a positive influence on our lives. They provide much of our learning, emotional support and physical and health care needs. For some people, however, the family can be a source of violence, crime, neglect and abuse, and these are the families that are most often known to local authority social services departments.

Family structures include:
- the *nuclear family* – a heterosexual couple and their children
- the *extended family* – more than one generation of the nuclear family living together or very close by
- the *lone-parent family* – a lone parent (most often the mother), plus the children
- the *reconstituted family* – adults forming new relationships including their children from a previous relationship.

### The changing face of the family

The structure of families continues to develop, with reconstituted families now being openly headed by heterosexual, lesbian or gay couples. These 'new' families continue to fight prejudice in some areas of society to gain equal rights with 'traditional' families.

A useful discussion on the definition and diversity of the modern family can be found in Walsh *et al.* (2000) – see *Bibliography and suggested further reading*, page 237.

**Professional Practice** Always remember that abuse occurs in all social classes, in all family structures and within all cultures.

### Different concepts of discipline

Families and cultures have different ideas about what is a suitable form of discipline for their children, with some leaving discipline to the father, seeing him as having the overall power within the family group.

a) Where discipline is left to the father in a family, what message is this likely to give to the children?
b) How might this confuse a child?

## Cultural practice

Terminology varies and what is meant by the word 'beat' in one culture is not the same as in another. Whatever your views on parents smacking their children, if a child told you that their father 'beat them last night' what would this conjure in your mind? In British culture most people would immediately think of forceful, heavy-handed hitting of a child. In Caribbean culture, however, the term 'to beat a child' is to smack a child. The difference in understanding here could be crucial.

**Remember!** It is important to consider cultural differences and practices before jumping to conclusions about a situation that raises concerns for you.

Some cultural practices, which are considered a normal part of life or a 'rite of passage' in some cultures, are considered to be acts of abuse in others. The most well-documented example is that of female circumcision, which is common in African cultures and is seen as a necessary act of presenting an 'unblemished' bride to her groom on their wedding day. Western societies consider it to be a barbaric act – it has been illegal in the UK since 1985, but it is suspected that the practice still continues, either covertly or by sending young girls on a 'cultural' visit back to their family's country of origin. The genital mutilation that the girls suffer frequently gives constant pain, and problems with menstruation, urination and childbirth in later years. Anyone caught perpetrating female circumcision in the UK faces prosecution.

Pressures on some cultures regarding what is acceptable 'behaviour' prior to marriage can also have an impact on a child's or young adult's ability to disclose the abuse they have suffered.

**Case Study**

### Sophie and Sungita

Sophie is fourteen years old and has been sexually abused by her uncle since she was nine. She has recently disclosed the abuse to a trusted adult and is now being supported by her parents in bringing charges against her uncle.

Sungita is also fourteen and has also been sexually abused by her uncle since she was nine. She is trying to raise the courage to disclose her abuse to her family. Sungita's family culture considers sexual contact before marriage for girls to be the ultimate disgrace for a family, and any girl known to have lost her virginity before marriage is disowned by both her family and the community.

Clearly the physical abuse and suffering has been similar for both Sophie and Sungita, but what extra pressure do you think Sungita faces as she considers disclosing?

For an in-depth look at the particular issues faced by children in minority cultures who are abused, refer to Jackson (1996) – see *Bibliography and suggested further reading*, page 237.

## Consequences of abuse

No child remains unscarred by the abuse they suffer, but some are able, or are enabled, to deal with some of what they experience and move on to lead fulfilling and positive lives. For those who are not so lucky, the future can be far bleaker. The effects of childhood abuse can be both short-term and long-term, affecting the choices they make as adults and the levels of achievement they reach, and limiting their feelings of self-worth.

The spidergrams below and opposite summarise the short-term and long-term effects of abuse. Bear in mind that the effects on individual children will vary greatly and not all the effects will be experienced by all children.

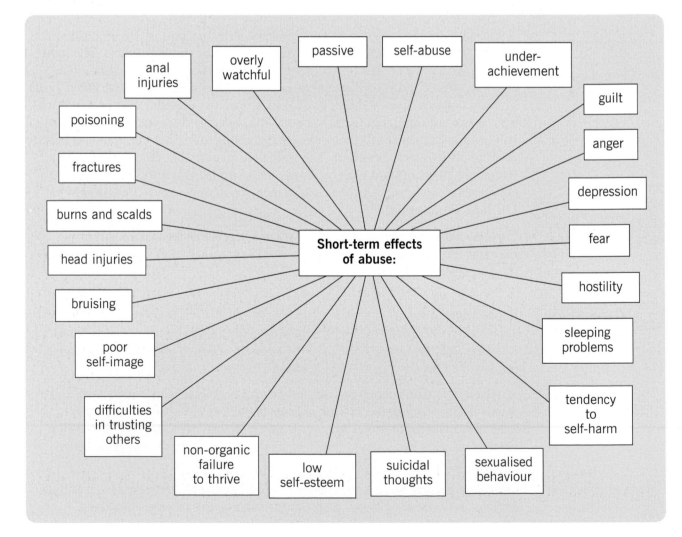

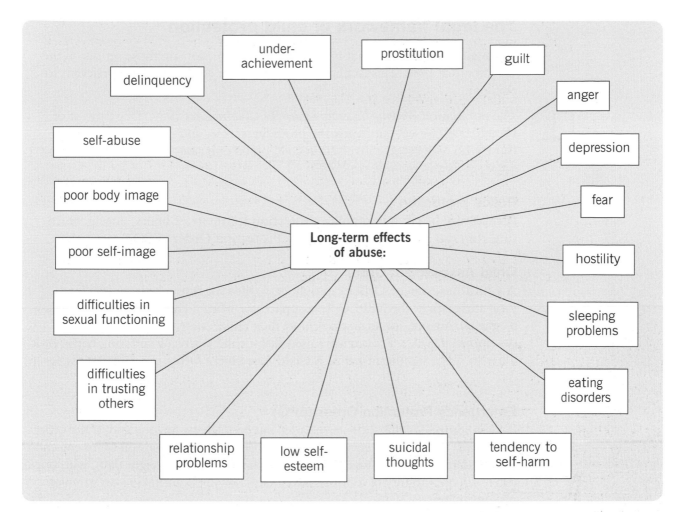

Long-term effects of abuse:
- under-achievement
- prostitution
- guilt
- anger
- delinquency
- depression
- self-abuse
- fear
- poor body image
- hostility
- poor self-image
- difficulties in sexual functioning
- sleeping problems
- difficulties in trusting others
- eating disorders
- relationship problems
- low self-esteem
- suicidal thoughts
- tendency to self-harm

**Activity**

Using the two spidergrams as a guide, discuss in a small group each effect. Consider:
a) the aspects of development affected, i.e. physical, emotional, social
b) the context in which the effects may be considered to be linked to abuse
c) the impact on families of children displaying these symptoms
d) the role of early years workers and other professionals (i.e. teachers, youth workers) in supporting the children
e) the role of early years and other professionals in supporting the children's families
f) how you could summarise the overall effects of abuse in your own words.

*Remember!*  Some of the behaviours and problems noted in the spidergrams can also be due to other reasons.

## The legal framework of child protection

The main aspects of law that impact on child protection are those set out in the Children Act 1989. This Act has brought together all the legislation relevant to children.

The publication *Working Together under the Children Act 1989* (Department of Health, 1991b) sets out clearly the procedures, roles and responsibilities of all those who may become involved in child protection cases – see *Bibliography and suggested further reading*, page 237.

### Police protection

A child may be taken into **police protection** for up to 72 hours, during which time they can apply for an **Emergency Protection Order** (EPO) – see below.

### Child Assessment Order

A **Child Assessment Order** can only be applied for through the courts by the local authority or the NSPCC. It is applied for when a child's parents are unlikely to give permission for an assessment of their child's state of health or level of development, when a concern is raised that a child is already suffering harm, or is likely to suffer significant harm. A Child Assessment Order can only last for seven days.

### Emergency Protection Order (EPO)

An application for this short-term order can be made by anyone and, if the order is granted, the applicant subsequently takes on parental responsibility for the child for the duration of the order. The order is usually issued for eight days, with one extension opportunity of a further seven days. An applicant taking on parental responsibility:

'must take (but may only take) action which is reasonably required to safeguard or promote the child's welfare '

Children Act 1989, *Guidance and Regulations*, Volume Two

This might include an assessment of the child, or decisions about how much contact or who has contact with the child.

An Emergency Protection Order is always followed by an investigation by the local authority.

### Recovery Order

A **Recovery Order** is designed to provide a legal basis for recovering a child who is subject of an Emergency Protection Order, a **Care Order** or who is in police protection. It is used in situations where a child has been unlawfully taken away, or is being kept away from the person who has parental responsibility for them. It also applies if the child runs away from the 'responsible' person or is considered to be missing.

The Recovery Order directs anyone who is in a position to do so to produce the child concerned, if asked to do so, or to give details of their whereabouts. The child will then be removed by the local authority. Police are authorised under the order to enter and search any premises as is necessary, using reasonable force.

### Supervision Order

On occasions a child is placed under the supervision of the local authority (for up to one year) if it is not felt that sufficient co-operation between the parents and the authority will ensure that the child is fully protected. Although the child continues to live at home, the local authority has a right of access to the child. The **Supervision Order** can be extended if deemed necessary.

### Care Order

As with the Supervision Order, a child continues to live at home under a Care Order. The local authority has a shared responsibility for the protection of the child, and its decisions hold the greater balance of power in any disputes between the authority and the parents. At any time the authority can remove the child from the parents' home without the need to apply to the courts for any other order. The Care Order can last until the child reaches the age of majority (18 years old).

## Area Child Protection Committees (ACPC)

Under the Children Act 1989, each area is required to have a joint forum for developing, monitoring and reviewing child protection policies. This is the responsibility of **Area Child Protection Committee (ACPC)**. ACPCs are made up of those persons who have contact with a child whose case comes before them, for example:
- social workers
- police officers
- medical practitioners
- community health team workers
- school teachers
- voluntary agencies.

An inter-agency approach to each case ensures that relevant information is passed on to all who need it.

## Referral procedures

Investigations into cases of abuse or suspected abuse, or where there is a concern that a child may be at risk, are carried out following a **referral**. Referrals can be made to the police, social services departments or to the NSPCC. Anyone can make a referral, and the impetus to do so may result from disclosure by a child to the individual making the referral, or their representative (early years settings and schools have a designated person who takes on this responsibility), or may result from the concern of an individual or a group of people represented by the individual. Referrals are also made by neighbours, family members and concerned members of the public. It is always preferred if individuals identify themselves when making a referral, but anonymous referrals are also accepted and investigated as necessary.

It is a misconception that following a referral the 'authority' goes immediately to the family and takes away the child. This only happens on rare occasions when there has been a clear case of abuse and the child faces imminent risk of further abuse. Most cases go through a set procedure to establish if the concern is justified, to explore the concerns raised with all those who are in contact with the child, or who might have relevant information, and to establish the level of risk to the child. A situation in which immediate action may be needed to remove the child to safety would be if physical violence is likely to increase following the referral being brought to the family's notice. If a child is not allowed to leave voluntarily, an Emergency Protection Order can be obtained.

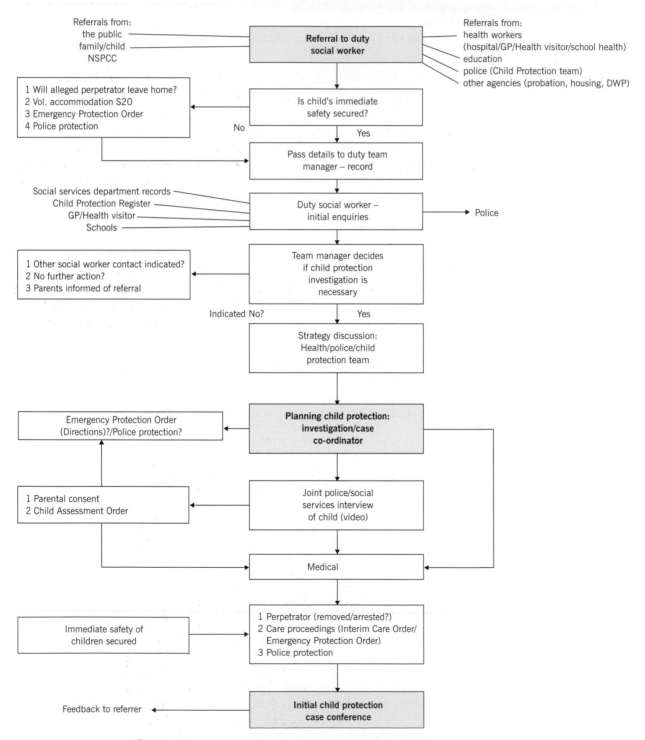

The investigation procedure in cases of suspected child abuse

**Activity**

Think about how you might feel if you had concerns about a child. What range of emotions would you expect to feel regarding:

a) the child who you are concerned about?
b) the perpetrator of any abuse?
c) the prospect of making a referral?

**Professional Practice**

- If, during your placement experience, you are concerned about a child for any reason, you should talk to your placement supervisor or, if you do not yet feel comfortable doing this, talk to your college tutor. They will help you to explore your concerns further and take action appropriately.
- It is never appropriate to simply talk to your friends about a concern, as **confidentiality** is of utmost importance in all cases, and information about any suspected case of abuse should only be discussed on a 'need to know' basis.

### Keeping records

In early years settings, clear record-keeping and report-writing help to provide all the details that may be asked of the setting in the event of an enquiry. Each setting should have an accident book, where all accidents and incidents are recorded, witnessed and signed by at least two members of staff. Many settings use 'body

A body map

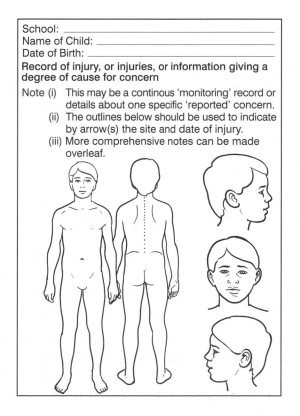

School: _____
Name of Child: _____
Date of Birth: _____
**Record of injury, or injuries, or information giving a degree of cause for concern**

Note (i)  This may be a continous 'monitoring' record or details about one specific 'reported' concern.
(ii)  The outlines below should be used to indicate by arrow(s) the site and date of injury.
(iii)  More comprehensive notes can be made overleaf.

maps' to record marks and bruises that have been identified and date them. This can form a useful piece of supportive evidence in a case involving physical abuse. It is important that staff are able to identify signs and symptoms of abuse on different skin tones.

**Case Study**

*Kieron*

Kieron arrives at nursery one morning with a bruise developing above his left eyebrow. Several staff members notice it, but no one mentions it to Kieron or his mother. At home time, Kieron's mother asks what has happened to Kieron for him to get such a nasty bruise. Staff are astounded at this, and protest that he arrived with it in the morning. His mother denies this emphatically and is angry with the staff, raising her voice and shouting her concerns about the quality of care and levels of safety in the nursery.

1 How could this situation have been avoided?
2 What should happen now?
3 How differently might staff view Kieron's mother and her relationship with Kieron from now on?

Building up good relationships with parents is important in order to provide the best care possible for their child. If the setting has a policy on child protection which states what will happen in light of any concerns, this lets parents know that you are making the welfare of their child of paramount importance, as set down by the Children Act 1989. This policy could include a clause stating that any child arriving in the setting with an injury will have it noted in the accident/incident book. This will offer added safety for the child, and added safety for the staff, avoiding the situation that arose in the case study above.

Each setting should have a child protection procedure which follows the guidelines provided by the local authority.

**Activity**

1 Ask to see a copy of the child protection guidelines and reporting procedures from both your local authority and from your work placement or place of employment.
2 If the guidelines are not clear, ask for an explanation.
3 Try explaining the guidelines and procedure to another person. If you can explain them clearly, it is likely that you understand them.

For further coverage of reporting procedures in child protection cases, it would be useful to refer to Hobart and Frankel (1998) – see *Bibliography and suggested further reading*, page 237.

## Child protection register

In the mid-1970s, **Child Protection Registers** were first set up within each local authority. A child's name is put on the register if there is concern about the safety of that child or their family. An unborn baby can be placed on the register, if there is a known abuser in the family.

The register contains relevant information (see below) about the child, so that the child's situation can be monitored and appropriate action taken when necessary. The child's case and inclusion on the register is reviewed regularly.

If a senior professional has a concern about a child, they can ask for a check to be made of the register for the name of that particular child or their family. These registers are now computerised and held centrally, enabling a fast checking facility. The information is not readily given out, and professionals wishing to consult them have their details and authority to apply to the register checked before information is released to them.

Deregistration can take place when a child's case is reviewed, if it is thought appropriate. Deregistration can occur if:
- the original points that led to registration no longer apply
- the child reaches the age of majority (18) and is no longer termed a 'child'
- the child dies.

## Contents of a register

The information held on a Child Protection Register includes:
- the child's name (and any other names they are known by)
- the child's address, gender, date of birth, culture and any known religion
- the name and contact details of their GP
- the name and details of their main carer
- details of any school or other setting the child is known to attend
- if applicable, the name and details of any person who has parental responsibility for the child (if different from above)
- outline details of any court orders
- an outline of the alleged or confirmed abuse that has previously occurred
- the date the child was placed on the register
- the name and details of the professional responsible for the child's case (the child's key worker)
- the date of the proposed review of the child's situation.

**Test Yourself**

1  Briefly describe the four main models of abuse.
2  Name the main types of family structure.
3  What is meant by the 'changing face of the family'?
4  Why is it important to consider cultural practice in child protection?
5  How would you explain the difference between the short-term and long-term effects of abuse?
6  Who can apply for a Child Assessment Order?
7  How long can police protection last initially?
8  What is an Emergency Protection Order?
9  When might a Recovery Order be implemented?
10  What is the difference between a Supervision Order and a Care Order?
11  What is the Child Protection Register?
12  When might deregistration take place?

# Methods of supporting parents in their parenting

The implementation of the Children Act 1989 in October 1991 placed emphasis on parental *responsibility*, rather than parental rights. This responsibility for children refers to the 'collection of duties, rights and authority' which a parent has regarding their child. Parental responsibility is automatically acquired by married couples and by unmarried mothers. Unmarried fathers can acquire it if they are made a legal guardian by the mother or by applying to the courts

Where it is in the interests of a child, parental responsibility can be granted to other adults, such as grandparents, step-parents or the local authority when a Care Order or Emergency Order has been obtained. The responsibility would automatically end when an Emergency (or other) Order ends, or in the case of step-parents where responsibility is gained through a Residency Order, if that order ends.

The Children Act lays emphasis on parental responsibility continuing after the separation or divorce of the parents unless otherwise stated by a court of law.

## Children's rights and parents' rights

Children have rights, and the United Nations Convention on the Rights of the Child, adopted by the United Nations in 1989, includes a range of rights directly relevant to child protection:

- Article 3 – The best interests of the child should always be taken into account.
- Article 12 – The child's viewpoint should always be considered in conjunction with an assessment of their age and level of understanding.
- Article 16 – Children have the right to privacy.
- Article 19 – Children have a right to be looked after properly, and protected from violence and kept safe from harm.
- Article 37 – Children should not be punished cruelly.
- Article 39 – A child who has suffered ill treatment should be helped to recovery.

Flekkøy and Kaufman (1997) offers a useful discussion of children's rights. Appendix 2 includes an 'unofficial' summary of the main provisions of the UN Convention on the Rights of the Child and is a useful point of reference. See *Bibliography and suggested further reading*, page 237.

## Good-enough parenting

A term that is used from time to time is **good-enough parenting**. Few people would describe themselves, or be described by others, as 'perfect' parents, nor is perfection necessary for a positive parent–child relationship to develop, or for children to feel cared for and loved. Overall, it is consistency of care and being valued and supported by parents that counts, providing it is 'good enough'.

**Activity**

1 The term 'good-enough parenting' does not have a specific definition.
   a) What does the term mean to you?
   b) In a small group, discuss what factors you consider would be 'good-enough' aspects of parenting and what would not.
   c) Consider what you are basing your ideas on.
   d) How well did you agree within your group?
   e) Discuss the differences in your ideas and what may have influenced them.

2 Sometimes parents need support to help them parent their children. Look at the spidergram below. In what ways do you think each form of support would help parents develop better parenting skills?

As you consider each point, think:
   a) about the impact on the child or children
   b) how the parent might feel about themselves as a parent
   c) how they might feel about themselves as a person.
   d) how early years settings can contribute.

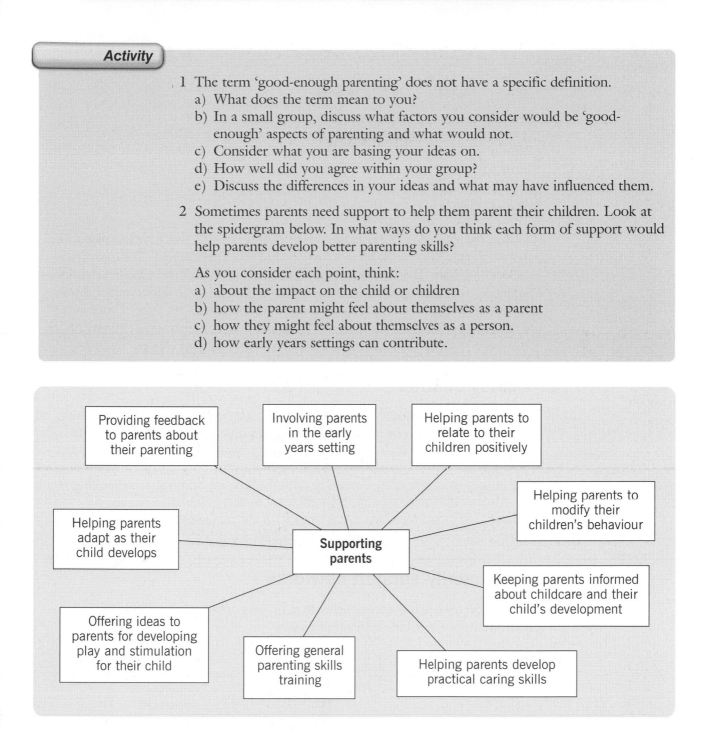

## Sources of advice

Help and advice can be given to parents by:
- known professionals, for example day-care providers, teachers, playgroup staff
- other professionals, for example health visitors, social workers, family support workers
- family members
- friends.

What examples can you give of sources of help and advice for parents in your area?

The level of support available to parents can make a huge difference, tipping the balance between 'good-enough' parenting and the need for intervention. Many of the same agencies are able to offer support informally as well as through case involvement.

## Sure Start

Government funding has been provided to focus on areas that have been identified as having an unacceptable level of poverty and social deprivation. The initiative is called Sure Start. The Sure Start ethos is to work with local communities to improve and increase the range of support and provision for young children (under three) and their families. Information on projects incorporating Sure Start in your area is available from the local authority Family Information Service, which was set up by the Early Years Development and Childcare Partnership (EYDCP).

## Family centres

A family centre is usually staffed by a multi-disciplinary team and offers a range of support. Centres can be used as access points for parents who have restricted or supervised access visits to their children. Many family centres receive funding through the Sure Start initiative. Some family centres run separate support sessions for fathers, with life skills, parenting skills, health, education and counselling being available to all family members. Families are mostly referred by health professionals, and there are strong links with the family support workers who are part of the social services children and families team.

## Community support networks

The professionals and agencies that may become involved in a child protection case are summarised in the diagram below.

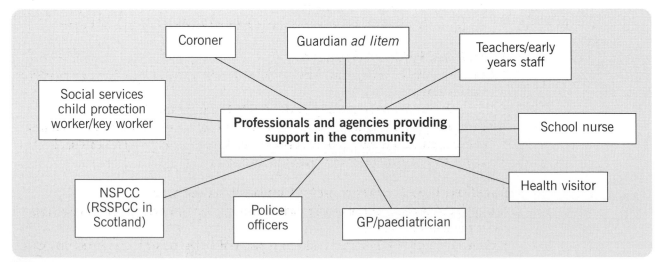

### Teachers/early years staff
- A designated person with responsibility for child protection issues should be named in each setting.
- Concerns should be taken to the designated person who will notify social services.
- Staff are trained in child development and are able to monitor signs of change or regression.
- Training in recognising and responding to signs of abuse should be undertaken.

### School nurse
- School nurses have close and regular contact with children.
- They are particularly involved with children with special needs.
- They are aware of child development and the signs of abuse.
- Some, but not all, are trained children's nurses.

### Health visitor
- Health visitors have on-going contact with families, particularly those with very young children.
- They are specialists in child development and one of their main concerns is with the welfare of children and monitoring of their development.
- Most early years settings have an established health visitor link.
- Health visitors will refer suspected cases of abuse to the police or social services.

### GP/paediatrician
- Children may be presented with injuries or health concerns either at their local GP surgery or at the casualty department.
- Community paediatricians may identify causes for concern during screening programmes for young children.
- Referrals will be made to police or social services.

### Police officers
- Police officers uphold the law.
- Referrals can be made directly to the police.
- They have a duty to protect children and to follow up any referrals or concern brought to their notice.
- Police officers have responsibility for the safe keeping of any evidence in cases which may end in a prosecution.
- The police have emergency powers to remove a child to a place of safety.

### NSPCC (RSSPCC in Scotland)
- Both organisations have qualified social workers who have powers to investigate cases of abuse.
- Referrals can be made directly to the NSPCC and to the RSSPCC.
- They can apply to remove a child to a place of safety, or start care proceedings.
- Both organisations have family support workers who work with families both during and after cases have been investigated.

### Social services child protection worker/key worker
- The social services social worker who takes on the case will be the key worker for the child or family.
- Staff can apply to remove a child to a place of safety or start care proceedings.

### Coroner

- The coroner is an independent law official who is involved in all cases of violent or unexplained death.
- Many coroners are also medical practitioners.
- They investigate a death to establish its cause.
- They are not involved in the prosecution of any perpetrator of abuse.

### Guardian *ad litem*

- A guardian *ad litem* is an independent person who is appointed by the court.
- They speak on behalf of children, ensuring that their welfare remains paramount.
- Where the child is sufficiently able, they will help the child to understand the proceedings they are the subject of.

**Test Yourself**

1 What is the United Nations Convention on the Rights of the Child?
2 What is meant by the term 'good-enough parenting'?
3 How does the Children Act 1989 define parental responsibility?
4 What support is available for parents in the community?
5 How will giving feedback to parents on their parenting help them develop their parenting skills?

# Strategies for supporting children and their families

Communication is an important aspect of supporting both children and their families. Good parent–staff relationships create a level of trust and respect that promotes honesty and openness and allows concerns to be raised more easily. An important aspect of this communication is to share information about the setting's child protection procedures with parents, so that in the event of an issue arising, it can be dealt with effectively.

Body language can also be part of an individual's personality.

BACK to Chapter 3, pages 89 and 101, to refresh your understanding of communication and the barriers that can exist.

---

**Professional Practice**

- In cases of child abuse, you need to be aware that (non-abusing) parents can sometimes be embarrassed to talk to early years staff if they feel they have let their child down by not protecting them.
- You will at times need to continue to communicate with a known or suspected abuser. This will not always be easy. Personal feelings must never be allowed to affect your professionalism.
- You can help parents by being a good role model in how you interact with children.
- Keeping communication open between staff and parents is an important part of supporting both the child and their family.

## Supporting children who disclose

When a child **discloses** abuse to an adult (i.e. tells an adult about it), they are likely to have chosen that person for a reason and taken a great deal of both time and courage to speak out. It is therefore crucial that they are given an appropriate response.

**Activity**

Often, the disclosure comes 'out of the blue'. How do you think you or another adult might feel if a child discloses to you? Horrified? Shocked? Anger at the abuser? Scared about what to do? What other emotions do you think you might feel?

It is important to explore these emotions in order to think through how you might deal with them if the need arises. The most important initial response to a child should be one of unconditional acceptance. By listening to a child, showing them that you believe them, and responding to them positively you will have provided the first stage of help for them.

In responding to disclosure you need to:
- reassure the child that they have done the right thing by telling someone
- assure them that you will help them in whatever way you can
- explain that you understand how hard it is for them to tell you this information
- find a more appropriate setting, or make arrangements to talk to the child somewhere else as soon as you can if you are not in a suitable place (for example, if it is very exposed to being overheard by others)
- remain calm
- keep your facial expressions and body language positive
- give the child time
- be a good listener
- be patient, the child will most likely need to stop to sort their thoughts out
- reassure the child that whatever the situation, they are in no way to blame
- ensure that you do not make promises that you cannot keep, i.e. you cannot keep disclosed information a secret, the child cannot come to your house to live
- explain that there are other people who you may need to contact
- explain that these people will also want to help them
- ask the child if they have told anyone else
- ask them who else they think they could tell – a parent, aunt, etc. – it may be appropriate to offer to help them tell that person
- maintain strict confidentiality, working on a 'need to know' basis
- follow the reporting guidelines for your setting
- write up a report of the disclosure immediately afterwards and date and sign it
- let the child know what will happen next
- keep the child informed until the situation is out of your hands.

It is important that you do not ask the child leading questions. They can invalidate a child's statement if there is a subsequent prosecution.

Disclosure can also come from an adult who has grown to trust you. This may be a friend or a work colleague. The same approach is needed here as it would be for a child. The adult may have waited a long time to speak out and your response will be as important to them as it would be to a child. You may feel shocked, or even guilty that you had not been aware of what had been happening to them. These are natural responses, but you should remember that your level of understanding and awareness has developed further, and you were less equipped in the past to identify signs of abuse.

*Remember !* If the abuse disclosed by another adult is current, consideration must be given to any children who may also be at risk.

## Confidentiality

All information that you receive about children and their families, verbal or written, is confidential. You have been trusted to receive it, and as part of your professional role, you must respond to that trust. To break confidence may put a child at further risk. It could have an impact on an investigation and it could place a slur on a person's character if the concern is subsequently unfounded.

**Professional Practice**
- Confidentiality is always important, but within child protection it is essential.
- You should never discuss a parent with other parents.
- You should work with facts, not with gossip.
- Information should only be shared on a 'need to know' basis.

## The impact of abuse on families

Families are not always aware of what has been happening to a child even if the perpetrator lives within the same house. A significant percentage of abuse is carried out by close relatives or persons known to the child and their family. In some families violence may be commonplace and adults dealing with their own suffering may not identify the suffering of their children, or may not have the physical or emotional energy to deal with it if they have.

As an early years worker, you will be dealing with the parents on a daily basis. If they are the subject of an enquiry instigated by the setting, you may have to face anger and hostility. If they had been unaware of the abuse and are in no way responsible, they are likely to feel distressed, guilty and saddened. They may wish to talk to staff who know their child well and require a greater level of feedback on their child's welfare and progress.

Parents who abuse are often in need of help and support themselves. This can be a difficult area to cope with. It is important that staff continue to interact with them positively, offering opportunities to talk where appropriate and being seen to be good role models with children.

**Case Study**

*Isobel*

Isobel, who has mild learning difficulties, is the single mother of James and was supported by staff at her local family centre in learning to look after James in his early weeks. They showed her how to prepare suitable foods for him when he was ready for solids and offered advice on developing a routine for him. Isobel has attended the family centre only occasionally since then as she often goes to stay with her mother, some distance away. In conversation with Isobel when she arrived today, it has become clear that she is very proud of the way she has managed to care for James, but you can see that she has not really moved James on very far in his development. James is now eleven months old and is still only being fed puréed foods, mostly from jars, with bottles of formula throughout the day. His playthings are still mostly rattles and soft toys and he is a very passive baby, showing no real interest in moving. There does not seem to be any cause for concern regarding James' weight. As Isobel has been away a great deal, she has not had recent contact with her health visitor.

1 What support and advice do you think Isobel needs first for James?
2 How could you help her develop more stimulating play for James?
3 What should be most important regarding your approach to Isobel?
4 What concern might there be for James' future if his mother did not have support offered to her?

## Alternative forms of care

For some children, even with the full support available within the community, a decision eventually has to be made to remove them from the direct care of their parents. This decision is not taken lightly and their age and situation is always assessed before they are placed in an alternative form of care. Some children are better placed as the youngest or only child within a family, while others will benefit by having other children around. Whenever possible, and appropriate, siblings are placed together.

There are a range of care alternatives for children, which can be either temporary or permanent, depending on circumstances.
• Temporary care, for example foster care, applies when a child needs emergency or short-term care, for example as a result of a Care Order or the ill health of the main carer.
• Permanent care, for example adoption, is needed if a child is orphaned, where there is no alternative option available, or where parental responsibility is permanently removed by law for any reason.

### Foster care

Foster carers undergo considerable assessment and in most areas receive training through the local authority. They need to have a high degree of emotional stamina, as many children they care for will have suffered trauma through abuse.

### Respite care

Respite care is offered to parents when they need regular breaks from their children in order to cope with their parenting requirements. This may be due to the parents struggling to cope generally, or due to specifically difficult circumstances being faced by that family. Respite care is also offered to families who care for a child with extreme physical needs or very challenging behaviour.

### Adoption

Adoption is the permanent handing over of all responsibility for a child to permanent replacement parents. Adoptions can be either closed or open.

- A closed adoption is a total breaking of ties between parent and child, although children can apply for information to trace their parents when they reach 18 years of age.
- An **open adoption** means that limited contact is kept between the child and the birth family. They may exchange letters and cards, and even meet on occasions, although this does not alter the permanency of the adoption. The birth parents have no responsibility for the child and are not entitled to any say in their upbringing.

### Residential care homes

It is now very unusual for young children to be placed in residential care; they are usually placed with foster families. Residential care no longer consists of dormitory-style wings in large centres, but is more likely to group children together in small family-sized units.

### Family support workers

Wherever possible, children are supported within their own homes. This can be with the support of a family worker. These workers may spend time in the family home at times that are proving difficult for the parents to manage. For example, they may be present at meal times to establish good eating habits, or at bedtime to help bring about an accepted regular bedtime routine. The support worker may also be involved with the child and/or the family in day-care settings or family centres.

## Alleviating the effects of abuse

Children who have experienced abuse or trauma need opportunities to express themselves when they are ready to do so. Usually their self-esteem is low and the consequent feelings of worthlessness and lack of value can lead to a downward spiral if help and support is not available to them. Professional counselling is offered to some children, and early years staff can support children by giving them time, space and praise. Another approach in which children can be helped is through **play therapy**.

### Play therapy

Play therapy is about showing children that they are valued and helping them to value themselves as they move through the healing process. Children have always re-enacted familiar situations through their play, exploring and making sense of roles and events, so on this basis providing therapy through play makes good sense. The purpose of therapy following abuse is to help children move on from being victims to become survivors. It needs to be a non-threatening experience for the child, be relevant to their age and stage of development and be carried out by people who understand what they are doing and the limitations of the therapy that they are providing. It is not something that untrained individuals should attempt to involve themselves in, although early years settings are an excellent source of creative opportunities for children who can express themselves through paint, clay, role play, and so on.

The timing of structured play therapy sessions needs to be carefully considered. Sometimes there will be a greater need for a child that must be fulfilled before successful therapy can begin. This might include establishing a more settled home life or setting up involvement with the child's family alongside the play therapy. Play therapists need to build up a trusting relationship with a child, and time for this will be incorporated into any programme that is devised. Trust is all important in helping a child relax, feel safe and understand that they are able to express themselves in safety. Most often, sessions with a play therapist take place weekly for an hour at a time. Children are (within safety limits) able to direct the play, deciding what they will do and how they will go about it. Therapy sessions are the child's own special time and the therapist, while being present throughout, is often subsidiary to the play, remaining alert to what is happening and ready to respond where it is felt to be appropriate.

A useful definition of play therapy was drawn up by the British Association of Play Therapists:

'[Play therapy is] the dynamic process between child and therapist, in which the child explores, at his or her own pace and with his or her own agenda, those issues past and current, conscious and unconscious, that are affecting the child's life in the present. The child's inner resources are enabled by the therapeutic alliance to bring about growth and change. Play therapy is child-centred, in which play is the primary medium and speech the secondary medium.'

Association of Play Therapists Newsletter, 1995

This definition encompasses the main focus of play therapy, in that it is largely a non-verbal experience. Play is the most natural way in which children express themselves. Babies make sense of their world exploring through play, and a similar process occurs for traumatised children. Play therapy gives them the opportunity to express and make sense of what they have experienced, supported by the experience and understanding of a specialist adult.

### Typical resources provided by play therapists

Some therapists will work from a specially set out room and will ensure that aspects of the room remain constant for the child to give added security. Others work peripetetically and may find themselves having to use a range of suitable (and barely suitable) places. Many of these therapists will establish a safe area for the child by using a rug or mat to define a special space, endeavouring to give some consistency to the sessions.

Puppets form an important part of most therapists' resources. They usually include puppets that represent dominant and passive individuals, puppets who might represent power, and also puppets of animals. These give opportunities for strength and power to be demonstrated (and overthrown), and to represent both victims and survivors. Using animals may be a less personalised way for some children to symbolise their lives and experiences.

Dolls of different sizes, cultures, genders, and states of dress are also common, with or without dolls' houses and vehicles. These offer scope for a child to illustrate their family members and the other significant adults in their lives within their play. Many children will have had a transient lifestyle and experienced multiple homes, therefore a considerable number of 'people' will allow for greater exploration for these children.

Monsters, bizarre creatures, snakes and worms are common items, allowing children to explore and deal with 'nasty', 'wicked' and 'evil' individuals.

Creative materials such as drawing, painting, collage, face painting and clay offer children the chance to immerse themselves in their chosen medium, and communicate some of their feelings, and sand play and water play are always therapeutic mediums through which children everywhere gain pleasure and express themselves. The trickling sensation of sand can be a very calming experience.

The following two titles give an interesting and accessible introduction to play therapy, offering examples drawn from experience: Cattanach (1992); Carroll (1998). For general accounts of the work of therapists the following books are wonderful examples: Bray (1991); Axline (1964). These two books are, however, quite explicit in content and you should be aware that they can at times be quite distressing. See *Bibliography and suggested further reading*, page 237.

**Test Yourself**

1 List ten examples of how you should respond if a child discloses abuse to you.
2 What impact can a disclosure of abuse have on a family?
3 Who is involved in an Area Child Protection Committee?
4 What is the role of the ACPC?
5 What alternative forms of care are there for children?
6 What is the difference between open and closed adoption?
7 What is the purpose of play therapy?
8 How would you describe a play therapy session?
9 Give examples of typical play therapy resources.

# Good practice in childcare settings

Security of early years settings has had to be reassessed in recent years after a number of incidents involving unauthorised entry into buildings, on occasions resulting in children being harmed or even killed (at Dunblane Primary School in March 1996, when 16 children and their teacher died). Security is increasingly being made a high priority by local authorities and private owners, with staff teams having to consider how easy it might be to access the premises and redefining who is allowed access.

# Building security

Asking for proof of identity from visitors, such as course tutors or health visitors, should now be mandatory, and children should only be handed over to known adults, or others by prior instructions from the usual parent collecting them. Most pre-school settings allow parents to stay for a short while to settle their child, but some degree of control of the numbers of visitors needs to be in place to ensure that children have a safe level of supervision at all times by the setting staff.

Visitors should never be allowed to take children anywhere on their own, and should not be involved in intimate care routines. Any child reluctant to work with a visitor should not have to do so, and staff need to monitor the effect that visitors have on the children in their care. If it is found that visitors disrupt the session to unacceptable levels or that children appear insecure, the frequency and level of involvement of visitors in the setting may need to be reassessed.

As an early years student, you too are a visitor, particularly in the early weeks of your placement. You will need to build up a rapport with the children and will not be involved in intimate care routines without supervision.

Outer doors should ideally be kept locked at all times, but if they need to be accessible by parents (for example, if a staff member leaving the room to answer the door would be the greater risk), they need to be alarmed to indicate an arrival, and staff should ensure that they know who has arrived and where they have gone to. Any visitors who are staying for a specific length of time should be signed in and out of the setting, and issued with a visitor badge, to be handed in as they leave.

A clear policy should be developed about not accepting visitors 'off the street'. All prospective visitors should make an appointment in advance and anyone interested in the welfare and safety of children will not have a problem with this. Unexpected visitors can cause problems in maintaining staff:child ratios and can cause disruption to the planned structure of the session. They should be politely asked to return at a mutually convenient time unless the manager is supernumerary to numbers and it is practical for them to accommodate unexpected visitors at that time.

**Case Study**

*Sarah*

Sarah is a BTec National student, currently on placement at Greenwood Primary School. It is mostly an open-plan site, with the classrooms along three sides of a square and side areas for creativity, music and PE along the fourth side. Sarah was preparing materials for a creative activity in one of the side areas when she was aware of a man walking slowly along the outside wall, looking through the windows. She watched him for a few minutes, but as he did not seem to be making any attempt to get into the building she did not do anything about it.

1  What would you have done if you had been Sarah?
2  What might this tell you about the security of the school building?
3  What would you do if you were trying to get into a school on the first day of your placement, but were unable to find an open entrance?

## Working patterns

Security can be helped by consistency of staffing. A key-worker system where a staff member has responsibility for a set group of children will ensure that there is always one specific person keeping records and making observations on each child, and this close relationship will enhance their ability to pick up any changes in a child's behaviour or problems with their development. They will also be more likely to build up a good relationship with the child's parents and be more likely feel able to ask if there is anything troubling the child or to raise a concern with them. This will be less easy if no relationship has been established.

### Activity

What might be the outcome for a troubled child where there is no consistency of care? Explore this both from the angle of the setting, and from the child's point of view.

## Teaching children self-protection

The most important skill that we can teach children regarding their personal safety is to speak out when they need to. Activities which encourage children to take a lead, to demonstrate, illustrate or describe something will help them grow in confidence. Giving praise for effort rather than just for achievement will boost a child's self-esteem, and giving them small responsibilities will make them feel valued and worthwhile as individuals.

Children need to learn that their bodies belong them, and that no one has the right to touch their body if they do not want them to. They need to know that this applies to all adults, but with exceptions for medical treatment, such as a doctor listening with a stethoscope or a nurse taking a blood sample or giving an injection. To a child, any of these procedures may be unwelcome. Another aspect of learning self-protection is to help children to build their confidence and explore the issue of secrets with them. Parents and early years staff need to encourage children to be open and honest and to learn to say 'No' when they feel they want to, or their space is being intruded upon. Michele Elliott of the organisation Kidscape says that adults spend a great deal of time teaching children to obey adults, when really there is a need to encourage them to say 'No' when they are unhappy or uncomfortable with anything they are asked to do.

### Activity

Read the following statements that might be made to a young child and consider the questions that follow:
- You must always do what an adult tells you.
- Always go where an adult tells you to go.
- Never disobey an adult.
- If you get lost, ask an adult to help you.
- It is rude not to speak to someone, when they have spoken to you.

a) What problems could arise from each of the statements?
b) What alternative instructions to those given above would you give to young children?

Children can learn that the areas of their body covered by their bathing suit are private to them and should not be touched by anyone else. It would be inappropriate to simply state that these are areas that 'should not be touched' as this implies that the child also should refrain from the natural exploration of their own body.

Everywhere under your bathing suit is private

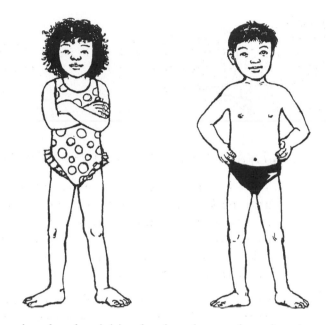

Games can be played and activities developed to explore situations and problems that might be faced by children and to build children's self-esteem, for example an activity about 'secrets'. Activities can be introduced within the general planning of the setting.

Secrets should be pleasurable and exciting, linked to birthdays, festivals and surprises, but for some children secrets mean abuse, with the abuser telling them 'This is our little secret' or 'Make sure you don't tell anyone about this, because …'. You need to be able to help children understand the difference and to know when they should tell their parents about a secret they have been asked to keep.

**Activity**

a) How could you introduce the concept of safe and unsafe secrets to a child?
b) What examples of safe and unsafe secrets would you give them?

 The television characters Cosmo and Dibs are featured in a useful video addressing safety issues, including safe and unsafe secrets.

 Karp and Butler (1996), which was originally produced as a therapeutic aid for children who have been abused, includes a range of activities that can be used to help define boundaries for young children and to establish where they feel safe, for example:

- The Private Triangle
- Colour in the Personal Space
- People I Trust – the child draws a picture of someone they trust.

The Private Triangle – dot to dot

The Private Triangle – cut and paste

- Connect the dots and colour your picture.

- Colour in the personal space.

- Cut out the triangle and paste it on the picture, showing where the private triangle should go.

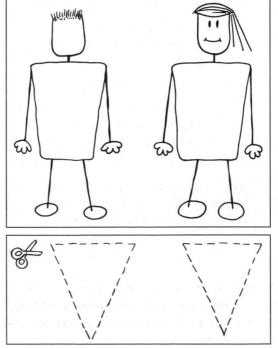

Colour in the Personal Space

## Paedophiles

The true definition of a **paedophile** is a person who is sexually attracted to children. However, the term is commonly used to describe adults who sexually abuse children. These abusers came from all walks of life and are often considered to be pillars of the community holding posts of responsibility and trust, and taking on roles that will bring them into regular contact with children, such as a scout group leaders, sports coaches, youth workers and teachers.

Paedophiles spend a great deal of time and effort setting the scene for their abuse, often building up relationships with a child's parent(s), increasing their level of trust in them. Children of single mothers can be particularly vulnerable as the mother may be pleased to encourage a male role model for her children, particularly if they do not see their father. This process is known as 'grooming'.

As the paedophile gains the trust of the family, closer physical contact develops, gradually moving towards sexual contact or involvement in pornography. Intimidation, bribes and threats often follow, in return for promises that the activity is kept secret.

---

### The Abel Study

232 abusers were involved in a research study by Gene Abel. These were 'first time' abusers who had no previous convictions for child sexual abuse. After serving their sentences, they were given immunity from further prosecutions and asked to relate the true number of children they had abused before they were caught and convicted.

This was done by asking them at what age they began abusing and approximately how many children they had abused per week (or month or year), so it is necessarily an estimate.

*232 'First Time' Abusers:*
- On average, each abuser attempted 238 offences.
- On average, each abuser completed 166 offences.
- On average, each abuser molested 75 children.

If you add up the total number of offences and attempts by these abusers:
- The 232 abusers attempted 55,216 offences.
- The 232 abusers completed 39,508 offences.
- The 232 abusers molested 16,400 children.

This means that a small group of compulsive child abusers can create a huge number of victims and that the victims were either silent about what happened or were not believed if they told.

from Elliott (1992)

---

**Professional Practice**
- If an individual person begins to be closely involved with a child or family other than their own it may be appropriate to monitor the situation closely.
- Paedophiles are devious people and many operate for many years before being caught.

**Remember !**

Paedophiles are skilful in identifying vulnerable children, such as a child who:
- is a loner
- lacks confidence
- is very trusting of adults
- who craves love and attention.

Motivation + Opportunity = Abuse

- Paedophiles have the *motivation* to abuse.
- They seek *opportunities* to abuse the children they have contact with.
- Early years staff can play a part in building up a barrier to their opportunities.

## Megan's Law

In the state of New Jersey in the USA, a young girl named Megan was sexually abused and killed. Following her death, a campaign was successfully carried out to change the law regarding sex offenders. Courts in many states in the USA now have to inform local communities when a convicted sex offender moves into their area.

Many people have called for a similar law to be passed in the UK, claiming that it will improve the safety of all children. Others argue that it infringes the human rights of the offenders and will cause social unrest in communities, with the risk of vigilante-style ousting of the offenders and the wrong identification of innocent people as abusers of children.

**Activity**

In a group, debate the arguments for and against Megan's Law being introduced in the UK.

◄◄ BACK to Chapter 3 and the activity on confidentiality (page 112). How does Megan's Law fit into the thinking on confidentiality? Do you still feel the same way about the situation there? If your views have changed, in what way have they changed, and why?

## Formulating a child protection policy

Each setting needs:
- a copy of the local authority guidelines
- a person specifically responsible for child protection
- setting guidelines for all staff regarding behaviour, responsibilities and recording procedures
- police screening of all staff
- whenever possible, police screening of students.

## Record-keeping

Any records made of children should be kept safely and only the appropriate member of staff (key worker, senior staff, manager, etc.) and parents should be allowed access to them. It is not usually appropriate for children's records to be shared with students, although in some settings this may be the case. As a student, you must be aware of the responsibility of being privy to this information and should ensure that you in no way pass any of it on.

In the case of a child protection concern, the records should make it clear what has been directly observed by staff and what information has been gathered from other sources. Records of any kind must always be dated and signed, and then witnessed by another person, usually a senior member of staff.

### Accurate records

On occasions 'hearsay' evidence may be accepted and included in a child's case. If a child has disclosed to you, it is important that you include the full details in your report. This must include any questions that you asked, the details of the disclosure and any non-verbal communication relevant to the disclosure, such as indicating a body part by pointing.

The facts will be the most important aspect of your report. However, for the future when you have more experience, a comment such as the example below may be appropriate if you are raising a concern following your own observations.

Example    'In my professional judgement, following 18 years as a senior nursery worker working with children aged 0–5 years, I consider the overt sexual nature of Joseph's interactions with both staff and children to be beyond what would be expected of children of his age, taking into consideration the natural curiosity and exploration of the age group.'

This example gives the opinion of an experienced professional early years worker, based on developmental norms and what has been observed.

*Remember!*
- The safety of the child is paramount.
- Early years settings have a duty to report any concerns about a child.
- If you have a concern, discuss it with your line manager or designated member of staff.

**Professional Practice**
- The worst situation that can arise is that your concern is unfounded. You may be embarrassed, but you will know the child is safe. If you had not raised a concern and a child suffered further, how might you feel then?
- It takes courage to raise a concern, but it is part of your professional role as an early years worker.

a) Why do you think it is important to date any comments recorded?
b) Why is it important to sign any comments you make?
c) Why should you get a witness to sign too?
d) Who is this protecting?

## Carrying out a safety audit of the setting

Early years staff should, from time to time, reassess the safety of the setting, asking themselves:

- What possibilities for abuse exist within the setting?
- What risks can be identified and how can they be reduced?
- How can the children be helped to lower the risk?
- What can the staff do?
- What external factors might impact on safety from abuse?

## Good practice when working with children

To ensure good working practice with children means ensuring that physical care is always appropriate. Ask yourself:

- How much can the child do for themselves when dressing?
- How much can the child do for themselves in the bathroom?
- How much privacy should I be giving them?
- Is it appropriate for the children to kiss me goodbye?
- Is it appropriate for the child to be having cuddles?
- Is it appropriate for the child to be sitting on my lap?
- Is the contact I have with the children fulfilling their need, or mine?

You will probably find that your answers will partly depend on the age of the child and their stage of development. It will also be determined by the environment in which you are working, and the role you have in the children's lives, as either a nanny, nursery manager, key worker, teacher, nursery nurse or student on placement.

*Remember!*

- Physical contact is permissible when a child needs comforting, during intimate care routines and at times when physical restraint might be required (such as a child about to run into a road).
- Children deserve respect at all times, and should not, for example, be sat upon a potty in full view of a multitude of other people, or asked to undress in front of a crowd.
- Children should not be photographed in early years settings partially clothed. Any photographs that are taken need to be shown to parents before being displayed. This is particularly important if any materials are likely to be published in local newspapers.

**Case Study**

*Abigail*

Abigail is three and has recently joined the local pre-school group. Little Monkeys Pre-school is situated in a large village on the outskirts of a country town. It has recently had a very successful fundraising event and wishes to advertise this in the local press. A member of staff contacted the local newspaper who sent along a photographer. All the children lined up and had their photo taken, and it was subsequently printed in the local free newspaper. Abigail's mother was very upset when she found out about this. She had recently moved to the area, having been relocated to a safe house supported by the Women's Refuge Organisation, having left a violent relationship with Abigail's father. She is very worried that he might see the photograph and trace them, as the paper is also distributed in the area in which he lives.

1 What should have been the procedure here?
2 Were the pre-school staff wrong do you think ?
3 Should Abigail have been missed out of the photograph?
4 How could this have been resolved satisfactorily?

## Allegations against staff

Although a vetting procedure will usually have been carried out on members of staff prior to them joining the setting, this only indicates when someone has been investigated and convicted. It does not tell you for certain that they are a 'safe' person. As was seen in the Abel Study on page 231, most convicted abusers have been offending for a long time prior to their conviction, and many of these individuals will have applied for posts working with children. Any teacher who is convicted of inappropriate conduct with children, or who is no longer considered safe to work with children, is placed on a list known as *list 99*. This list can be accessed by employers.

To prevent false allegations being made against innocent members of staff, early years settings need to look at ways of staff safe-guarding themselves. These safe-guards should form part of the setting's child protection policy, for example:
• Avoid unnecessary intimate care.
• Record all accidents or incidents and have them witnessed by another member of staff.
• If a child acts or talks in a sexually inappropriate way to you, record it and tell your manager.
• Avoid spending time alone with individual children.

**Activity**

What other guidelines could be included? Consider this in light of:
a) working with pre-school-age children
b) working in a primary school
c) working in residential care
d) being part of an organised trip.

**Professional Practice**

- The same rules of confidentiality apply to staff facing an allegation as they do with parents.
- Information will be given on a 'need to know' basis.
- Speculation and gossip is never helpful.
- Discussion with, or reassurance of, parents will be the responsibility of the manager of the setting or a designated senior member of staff.
- You should pass any enquiries on, rather than deal with them yourself.

Child protection, whilst being a difficult and sensitive area of the early years profession, is very rewarding. If, through your knowledge, understanding, observation or support, you are able to help lessen the trauma for just one child by your words or actions, it will have been an important element of your professional career.

**Test Yourself**

1. How can access to early years settings be monitored safely?
2. In what way can the key-worker system contribute to the safety and welfare of children?
3. What examples can you give of teaching children self-protection strategies?
4. What should we teach children about secrets?
5. Why is confidentiality important?
6. Explain the importance of clear records in early years settings.
7. What should you consider when involved with a child's physical care?
8. Why is it important to gain permission from parents before taking and displaying photographs?
9. What is a paedophile?
10. Why is it important to understand how paedophiles operate?
11. What is Megan's Law?

# Key terms

**You should now understand the following words and phrases. If you do not, read through the chapter again and review them.**

accurate records
alternative forms of care
Area Child Protection Committee (ACPC)
Care Order
changing face of the family
Child Assessment Order
Child Protection Register
confidentiality
disclosure
Emergency Protection Order

emotional abuse
EPOCH
feminist model
good-enough parenting
historical perspective
incest
indicators of abuse
long-term effects of abuse
medical model
neglect

| | |
|---|---|
| open adoption | Recovery Order |
| paedophile | referral procedures |
| paramountcy principle | self-protection strategies |
| physical abuse | sexual abuse |
| play therapy | short-term effects of abuse |
| police protection | sociological model |
| predisposing factors | Supervision Order |
| psychological model | UN Convention on the Rights of the Child |

## Bibliography and suggested further reading

Axline, V. (1964) *Dibs: In Search of Self*, Penguin

Bray, M. (1991) *Poppies on the Rubbish Heap: Sexual Abuse – The Child's Voice*, Canongate Press

Carroll, J. (1998) *Introduction to Therapeutic Play*, Blackwell, Oxford

Cattanach, A. (1992) *Play Therapy with Abused Children*, Jessica Kingsley Publishers, London

Carver, V. (1980) *Child Abuse: A Study Text*, Open University Press, Milton Keynes

David, T. (1993) *Child Protection and Early Years Teachers*, Open University Press, Milton Keynes

Doyle, C. (1990) *Working with Abused Children*, Macmillan, London

Elliott, M. (ed.) (1992) *Protecting Children Training Pack*, HMSO, London

Elliott, M. (ed.) (1993) *Female Sexual Abuse of Children: The Ultimate Taboo*, Longman, Harlow

Flekkøy, M. and Kaufman, N. (1997) *The Participation Rights of the Child*, Jessica Kingsley Publishers, London

Hobart, C. and Frankel, J. (1998) *Good Practice in Child Protection*, Nelson Thornes, Cheltenham

Jackson, V. (1996) *Racism and Child Protection*, Cassell, London

Karp, C. and Butler, T. (1996) *Treatment Strategies for Abused Children*, Sage

Kempe, C.H. (1992) in Elliott, M. (ed.), *Protecting Children Training Pack*, HMSO, London

Meadows, R. (1993) *ABC of Child Abuse*, 2nd edition, BMJ Publishing, London

Murphy, M. (1995) *Working Together in Child Protection*, Arena, Hants

Oaklander, V. (1988) *Windows to Our Children*, The Gestalt Journal Press, USA

Reder, P., Duncan, S. and Gray, M. (1993) *Beyond Blame: Child Abuse Tragedies Revisited*, Routledge, London

Sereny, G. (1999) *Cries Unheard: The Story of Mary Bell*, Macmillan, London

Department of Health (1991a) *Child Abuse: A Study of Inquiry Reports 1980–1989*, HMSO, London

Department of Health (1991b) *Working Together under the Children Act 1989*, HMSO

Department of Health (1995) *Child Protection: Messages From Research*, HMSO, London

Walsh, M., Stephens, P. and Moore, S. (2000) *Social Policy and Welfare*, Nelson Thornes, Cheltenham

Waterhouse, L. (ed.) (1993) *Child Abuse and Child Abusers*, Jessica Kingsley Publishers, London

# Childcare Practice

**This chapter covers:**

- The healthy development of babies
- The healthy development of children
- Children's behaviour
- Creating a safe, secure and stimulating environment.

## Introduction

The Childcare Practice unit forms the foundation of professional practice within the BTec National courses, looking at the specific needs of babies and how routine plays a part in their development, and considering the nutritional, environmental and stimulation needs necessary for them to develop fully. Information on diet and nutrition is provided, enabling you to plan, prepare and support the feeding of both babies and young children, and strategies for managing behaviour are discussed, offering suggestions for dealing with unwanted behaviour. This is a vital aspect of children's overall development, particularly socially and emotionally. Brief reference is made to safety and security of the environment, although these issues are covered more fully in Chapter 5.

## The healthy development of babies

Human infants are totally dependant on their carers for all their health, care and developmental needs. Caring for babies takes a great deal of time, patience and energy. It is, however, extremely rewarding. Babies are usually very responsive to the adults who care for them, showing enjoyment of cuddles and close contact, and rewarding them with smiles and by vocalising. The needs of young babies are simple – they need to be kept warm, clean, fed and happy. Their care should be viewed holistically (looking at the baby as a whole person), rather than compartmentalising their care into feeds, physical care and stimulation, as each of these areas is inter-related. Caring for babies includes caring for their environment, their diet, establishing a daily routine, providing stimulation and managing their times of distress. Caring for their physical needs includes their skin, hair and tooth care, bathing and nappy changing, rest, sleep and play routines.

**Continuity of care** is important as it is central to making babies feel secure. Care can involve a range of carers, but they must each be familiar to the individual baby, and in a day-care setting it is particularly important that the baby has one main carer (their key worker). Assessing the needs of a baby involves knowledge of their stage of development, their current state of health, usual feeding patterns and any specific requirements or parental choices. Each baby should have a **routine** that suits them; they should not all be included in a routine care 'regime'.

FORWARD to pages 259, 278–9 and 280 for discussion and activities on routines in day-care settings.

---

**Activity**

During your placement with babies, ask to see the planning and assessment charts held by the staff. Ask yourself:

a) How clearly can the charts be followed?
b) What aspects of the charts are most significant, do you think?
c) Do the charts give you sufficient information for you to care for the relevant baby?
d) If not, what else would you like to see included?

---

Human infants are totally dependent on their carers for all their health, care and developmental needs

## Care of the environment

One of the first points regarding the care of babies that you will need to understand is how to prepare a suitable environment. Room temperature and suitable levels of ventilation are an important factor in looking after a baby, and any room where a baby spends much of their time should be a constant 20°C (68°F) day and night. A room thermometer should be placed on the wall in the baby room of any early years setting and be checked regularly, adjusting the heating accordingly when necessary. Overheating of babies is thought to be a contributory factor in Sudden Infant Death Syndrome (cot death), and recommendations are that babies should not be piled high with blankets – just a sheet and two layers of blankets are normally be sufficient. Duvets and baby nests are no longer recommended, as they do not allow for temperature regulation. Cot bumpers are also advised against as they add extra warmth to a baby's cot, as well as having the potential for suffocation. Having a well-ventilated room will help to prevent cross-infection and make the working or living environment a more pleasant place to be, both for the babies and their carers.

*Remember!* A blanket folded in half counts as two layers.

**Professional Practice**

- You can check if a well baby is too warm or too cool by feeling their abdomen. If it feels warm and clammy, then they are hotter than necessary. A slightly cool-to-touch abdomen is usual. Removing a layer of clothing should be sufficient to keep the baby at a more comfortable temperature.
- Cool hands and feet do not automatically indicate a 'cold' baby. Young babies are not able to regulate and control their temperature as well as adults and older children, and many babies have cool extremities, especially before they become mobile.
- If you are concerned that a baby is unwell or has a raised temperature, always check it with a thermometer and seek medical advice as necessary.

### A high temperature (pyrexia)

Normal body temperature is between 36 and 37°C. A temperature above 37.5°C indicates **pyrexia** (fever). Young children's temperatures are often a sensitive indicator of the onset of illness and a raised temperature should never be ignored.

**Professional Practice**

- Deal with for overheating in the first instance by:
  - removing clothing or a layer of bedding
  - reducing the temperature of the room
  - sponging the child with a cool flannel.
- If fever is suspected:
  - Take the child's temperature and record the outcome.
  - Remove clothing or a layer of bedding.
  - Sponge with a cool flannel.
  - Offer plenty of fluids.
  - Use a fan to circulate cool air around them.
  - Observe the child carefully, particularly very young babies.
- Febrile convulsions can occur in some children when their temperature rises, involving loss of consciousness, flickering of eyes and general jitteriness.

– A child who has one febrile convulsion is more likely to have another. It does not however mean that they have developed epilepsy.
– Medical advice should be sought if a febrile convulsion occurs.
– The child should be placed in the recovery position when the convulsion is over whilst medical advice is sought.
– The child needs reassurance and rest following a febrile convulsion.

BACK to Chapter 5, page 162, for information regarding emergency first aid.

**Activity**

Ask your placement supervisor about the setting's policy on dealing with a child with a raised temperature.

## Types of thermometers

### Mercury thermometer

Mercury thermometers should never be used in childcare settings, but are sometimes still used in the family home. They are made of glass and should never be placed in the mouth – mercury is a poison and any breakage would mean a high risk of mercury poisoning. It takes a few minutes to get an accurate reading, which is not practical with very young children. This type of thermometer is normally placed under the armpit. It is less frequently used nowadays, being replaced by the digital thermometer.

### Digital thermometer

A digital thermometer is a popular alternative to the mercury thermometer. It gives a quick and accurate reading. It is usually placed in the armpit and offers no chemical risk. It should be cleaned after each use.

### Temperature strip thermometer

The temperature strip thermometer is placed on the forehead. It is easy to use but less accurate than the digital or mercury thermometers.

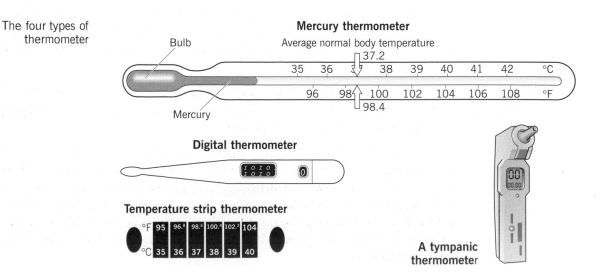

The four types of thermometer

**Mercury thermometer**
Average normal body temperature
Bulb
37.2
35 36 37 38 39 40 41 42 °C
96 98 100 102 104 106 108 °F
98.4
Mercury

**Digital thermometer**

**Temperature strip thermometer**
°F 95 96.8 98.6 100.4 102.2 104
°C 35 36 37 38 39 40

**A tympanic thermometer**

**Tympanic thermometer**

The tympanic thermometer is favoured in hospitals. It is funnel-shaped and is placed in the outer ear. It gives a quick and accurate reading. A disposable ear-piece is used each time, and then discarded.

*Remember !*  Parents should always be informed if a child has become unwell at an early years setting, even if they appear well again by the time they are collected.

Keene (1999) is a useful source of further information on febrile convulsions and managing ill health in young children – see *Bibliography and suggested further reading*, page 294.

## Feeding and nutritional needs

The decision whether to breast- or bottle-feed is a personal one, and a mother's choice should be respected. However, all health professionals agree that the best start for any baby is to be breast-fed, as this is the most natural and well-prepared food they can be given. For the first four months of life, most babies will need only milk feeds, either breast or bottle, to give them all the nutrients they need for their development.

### Breast-feeding

Breast milk offers a degree of **natural immunity** to the infant through the mother's own immunity, and it is considered to be nature's 'designer food' because, as the infant grows, the mother's breast milk changes to meet her child's developing needs. The colostrum-rich early milk (a thick, yellowish substance with a high protein content, secreted prior to the mother's full milk production) offers some protection against common infections and is particularly important to newborn infants. Even when mothers are not intending to breast-feed long term, they are encouraged to do so for the first few days to allow their babies to benefit from this.

For breast-feeding to be successful, the mother needs to eat well and drink plenty of fluids. The more the baby feeds, the more milk is produced, working on a supply-and-demand basis. Once the initial stages of breast-feeding are passed, and any soreness or discomfort has been overcome, breast-feeding is usually considered a pleasurable part of mothering.

Refer to Dare and O'Donovan (1998) for an explanation of lactation (how breast milk is produced) and how it is released (the let-down reflex) – see *Bibliography and suggested further reading*, page 294.

Babies suckle for different lengths of time – some will take all they need in just a few minutes, while others will suck for far longer. Letting the baby decide the length of a feed maintains a balance and helps to prevent engorgement of the breasts. At each feed the baby initially receives the 'fore' milk, which offers satisfaction in the short term, but the richer 'hind' milk which follows often gives satisfaction for a longer period. It is usual for babies to feed from alternate breasts at alternate feeds.

Breast milk offers the
baby natural immunity

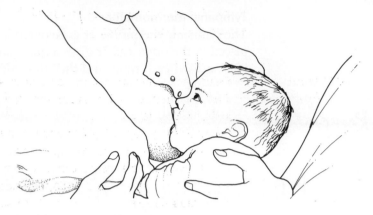

### Expressing breast milk

Many mothers choose to express some of their breast milk which can be given in a bottle or cup, and this can be a useful solution to the question of how to continue breast-feeding when returning to work. Breast pumps can be either manual or mechanical and they produce a vacuum which draws out the milk in much the same way as the baby's sucking. Battery or mains-operated pumps are far quicker to use than expressing by hand, and are suitable for expressing significant quantities.

Expressed milk can allow other family members to enjoy feeding the baby too. It can give the mother some time for herself and can alleviate any issues of embarrassment or cultural indiscretions regarding feeding in front of other people.

Expressed milk needs to be kept in sterile containers and refrigerated until needed. Breast milk can be frozen (ice-cube trays are useful for this) and used in preparing solid food when the baby reaches the onset of mixed feeding. The usual sterilising procedures should be followed.

FORWARD to pages 245 and 248 information on sterilising and making up a formula feed.

### The diet of a breast-feeding mother

As well as eating well, a lactating mother needs to be aware that whatever she eats will be passed on to her child. This includes alcohol, spicy food, medication and the effects of smoking. Medication should never be taken without checking that it is safe for the breast-feeding child too. This applies to cough and cold remedies as well as prescribed items.

Breast-feeding mothers need plenty of support, especially in the early days and weeks. It can be very tiring, as the mother is usually needed at each feed time and may have few uninterrupted rest periods. At times, breast-feeding can be hard to establish and the sensitive support and encouragement of health professionals and early years workers can be crucial to whether a mother feels able to continue. Support can be given in the form of:
- encouragement
- help with positioning of the infant
- advice on length of suckling
- advice regarding 'latching' the infant on to the breast
- advice regarding removing the infant from the breast.

Each of these are necessary to establish a feeding process which is free form soreness and discomfort.

> **Professional Practice**
> - Feeding on demand allows babies to satisfy their hunger.
> - If a baby sleeps well between feeds, it usually means they are getting sufficient nutrients.
> - Regular weighing of babies allows mothers to monitor the sufficiency of their milk production and gives them peace of mind.
> - Green slimy stools may indicate that a baby is not getting enough feeds – longer or more frequent feeds may need to be encouraged.
> - The breast-feeding mother needs to sit comfortably, with her back supported. The baby sucks with lips curled back and takes the whole of the areola (the pigmented area around the nipple) into the mouth. Eye-contact is made between mother and child and as the baby develops they pat the breast contentedly.

*Remember!* Breast-feeding is *always* the best choice for a baby, although as an early years professional you should respect the choices made by others and offer support accordingly.

### Formula feeding

Formula milk is an alternative to breast milk, but no artificial milk can be as ideal for a baby's stomach as breast milk. As the baby's nutritional needs change, parents need to decide when the next stage formula is needed, whereas with breast-feeding this occurs naturally. It is linked to the growth rate of the baby and their levels of hunger.

In early years settings, babies' feeds will usually be supplied ready prepared by the parents and will need to be stored in a refrigerator until needed.

The baby should be held securely, with good eye-contact

**To make a formula feed**

*Preparation:* You will need:

- formula feed
- bottle
- teats
- knife
- kettle of water, pre-boiled and allowed to cool
- sterilising equipment.

*Method*

1 Boil the kettle in advance and allow the water to cool.
2 Remove bottle from steriliser unit and rinse with boiled water.
3 Pour sufficient **cooled boiled water** into the bottle for the feed required following the manufacturer's guidelines.
4 Check the level is accurate.
5 Open the tin of formula.
6 Using the scoop enclosed in the tin, add the correct number of scoops to the bottle. Level each scoop off with a flat knife.
7 If using straightaway, put on the teat, ring and lid, and shake gently to dissolve the formula.
8 The feed is ready for use after checking the temperature is OK (see page 247).
9 If storing the feed for later, put a disc and ring on the bottle and shake gently to mix.
10 Remove disc and replace with upside-down teat (**do not** allow formula to touch the teat, as bacteria could begin to form).
11 Cover with disc and lid and refrigerate until needed.

*Remember!*

- It is important that the scoops of formula are *level*. Heaped scoops or packed down scoops lead to over-feeding, and over-feeding can lead to excessive weight gain, high levels of salt intake and possible kidney strain. Insufficient scoops of formula to the number of ounces of water leads to under-feeding, and under-feeding can lead to poor weight gain and a hungry baby.
- A baby needs 75 ml of formula per 500 g of body weight (2½ fl oz per pound) in each 24-hour period.

**Professional Practice**    It is easier to make up enough feeds for the day in one go if suitable refrigeration is available. This is particularly useful for families with twins or other multiples.

**Activity**

Calculate the amount of formula needed in each bottle for the following babies:

a)  Colin, who weighs 5.5 kg and is having seven feeds in each 24-hour period
b)  Alice, who weighs 8.0 kg and is having six feeds in each 24-hour period.

### Giving a formula feed

It is important to be prepared in advance, with everything that you might need easily to hand. You should be seated comfortably and able to give the baby your full attention. Often a baby will be more comfortable having their nappy changed prior to feeding, but individual routines will vary.

*Remember!*    Wash your hands thoroughly before feeding a baby or handling feeding equipment.

1  Have all equipment together and suitably covered. The bottle can be kept warm in a jug of hot water whilst you settle with the baby.
2  Hold the baby close to you, offering a sense of security and pleasure.
3  Test the temperature of the formula against the inside of your wrist. It should feel warm, not hot.
4  Check that the milk is flowing at the appropriate rate for the baby you are feeding. Several drops per second is usual, but rates do vary from baby to baby.
5  Encourage the onset of feeding by touching the teat against the baby's lips before placing the teat into the mouth. The milk should always cover the whole teat to stop the baby taking in excess air and becoming frustrated at not receiving enough milk at a time. If the baby is reluctant to suck, pull the teat gently, as the tension of this will often give them the impetus to suck harder.
6  About half way through the feed, stop and wind the baby (see page 248).
7  Wind again when the feed is over and settle the baby down. They may need another nappy change.
8  When a baby has finished feeding, discard any remaining formula and wash the bottle thoroughly before placing in a steriliser.

*Remember!*    Always throw away left over milk and *never* use the same bottle twice without sterilising.

### Winding

Winding a baby is the process of helping them release any trapped air taken in during the feeding process. They are best held in an upright position to allow the air to rise. Useful positions for this include:

- sitting the baby forward, resting against your hand, which allows you to rub or gently pat their back with your other hand
- placing the baby on your shoulder and rubbing or gently patting their back
- resting the baby along your forearm (very young babies only) and rubbing their back
- for some babies laying them prone across your lap and rubbing their back works well.

---

**Professional Practice**

- It is always useful to have a cloth handy as many babies posset (regurgitate) some milk during the winding process.
- Remember to keep the head and neck of young babies well supported.

---

**Activity**

You have been asked to prepare a leaflet on feeding choices for your local antenatal class. This needs to set out the advantages and disadvantages of both breast- and bottle-feeding and you should also include health, social, cultural and environmental factors in your information.

---

*Remember !* A mother has the right to choose the feeding method that suits her needs and your information should simply inform and not judge or advise.

---

### Sterilising techniques

Bottles and all other feeding utensils need sterilising to prevent illness occurring from the growth of bacteria. There are various methods to choose from.

### Cold water sterilisers

This method of sterilising uses chemicals either in solution or tablet form. The steriliser needs to be filled to the required capacity and the solution added (or sterilising tablet allowed to dissolve) before adding bottles and other feeding equipment. Each bottle, teat or other item needs to be fully submerged, and held under water by a float. Sterilising takes 30 minutes from the time the last piece of equipment has been added. The solution needs to be replaced every 24 hours and most tanks hold a large amount of feeding equipment.

---

*Remember !* Fully submerging items such as bottles means ensuring that all air bubbles are released – an air bubble leaves an area unsterilised and therefore a potential site for bacteria growth.

A microwave steriliser

### Steam sterilisers

The steam sterilising method is quick and efficient, but is expensive, and once opened the bottles need to be prepared within a short period of time, as opening the steriliser allows the potential growth of bacteria. There is a risk of scalding from the release of steam if the unit is opened whilst still very hot, so care must be taken. Steam sterilisers usually hold six or eight bottles at a time. They are ready for use within approximately 12–15 minutes from switching the unit on.

### Microwave sterilisers

This method works on the same principle as the steam steriliser. The units usually only hold four bottles, but the method is quick. Metal objects cannot be placed in the microwave steriliser.

### Boiling method

Boiling an infant's feeding equipment is cheap, but no longer a popular choice. It has considerable potential for accidents due to the large quantities of boiling water used. It can, however, give reassurance that equipment is clean and free from germs if no other form of sterilising is available. This method only needs ten minutes of boiling time to be ready. All equipment must be fully submerged, as with the cold water method.

**Case Study**

*Janice*

Janice is shortly due to give birth to her first baby and is unsure which sterilising method to use. She is currently on maternity leave and is due to return to work when her baby is about three months old. Janice intends to breast-feed for the first few weeks, moving her baby onto formula feeds by about two months as she will be working full-time and this will be a more practical option for her.

Janice has asked for your advice.

1  What advice would you give Janice?
2  What are the advantages and disadvantages of the various sterilising methods?

### Weaning and feeding older babies

From about four months onwards, babies begin to be less satisfied with what they receive from breast or formula milk and an introduction to solid food becomes appropriate. It is usual to introduce solids to babies before they reach six months, and this transition into mixed feeding is called **weaning**. Breast and formula milk do not have sufficient iron for continued healthy development, and prolonged (exclusive) milk feeding will therefore not provide enough of this important mineral. Up to four months old, the baby has sufficient stocks of iron taken from their mother during pregnancy, and below four months the baby's digestive system is not usually mature enough to cope with the components of solid food.

Weaning should be a pleasurable experience for both carer and child, encouraging them to explore new tastes over a period of time. It should not be a situation of stress or tension. At times it can be difficult to get a baby interested in trying to take solids from a spoon, but it is important to keep on trying, without worrying about regular refusals. The baby will get there in time and in the early stages of weaning the baby will still be having all of their milk feeds and so will not be losing out nutritionally.

Babies progress quickly onto other foods once they are used to taking food from a spoon

### Suitable foods for babies

Most babies start with a baby rice, which is bland in taste and very smooth. They usually progress quite quickly onto other puréed foods once they are used to taking food from a spoon. Whenever possible, freshly prepared foods should be given, rather than packets, jars or tins, as this will enable the carer (you) to control what the baby is eating more fully, particularly regarding additives such as sugar, salt, colourings and preservatives. Preparing fresh food helps to integrate the baby into family mealtimes. Convenience foods are ideal as emergency options or when travelling and many commercially prepared foods now have symbols showing whether they are sugar-free, salt-free, gluten-free, and so on.

All babies should avoid foods containing wheat or gluten (a protein found in wheat, barley and rye) up to six months of age, with oats (which also contains the protein gluten) only being allowed from four months if there is no family history of coeliac disease – there is a suspected link between early introduction of these products and the development of coeliac disease later on. Nuts or products containing nuts should be avoided completely as early introduction to these has been linked to later development of nut allergy.

▶▶ FORWARD to Chapter 10, page 480, for an description of coeliac disease.

| **Professional Practice** | • Milk remains an important part of the baby's diet and will remain so until at least a year old.<br>• The aim of weaning is to introduce babies to a variety of textures, tastes and experiences to integrate them fully into family mealtimes.<br>• Do not introduce weaning (or a new food) when the baby is unwell or tired.<br>• Offering half of the milk feed before the solids and half afterwards works well for most babies, but each baby is different and they will soon indicate their preference! |
| --- | --- |

**A suggested weaning plan**

| Age/months | 4 months | 4½ months | 5–6 months | 6–7 months | 7–8 months | 9–12 months |
|---|---|---|---|---|---|---|
| On waking | Breast- or bottle-feed | Breast- or bottle-feed | Breast- or bottle-feed | Breast- or bottle-feed | Breast- or bottle-feed | Breast- or bottle-feed/cup |
| Breakfast | 1–2 tsp baby rice mixed with milk from feed or with water; breast- or bottle-feed | 2 tsp baby rice mixed with milk from feed or with water; breast- or bottle-feed | Baby rice or cereal mixed with milk from feed or with water or pureed banana; breast- or bottle-feed | Cereal mixed with milk from feed or with water; fruit; toast fingers spread with unsalted butter | Cereal, fish or fruit; toast fingers; milk | Cereal and milk; fish, yogurt or fruit; toast and milk |
| Lunch | Breast- or bottle-feed | 1–2 tsp puréed or sieved vegetables or vegetables and chicken; breast- or bottle-feed | Puréed or sieved meat or fish and vegetables, or proprietary food; followed by 2 tsp puréed fruit or prepared baby dessert; drink of cooled, boiled water or well-diluted juice (from cup) | Finely minced meat or mashed fish, with mashed vegetables; mashed banana or stewed fruit or milk pudding; drink or cooled boiled water or well-diluted juice in a cup | Mashed fish minced meat or cheese with vegetables; milk pudding or stewed fruit; drink | Well-chopped meat, liver or fish or cheese with mashed vegetables; milk pudding or fruit fingers; drink |
| Tea | Breast- or bottle-feed | Breast- or bottle-feed | Puréed fruit or baby dessert; breast- or bottle-feed | Toast with cheese or savoury spread; breast- or bottle-feed | Bread and butter sandwiches with savoury spread or seedless jam; sponge finger or biscuit; milk drink | Fish, cheese or pasta; sandwiches fruit; milk drink |
| Late evening | Breast- or bottle-feed | Breast- or bottle-feed | Breast- or bottle-feed if necessary | | | |

from Dare and O'Donovan (1998), page 121

As the level of solid food intake increases, the milk feeds will decrease until the baby is having sufficient solid food at a meal time to be satisfied with a drink of water to accompany it. The table on page 251 sets out a sample programme for weaning a baby.

**Activity**

a) Using the table on page 251 as a guide, plan a week's menu for a baby aged either:
   • 6–7 months or
   • 8–9 months.
b) Compare your menu with another student.
c) How much of your menu could easily be prepared fresh?
d) How much of your menu could be taken from the family meals?

**Professional Practice**

A Bristol University research project into children's development has shown that babies who are not introduced to mashed (rather than puréed) food by ten months of age are likely to be fussier eaters later on in their life.

## Caring for babies

### Skin care

Care of the skin is important as it is one of the body's front-line defences against infection. Protecting the skin against damage has short-term benefits (from discomfort and infection) and long-term benefits (from sun damage and scarring). Babies have sensitive skin and many of our everyday products are far too harsh for them. It is therefore important to use specially prepared baby products suitable for sensitive skins during all care routines.

Skin types vary, as do cultural practices, and it is important that in any early years setting the preferences of parents are taken into account. For example, many parents of black babies prefer their baby to have cocoa butter rubbed into their skin after bathing, as black skin often has a tendency towards dryness. Some babies will also require a daily massage with an oil to alleviate the dryness. Most day-care settings ask parents to provide their own products and these are clearly labelled and kept solely for the use of their baby.

**Professional Practice**

• Any oil used on babies and young children should be free of nut traces (almond oil used to be popular but is no longer used), as there is concern about links with the increase in nut allergies in young children.
• Many specialists recommend the use of organic sunflower oil.

A common skin complaint in young children is eczema.

 FORWARD to Chapter 10, page 481, for details of how to care for a child with eczema.

A range of other skin problems are described in Keene (1999) – see *Bibliography and suggested further reading*, page 294.

### Care of hair

Hair care is necessary to prevent infestation from headlice and to encourage good grooming for the future. Cultural practices differ, for example Muslim babies will have their heads shaved within forty days of birth as part of cultural tradition, and many Caribbean parents traditionally weave and plait their babies' hair at a very early age.

Washing babies' hair can at times be traumatic, as not all babies are happy to have water in their eyes. Hair rings are available which prevent water from reaching the eyes and can make for a happier bathtime. Hair washing products should be 'non-stinging' for the eyes and specially formulated for babies.

FORWARD to *Bathing and nappy changing,* below, for advice on how to wash a baby's hair.

### Care of teeth

Brushing of teeth should commence as soon as the first ones arrive, and definitely when a baby has corresponding teeth top and bottom. Soft baby toothbrushes are specially designed for the delicate gums and first teeth, and their regular use will encourage the baby into a habit of good oral health care. In day-care settings, each baby should have their own toothbrush which should be labelled and kept separately from others.

The usual order in which milk teeth appear

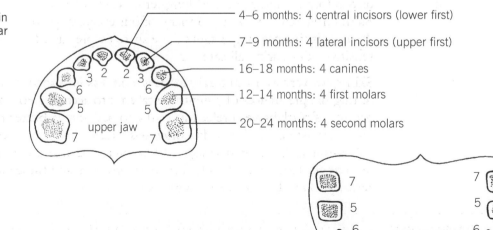

4–6 months: 4 central incisors (lower first)
7–9 months: 4 lateral incisors (upper first)
16–18 months: 4 canines
12–14 months: 4 first molars
20–24 months: 4 second molars

### Bathing and nappy changing

Hygiene is top priority when dealing with body fluids of any kind, and in day-care settings the use of disposable gloves is now the norm. In the home, good personal hygiene practice should be sufficient.

BACK to Chapter 5, for information on health, safety and personal hygiene practice.

Babies are usually topped and tailed in the mornings and bathed at night before being put to bed.

### Topping and tailing

**Topping and tailing** involves washing the face and refreshing the top half of the body, and changing the nappy.

*Preparation:* Get everything ready in advance. You will need:
- towel
- changing mat
- bowl of cooled boiled water
- bowl of warm water
- cotton wool
- barrier cream (if using)
- clean nappy
- fresh set of clothes
- access to nappy bucket (for towelling nappies) or a nappy sack (if using disposables)
- access to laundry basket for clothes.

*Method*
1. Place baby on changing mat and undress to their vest and nappy.
2. Using the cooled boiled water and cotton wool, wipe each eye from the nose corner outwards, using each piece of cotton wool only once.
3. Repeat two or three times for each eye.
4. Dry gently with corner of a clean towel.
5. Gently clean ears and around the face using moistened cotton wool, ensuring that you reach all the creases, particularly under the chin and behind the ears. Dry gently.
6. Using a larger piece of moistened cotton wool, freshen up the baby's armpits and hands, removing all fibres collected between the fingers. Dry gently.
7. In newborn babies, check that the umbilical stump is clean, but do not clean unnecessarily. Whenever possible, it should be left alone. (It tends to shrivel up and drop off 7 to 10 days after birth.)
8. Remove soiled nappy and place in bucket or nappy sack.
9. Clean the nappy area thoroughly, with warm water (or baby wipes if used), ensuring that you clean all creases, wiping from the front to the back.
10. Put on clean nappy (applying barrier cream if used), dress and have a cuddle!

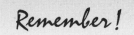 **Remember!**
- When changing a baby girl's nappy, always wipe from the front to the back to avoid any infection from the bowels passing into the vaginal area.
- When changing a baby boy's nappy, do not pull back the foreskin. Excessive cleaning can cause irritation and infection, rather than prevent it.

### Bathing

Bathing babies can be carried out by the traditional method or the modern method. Early years professionals need to be proficient at both, to meet with parental preferences.

*Traditional method:* Prepare everything in advance, ensuring that the temperature of the room is suitable (at least 20°C/68°F) with no draughts, and that all windows and doors are closed. All that you will need must be to hand and the bath should be in a safe and secure place. A special bath stand or a firm surface is ideal, but many people choose to place the baby bath in their own bath or on the floor. Any of these options are acceptable.

You will need:
- bath, with water at 37°C – *always check* this (preferably with bath thermometer or use your elbow) before putting the baby in
- changing mat
- towels
- cotton wool
- bowl of cooled boiled water (for the eyes)
- baby shampoo (if using)
- soap
- barrier cream (if using)
- clean nappy
- fresh set of clothes
- access to nappy bucket (for towelling nappies) or a nappy sack (if using disposables)
- access to laundry basket for clothing.

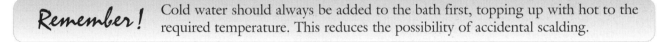

*Remember!* Cold water should always be added to the bath first, topping up with hot to the required temperature. This reduces the possibility of accidental scalding.

**The traditional method for bathing a baby**

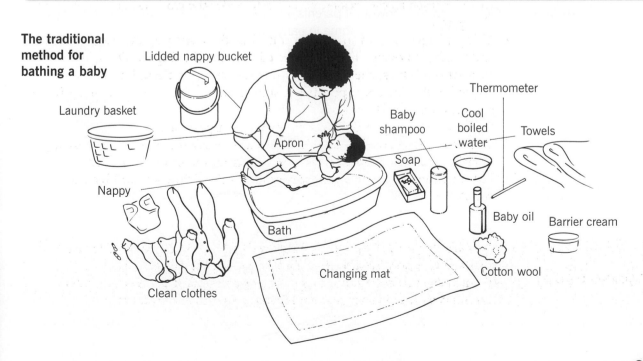

Lidded nappy bucket

Laundry basket

Apron

Baby shampoo

Soap

Thermometer

Cool boiled water

Towels

Nappy

Bath

Baby oil

Barrier cream

Changing mat

Cotton wool

Clean clothes

Method:

1 Undress baby to just the nappy and wrap in towel with the top corner folded away from you.
2 Wash the baby's eyes and face as in topping and tailing.
3 Hold baby (still wrapped in towel) under your arm with the head over the bath, resting on your hip.
4 Gently wet the hair all over.
5 Add shampoo or soap and rub in gently but firmly.
6 Rinse hair by leaning baby backwards over the bath. Towel dry the hair with the folded-over corner of the towel
7 Lay the baby across your lap and remove nappy, cleansing away excess faeces.
8 With your spare hand, gently wet and soap baby all over, turning them onto their tummy by pulling them over towards you, holding shoulder and thigh. When their back and bottom are also soaped, turn again in the same way (always towards you).
9 Supporting baby's head and neck with one hand and their bottom with the other, lower them into the bath.
10 Gently rinse the baby all over, continually supporting the head and neck, and holding their shoulder and arm.
11 When ready to be dried, lift the baby onto your lap, wrap in towel and cuddle dry!
12 Apply nappy and clothing as before.
13 Brush or groom hair as appropriate.
14 Trim nails as necessary using blunt baby scissors (with parents' permission).

---

*Remember !* Always keep hold of the baby, by firmly holding the arm and shoulder furthest away from you. Even very young babies can move suddenly.

---

**Professional Practice**
- Babies usually have a feed after a bath and are then put down to sleep.
- Only use talcum powder if parents insist. It has been suggested that it may link to the development of asthma in early childhood.
- Cultural practice regarding hair care, use of oils and creams should be adhered to.
- *Never* poke cotton buds into ears, noses, and so on.
- Babies need total supervision by a responsible adult at all times when being bathed.

Support the baby's head and neck while holding their shoulders and arm

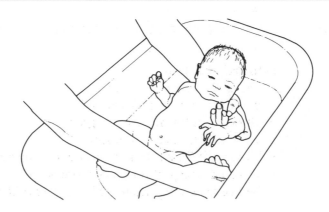

*Modern method*

1  Prepare bath water, clothing and so on in the same way as the traditional method.
2  Add a bathing preparation to the water.
3  Lower the baby into the water after the eyes and face have been washed.
4  Soap the baby using the 'bubble bath'.
5  Continue as in the traditional method.

*Remember !*  Using a bathing preparation can make the water (and baby) quite slippery, so particular care is needed to hold the baby securely.

**Professional Practice**
- If a bathing preparation causes irritation of the baby's skin, do not continue to use it.
- Some preparations irritate a baby's skin in the early weeks but can be used later on.

### Bathing older babies

From seven or eight months onwards, babies can progress into the family bath, although some babies will prefer the security of the baby bath for far longer. They are usually much more active by this time and the additional room for splashing is appreciated. Babies are often able to sit alone quite well by this stage, but remember that the water will make them buoyant and you will need to be ready to support them if they slip.

**Professional Practice**
- The same precautions are needed regarding temperature, preparation and supervision as with younger babies.
- Ensure that baby cannot touch the hot tap, which remains hot for some time after use.
- Do not have the water too deep, or the baby will 'float'.
- Sitting on a rubber mat can help the baby feel more secure.
- Provide a range of containers and bath toys for the baby to play with.
- Many babies enjoy bathing with a parent.
- *Never* leave a baby under the supervision of an older child.
- No child under eight years of age should be left alone in the bathroom at any time.

### Babies' clothing

Clothing for babies needs to:
- be easy to put on and take off
- allow room for the baby to grow
- allow unrestricted movement
- be suitable for the time of year and temperature of the environment they are in
- avoid cramping of toes (all-in-one suits)
- be free from long ties or ribbons (to avoid choking)

- be free from loose buttons or poppers (another choking hazard)
- be free from looped edgings on seams
- avoid lacy designs that may catch small fingers
- be easy to wash and dry
- be made of natural materials to allow skin to breathe
- not involve fluffy materials or wools such as mohair
- be of a suitable length – not long enough for dresses to get caught when toddling or crawling.

Babies' clothing should be suitable for the time of year and the environment they are in

**Professional Practice**  It is better for babies to be dressed in several layers of clothes that can be removed or replaced according to temperature, rather than one warmer layer which offers no opportunity for adjustment, as babies are not able to control their body temperature and could therefore become overheated.

### Care of babies' feet

Babies' feet are very delicate and their bones are still forming, therefore they should not be given shoes before they are able to walk, as this will hinder the natural growth of their feet, causing deformity. Socks, all-in-one suits and bootees should all have sufficient room for natural movement and growth.

Soft, roomy boottees are the ideal first footwear

<table>
<tr><td>Professional Practice</td><td>When babies are ready for their first pair of proper shoes, it is important to have their feet measured and shoes fitted by a footcare specialist.</td></tr>
</table>

### Rest, sleep and play routines

Babies need a routine which is not rigid but which provides continuity and security for them – a secure baby is usually a settled baby. Babies have periods of wakefulness and periods of deep sleep. They can appear very alert and content at times and restless and irritable at others.

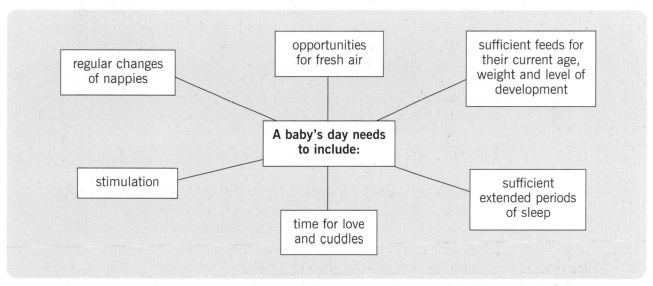

regular changes of nappies

opportunities for fresh air

sufficient feeds for their current age, weight and level of development

**A baby's day needs to include:**

stimulation

time for love and cuddles

sufficient extended periods of sleep

<table>
<tr><td>Case Study</td><td>Jefferson, Chloe and Ainsley</td></tr>
</table>

Jefferson is six weeks old, Chloe is five months old and Ainsley is ten months old. Each of them is the first child. Imagine that they all have a non-working parent at home to look after them each day.

1  What similarities and differences will there be in their daily needs?
2  Plan a suitable day for each baby.

Imagine that all three babies now attend the Lilac Tree Nursery, where the following routine is set out for the baby room:

| | |
|---|---|
| 8.30 a.m. | Arrival, settling in and play with key worker |
| 10.00 a.m. | Feed or snack; nappy change |
| 10.30 a.m. | Walk around the nursery grounds in prams/buggies |
| 11.15 a.m. | Play with key worker and other staff |
| 12.15 p.m. | Feed and/or lunch; nappy change and sleep |
| 1.45 p.m. | Play with key worker and other staff |
| 3.00 p.m. | Feed or snack; nappy change |
| 3.30 p.m. | Play or fresh air |
| 4.00 p.m. | Play until collected |

Imagine that Jefferson, Chloe and Ainsley are cared for each day in this baby room.

1 How well do you think the routine will meet the needs of these children?
2 What might indicate to you that the needs of a baby are not being met by the routine?
3 What changes would you make if you could?

## Communication with babies

Taking time to observe an adult with a young baby will give you an example of pre-verbal communication, as the adult encourages the baby to take a share in the conversation, asking them questions and supplying them with answers or making reaffirming comments following their own vocalisations. Welcoming the vocal sounds of babies encourages them to vocalise further, and responding to babies and watching them respond to you will enhance their communication with you.

Adults communicate with babies in many ways. This can be through:
* eye-contact during breast or formula feeds
* **turn-taking** vocally or visually
* initiating 'conversations' with babies as you play
* observing their needs through their body language or facial expression
* responding to their cries, for example, by giving them a cuddle
* encouraging them to vocalise, for example, by clapping and smiling
* showing appreciation of their vocalising, for example, by clapping and smiling
* giving praise, for example, by clapping and smiling
* calling to them when out of their visual range
* **aural stimulation**, for example singing to the baby
* **visual stimulation**, for example, holding a mirror in front of the baby.

### Activity

Take time to observe an early years worker in a baby room setting, working with young babies.

a) Which forms of communications listed above did you see?
b) Were there opportunities for any other form of communication to have taken place, do you think?
c) Do you think the adult you observed missed any opportunities for communication? If yes, what were they?
d) What might be the outcome for a baby who does not have opportunities for communication?

### Baby massage

**Baby massage** can improve communication between a parent and their baby, as it enhances the parent's understanding of their baby's needs. Baby massage involves eye-contact, touch, smiling and other pleasurable facial expressions, and as it involves such close contact, interaction between parent and baby is heightened. Baby massage is used by therapists to help mothers who are suffering from postnatal depression. It strengthens their contact with their baby and encourages bonding.

Baby massage can improve communication between a parent and their baby

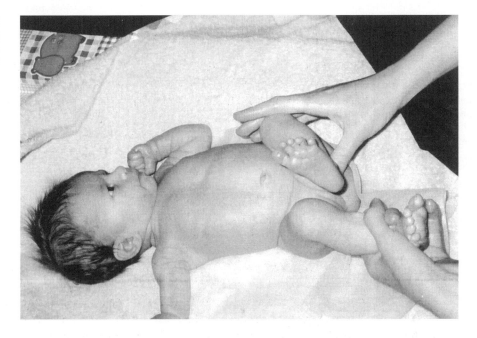

FORWARD to Chapter 9, page 394, for a table showing how babies' language develops.

### Baby-signing

**Baby-signing** has been developed as a means of additional communication for hearing babies. The range of simple signs can be introduced very early on and babies of just over a year old have been seen to communicate in this way, alleviating some of the frustration of not making their needs clear.

Garcia (2000) is a useful reference on baby-signing – see *Bibliography and suggested further reading*, page 294.

## Management of a distressed baby

Babies become distressed for lots of reasons. It may be because they are tired, wet, hungry, uncomfortable, unwell, teething or simply bored. Working out the cause of their distress is not always easy.

**My tummy hurts**
If a baby is distressed at the same time of day every day, it can often be attributed to **colic**. Colic is a painful condition, common in the first four months, in which the baby pulls up their legs indicating abdominal pain and is very difficult to console. There is no known cause for colic and it tends to disappear by itself by the time the baby reaches four months old. It is, however, distressing for both baby and carer and advice from a health visitor is advisable. The baby is usually thriving well in spite of the colic and no other symptoms are displayed.

**I'm tired**
Babies become over-tired if they do not have sufficient periods of restful sleep, and a baby who is constantly disturbed may become irritable. It is important to allow babies an extended period of sleep whenever possible.

**I want my nappy changed**
A wet or soiled nappy is uncomfortable, and most babies prefer to be clean and dry. Regular changing of babies helps prevent the development of nappy rash, as does allowing fresh air to their bottoms by leaving them to kick freely at some point each day.

**I'm so bored**
Sometimes, however, babies are simply bored, and so it is important to offer them stimulation. Mobiles over the cot or hanging from the ceiling are ideal visual stimulants and musical toys will stimulate them aurally. Babies also enjoy the company of their carers and will respond with pleasure and recognition from a very early age.

**Why is the baby crying?**

**Please leave me alone**
Sometimes babies become distressed when being handled, but this is usually a stage that passes quickly. Handling should be gentle and kept to a minimum until they find it more pleasurable.

**I'm too hot**
A baby who is too hot or too cool may also cry in discomfort. Adjusting the temperature of the room or their clothing will usually help.

**My gums hurt**
If a baby is unwell or teething, they may simply want to be cuddled. For a teething baby, a refrigerated teething ring will help cool down their gums and firm flexible teething toys will give them something appropriate to chew hard on. Preparations are available to rub onto the gums to alleviate discomfort of the gums and paediatric paracetamol can be given in times of extreme discomfort.

**I want my bottle**
A hungry or thirsty baby is often the easiest to identify as they tend to root for the breast or bottle when picked up or suck on whatever passes their mouth. In a day-care setting, making a note of the time and amount of feed taken by the baby helps you to anticipate their next feed time and is a general requirement of those caring for babies.

*Remember !* Babies sometimes want a drink in the same way as adults and older children do. Small amounts of cooled boiled water can be introduced to even very young babies, especially in hot weather.

 FORWARD to Chapter 10, page 469, *Common childhood illnesses*.

**Professional Practice**
- Every baby is different and has their own individual personality.
- Some babies cry much more than others.
- It is possible to over-stimulate a baby, tiring them and causing irritability
- Illness must never be ruled out, but will usually be considered when other causes have been eliminated unless additional symptoms are present.
- Offer support to the parents of a constantly crying baby as it can be very draining.

**Case Study**

*Rosie*

Rosie is seven months old and is teething. She has been unsettled for the past week during the day, and has hardly slept for the past two nights. Her mum is exhausted as she is a single parent and she has sole responsibility for Rosie and her three older brothers aged two to seven. You live next door to Rosie's family and want to help.

1 What could you do to help?
2 What advice could you give Rosie's mum?
3 You have heard of a phone line called Cry-sis for parents with fretful babies. Where could you find out more about the help they offer?

**Test Yourself**

1 At what temperature should a baby's room be?
2 Why are a baby's feet and hands sometimes cold even when their temperature is considered to be normal?
3 What body temperature indicates a potential fever?
4 What is a febrile convulsion?
5 Where is the temperature taken if using a tympanic thermometer?
6 What are the main benefits of breast-feeding?
7 Why is it important to add the correct ratio of formula to water when making a bottle feed?
8 What is meant by 'posseting'?
9 Name four methods of sterilising infant feeding equipment.
10 Why is four months the recommended age to introduce solid food to babies?
11 What type of skin has a particular tendency towards dryness?
12 List five points to remember about clothing for babies.
13 Why are nut oils not recommended for use in baby massage?
14 Why are mothers suffering from postnatal depression often encouraged to massage their babies?
15 What concern has been raised about the use of talcum powder on babies?
16 What temperature should a baby's bath water be?

# The healthy development of children

Like babies, children require a suitable temperature in which to play, work and sleep and in an early years setting the room temperature should not drop below 18.5°C/65°F. A wall thermometer should be displayed and regularly monitored. Maintaining and promoting the healthy development of children includes consideration of their diet and daily routine, and ensuring that they are clothed appropriately for the time of year and the activities they are engaged in.

## Principles of diet and nutrition

A good balanced diet is one which includes all the nutritional requirements for the growth, maintenance and development of the body. The food we eat helps us maintain and repair our body tissues, keeping muscles and organs functioning. It also helps to prevent infection and supplies us with our energy needs. A balanced diet should include elements from the four main food groups:

- *proteins*, which help growth, development and tissue repair
- *carbohydrates*, which provide energy
- *vitamins, minerals and fibre*, for general good health and the prevention of illness
- *dairy products*, which are high in calcium, enhancing and maintaining bones and teeth.

A fifth food group – *fats and oils* – are higher-level energy-giving foods which should be consumed sparingly by adults.

Many foods contribute to more than one food group, for example, meat is a good source of iron, and pulses are a good source of fibre, but the illustration below indicates where the main benefits of each food lie.

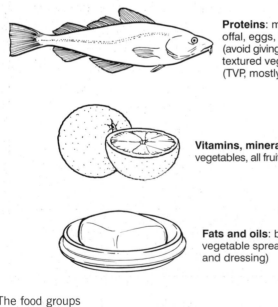

**Proteins**: meat, fish, poultry, offal, eggs, pulses, nuts (avoid giving to young children), textured vegetable protein (TVP, mostly made from soya)

**Vitamins, minerals and fibre**: all vegetables, all fruits, fresh and dried

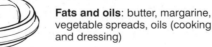

**Fats and oils**: butter, margarine, vegetable spreads, oils (cooking and dressing)

**Carbohydrates**: cereals, breads, pasta, rice, starchy vegetables (e.g potato, yam, plantain)

**Dairy products**: milk, cheese, yoghurt, fromage frais

The food groups

The following tables show the benefits of a range of vitamins and minerals and the possible problems that can occur if there is a deficiency.

## The main vitamins

| Vitamin | Food source | Function | Notes |
|---------|-------------|----------|-------|
| A | Butter, cheese, eggs, carrots, tomatoes | Promotes healthy skin, good vision | Fat-soluble, can be stored in the liver; deficiency causes skin infections, problems with vision |
| B group | Liver, meat, fish, green vegetables, beans, eggs | Healthy working of muscles and nerves; forming haemoglobin | Water-soluble, not stored in the body, so regular supply needed; deficiency results in muscle wasting, anaemia |
| C | Fruits and fruit juices, especially orange, blackcurrant, pineapple; green vegetables | For healthy tissue, promotes healing | Water-soluble, daily supply needed; deficiency means less resistance to infection; extreme deficiency results in scurvy |
| D | Oily fish, cod liver oil, egg yolk; added to margarine, milk | Growth and maintenance of bones and teeth | Fat-soluble, can be stored by the body; can be produced by the body as a result of sunlight on the skin; deficiency results in bones failing to harden and dental decay |
| E | Vegetable oils, cereals, egg yolk | Protects cells from damage | Fat-soluble, can be stored by the body |
| K | Green vegetables, liver | Needed for normal blood clotting | Fat-soluble, can be stored in the body |

from Beaver *et al.* (2001) page 345

## The main minerals

| Mineral | Food source | Function | Notes |
|---|---|---|---|
| Calcium | Cheese, eggs, fish, milk, yoghurt | Essential for growth of bones and teeth | Works with vitamin D and phosphorus; deficiency means risk of bones failing to harden (rickets) and dental caries |
| Fluoride | Occurs naturally in water, or may be added artificially to water supply | Combines with calcium to make tooth enamel more resistant to decay | There are different points of view about adding fluoride to the water supply |
| Iodine | Water, sea foods, added to salt, vegetables | Needed for proper working of the thyroid gland | Deficiency results in enlarged thyroid gland in adults, cretinism in babies |
| Iron | Meat, green vegetables, eggs, liver, red meat | Needed for formation of haemoglobin in red blood cells | Deficiency means there is anaemia causing lack of energy, breathlessness; vitamin C helps the absorption of iron |
| Sodium chloride | Table salt, bread, meat, fish | Needed for formation of cell fluids, blood plasma, sweat, tears | Salt should not be added to any food prepared for babies: their kidneys cannot eliminate excess salt as adult kidneys do; excess salt is harmful in an infant diet |

Other essential trace minerals include: potassium, phosphorus, magnesium, sulphur, manganese and zinc.

from Beaver *et al.* (2001) page 246

A healthy diet offers a range of foods from each food group, ensuring that the diet is well balanced, and is not deficient in any area. Encouraging children to try foods from a range of cultures and from amongst seasonal fruits and vegetables will encourage a healthy and diverse approach to diet throughout life.

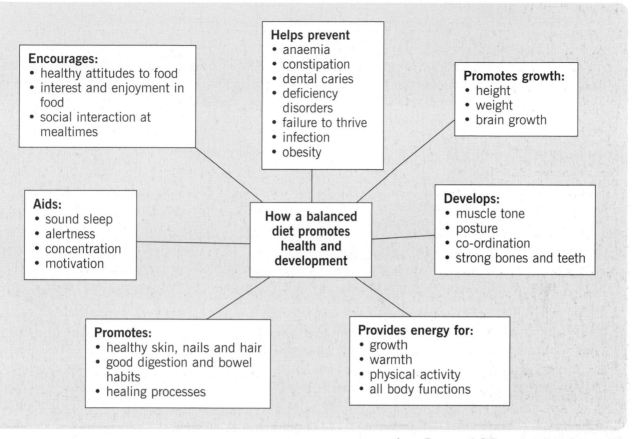

from Dare and O'Donovan (1996) page 32

## Planning a diet for children

- Children need a diet that is high in protein and carbohydrates to meet their high energy needs. The carbohydrates should ideally come from starchy foods such as potatoes, breads and cereals.
- Think about both colour and texture when planning meals, as an attractive meal will be more appealing, especially to a fussy or reluctant eater.
- Vary the meals that are offered to children, but do not offer more than one new food at a time.
- Large portions can be off-putting. It is better to have all of a small meal eaten, than half of a larger one, as it encourages good habits.

*Remember!*  Children have preferences too.

### Daily portions for children
As a guideline for planning the dietary needs of young children, a good daily balance would include:
- five portions of fruit or vegetables
- two portions of protein foods
- two portions of dairy foods plus 1 pint of milk
- four portions of carbohydrates.

### Snacks

Most children will also need to be offered snacks. It is important that these are mostly nutritional and healthy.

Snacks are an important part of a child's nutritional intake. Children use a lot of energy in their play and often need an energy boost in the middle of the morning or afternoon. This is particularly important if they are at a stage of developing particularly quickly physically, or becoming more active than usual.

**Case Study**

*Redhouse Nursery School*
Redhouse Nursery School has a fruit-only policy for snacktime. Many children bring an apple or a carrot, but still seem to be flagging at the end of the morning.

1 Why is this do you think?
2 What fruit would offer them a greater energy boost?
3 Is a fruit-only policy a good idea?
4 What other healthy options could be included?

Snacks need to be nutritional to be of benefit to a child; this should set them a healthy example for the future (see table opposite).

**Activities**

1 Plan a midday meal for a group of four-year-olds, ensuring that there are three colours and three textures within the meal. You can plan a meal from any culture you wish.

 a) What have you included for colour?
 b) What textures have you provided?
 c) What food groups have you incorporated into your meal?
 d) Are any food groups not represented? Is this a problem, do you think?

2 Pollect labels from a range of frequently-used processed products that are enjoyed by children.

 a) What proportions are the ingredients in?
 b) How near to the top of the list are sugar or salt?
 c) What does this tell you about processed foods?
 d) What alternatives could you offer in their place?
 e) Look at the table on page 270. How much of the EARs would the processed foods you looked at meet?

**Professional Practice** There are many hidden extras in processed foods, particularly sugar and salt. Whenever possible, offer fresh foods to children and do not provide salt or sugar on the table for them to add to their foods.

**Ideas for healthy snacks**

| Good as regular snacks | Occasional snacks, not regular |
|---|---|
| Fresh fruit:<br>banana<br>orange<br>pear<br>kiwi<br>melon<br><br>Raw vegetables<br>(washed thoroughly):<br>celery<br>carrot<br>tomato<br>cabbage leaves<br>Chinese leaves<br><br>Dried fruits:<br>raisins<br>sultanas<br>banana<br>dates and figs<br>apple rings<br>apricots<br>Small cubes of cheese<br>Sandwiches (savoury fillings)<br>pitta breads (savoury fillings) | Crisps<br>Sweet biscuits<br>Chocolate biscuits<br>Chocolate and sweets<br>cakes |

| Healthy drinks | Less healthy drinks |
|---|---|
| Milk<br>Water<br>Milkshakes (fresh fruit)<br>Fruit juices | Milkshakes (powdered)<br>Squashes<br>Carbonated drinks<br>(Coke, Cola, etc.) |

**Estimated Average Requirements (EARs) for energy in the UK (per day)**

| Age range | Males | | Females | |
|---|---|---|---|---|
| | MJ | kcal | MJ | kcal |
| 0–3 months (formula fed) | 2.28 | 545 | 2.16 | 515 |
| 4–6 months | 2.89 | 690 | 2.69 | 645 |
| 7–9 months | 3.44 | 825 | 3.20 | 765 |
| 10–12 months | 3.85 | 920 | 3.61 | 865 |
| 1–3 years | 5.15 | 1230 | 4.86 | 1165 |
| 4–6 years | 7.16 | 1715 | 6.46 | 1545 |
| 7–10 years | 8.24 | 1970 | 7.28 | 1740 |

from Dare and O'Donovan (1996), page 7

Further information on nutritional sources can be found in Dare and O'Donovan (1996) or Walker (1998), which includes a CD-ROM, the CHOMP menu planner, to help with menu planning and nutritional advice for young children in all early years settings. See *Bibliography and suggested further reading*, page 294.

**Activity**

Using a chart like the one below, plan a range of meals and snacks for a group of similar-aged children in a day nursery. Take into account their age, level of activity and the appropriate guidelines regarding EARs. National guidelines state that children in full day care (over eight hours) should be provided with 70 per cent of the EARs by the setting. Assume that all the children in your chosen group are in this category.

| | Monday | Tuesday | Wednesday | Thursday | Friday |
|---|---|---|---|---|---|
| On arrival | | | | | |
| Morning snack | | | | | |
| Lunch | | | | | |
| Afternoon snack | | | | | |
| Tea | | | | | |

## Cultural and dietary needs

Children have their own preferences regarding food, which should be accommodated up to a point. A balance is needed between allowing a child to select what they eat or do not eat, and encouraging them to try a range of new and familiar foods. When preparing meals for children, dietary needs also need to be considered. This includes children with a food allergy, family requirements such as vegetarian or vegan diets and cultural needs. The table below sets out the food-related customs of a range of cultures.

### Food-related customs

|  | Jewish | Hindu[1] | Sikh[1] | Muslim | Buddhist | Rastafarian[2] |
|---|---|---|---|---|---|---|
| Eggs | No blood spots | Some | Yes | Yes | Some | Some |
| Milk/yoghurt | Not with meat | Yes | Yes | Yes | Yes | Some |
| Cheese | Not with meat | Some | Some | Possibly | Yes | Some |
| Chicken | Kosher | Some | Some | Halal | No | Some |
| Mutton/lamb | Kosher | Some | Yes | Halal | No | Some |
| Beef and beef products | Kosher | No | No | Halal | No | Some |
| Pork and pork products | No | No | Rarely | No | No | No |
| Fish | With fins and scales | With fins and scales | Some | Some | Some | Yes |
| Shellfish | No | Some | Some | Some | No | No |
| Butter/ghee | Kosher | Some | Some | Some | No | Some |
| Lard | No | No | No | No | No | No |
| Cereal foods | Yes | Yes | Yes | Yes | Yes | Yes |
| Nuts/pulses | Yes | Yes | Yes | Yes | Yes | Yes |
| Fruits/vegetables | Yes | Yes[3] | Yes | Yes | Yes | Yes |
| Fasting[4] | Yes | Yes | Yes | Yes | Yes | Yes |

from Walker (1998), page 68

'Some' means that some people within a religious group would find these foods acceptable.

1   Strict Hindus and Sikhs will not eat eggs, meat, fish, and some fats.
2   Some Rastafarians are vegan.
3   Jains have restrictions on some vegetable foods. Check with the individuals.
4   Fasting is unlikely to apply to young children.

## Activities

1 The menus for young children shown below do not take into account any special dietary requirements. You have been asked to suggest alternatives for Monday and Wednesday to accommodate a child with coeliac disease, and for Thursday and Friday to accommodate a child from a practising Buddhist family.

a) What will you change?
b) What difference will this make to the nutritional balance?
c) How will you ensure that the children are not made to feel different from anyone else?

▷▷ FORWARD to Chapter 10, page 480, for details of coeliac disease.

### Monday

| On arrival | Diluted fruit juice, slice of bread with margarine, jam or marmite |
| --- | --- |
| Morning snack | Milk or diluted juice and toast |
| Lunch | Minced lamb, rice and peas<br>Stewed apple and custard<br>Water |
| Afternoon snack | Bread with cheese spread<br>Apple slices<br>Milk or diluted juice |

### Tuesday

| On arrival | Diluted fruit juice, slice of bread with margarine, jam or marmite |
| --- | --- |
| Morning snack | Milk or diluted juice and oatcake |
| Lunch | Pork hotpot, potatoes and carrots<br>Custard tart<br>Water |
| Afternoon snack | Egg sandwiches<br>Banana<br>Milk or diluted juice |

### Wednesday

| On arrival | Diluted fruit juice, slice of bread with margarine, jam or marmite |
| --- | --- |
| Morning snack | Milk or diluted juice and toast |

| Lunch | Bean and vegetable pastabake<br>Milk pudding<br>Water |
|---|---|
| Afternoon snack | Toast and marmite<br>Yoghurt<br>Milk or diluted juice |
| **Thursday** | |
| On arrival | Diluted fruit juice, slice of bread with margarine, jam or marmite |
| Morning snack | Milk or diluted juice and rice cake |
| Lunch | Pork curry and rice<br>Fruit fool<br>Water |
| Afternoon snack | Fruitbread<br>Apple slices<br>Milk or diluted juice |
| **Friday** | |
| On arrival | Diluted fruit juice, slice of bread with margarine, jam or marmite |
| Morning snack | Milk or diluted juice and toast |
| Lunch | Fish cakes, mashed potato and baked beans<br>Cake and custard<br>Water |
| Afternoon snack | Bread with cheese spread<br>Banana<br>Milk or diluted juice |

2  With a partner, discuss the following statements made to children:
   • 'No you can't have pudding unless your dinner is eaten up'.
   • 'Everybody is given the same amount, otherwise it is not fair.'
   • 'Of course you like peas, everyone likes peas.'
   • 'You can have a drink after you have finished.'
   • 'No, you're a coeliac, you can't have the pie.'

   a) What would concern you if you heard these statements being made?
   b) What messages are being given to the children?
   c) How would you feel if the statements were made to you during your meal?

**Professional Practice**

- Meal times should be a time of pleasure and socialising.
- Forcing a child to eat more than they want to may make them resent food, or even vomit.
- The pudding should be an integral part of the meal, not a prize for those who eat their dinner.
- Some children have far greater appetites than others, so will need larger portions.
- Making meals exciting can entice children to eat foods they may usually refuse.

**Ways of making foods more interesting**

- Sandwiches can be cut into interesting shapes:
  - boats: an oblong with two triangle sails (from one round of sandwiches)
  - use large pastry cutters: trees, stars, moons, and so on.
- Arrange food on plates into pictures: faces, clowns, cat with whiskers.
- Give meals exciting names: magic mash, nursery noodles, rocket of rice, planet of pasta.

## Caring for children

### Skin and hair care

Skin and hair care applies to children in the same ways as it does to babies. It involves encouraging regular washing, bathing and teeth cleaning. Children may now, however, be able to tolerate some of the bath products that were unsuitable for the more sensitive skin of younger babies. Whenever a new product is used, it is sensible to watch for any reaction such as a slight rash or irritation. If a reaction occurs, refrain from using the product.

Skin care includes using sun block whenever exposed to the sun. Early years settings need a clear policy regarding outdoor activity and sun-screening, and parents should be responsible for putting sunblock on their child before leaving them at school or the day-care setting in hot weather. With parents' written permission, early years staff must take on this responsibility, following parents' instructions.

*Remember!* Children and babies should not be exposed to the sun for more than a short period of time. Babies should be kept in the shade whenever possible (watch out for the sun moving round) and outdoor play should be restricted, particularly around midday when the sun is at its highest point.

Children and babies should not be exposed to the sun for more than a short period of time

**Professional Practice**

- Children who suffer any chronic skin problems, such as eczema, should not use perfumed bathtime products, unless sanctioned by their doctor, as these are likely to irritate the skin further.
- Total sunblock should be used on babies and young children.

### Dental care
All children should be encouraged to clean their teeth after each meal and before bedtime, to prevent a build up of tartar and tooth decay.

### Toilet training
By around eighteen months, many toddlers are ready to start potty training, but others will not be ready to start until quite a few months later. Bladder and bowel control cannot be achieved until the nervous system is mature enough for the child to register that they want to use the potty and their muscles are able to control the process. Many people recommend having a potty around the house so that it becomes familiar to the child, eventually encouraging them to sit on it. When this coincides with a successful 'outcome', much praise should be given (**positive reinforcement**).

The wishes of parents should be respected regarding potty training, but this should in no way result in a child becoming anxious or upset about the process. A calm, patient approach is likely to be the most successful.

## Clothing

Adults need to be responsible for what the children in their care wear, as young children are not able to make an informed choice, but will state preferences with little regard to temperature, weather or planned activity.

Clothing for children needs to:
- be easy to put on and take off, to encourage independence
- allow for growth, as the growth rate of children is so rapid
- allow unrestricted movement, particularly for outdoor play
- be suitable for the time of year and temperature of the environment they are in
- be free from long or loose ties or ribbons that could get caught during play
- be kept in good repair and regularly washed, setting a good example regarding cleanliness
- be easy to wash and dry
- be made of natural materials to allow skin to breathe
- be of a suitable length to avoid the possibility of tripping
- be suitable for the activities being undertaken.

Children's clothing should be suitable for the activities being undertaken

### Footcare

Children's feet develop quickly and it is not uncommon for a child to need four pairs of new shoes during the course of one year. Foot-care specialists recommend that children should have their feet measured every twelve weeks, and sooner if there is any concern about cramping of toes or if soreness occurs.

**Professional Practice**

- Shoes made of leather allow children's feet to breathe and it is therefore the ideal choice of material.
- It is unhealthy for children to wear trainers or similar footwear for long periods of time.
- Sock sizes should also be monitored – socks that are too tight can cause damage to the structure of a child's foot.
- It is better for children to wear several layers of clothes that can be taken off or replaced according to temperature, rather that one warmer layer which offers no adjustment.
- Children should be able to play happily without worrying about getting their clothes messy.
- Aprons for painting and water play are of course appropriate precautions to take in school or day care.

**Test Yourself**

1  What are the main food groups?
2  What are the guidelines regarding daily portions for young children?
3  Why is it important to vary the colour and texture of meals for children?
4  Outline the food customs of one culture or religion.
5  List five points regarding clothing and shoes for young children.

# Children's behaviour

Children need adult guidance and example to help to learn the social rules of the society into which they are born. In every family the routines and boundaries vary, but whatever they may be, they are a crucial aspect of family life for a household to run smoothly and for the children to feel secure.

The **boundaries** set by parents need to be reasonable without being too rigid and, once agreed, it is important to keep to them, otherwise children will continually test them. Boundaries allow children to explore ever-increasing elements of their world, safe in the knowledge that the adults in their life are in overall control of the situation and are taking care of them.

The individual personality of each child will also have an impact on their behaviour.

 FORWARD to Chapter 9, page 371, for more about personality.

## Setting boundaries

*Caleb*

Mr Collins takes Caleb to the supermarket to do some shopping. He usually buys Caleb some sweets in the supermarket when they shop on Saturdays, but not when they shop midweek. It is Tuesday and Caleb decides he wants some sweets and he wants them *now*! He shouts and stamps his feet and Mr Collins is so embarrassed, he buys Caleb what he wants and quickly leaves the shop.

1 What has Caleb learned?
2 What should Mr Collins have done (ideally)?
3 What might be the long-term implications of this incident?
4 What does this tell you about boundaries?

Children need clear, consistent and fair boundaries

## Setting goals and boundaries in early years settings

Early years professionals need to set boundaries and make clear their expectations of children when they are in the school or pre-school setting. These boundaries need to be reasonable, consistent and fair. This will contribute to the social and emotional stability of the children within the setting and to their development in general.

Children need to learn the social rules of their own culture (their primary socialisation) in order to be fully accepted by others within that culture. Each culture places its own emphasis on certain social skills and children will be encouraged to comply with these, by noting the responses they receive. This links to Albert Bandura's social learning theory.

FORWARD to Chapter 9, page 374, for information on social learning theory.

An approving look, a smile or a word of praise encourages a child to repeat an action, gesture or response, whereas a disapproving look or negative verbal comment is more likely to deter a child from repeating something. Parents and early years professionals should lead by example.

**Activity**

Think of an incident where children were learning by example.

a) Was this important, do you think?
b) What might have been the outcome had there been no example for them to follow?

**Case Study**

*Desmond*

Desmond is six years old and is an only child, born to his mother, Denise, when she was just fourteen. Desmond and his mum lived with her parents for four years until she felt able to cope with him on her own. Desmond is a very lively little boy who is awake by 6.00 a.m. every morning and does not go to bed until Denise does, usually at around 11.30 p.m. Desmond's grandparents doted on him when he lived with them, giving him all that he asked for. They still come and see him most evenings, usually at around 9.00 p.m. This allows Denise time to tidy up a bit as she gets nothing done with Desmond there. In school, Desmond is difficult to manage, being irritable and unwilling to share. He clamours for the attention of the class teacher throughout the day.

1 What is going wrong for Desmond?
2 What is Desmond learning from the adults around him?
3 What would be the first issue you would want to tackle for Desmond?
4 How could Denise help Desmond?
5 How could the grandparents help Desmond?
6 How could the class teacher help Desmond?

Sometimes we need to take a firm stand on issues for the long-term good of the child. Getting the balance right often comes with experience.

In setting boundaries for children, it is important to think them through carefully, considering how important each 'rule' or boundary actually is. In a busy early years setting you do not want to be constantly reminding children of boundaries, as life will soon be come very negative, regularly repeating 'Don't do that please', 'Off there please', and so on.

**Professional Practice**

- Children will test boundaries if they are not seen to be both clearly set and consistent, which is why a few really important boundaries are better than a whole range of desirable ones.
- Newly qualified early years staff will benefit from observing the approaches taken by more experienced staff in setting and maintaining boundaries.
- It is important that any reference to unwanted behaviour is made clear that it is the *behaviour* that is unwanted, and not the child.

**Activity**

Think about the following statements and discuss them with a partner:
- Children must say please and thank you before they get their snack.
- Only the child holding the teddy at circle time is allowed to speak.
- Children should *never* interrupt an adult.
- Only three children are allowed in the sand tray at a time.
- No more than five children are usually allowed in the play house.
- No more than five children are allowed on the climbing frame.

a) How important to you consider each statement to be?
b) Which could be described as a clear and consistent boundary?
c) What makes them a clear boundary?

Only the child holding the teddy at circle time is allowed to speak

**Case Study**

*Orange Blossom and Hillview Nurseries*

Orange Blossom Nursery has recently opened, and can accommodate twenty-four children aged two to five years. They currently have fourteen children each day, mostly aged three. The managers of Orange Blossom have decided to run the nursery as a free-play nursery, and have interpreted this as allowing the children to play with whatever they like, whenever they want to, with no restrictions on how many children can play with any one resource.

You are visiting Orange Blossom as part of a professional practice studies task which asks you to make a comparison between different types of provision. You have already written notes on Hillview Nursery which tries to ensure a balanced approach between free play and structured activities. At Hillview, the free-play activities are restricted to a range of resources predetermined by the staff and there are guidelines for the children as to how many children can play in any one place, whereas at Orange Blossom the children select or ask for whatever resources they want and play within small or large groups as they choose.

1 What are your first thoughts about the ethos of Orange Blossom Nursery?
2 What are you first thoughts about the ethos of Hillview Nursery?

3  Draw up a list of benefits and drawbacks for each nursery.
4  How might the children's developing understanding of boundaries be affected at Orange Blossom?
5  How might this freeplay approach affect the working practice of the staff?
6  What might the children miss out on at Orange Blossom?
7  Would you have any other concerns? What are they?

| Professional Practice | • Children feel secure with boundaries, and their understanding of them is made clear when they are heard trying to enforce them on others in the setting, for example 'You're not allowed to do that'.<br>• It helps children to understand the need for boundaries if you can give explanations to reinforce them whenever opportunities arise. |
|---|---|

**Example**  Following an incident on the climbing frame, the nursery manager of Hillview Nursery talked to the children, saying:

'Jenny has had a nasty fall from the climbing frame, which is a shame, but too many children were trying to use it at the same time and were not listening to Monica who was asking Jenny and Sarah to get off and wait their turn. Hopefully everyone will remember this; it is why we only allow five children on the frame at the same time.'

This was a clear explanation that had meaning for the children. It is more likely to be remembered by them for the future.

## Managing unwanted behaviour

Children can at times display a range of unwanted behaviours, and responding to them in a positive and consistent manner will help them to learn what is and what is not acceptable. Certain behaviours may need to be elimited because they:
• breach the boundaries of the setting
• affect the enjoyment and/or learning of others in the setting
• affect the enjoyment and/or learning of the child themselves
• are dangerous for the child or for others.

When challenging a child's behaviour, you need to be aware of what expectations are made of the child at home, and how your views of their behaviour will be interpreted. It is important that a child's home life is not seen to be criticised or devalued, whilst still maintaining the boundaries of the setting.

It is common in many schools for each class to display a list of the school 'rules'. These include statements such as 'We will not run in school', 'We will be nice to everyone', and so on. These statements make it clear what is acceptable or not acceptable within the setting and make no judgements about any one child's upbringing.

**Example**  Kieron loves to jump on and off the tables. This is a game that he plays at home with his brothers who are both older than him. It will be far better for you to explain to Kieron that he cannot jump on and off the tables in nursery because he might hurt himself on the nursery floor, or that the younger children may try to copy him and hurt themselves, rather than simply telling him that it is wrong to jump off furniture. In Kieron's home it may not be considered wrong and this could cause him confusion.

Similarly, it is better to explain to Maisie that shrieking at the top of her voice in the village hall (where she attends your pre-school group) cannot be allowed, as it echoes around and disturbs everyone, but is much more acceptable in the farmyard of the farm house where she lives, because it is an open space and the cows probably love to hear her coming to see them.

**Professional Practice**
- Children need to be given reasons and explanations which have meaning for them.
- On issues of health or safety, there is no room for negotiation. No must mean no.

**Activity**

a) What forms of behaviour do you consider to be unwanted, and why? Copy the table and try listing them under appropriate headings.

| Breaches boundaries | Affects others | Affects the child themselves | Dangerous for child or others |
|---|---|---|---|
| | | | |

b) Where would you place the following behaviours in the table?

tantrums
jealousy
withdrawn behaviour
extreme shyness
isolating behaviour
child without friends
repetitive crying
constantly seeking attention

telling tales
hitting
pushing over
bullying
taking somebody's toy
rudeness
refusing to share
group running away from another child

teasing
using aggression
defiance
disobedience
destruction of others' activities or drawings, etc.

c) What can you add to the list?

Examples of strategies you could take in exploring and managing behaviour are set out below, based on some of the behaviours listed in the activity above.

Examples    **A The child without friends**

1 Produce a sociogram of friendships within Child A's class or group.
   a) Who does Child A indicate as their friends?
   b) Which children indicate Child A as a friend?

 FORWARD to Chapter 9, page 405, for observation techniques.

2 Consider the interests and personalities of the children identified in the observation above. Think about who most closely relates to the interests and personality of Child A.
3 Initiate activities to bring the children together (one or two at a time). It may be helpful to involve an adult working alongside them to start with.
4 Monitor the progress of the 'friendship' and if it does not last, note what went wrong.
5 Use any information gained (from 4) to inform you in helping the child in developing another friendship.

Professional Practice
Sometime children need to be taught how to respond to others. If a child has a naturally 'neutral' facial expression, they may need help in learning to make eye-contact and give a welcoming look to others.

**B The destructive child**

1 Make a note as to whose belongings the child destroys.
   a) Anybody's?
   b) Their own?
   c) The belongings of children of a particular social group or culture?
2 Does the child seem to want to 'get back at' anyone in particular? If so, monitor for antecedent behaviour (see **ABC strategy**, page 286).
3 Does the child seem angry or frustrated? Offering opportunities for releasing anger and frustration may help.
4 Has the behaviour started suddenly? It may be appropriate to consider what is happening at home. The child may be taking out their confusion or unhappiness in the setting because they are unable to express it at home. Giving opportunities to be creative and to talk may help.

Professional Practice
- Whenever possible, ignore destructive behaviour (but comfort any child affected by the destruction), as sometimes the child's aim is to get your attention!
- Reward good behaviour with praise as this positively reinforces desirable behaviour.
- Whenever possible, work in partnership with parents to improve behaviour both at home and in the setting.

### C The withdrawn child

1  Make a note of how significant the problem is:
   a) How easy is it to involve the child in everyday activities?
      Easy? Sometimes difficult? Always difficult?
   b) How regularly does the child seem withdrawn?
      Occasionally? Regularly? All the time?
   c) How much do you consider the child's learning or activity to be affected?
      A little? Quite a lot? Almost totally?

2  It is important to establish whether the child is withdrawn in all situations, or just in the early years setting.
   If it is just in the setting, you will need to observe closely to identify where the problem lies.
   a) Is it linked to separation anxiety?
   b) Is the child being bullied?
   c) Is there a problem at home?
   d) Is the ABC strategy relevant (see page 286)?

3  Use of observation should guide you as to the best approach to take. Approaches might include:
   a) encouraging greater parental involvement to help the child feel more secure
   b) identifying children you need to keep separated from the withdrawn child, hoping to break the cycle and restore the child's confidence
   c) involving an adult in activities to help the child to develop 'joining in' skills.

**Professional Practice**   Use your understanding of child development to help you approach the child concerned appropriately.

### D The attention-seeking child

1  Consider whether the attention-seeking behaviour is due to:
   a) not being accepted by others in the class or group
   b) problems at home (feeling rejected, lack of interest shown in them)
   c) anxiety in new situations
   d) the child being bored with the activities offered or the work set
   e) the child finding the activities or work too challenging, and therefore lacking a sense of achievement.

2  Use observation skills to identify when attention-seeking behaviour occurs.

3  Adult involvement in group situation may help alleviate any 'social' problems.

**Professional Practice**
- Giving plenty of praise and attention where appropriate can be beneficial. This will indicate to the child that you are willing to give them your attention, but at appropriate times.
- Providing more differentiation in the activities offered or the work set may help the child find the appropriate balance of stimulation and achievement.

### Developmental affects on behaviour

The age or stage of development a child has reached will of course have a bearing on the expectation of how a child behaves and how best to manage their behaviour if it becomes unacceptable.

**Activity**

Think about how you would manage the following:
a) a five-year-old making a racist remark to another child
b) a two-year-old repeatedly undressing themselves on a very cold day
c) a seven-year-old actively encouraging his little sister to flick paint across the kitchen.

The ages of each child will influence how you respond to each incident. Now swap round the ages and think them through again. What difference would this make?

**Professional Practice**

What is acceptable at two is not always acceptable at four or older.

**Example**

A two-year-old who crayons on another child's drawing has not yet learned that this is not 'fun'. A four-year-old who does the same (usually) knows that it is not appropriate, but could be doing it for a number of reasons, for example:
• to try to gain your attention
• because they are jealous of the other child
• in retaliation for a previous act.

Before jumping to any conclusion, it is important to establish the facts, ensuring that the act itself is clearly acknowledged as unacceptable, but exploring any other issues and helping the children to reach a resolution between themselves if one is required.

**Professional Practice**

• Explanations will only work if the child concerned has the ability to understand.
• Children's behaviour often regresses during illness or times of stress.

FORWARD to Chapter 10, page 485, for further information about children who are ill. Refer also to the strategies below.

### Behaviour policies

Any strategy used by early years staff will work best if supported by the parents and carers of the children who attend the setting. This is why having a behaviour policy is important. It sets out what is acceptable to the setting and how unacceptable behaviour will be handled.

Activity

With a group of other students, collect a range of behaviour policies from a range of different settings. Having removed any form of identification of the settings from the policies, discuss the contents of each behaviour policy.

a) How do they compare?
b) Which policies do you think would be most useful to the staff in the setting?
c) Which would be least helpful? Why is this do you think?

For examples and discussion of behaviour (and other) policies, refer to Sadek and Sadek (1996) – see *Bibliography and suggested further reading*, page 294.

### Strategies for dealing with behaviour

Strategies include:

- the ABC strategy
- containment
- setting goals
- helping children cope with change.

### ABC strategy

Behaviour, whether acceptable or not acceptable, follows the same process. The ABC strategy is based on social learning theory. ABC stands for:

- *antecedent* – what occurs immediately before the behaviour
- *behaviour* – the incidence of behaviour being referred to, whether acceptable or not acceptable
- *consequence* – the outcomes following the behaviour, which will be either positive or negative.

Positive antecedent + Positive behaviour = Positive consequence
Negative antecedent + Negative behaviour = Negative consequence

FORWARD to Chapter 9, page 374, for social learning theory.

### Case Study

*Cleo*

*Incident A:* Cleo had been happily making a model using junk boxes for almost twenty minutes when Samuel came along and started telling her what to do next and interfering with his model. Cleo lost interest and went to play elsewhere.

*Incident B:* Cleo and Ginny were playing in the sand tray, driving cars through the sand. When Samuel joined them Cleo left immediately and went to play in the water.

*Incident C:* The whole group were playing circle games, and you became aware that Cleo was avoiding being next to Samuel, specifically changing places to avoid him.

Clearly something is not right here. How do you think using observation skills will help you get to the bottom of this situation?

FORWARD to Chapter 9, page 405, *Observational techniques.*

| **Professional Practice** | • Noting and responding to antecedent behaviour is a good way of starting to manage children's behaviour.<br>• Your role as an early years professional would be to intervene in a situation before the antecedent behaviour is put into effect. |
|---|---|

| Example | In the three incidents described in the case study, the antecedent was clearly Samuel, although he did not appear to be doing anything significant to upset Cleo (apart from some interference in incident A). Observation skills could be of importance here, in that taking time to observe Samuel, particularly when in close proximity to Cleo, could indicate why Cleo is anxious in his presence. |
|---|---|

| **Professional Practice** | Sometimes a child can be anxious due to the larger size or louder personality of another child. The adult's role here would be to join in and help show the wary child that they can play or work on equal terms with the other child. |
|---|---|

### Activity

With advice (and permission) from your placement supervisor, observe a child over a period of time and note any situations where the antecedent affects subsequent behaviour. If these were negative effects, think through what could be done by the adults responsible to alter the situation and avoid it being repeated.

### Containment

Sometimes a child's frustration or anger overwhelms them and they are unable to deal with it themselves. At this point, a sensitive adult can step in and 'contain' their emotions for them, holding them calmly and preventing them for losing control, gradually easing them back into a relaxed state.

It is important for you as the adult to remain unflustered, offering children examples of how to behave another time by outlining alternative measures they could have taken, where appropriate.

| **Professional Practice** | • Different cultures place different values on possessions and this can at times be a cause of conflict.<br>• Clear explanations must always be given to a child as to why their behaviour is not acceptable.<br>• Some children will benefit from taking 'time out' of the activity, to calm down, relax and compose themselves once again.<br>• Sanctions should be used only as a last resort, and if sanctions are indicated |
|---|---|

to a child, they need to be carried through (part of setting boundaries for the setting).

- Sometimes, children need opportunities to express anger. Providing them with clay, wood-working or a similar activity can be helpful.
- Distracting a child away from whatever is the problem can work well. This strategy can be particularly useful with younger children.
- If children continually have negative interactions with others, it may be helpful for an adult to join them in their work or play and help to direct their interactions, demonstrating a more positive way to play or work with others.

### Setting goals for behaviour

Self-esteem plays a large part in children's behaviour. If they are secure and feel confident, they are less likely to display unwanted behaviour. There are many ways of encouraging good behaviour and using reward stickers and star charts has become a popular approach. Some of these are aimed at building self-esteem, for example:

- 'I have good thinking skills'
- 'I am a kind person'
- 'I have done really well today'.

Others will be direct rewards, such as:

- 'Good work'
- 'Well done'
- 'A kind act'.

Whole-class rewards are given in some schools by using Golden Time or something similar. Golden Time is often on a Friday afternoon and children are given a greater autonomy regarding what they do. In some schools, children can even change to another class for the Golden Time session.

Setting targets for children can be successful, particularly if the children can see a tangible reward outcome. Many primary school classes use charts to indicate which books have been read, or how often good behaviour has been noted, and so on. These give positive reinforcement to the children and encouragement to continue.

### Helping children cope with planned and unplanned change

The flexibility built into the daily routine of a school or day-care setting offers security for children, enabling them to face changes in other situations too, whether planned or spontaneous. This is another good reason why the routine in any setting should never be too rigid.

**Test Yourself**

1. What is a boundary?
2. Why do children need boundaries?
3. What effect can a lack of consistent boundaries have on children?
4. Why is structure and routine important in early years settings?
5. What is meant by positive reinforcement?
6. What does the ABC stand for in the ABC behaviour management strategy?
7. What is meant by containing a child's emotions?

# Creating a safe, secure and stimulating environment

Issues of safety and the security of early years environments are covered in Chapter 5.

 BACK to Chapter 5 for a discussion of personal hygiene, cross-infection, accident prevention and risk assessments (including health and safety legislation) both in early years settings and on outings. Reference is also made to the safe care of equipment and resources.

**Activity**

Having referred back to Chapter 5, consider how you could encourage children to plan an activity that would show their awareness of the importance of personal hygiene.

a) What topics could they include?
b) What could they involve in their activity?
c) How might an activity differ for children aged four and children aged seven?
d) Compare your ideas with a partner.

## Stimulating play environments

**Stimulating play** is an essential part of a child's daily experience and as an early years professional you will be responsible for providing the children in your care with a range of stimulating opportunities, both indoors and outside.

 There are a number of excellent publications outlining ideas for providing stimulating play. One of these is Hobart and Frankel (1999). This book considers the planning of activities, the range of resources usually provided, the aims of the activities and how to evaluate their success. See *Bibliography and suggested further reading*, page 294.

### Stimulating play for very young babies

Very young babies initially obtain most of their stimulation from the interactions with their mother or main carers, through feeding, care routines, gentle rocking and soothing and the calming tone of their voice. By about six weeks, babies demonstrate that they have become much more visually alert, are usually smiling and focusing on the faces of their carers and familiar objects. By this time they will enjoy stimuli which hold their attention such as mobiles, which should be brightly coloured and three-dimensional. Many have a musical element which adds to the stimulation.

By about six weeks, babies enjoy stimuli which hold their attention

From here, babies benefit from progressing to an activity frame or something similar which can be placed above them, encouraging them to focus visually and aurally on the items hanging in front of them and enjoying tactile experiences too as they come into contact with the items during their natural body movements. Eventually, these movements become more intentional, and repeated actions will be observed, often in response for the 'reward' of a noise or visual 'experience' (movement, reflection or fluttering of material). Opportunities to play at bathtime or when having their nappy changed gives freedom from the restriction of clothes, allowing full leg mobility, and should be encouraged as often as possible.

Babies love music, and many will respond well to music familiar to them from the womb. They listen carefully to all that goes on around them and can often be seen to respond to both gentle music (which has a soothing affect) or lively music (which can agitate or excite).

Babies also enjoy books and pictures from a very early age and there is now a scheme specifically designed for them: *Books for Babies* (published by Friends of Libraries USA – FOLUSA) is a literacy programme that helps parents understand the importance of books in a baby's development.

Reading with a baby involves close and pleasurable contact. It also encourages an early interest in literature as a medium of pleasure.

### Outside
Babies enjoy being outside watching the leaves on trees flickering and taking in the sounds and smells of the garden. Fresh air is good for them, but they should never be left unsupervised and care should be taken to ensure that prams are not positioned in the sun, as a baby's delicate skin burns extremely quickly. Whenever possible, allow a baby to lay out of doors in warm weather without a nappy on, as exposure of the nappy area to fresh air is healthy and stimulating for their skin too.

Although most professionals agree that taking a baby out each day is a good idea, this does not apply if the weather is particularly cold or foggy.

**Professional Practice**

- Babies absorb information from all around them and benefit from as many experiences as it is possible to give them.
- It is, however, important not to over-stimulate them at any one time, as this can cause them to become tired and irritable.

An activity frame encourages babies to focus visually and aurally on the items in front of them

### Stimulating play for older babies

As they develop, older babies will be interested in a range of household articles. Sturdy boxes can be handled easily, being passed from hand to hand from about six months and knocked together as manipulative control is developed. They will also enjoy banging things in order to make a noise. A useful item for this is a wooden spoon on a saucepan lid or the tray of their high chair.

### Treasure baskets

Babies enjoy activities which enable them to explore through all of their senses and an excellent resource for this is a **treasure basket**. A treasure basket includes a range of objects that are made of natural materials that can be easily handled by the infant. They should be selected carefully to stimulate all the senses, and they should be completely safe. Nothing in a treasure basket should be made of plastic or any man-made materials.

Infants of about six months will enjoy exploring a treasure basket. They ideally need to be able to sit up securely in order to benefit from the freedom to explore. They should be allowed to focus on the objects they are handling without distraction from the adult or older children.

From about the age of six months, a baby will enjoy exploring a treasure basket

**Case Study**

*Nasreen and Claire*

Nasreen and Claire have been asked to prepare a treasure basket. They have selected the following items:

a silk hankie
a fir cone
an orange
a natural sponge
a wooden spoon
a glass paper weight
a loofah
a sheet of sandpaper

a bag of lavender
a wooden 'egg' permeated
　　with lemon scent
corrugated cardboard
a large shell
a wooden clothes peg
a large cork.

1 Are all the items suitable, do you think?
2 Would you remove any of the items? If yes, which ones and why?
3 What else would you add to the basket if you were preparing it?
4 Have Nasreen and Claire provided stimulation for all the senses?

*Remember !*

The objects included in a treasure basket need to be kept very clean. They should not have sharp or rough edges or be at risk of coming apart, and none should be small enough to be swallowed, or put up noses. The infant will need supervision whilst exploring their treasure basket, but not direct adult intervention.

**Professional Practice**

• The adult's role is to provide, to oversee and to allow freedom of exploration.
• Some older children with a special need may also benefit from exploring a resource prepared along the lines of a treasure basket.

## Stimulating play for toddlers

As they reach the toddler stage, children need opportunities to develop their large motor skills, particularly direction and spatial skills. Once walking, the use of push-a-long toys will help them become more stable and co-ordinated. Children at this stage need space, and careful positioning of unavoidable obstacles around the nursery room will help them develop spatial awareness and control.

The use of boxes, and tables and chairs as places to hide is common and rewarding for children of this age and opportunities to learn to climb skilfully will be beneficial. Indoor slides and mini climbing frames are ideal.

The interest in boxes and placing items in and taking them out is gradually replaced by the building of towers, and grading toys enhance both manipulative dexterity and early problem-solving.

### Outside

Wheeled toys are enjoyed, including ride-along toys and tricycles. Balls and beanbags, whilst possible to use indoors, are a real asset in the garden. Controlling large and small balls takes differing skills and paired games with an adult or an older child helps develop physical as well as social development.

## Stimulating play for older children

Activities should be planned to meet the needs of all children in the group or class, taking into account the differentiation of need. The stages of development set out in Chapter 9 are only a guide. Many children will be ahead of the 'norms' and some will still be developing towards them. An environment in which there is too little stimulation will result in children who are bored and potentially disruptive to others in the group. An environment in which there is little opportunity to achieve will result in children who are frustrated, disappointed and whose self-esteem could be affected negatively.

### Outside

Playing out of doors needs careful supervision as it does with younger children because as children become more independent they sometime take risks. Their interest and wishes to climb higher, run faster, and so on, often outstrip their ability to carry the activity out safely. If climbing frames and other large items of play equipment are provided, they must be supported by safety surfaces.

BACK to Chapter 5, page 183, for information on safe play surfaces.

**Test Yourself**

1  What is a treasure basket?
2  At what age would you usually introduce treasure basket exploration?
3  Name five items that could be included in a treasure basket.
4  What is meant by a tactile experience?
5  Why do older children need careful supervision?

# Key terms

You should now understand the following words and phrases. If you do not, read through the chapter again and review them.

| | |
|---|---|
| aural stimulation | principles of diet and nutrition |
| baby massage | pyrexia |
| baby-signing | routines |
| behaviour policies | setting boundaries |
| care of the environment | skin care |
| colic | sterilising techniques |
| containment | stimulating play |
| continuity of care | the ABC strategy |
| cooled boiled water | topping and tailing |
| food related customs | treasure baskets |
| managing unwanted behaviour | turn-taking |
| natural immunity | visual stimulation |
| positive reinforcement | weaning |

## Bibliography and suggested further reading

Abbott, L. and Moylett, H. (1997) *Working with the Under-3s: Responding to Children's Needs*, Open University Press, Milton Keynes

Beaver, M., Brewster, J. *et al.* (2001) *Working with Babies and Young Children, Nelson Thornes*, Cheltenham

Dare, A. and O'Donovan, M. (1996) *A Practical Guide to Child Nutrition*, Nelson Thornes, Cheltenham

Dare, A. and O'Donovan, M. (1998) *A Practical Guide to Working with Babies*, 2nd edition, Nelson Thornes, Cheltenham

Dowling, M. (2000) *Young Children's Personal, Social and Emotional Development*, Paul Chapman Publishers, London

Garcia, J. (2000) *Sign With Your Baby*, Northlight Communications, USA

Hobart, C. and Frankel, J. (1999) *A Practical Guide to Activities for Young Children*, 2nd edition, Nelson Thornes, Cheltenham

Keene, A. (1999) *Child Health: Care of the Child in Health and Illness*, Nelson Thornes, Cheltenham

Mukherji, P. (2001) *Understanding Children's Challenging Behaviour*, Nelson Thornes, Cheltenham

Sadek, E. and Sadek, J. (1996) *Good Practice in Nursery Management*, Nelson Thornes, Cheltenham

Walker, C. (1998) *Eating Well for the Under-5s in Child Care*, The Caroline Walker Trust, St Austell

# 8 Learning in the Early Years

---

**This chapter covers:**

○ **Theories of how children develop and learn**

○ **The work and influence of early educators**

○ **The role of play in the development of early learning**

○ **Identifying and promoting learning opportunities.**

---

## Introduction

Early years education has seen many changes in recent years as the learning needs of young children have gained greater status. The stage of a child's learning is now recognised as an important stage in its own right, rather than simply as a springboard for learning in later years.

Across the world, children's experiences of early learning vary considerably, with the starting age of formal education differing quite significantly between countries. Until recently, in the UK, learning opportunities across the range of settings offered have also varied a great deal. Government input, both educational and financial, has tried to address some of the imbalance between settings by introducing a comparable learning experience for all children of similar ages. This begins with the Early Learning Goals in the **Foundation Stage Curriculum** (the Cwricwlwm Cymreig in Wales) when children reach their third birthday (see below). This curriculum continues through to the traditional Reception class year, enabling children to enjoy a learning environment where play still has high status, while at the same time preparing them for Year 1 when they move into Key Stage 1 of the **National Curriculum**.

FORWARD to page 313 for more about the National Curriculum.

## The Foundation Stage Curriculum

The Foundation Stage Curriculum is made up of six areas of learning:
• Personal, social and emotional development
• Communication, language and literacy
• Mathematical development
• Knowledge and understanding of the world
• Physical development
• Creative development.

Each child will have their own individual experience of early years care and education before entering school, as there are many different types of pre-school provision available. Any setting which receives funding from the nursery education grant needs to provide evidence of a high standard of care and a planned environment, which offers opportunities for children to progress through the Early Learning Goals. These goals are achieved in most cases by the time a child leaves the Foundation Stage, and an understanding of how children learn is a mandatory requirement for all professionals working in the early years field.

Why, how and when to introduce new learning to children is discussed in this chapter, together with influences on the types of activities that can be offered and how they are presented. Advice is offered on how to extend and identify appropriate opportunities for learning within activities, enabling differentiation of need within any group of children.

A range of theories on the develoment of learning and educational theories are described in this chapter, illustrating how the theorists have had an influence on early learning in the past and how their theories influence current thinking and practice.

FORWARD to page 310 for more about the Foundation Stage Curriculum, and page 327 for more about the Early Learning Goals.

# Theories of how children develop and learn

As with general development, a child's rate of learning is influenced by a range of factors. *Development* can be described as a progression or expansion of past achievements, building on previously-set foundations, for example walking before running or sitting before standing, whereas *learning* is the process of acquiring new knowledge or a skill due to a certain set of circumstances, for example being able to roll a ball and then learning to play the ball game, boules.

Children's development and learning is most usefully seen as a continuum, along which they progress according to the influences and opportunities available to them. Each stage of development is a defined part of the overall human life-span. It should not be seen as merely a prelude to the rest of life. The term 'life-long learning' is commonly used to describe how we all continue to develop our knowledge, understanding and skills throughout our lives, both formally or informally.

## Factors affecting development and learning

Both development and learning are influenced by:
• health
• genetics
• environment
• support levels
• timing.

### Health

The health of a child impacts on both development and learning – a child who is unwell, undernourished or who has a chronic health problem is likely to be at a disadvantage due to repeated health-care needs. A hungry child will lack the energy levels usually associated with young children. Chronic health needs include asthma, diabetes, sickle cell anaemia or severe eczema. To be fully able to learn, a child needs to be physically and mentally alert. Therefore, a child who is distracted by discomfort or pain will be less able to assimilate learning at the rate of their peers and will move more slowly along the development continuum.

**Case Study**

*Stewart*

Stewart is five and has chronic asthma. He tends to need to sit quietly and use his inhaler several times during an average school day.

1  How might this affect Stewart in the classroom?
2  How might he be affected in the playground?
3  What impact might this have on Stewart's learning overall?

FORWARD to Chapter 10 for information on child health and to page 475 for information on asthma.

### Genetics

Genetic inheritance and how it influences children's learning has been much debated, with the nature theorists (**nativists**) purporting that genetic factors influence behaviour and learning, i.e. we are born ready primed for what we will achieve. The nurture theorists (**empiricists**) by contrast, claim that environmental factors are the main influences on learning, i.e. the circumstances we are born into and raised within will determine our achievements. This is the **nature–nurture debate**.

Biological factors, such as chromosome make-up and dominant and recessive genes determine the physical characteristics of each individual, and these factors influence the achievements and choices that we each make and therefore the rate of progress is open to greater debate. The line between nature and nurture becomes blurred when factors present at birth are influenced by social factors, for example the effects of foetal alcohol syndrome (FAS) or of maternal drug use. Both of these factors can give rise to malformations, impaired cognitive development and either hyperactivity (associated with FAS) or lethargy (associated with drug use), and so both will have an impact on learning.

At times adverse circumstances, either social or familial, do not have a negative affect on development, and in some cases, the adverse affects present in the early years can be reversed later on in life with relevant support.

FORWARD to Chapter 9, page 336, for information about the genetic effects on development and page 339 about foetal alcohol syndrome.

### Environment and support

Most modern-day theorists take a nature *plus* nurture approach to learning, considering that the genetic start we each have (nature) is enhanced by experience (nurture). Most agree that the environment in which a child is brought up and educated has an effect on the rate at which they develop and learn and how well they achieve their potential. Factors such as a stable home life, the interest of parents in their children, the encouragement, provision of resources, opportunities for new experiences and emphasis on raising self-esteem are all seen as important.

### Timing

Offering children opportunities at appropriate times ensures the best learning experiences. Some theorists in the past believed that children have 'critical' or 'sensitive' times for learning – learning can be missed altogether if it does not occur at a certain point in a child's life. Modern theorists do not generally agree with this, but consider that most children are able to catch up on lost time once they have learned a new skill or been introduced to a new experience, but may lack confidence and self-esteem due to being slightly 'behind' their peers. Children who have been pushed on too fast at too early an age (**hot-housing**) are at risk of losing interest in learning (**burn-out**). The most successful approach to providing positive learning experiences for children is to direct the learning to each child's individual stage of development.

| **Professional Practice** | A child who is tired will gain less from a new experience that a child who is fresh and alert. The end of the day is not a suitable time to introduce an exciting new activity as children may be starting to go home, leaving some frustrated at missing out, whereas others may be too tired to appreciate the potential of the activity. |
| --- | --- |

## Models of learning

There are three main models of learning:
- the **transmission model**
- the *laissez-faire* **model**
- the **social constructivist model**.

### Transmission model of learning

The seventeenth-century philosopher John Locke (an empiricist, see page 297) considered that children were a blank page to be written on by adults. His view was that children were born with differing potentials for intelligence and temperament, but they had no facilities of innate learning. Therefore Locke believed solely in the influences of nurturing. Classical conditioning (a stimulus which repeatedly causes a response) and **operant conditioning** (positive reinforcement of behaviour) are part of this philosophy.

The transmission model of learning is one in which adults keep control of the situation. The adult determines what learning will take place by their own direct involvement, controlling the learning process and suppressing the children's initiative. Children remain passive in these situations, and in the long term are less likely to try out new experiences because they are concerned about failing.

FORWARD to Chapter 9, page 386, for more about operant conditioning.

### *Laissez-faire* model of learning

The *laissez-faire* model of learning is based on the thinking of Jean Jacques Rousseau (a nativist, see page 297) in the eighteenth century. He considered that children learn naturally, following pre-set biological processes, and that these biological processes would be best developed if supported by caring adults, who oversee what children are doing but do not intervene in the learning process.

The *laissez-faire* model of learning allows for exploration and choice. However, it lacks adult input which limits any extension of the learning by example, or by **scaffolding**. It is possible that with this approach children may not reach their potential due to the adult hesitating to 'interfere' with the learning.

FORWARD to page 302 for more about scaffolding and Jerome Bruner.

## Social constructivist model of learning

This model of learning is based on the interaction of a child with their environment. The emphasis is that children learn through practical experience. Jean Piaget, Lev Vygotsky and Jerome Bruner all identify with this philosophy.

### Jean Piaget (1896–1980)

Jean Piaget was a Swiss psychologist who originally studied biology. He became interested in knowledge and its origins, which he called the 'embryology of intelligence'. He was particularly interested in the way that children think, and concluded that the thinking of children was different to the thinking of adults. Piaget considered the interaction between the child and their environment to be the main factor in influencing **cognitive development** (the development of learning through thinking and problem-solving), and this active involvement in their own learning is described by Piaget as a series of **schemas** (principles). During the early years, Piaget considered that these schemas changed and developed through the processes of assimilation and accommodation.

FORWARD to Chapter 9, pages 380–2, for an explanation of assimilation and accommodation.

Piaget proposed four stages of cognitive development:

1 Sensorimotor stage (0–2 years)
2 Pre-operational stage:
   Pre-conceptual (2–4 years)
   Intuitive (4–7 years)
3 Concrete operations stages (7–11 years)
4 Formal operations stage (11 years onwards).

Piaget's first two stages
of cognitive development

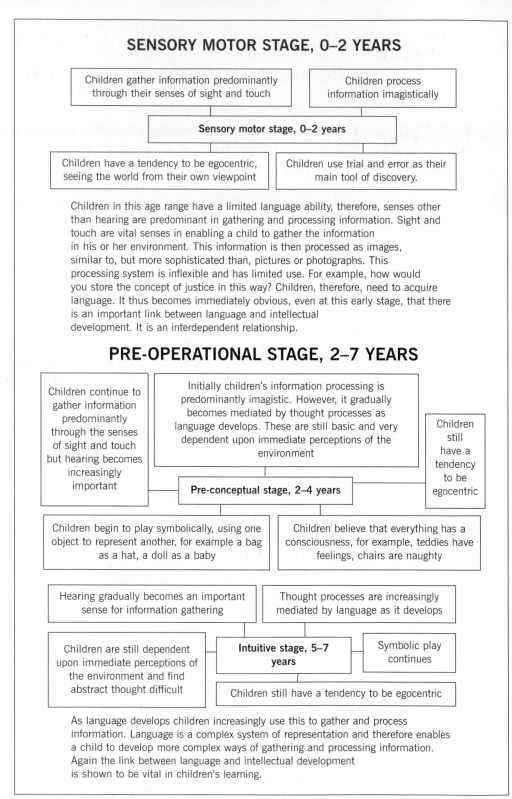

## SENSORY MOTOR STAGE, 0–2 YEARS

| | |
|---|---|
| Children gather information predominantly through their senses of sight and touch | Children process information imagistically |

**Sensory motor stage, 0–2 years**

| | |
|---|---|
| Children have a tendency to be egocentric, seeing the world from their own viewpoint | Children use trial and error as their main tool of discovery. |

Children in this age range have a limited language ability, therefore, senses other than hearing are predominant in gathering and processing information. Sight and touch are vital senses in enabling a child to gather the information in his or her environment. This information is then processed as images, similar to, but more sophisticated than, pictures or photographs. This processing system is inflexible and has limited use. For example, how would you store the concept of justice in this way? Children, therefore, need to acquire language. It thus becomes immediately obvious, even at this early stage, that there is an important link between language and intellectual development. It is an interdependent relationship.

## PRE-OPERATIONAL STAGE, 2–7 YEARS

| | | |
|---|---|---|
| Children continue to gather information predominantly through the senses of sight and touch but hearing becomes increasingly important | Initially children's information processing is predominantly imagistic. However, it gradually becomes mediated by thought processes as language develops. These are still basic and very dependent upon immediate perceptions of the environment | Children still have a tendency to be egocentric |

**Pre-conceptual stage, 2–4 years**

| | |
|---|---|
| Children begin to play symbolically, using one object to represent another, for example a bag as a hat, a doll as a baby | Children believe that everything has a consciousness, for example, teddies have feelings, chairs are naughty |

| | |
|---|---|
| Hearing gradually becomes an important sense for information gathering | Thought processes are increasingly mediated by language as it develops |

| | | |
|---|---|---|
| Children are still dependent upon immediate perceptions of the environment and find abstract thought difficult | **Intuitive stage, 5–7 years** | Symbolic play continues |

Children still have a tendency to be egocentric

As language develops children increasingly use this to gather and process information. Language is a complex system of representation and therefore enables a child to develop more complex ways of gathering and processing information. Again the link between language and intellectual development is shown to be vital in children's learning.

from Neaum and Tallack (2000), page 24

**Professional Practice**
- At what stage of Piaget's cognitive development are the children at your current placement?
- What examples could you give to evidence their stage of development?

**Case Study**

*Donovan*

Donovan is two years old. He is using clay and is trying to squeeze it in his hands. He says the word 'ball' twice. Eventually, Donovan leaves the clay and moves to play with the salt dough. Again, he tries to squeeze the material in his hands. He smiles as he is successful.

Which of Piaget's stages of cognitive development would you place Donovan in?

FORWARD to  Chapter 9, page 380, for more about Piaget.

### Lev Vygotsky (1896–1935)

Vygotsky also believed that children learn by active involvement, and saw the adult role as a crucial part of the learning experience, developing the theory known as the **zone of proximal development (ZPD)**, see the diagram below.

Vygotsky's zone of proximal development

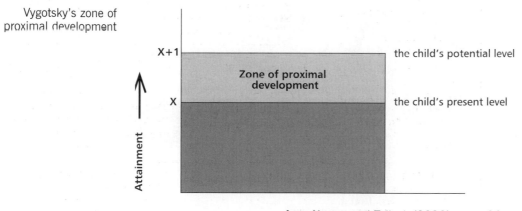

from Neaum and Tallack (2000), page 36

Vygotsky argued that children could often understand more than they demonstrated – while they were able to show understanding of some concepts through their play, the more abstract concepts, if introduced by an adult, could enhance their learning further. Children can therefore achieve more than if there had been no adult involvement. This highlights the important role that a (more able) individual (usually an adult) can have in helping develop the learning of a (less able) individual (usually the child) by extending opportunities for experience.

**Case Study**

*Yasmin and Thalia*

Yasmin and Thalia were at the sand tray and were trying to make sand pies with a small bucket. The sand was very fine and dry and they were not succeeding. Jenny, a member of staff, told them to add water to the sand. This they did, in large quantities, and saturated the sand tray. Yasmin and Thalia were still unable to make a sand pie as the sand had become too wet to turn out.

There was clearly an opportunity for Jenny to have extended the learning for Yasmin and Thalia here, but it did not happen.

1  What went wrong?
2  How should Jenny have approached the situation?
3  How do you think Yasmin and Thalia might have felt?

FORWARD to Chapter 9, page 384, for more about Vygotsky.

### Jerome Bruner (1915–)

With its basis in Vygotsky's ZPD, Jerome Bruner built his theory known as scaffolding. This again involves the adult in supporting the learning experience of the child by enhancing learning through the introduction of manageable levels of information. This supporting of learning enables the child to solve a problem, or to achieve further.

Bruner felt that children move through three main stages of thinking:

1 **enactive thinking**, where information is recorded mentally and linked to physical activity. This is the stage of most infants under one year old
2 **iconic thinking**, where the mental images are linked to the senses. This stage is associated with children aged one to seven years
3 **symbolic thinking**, using a range of representative forms to demonstrate their learning. This stage is seen mostly from seven years onwards.

 FORWARD to Chapter 9, page 385, for more about Bruner.

## Activity

Consider the three models of learning discussed on pages 298–303. Make a copy of the table below. Think of at least three statements to sum up each model and list them in the appropriate column. For example, under which heading would you place 'Believes that children achieve best if directed by an adult'? Compare your statements with another student.

| Transmission model | *Laissez-faire* model | Social constructivist model |
| --- | --- | --- |
| | | |

## Professional Practice

When planning an activity for children, you need to consider the level of adult involvement required and include it in your planning.

## Links to current research

## Activity

Using the academic and media resources available to you in your college resource centre, together with the Internet, explore current research linked to early years learning and find out about the perceived role of the adult in any proposed developments.

 One useful source could be the journal *Early Childhood Practice: The Journal for Multi-Professional Partnerships*, edited by Professor Tina Bruce.

## Links to your own experience and practice

As a student, you will see many examples of good practice during your placement experience. This is an important learning opportunity for you. However, on occasions, less ideal practice may be evident, which is unfortunate, but will add to your knowledge base as a professional early years worker, reminding you how *not* to approach certain situations.

 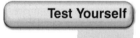
## The work and influence of early educators

A number of early educators have had a significant influence on the practice of modern early years professionals, enabling a greater understanding of how children learn and what impacts on the learning process. This section summarises some of the most influential early pioneers.

## Fredrich Froebel (1782–1852)

Fredrich Froebel considered parents to be the main educators of their children. He founded the first kindergarten in 1840 and the children who attended were given the opportunity to learn through **exploratory play**, particularly with natural materials. His emphasis was that children learn best when they are well motivated, and he focused on offering opportunities for a positive relationship between the child's home, their school and the wider community. Froebel encouraged **symbolic play**, and what is known today as **free-flow play**. He developed a set of learning materials which he called 'The gifts' and these materials went on to influence the work of Maria Montessori. Froebel's emphasis was always on the linking together of materials, and learning by their differences in a non-directed way.

**Froebel: key concepts**

| Key concepts | Types of play | Materials and resources |
|---|---|---|
| Parents as the main educators of their children<br><br>Interaction between home, school and the community<br><br>Non-directed learning<br><br>Focus on the whole child<br><br>No formal learning under seven | Exploratory play<br><br>Learning through nature<br><br>Symbolic play | The 'gifts' |

FORWARD to page 317 for more about free-flow play and page 306 for Maria Montessori.

## Rudolph Steiner (1861–1925)

Rudolph **Steiner** saw the child as having three developmental stages which they pass through on their way to adulthood:
- Up to seven years of age he considered that the emphasis of learning should be on the will (the active stage).
- From seven to fourteen years years old he proposed that the emphasis moves to the heart (the emphasis is now on feelings).
- From fourteen years onwards the head was considered by Steiner to be of greatest importance (the cognitive stage).

Like Froebel, Steiner considered the child holistically (as a whole), maintaining that each stage of learning was fostered by the interaction of prior experience.

He firmly believed that formal reading and writing should not be introduced at an early age, but should occur naturally at a child's own pace, fostered by opportunities for creativity. He also encouraged the use of natural materials and felt that learning should be initiated by the child – it should come from within.

Steiner settings offer a carefully structured environment which particularly fosters non-pressurised personal and social learning. He promoted what was known as curative education for children with emotional, behavioural and learning difficulties. The use of textbooks was only seen as a support to the learning that was already developing, they were not used to initiate it. The main emphasis of the Steiner approach is on learning from life's experiences.

Steiner Waldorf schools are run as private schools, but parents usually only pay according to their means. Some (but not all) children are integrated back into the state sector when they reach the GCSE and post-GCSE stage of their education.

### Steiner: key concepts

| Key concepts | Types of play | Materials and resources |
| --- | --- | --- |
| Three stages of learning:<br>• the will<br>• the heart<br>• the head<br><br>Learning at own pace<br><br>Focus on the whole child | Freeplay<br><br>Exploratory play<br><br>Learning through nature | Natural materials |

FORWARD to page 316 for more about the Steiner approach.

## Maria Montessori (1870–1952)

Maria Montessori believed that, given the right stimuli, children are naturally self-motivating. She saw children as active learners in much the same way as Piaget did, but she did not value play in its free-flow sense, believing that children became independent learners if they are encouraged to work alone.

Montessori believed that the child needed to work through the range of learning materials she developed before they were ready to express their own ideas. This range of materials particularly encouraged dexterity, and as they worked with them the child was guided from the simple to more the complex tasks. This included activities to learn particular skills. Montessori believed that each activity should only be used for the purpose for which it was designed and did not value imaginative play.

She encouraged children to learn to form letters through sand and finger play and no methods involving the formal learning of reading and writing were seen in a Montessori nursery, although a great emphasis was placed on the richness of literature and use of language. Montessori encouraged independence and considered that children had reached the highest point of their learning when they were silently absorbed in their activity. She referred to this as the 'polarisation of the attention'.

Montessori believed that the adult's role is to 'follow the child'. She based her theories on extensive observation of children and the acceptance today of children being eager learners from birth is often attributed to her theories.

### Montessori: key concepts

| Key concepts | Types of play | Materials and resources |
|---|---|---|
| Children are self-motivating<br><br>Independent learning was encouraged<br><br>Planned environment<br><br>Adult should follow the child | Free-flow play not valued<br><br>Sensory learning<br><br>Encouraged dexterous activity | Developed own range of equipment |

FORWARD to page 315 for more about the Montessori approach.

## Margaret McMillan (1860–1931)

Margaret McMillan was influenced by Froebel and like him she was interested in children learning both freely and naturally. She considered that play helped children demonstrate their knowledge and understanding of materials and situations, and placed emphasis on manipulative dexterity which was later favoured by Montessori.

McMillan was the pioneer of nursery schools, school meals and medical services. She initiated the viewpoint that a hungry child or a sick child will be unlikely to reach their potential so the need to feed them and monitor their health was crucial to the learning process.

She considered that children expressed what they had learned through their play and she was a pioneer of working in partnership with parents, encouraging them to learn alongside their children. McMillan's later work promoted the importance of the training of adults to enable them to work with young children in an informed manner.

### McMillan: key concepts

| Key concepts | Types of play | Materials and resources |
|---|---|---|
| Emphasis on manipulative dexterity<br><br>Pioneer of nursery schools<br><br>Initiated schools meals and health services<br><br>Partnership with parents<br><br>No formal learning before seven<br><br>Promoted training for adults | Free-play<br><br>Natural play<br><br>Exploratory play | No special resources |

## Susan Isaacs (1885–1948)

Also influenced by the work of Froebel, Susan Isaacs believed that children should not enter formal learning situations before the age of seven. She considered that they should be allowed to learn through free-play and individual experience and she placed great emphasis on the need for movement in their play and learning.

Isaacs also believed in the role of parents as the main educators of their children and was interested in children's feelings and emotions, an influence from the work of Melanie Klein (a psychoanalyst). Isaacs believed that children were able to move in and out of reality during their play, learning to cope with their feelings. This was important to their emotional security.

### Isaacs: key concepts

| Key concepts | Types of play | Materials and resources |
|---|---|---|
| Emphasis on need for movement<br><br>Play fundamental to learning<br><br>No formal learning before seven<br><br>Parents as main educators<br><br>Emotional regression common on entering school | Free-play<br><br>Active play | No special resources |

Isaacs made observations of children and recorded them, following them up after they had left the nursery. She noted that a marked regression in development was common when children entered formal schooling.

---

**Professional Practice**    Each of the five early educators have directly influenced some aspect of your professional practice experience. Think of an example relevant to each of them.

---

**Activity**

Using outdoor play as the basis for planning activities for children in your current placement, plan activities which could be directly relevant to the thinking of each of the five early educators.

a) How might the activities differ?
b) How might they be similar?

---

**Test Yourself**

1 Which of the early educators supported learning through exploratory play?
2 Who initiated school meals and health services?
3 Whose philosophy believed that textbooks should support, not initiate, learning?
4 From which age did Steiner believe children learned particularly through feelings?

## Provision and principles of practice

Most children will at some point attend a registered early years setting, which could include full or sessional day care, or after-school and wraparound facilities such as breakfast clubs. They may be registered through the private, statutory or voluntary sectors, each being overseen by government-led inspection processes. Facilities will be classified under a range of headings, for example:
• day nurseries
• nursery schools
• creches
• pre-schools
• playgroups
• play schools
• childminders
• nannies for pre-school age children.

Older children may be dropped off and collected from school by childminders and nannies, but also have opportunities to attend after-school clubs and wraparound facilities.

Makins (1997) offers a useful description of a range of multi-agency settings who were awarded early excellence status in the first round of the government's Early Excellence initiative. See *Bibliography and suggested further reading*, page 331.

All settings offering the Foundation Stage Curriculum and achieving satisfactory inspection outcomes from OfSTED receive funding for their four-year-olds (and in some areas three-year-olds too) from the Nursery Education Grant.

## Foundation Stage Curriculum

The Foundation Stage Curriculum is offered from the age of three, up until the child begins to follow the National Curriculum and its principles should be the basis of all future learning (QCA, 2000) by:

'supporting, fostering, promoting and developing children's:

**Personal, social and emotional well-being:** in particular by supporting the transition to and between settings, promoting an inclusive ethos and providing opportunities for each child to become a valued member of that group and community so that a strong self-image and self-esteem are promoted;

**Positive attitudes and dispositions towards their learning:** in particular an enthusiasm for knowledge and learning and a confidence in their ability to be successful learners;

**Social skills:** in particular by providing opportunities that enable them to learn how to co-operate and work harmoniously alongside and with each other and to listen to each other;

**Attention skills and persistence:** in particular the capacity to concentrate on their own play or on group tasks;

**Language and communication:** with opportunities for all children to talk and communicate in a widening range of situations, to respond to adults and to each other, to practise and extend the range of vocabulary and communication skills they use and to listen carefully;

**Reading and writing:** with opportunities for all children to explore, enjoy, learn about and use words and text in a broad range of context and to experience a rich variety of books;

**Mathematics:** with opportunities for all children to develop their understanding of number, measurement, pattern, shape and space by providing a broad range of contexts in which they can explore, enjoy, learn, practise and talk about them;

**Knowledge and understanding of the world:** with opportunities for all children to solve problems, make decisions, experiment, predict, plan and question in a variety of contexts, and to explore and find out about their environment and people and places that have significance in their lives:

**Physical development:** with opportunities for all children to develop and practise their fine and gross motor skills and to increase their understanding of how the body works and what they need to do to be healthy and safe;

**Creative development:** with opportunities for all children to explore and share thoughts, ideas and feelings through a variety of art, design and technology, music, movement, dance and imaginative and role-play activities.'

QCA (2000), pages 8–9

**Parents as partners**

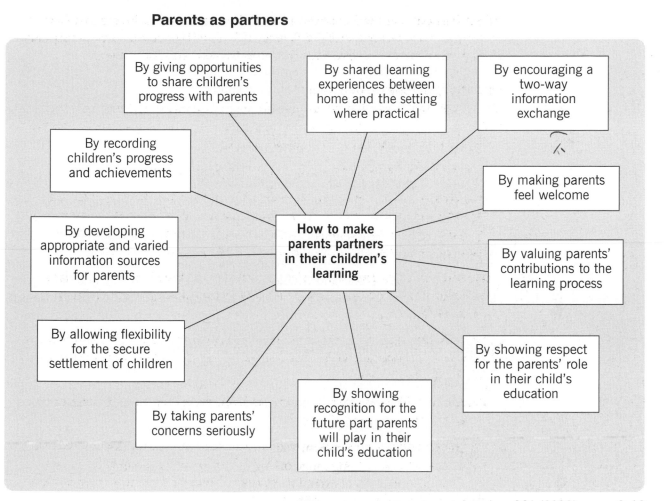

By giving opportunities to share children's progress with parents

By shared learning experiences between home and the setting where practical

By encouraging a two-way information exchange

By recording children's progress and achievements

By making parents feel welcome

By developing appropriate and varied information sources for parents

**How to make parents partners in their children's learning**

By valuing parents' contributions to the learning process

By allowing flexibility for the secure settlement of children

By showing respect for the parents' role in their child's education

By taking parents' concerns seriously

By showing recognition for the future part parents will play in their child's education

based on QCA (2000), pages 9–10

An effectively planned educational provision will include:
- a high quality of staffing, planning and resources
- positive relationships between adults and children
- opportunities for children to build on what they already know
- equality of opportunity regarding ethnicity, culture, religion, disability and gender
- differentiated plans to incorporate all children's developmental levels
- a balance of adult- and child-initiated activities
- adults who are able to intervene in the learning process appropriately to help extend learning.

### Children with special educational needs and disabilities
For children with special needs, individual education plans (IEPs) need to be drawn up and the focus placed on removing as many barriers as possible so the child can access the mainstream curriculum. Early years settings will either have, or be linked to, a special needs co-ordinator (SENCO) who will oversee the IEPs and support children and their families, and will usually also have a link with an educational psychologist and other members of the multi-disciplinary education and health care teams.

IEPs should:
- assess the level of a child's difficulty
- give an overview of what intervention is needed
- outline what SEN provision is required
- identify who is currently supporting the child
- suggest time scales and review dates.

There is a five-stage Code of Practice for special needs:
- Stage 1: A concern is expressed by parent, teacher or health professional
- Stage 2: Involvement of a SENCO and the development of an IEP
- Stage 3: Outside help from an educational psychologist is required
- Stage 4: A detailed assessment by the local authority in conjunction with parents and school
- Stage 5: A binding document (the statement) setting out the agreed provision for the child by the local authority.

 DfEE (1994) gives a clear and detailed explanation of the whole Code of Practice. It should be noted, however, that the Code of Practice is currently being reviewed and changes to the assessment process may be put into practice in the near future.

### Children with English as an additional language

The curriculum of any setting will need to plan for supporting a child in developing their English and, where possible, enabling the child to use their home language too. This should help both languages to develop alongside each other.

 Siraj-Blatchford and Clarke (2000) is an excellent source of reference – see *Bibliography and suggested further reading*, page 331.

---

**Professional Practice**    Remember that children learning a new language will usually understand a considerable amount of what they hear before they attempt to use the new language vocally. You will need to give continued emphasis to supporting spoken language, with visual cues such as pictures, signs and artefacts.

---

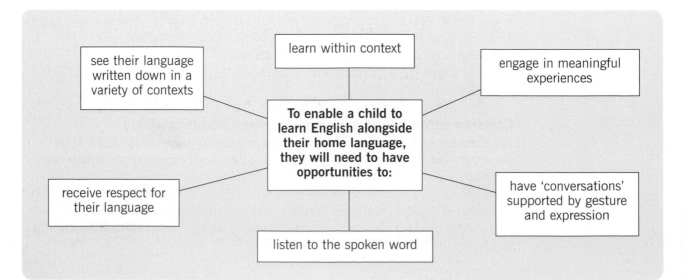

see their language written down in a variety of contexts

learn within context

engage in meaningful experiences

**To enable a child to learn English alongside their home language, they will need to have opportunities to:**

receive respect for their language

have 'conversations' supported by gesture and expression

listen to the spoken word

# The National Curriculum

The National Curriculum is a mandatory curriculum for all schools within the maintained sector. Privately-funded schools are not obliged to follow the same guidelines, but in practice many of them do.

The National Curriculum is divided into key stages.

### National Curriculum key stages

| Key stage | Age | Year groups |
|-----------|-----|-------------|
| Key Stage 1 (KS1) | 5–7 years | 1–2 |
| Key Stage 2 (KS2) | 7–11 years | 3–6 |
| Key Stage 3 (KS3) | 11–14 years | 7–9 |
| Key Stage 4 (KS4) | 14–16 years | 10–11 |

The key stage that follows on from the Foundation Stage is Key Stage 1. You will work with children following this stage during placement experience in a Year 1 or Year 2 class.

At the end of each key stage there are a number of tests known as **Standard Attainment Tasks (SATs)**, which all children must complete. The purpose of SATS is to monitor each individual child's performance as they progress through school.

### Key Stage 1

Key Stage 1 includes:
- English
- Mathematics
- Science
- Technology (Design and Technology and Information Technology)
- History
- Geography
- Art
- Music
- Physical Education.

The attainment targets at the end of Key Stage 1 are based around the following areas of learning:
- English
  - Speaking and listening
  - Reading
  - Writing
- Mathematics
  - Using and Applying Mathematics
  - Number and Algebra
  - Shape, Space and Measure
  - Handling Data

- Science
  - Experimental and Investigative Science
  - Life Processes and Living Things
  - Materials and their Properties
  - Physical Processes
- Design and Technology
  - Designing
  - Making
- Art
  - Investigating and Making
  - Knowledge and Understanding
- Music
  - Performing and Composing
  - Listening and Appraising.

 For each of the other subjects, teachers make a decision about the level attained, based on the range of descriptions set out for each key stage level. Details of these can be found in DfEE (1995) – see *Bibliography and suggested further reading*, page 331.

**Case Study** | *Acorn Group*
The Acorn group in Class 1 are growing beans in jars. Each child has their own bean.

1 Which elements of the National Curriculum could you link to this activity?
2 How could the activity be extended further?

**Professional Practice** | Most activities at both Foundation Stage and Key Stage 1 are cross-curricular, covering a range of learning intentions.

## Curriculum models outside mainstream provision

Approaches to education outside the main curricula are more often found in privately-funded settings, but elements of these approaches may be incorporated into the curriculum and planning of maintained settings.

### Highscope

The **Highscope** curriculum encourages children to take responsibility for their own learning, making choices, planning their activities and reviewing them collectively at a set point. Highscope is associated with the statement **plan, do and review**.

### Plan

Children decide, often with an adult, what they will do during the session. There are different ways in which a child can relay their plans to others in their group, through words, actions or simple gestures. The session often starts with a circle time, in which the whole group sits together, perhaps for weather-board or news time. They then divide into smaller groups for planning. In many settings, as a student you would simply observe at this stage until the student supervisor is confident that you are able to support the planning process appropriately.

### Do

Children select, use and put away their planned activities during the main 'work' time. The equipment is made easily accessible to the children with clear visual labels to enable them to identify and select for themselves. As independent learning is encouraged, the children develop responsibility and a sense of being part of the setting. Selecting and replacing resources becomes part of each day, adding to their social skills development.

The children make choices, exploring their environment freely and initiating ideas based on their interests and prior experiences. The adult role is to support those choices by providing an appropriate overall framework. As an adult working within this curriculum, you will encourage children to question, and to find the answers for themselves wherever possible. The Highscope curriculum requires a well-balanced level of child–adult interaction and many decisions are left to the child which you may at first find strange. The joint child–adult-led interactions, in which you join the child at their level, is an important aspect of the Highscope philosophy. Use of observation skills will enable you to identify when it is appropriate to involve yourself in a child's activity, to extend their learning, and when to hold back.

---

**Professional Practice** — It is important that you ask for advice and guidance when you are unsure. You will not be expected to know everything and will be respected for your honesty.

---

### Review

At the end of the Highscope session, each child describes what they have been doing, often displaying the creative outcomes. This time of recall and reflection is led by an adult, usually in a small group setting.

The Highscope curriculum promotes active learning, and adults assist and encourage the children, but do not direct them. Each adult responsible for a group of children (key worker) keeps a written record of individual children's plans. This helps identify aspects of the setting that the child does not particularly enjoy and areas of special interest to them.

The plan, do, review approach is regularly incorporated into non-Highscope schools and nurseries.

## Montessori

The Montessori philosophy initiated the need for child-sized equipment, including display tables and storage facilities, to allow children to select and return their chosen activities, linking with the Highscope approach too. Montessori settings also favour rugs, mats and cushions for the children to use at floor level and children will often be seen selecting an activity, for example a grading board, and taking it to a mat (carpet square) to explore it. Each activity is to be used for its intended purpose, and imaginative play is not actively encouraged in most settings.

The adult role within a Montessori setting is to observe and guide, using your understanding of a child's needs to indicate when adult intervention is needed.

Montessori produced a range of materials to encourage dexterity. They are still used in Montessori settings today, although the overall curriculum is generally more varied.

### Steiner

The Steiner setting places a great emphasis on imaginative play and creativity. There are many opportunities for self-expression through music, dance, drama and art. A range of objects are provided to encourage imagination, with a marked lack of commercially-produced artefacts.

The role of the adult is to guide and supply materials to enhance the child's creativity. Play is child-initiated and adults join them as appropriate.

| **Professional Practice** | Although the Steiner philosophy attracts a significant following, there are limited opportunities for placement experience. If you are fortunate to gain a place in a Steiner setting, remember to share your experience with others, enhancing their learning too. |
| --- | --- |

## The role of play in the development of early learning

Janet Moyles (1989) states that play should be 'viewed as a process'. She makes reference to Bruner who wrote:

> 'For the main characteristic of play – whether of child or adult – is not its content but its mode. Play is an approach to action, not a form of activity.'

Moyles introduced the idea of us 'playing at our work' and 'working at our play'. If as adults we enjoy our work and it is stimulating, interactive and challenging, it is likely to be fulfilling the same desires and needs as our leisure activities, i.e. our play! Similarly, children can often be seen concentrating hard on what they are doing, with their tongue sticking out as they focus their attention. They are indeed 'working' at their play. When as an adult, we buy a new 'toy', for example a camcorder or music system, we experiment with it, 'testing it out', seeing how it works and discovering its limitations. Basically we are playing with it, learning about it in much the same way as children experiment and learn through their play.

Children can often be seen concentrating hard on what they are doing

# Definitions of play

There are many different types of play. They can broadly be described as:

- **free-flow play**
- **structured play**
- **spontaneous play**.

Understanding what each type of play involves is important.

**Activity**

1  What do the terms 'free-flow', 'structured' and 'spontaneous' mean to you? Think where else you have heard them. What do you associate them with?
2  What do you remember about play in your childhood?
   a)  Did you explore outdoors? Or were you encouraged to stay near to home?
   b)  Were you provided with lots of commercial resources, or did you make your own?
   c)  Which aspects of play are most memorable for you? Why is this, do you think?
   d)  When you have read the following summaries of the three main types of play consider which mostly applied to your childhood experiences.

## Free-flow play

Free-flow play is described by Tina Bruce (1991) as the only true concept of play. It is often referred to as imaginative, pretend or ludic play – it allows children to learn by discovery.

> 'Games help children to understand external pressures and constraints; free-flow play helps children to see the function of rules for themselves.'
>
> Bruce (1991)

Bruce illustrates her definition of free-flow play as follows:

$$\text{Free-flow play} \; = \; \begin{array}{l} \text{Wallowing in ideas,} \\ \text{feelings and} \\ \text{relationships} \end{array} \; + \; \begin{array}{l} \text{Application of competence} \\ \text{and technical prowess that} \\ \text{has already been developed} \end{array}$$

Tina Bruce's twelve features of free-flow play are summarised as follows:

- It is an active process without a product.
- It is intrinsically motivated.
- There is no external pressure to conform.
- It is about lifting the 'players' to their highest levels of functioning, involving creativity and imagination.
- It involves reflection, the wallowing in ideas.
- It actively uses previous firsthand experiences.
- It is sustained and helps us to function ahead of our real-life ability levels.
- It allows control, using competence previously attained.
- It can be initiated by child or adult, but adults need to be aware of not imposing rules, or directing activity.
- It can be a solitary experience.
- It can be in partnership with others.
- It brings together what we learn, feel and understand.

Tina Bruce, *Time to Play in Early Childhood Education* (1991), Hodder & Stoughton Ltd; reprinted by permission of Hodder & Stoughton Educational

Bruce (1991) offers a detailed and fascinating explanation of play, bringing together the thinking of many theorists and educationists – see *Bibliography and suggested further reading*, page 331.

| **Professional Practice** | Think where you have identified the greatest amount of free-flow play occurring. What was special about the play? |
|---|---|

### Structured play

Structured play is planned and led by an adult, who may or may not work alongside the child during the activity. Most people agree that children benefit from a degree of structure, and every setting has its constraints regarding time, space and staffing which leads to the need to 'frame' the daily routine. This should not, however, lead to lack of flexibility and lack of opportunity for play to flow. A balance needs to be achieved with the structured introduction to a new experience leading the child to further (free play) exploration of the material or subject.

BACK to Chapter 1, page 35.

| **Professional Practice** | Give an example of a structured play activity. |
|---|---|

*Remember !* If children are continually led by an adult, they are likely to be less involved in the process of their play, and some opportunities for learning will be missed.

### Spontaneous play

Spontaneous play allows children to develop their play ideas for themselves, with the adult providing a range of resources and materials. Children learn successfully if they are allowed to 'seize the moment' and this is where adult flexibility is vital. The child who unexpectedly brings a jar of snails into the nursery offers the opportunity for an 'on the spot' discussion of minibeasts, life forms, houses, bodily needs (food, water, and so on). The interest of the children will be captured by the excitement of the snails' arrival, and therefore opportunities for learning are high. Similarly, the child who makes a pretend kite (perhaps triggered by observation of kites elsewhere) and runs around the garden trying to fly it, will be learning the basis of aerodynamics, as well as having fun and fulfilling a spontaneous need to try something new.

### Combining types of play

Janet Moyles developed the play spiral (see opposite). It encorporates free play with directed (structured) play, showing how the child moves in and out of each mode as their learning develops, leading to the development (accretion) of knowledge, understanding and new skills. Once you have studied and understood the play spiral, try to think of a child in your placement who you have specifically noticed developing in this way.

Moyles' play spiral

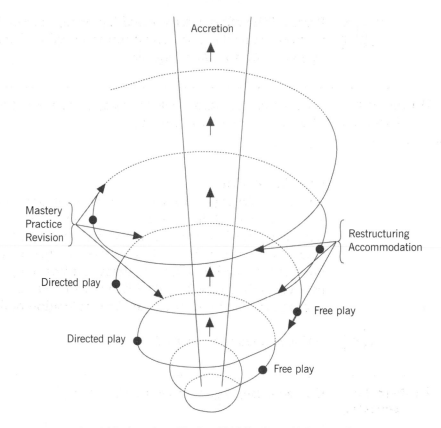

Janet Moyles, *Just Playing* (1989), Open University Press, page 16

---

**Activity**

Think back to the activity on page 317.
a) Was your childhood play mostly free-flow play, structured play or spontaneous play?
b) What determined the mode of play you mostly experienced?

---

**Professional Practice**  Children learn through stimulus. They need a range of activities that will keep their interest and enhance their experience.

---

There is a fourth type of play – **therapeutic play** or play therapy, which helps children who are troubled in some way to begin to explore their troubles and work through them. It is also a medium of play used in preparing children for health care interventions and procedures, and with children who have a life-limiting illness who may need to act out negative emotions, fear or stress.

BACK to Chapter 6, page 224, for information on play therapy.

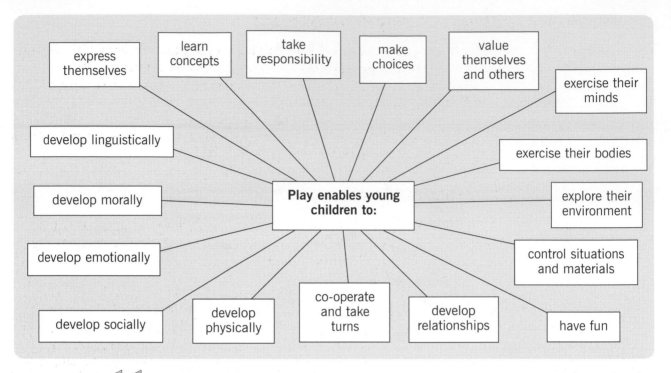

express themselves

learn concepts

take responsibility

make choices

value themselves and others

exercise their minds

develop linguistically

exercise their bodies

develop morally

**Play enables young children to:**

explore their environment

develop emotionally

control situations and materials

develop socially

develop physically

co-operate and take turns

develop relationships

have fun

BACK to Chapter 1, page 37, to remind yourself of the Rumbold Report, 1990. Link what you read there to the spidergram above. How well does it compare?

---

**Activity**

Consider each of the three broad categories of play in conjunction with the range of practical activities listed below. How do they each link to the spidergram above? For example, which of the practical activities do you think would enable children to develop relationships? Learn concepts? Exercise their bodies, and so on?

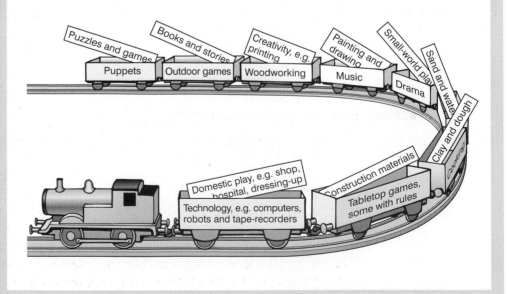

Puzzles and games — Puppets
Books and stories — Outdoor games
Creativity, e.g. printing — Woodworking
Painting and drawing — Music
Small-world play — Drama
Sand and water
Clay and dough
Cooking
Construction materials — Tabletop games, some with rules
Domestic play, e.g. shop, hospital, dressing-up
Technology, e.g. computers, robots and tape-recorders

## Stages of play development

Play develops in stages, as children develop socially from **solitary play** (playing alone), to **parallel play** (alongside other children), to **associative play** (watching and copying other children) and finally to **co-operative play** (playing with other children).

▶▶  FORWARD to Chapter 9, page 373, where play development is discussed in detail as part of social development.

## The role of the adult

The spidergram below shows how adults support learning through play. You will find it helpful to refer back to this as you read through the section on *Planning activities to support early learning*, page 327.

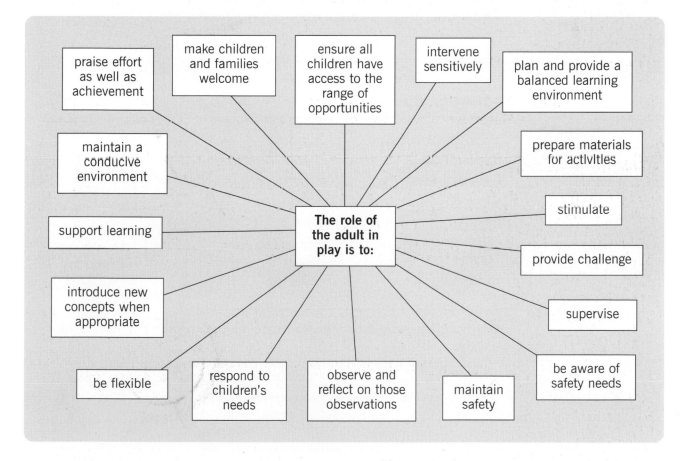

**Professional Practice**    A planned setting is usually a successful setting in which the effective deployment of adults impacts positively on the development of the children. Whatever the approach to play, directed or non-directed, there is always a need for careful adult supervision and childcare workers are responsible for the safety of all situations, including the range of equipment and resources.

BACK to Chapter 5 and Chapter 1, page 32.

> *Remember!* Safety awareness involves assessing the suitability of resources for the age groups present, removing small articles from the environment of the youngest children and giving guidance on safe use of utensils and materials to all children.

### Adult–child relationships

The relationship between adult and child impacts on the overall experience for the child. As you develop professionally, you need to consider how you build your relationships with the children in your care.

**Activity**

The role of the adult is to facilitate learning. Consider the analogies (examples with similarities) of adult–child relationships in the table below.

| Adult role | Child role |
| --- | --- |
| Conductor | Orchestra |
| Chef | Ingredients |
| Sales representative | Customer |
| Police officer | Citizen |
| Sergeant Major | Soldier |
| Gardener | Flower |
| Parent | Child |
| Potter | Clay |
| Teacher | Student |
| Performer | Audience |

a) Which analogies represent the ideal relationships between early years worker and child?

b) Which represent relationships you have experienced in settings known to you?

c) Which link to the transmission, *laissez-faire* or social constructivist models?

d) Which most closely represent your own relationships?

**Professional Practice**
- What have you learned about yourself as a facilitator of children's learning from the activity above?
- How will it affect your future professional practice?

**Test Yourself**

1 Which curriculum model includes the plan, do and review process?
2 What is an IEP?
3 How would you describe free-flow play?
4 What does Moyles' play spiral illustrate?
5 In what ways can an adult impact on a child's learning?

# Identifying and promoting learning opportunities

## Characteristics of the early years curriculum

Every adult is a potential human resource, extending learning and developing language by contributing to a child's play. Any curriculum for early years needs to be broad and balanced, involving a range of people, situations, values and resources. Learning takes place at all times, in all situations, and is enhanced by visits to places of interest and by the inclusion of visitors to the setting from the wider community.

## Curriculum provision

Providing appropriate resources to support the learning environment includes planning, storage and organisation of the resources, as well as the actual resources themselves. Each area of learning can be incorporated within most activities in some way or other. A range of these activities are explored here, linked to:
• Personal, social and emotional development
• Communication, language and literacy
• Mathematical development
• Knowledge and understanding of the world
• Physical development.
• Creative development

**Activity**

a) Which areas of learning are supported by the activities listed in the table on page 324? Copy and complete the table.
b) In what way do the activities support a child's learning?
c) Return to this table once you have read the whole chapter and see what else you might add.

| Activity | Personal, social and emotional development | Communication, language and literacy | Mathematical development | Knowledge and understanding of the world | Physical development | Creative development |
|---|---|---|---|---|---|---|
| Settling into a group | | | | | | |
| Sand and water play | | | | | | |
| Shape sorting | | | | | | |
| Puzzles | | | | | | |
| Cooking | | | | | | |
| Role play and dressing-up | | | | | | |
| Small world play | | | | | | |
| Woodwork | | | | | | |
| Sorting and classifying | | | | | | |
| Sequencing games | | | | | | |
| Handwashing and toileting | | | | | | |
| Interest tables | | | | | | |
| Music and movement | | | | | | |
| Book corner | | | | | | |
| One-to-one stories | | | | | | |
| Group storytime | | | | | | |
| Drawing and colouring | | | | | | |
| Clay and dough | | | | | | |
| Climbing frames and large equipment | | | | | | |
| Bikes and sit-ons | | | | | | |
| Using scissors | | | | | | |
| Helping to clear up | | | | | | |
| Construction resources – small-scale | | | | | | |
| Construction resources – large-scale | | | | | | |
| Turn-taking games | | | | | | |
| Board games | | | | | | |
| Circle time | | | | | | |

NB This is not an exhaustive list.

Examples of the learning outcomes have already been given, but QCA (2000) provides a full details of the goals for each area of learning – see *Bibliography and suggested further reading*, page 331

### Storage of resources

Good storage methods enable easy access to resources and keep them in good condition. A separate area is needed for 'messy' resources, such as paint, glue, clay, collage items and junk modelling boxes. Clay needs to be kept slightly moist, otherwise small hands will not be able to manipulate it. Paint pots and spatulas need to be washed regularly and brushes need thorough cleaning to keep the bristles soft and pliable. Glue lids need to be secured to prevent a skin forming.

Ideally surplus resources should be kept in a trolley or cupboard (most are now mobile). Items such as scissors are best kept in designated holders and paper is ideally stored in a purposely-designed storage unit. Keeping paper flat will keep it free of tears and easier to handle.

A pyramid for storing paper

You need to consider how you will store paintings and models. An old clothes horse can be useful, but a special drying frame is even better, with a shelf or spare surface area for models.

A drying rack for paintings

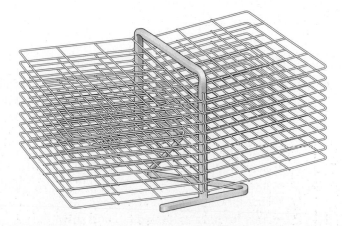

Storage boxes for items such as dressing-up clothes, construction kits and puppets can be purchased quite cheaply and encourage children to take responsibility for clearing away.

A multitude of small items can be stored in trays and placed in cupboards and again specially-designed tray storage units can be purchased.

A tray storage unit

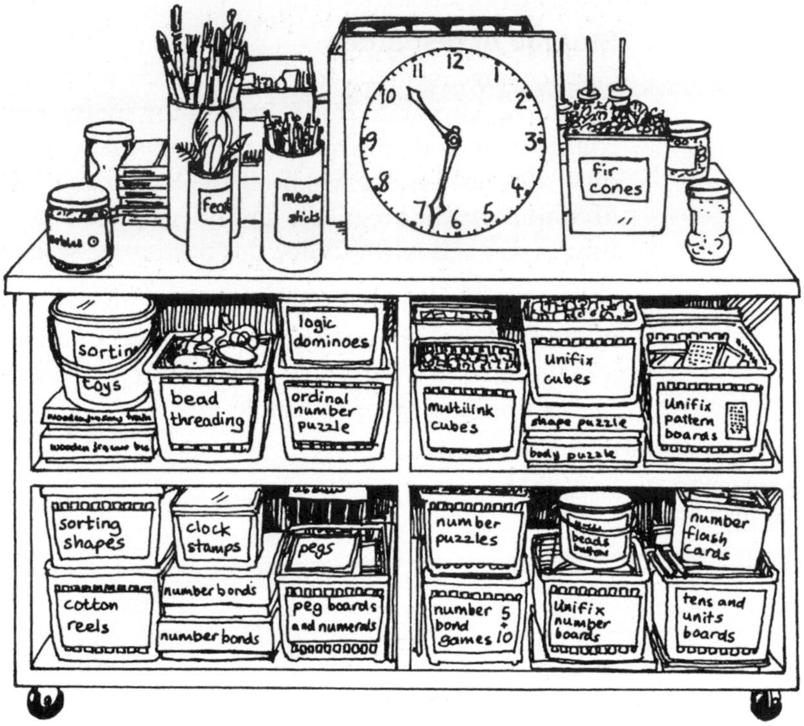

## Organisation of resources

Organising where resources and activities are placed within the setting needs careful consideration, including:

- the amount of space needed for the activity
- the number of children likely to use the activity at any one time
- the importance of a quiet area for the activity
- whether handwashing facilities are needed nearby
- the level of adult involvement needed (affecting deployment of staff)
- any level of interruption that could be posed to the activity by doorways, access points, etc.

**Case Study**

*Fountain Park Nursery*

Fountain Park Nursery is shortly opening in its new premises. The staff have each been asked to plan where they would position the range of everyday activities. They have been given a copy of the blank floor plan shown opposite and the following list of what to include:

- water tray
- sand tray
- indoor slide
- mat for cars, farm, and so on
- area for puzzles, threading, and so on
- book corner
- painting easels

- a creative activity
- drawing and writing
- dough (or clay)
- role-play area with dressing-up clothes
- large-scale construction
- small-scale construction
- a topic table.

Not all the activities need to be available all of the time, but each are offered in some way every day.

1 How would you set out the nursery if you were asked?
2 What would determine your decisions?
3 Which areas would you consider needed to be static, and why?
4 Which areas would you consider could be moved around?

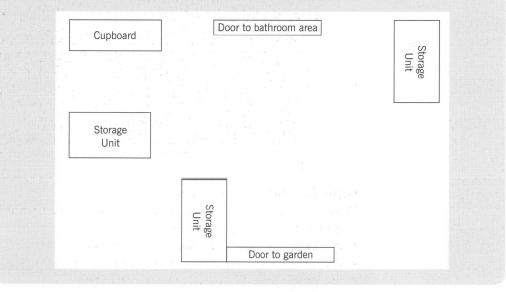

## Planning activities to support early learning

### The Early Learning Goals for personal, social and emotional development

The Early Learning Goals for personal, social and emotional development are as follows.

'By the end of the Foundation Stage, most children will:
- continue to be interested, excited and motivated to learn;
- be confident to try new activities, initiate ideas and speak in a familiar group;
- maintain attention, concentrate, and sit quietly when appropriate;
- have a developing awareness of their own needs, views and feelings and be sensitive to the needs, views and feelings of others;
- have a developing respect for their own cultures and beliefs and those of other people;
- respond to significant experiences, showing a range of feelings when appropriate;

- form good relationships with adults and peers;
- work as part of a group or class, taking turns and sharing fairly, understanding that there need to be agreed values and codes of behaviour for groups of people, including adults and children, to work together harmoniously;
- understand what is right, what is wrong, and why;
- dress and undress independently and manage their own personal hygiene;
- select and use activities and resources independently;
- consider the consequences of their words and actions for themselves and others;
- understand that people have different needs, views, cultures and beliefs, which need to be treated with respect;
- understand that they can expect others to treat their needs, views, cultures and beliefs with respect.'

from QCA (2000)

In order to foster these goals, children need opportunities to work both alone and in groups of different sizes. They need to develop independence and be able to both lead and follow.

## Case Studies

### Maya

Maya brought a jar of caterpillars into the nursery. Her key worker, Savita, showed immediate interest and placed them on a table to display them. Maya and the other children went into the nursery garden to find 'treats' for them. They returned with some dandelions, daisies, grass and a few leaves. Savita helped them to open the jar and to gently add a selection from the garden. She talked to the children about the caterpillars asking Maya where she had found them. As a group, they explored the book corner to find information on caterpillars, which they looked at together. Later in the day, Maya let the caterpillars go in the shrubbery. When she was collected, she gave an excited account to her mother of what she had done.

1 Which Early Learning Goals for personal, social and emotional development were supported here?
2 How well do you think Savita responded to the arrival of the caterpillars?
3 Would you have done anything else?

### Fircone Class

Fircone Class are cooking with a parent, Mrs Behera. They are making chapattis, and have each put on an apron and a cook's hat. Kamala's mother talks to the children about the process of kneading and flattening the dough and the importance of washing their hands. Kamala shows how she has brought chapattis in her lunch box, along with some dahl and fruit. Rajan says that he too brings chapattis for lunch. All the children are keen to try the chapattis when they are ready. They compare them to different types of bread (focaccia, rye bread, and so on), discussing the differences in texture and identifying the cultural origin of each food.

1 Which Early Learning Goals for personal, social and emotional development are supported here?
2 What is the particular significance of Mrs Behera leading the cooking activity?
3 How can the activity be extended?

**Professional Practice**     Refer to a copy of the Early Learning Goals in your college library and identify which goals from the other areas of learning were also being supported in the case studies above.

### The Early Learning Goals for mathematical development

The Early Learning Goals for mathematical development are as follows.

'By the end of the foundation stage, most children will be able to:
- say and use number names in order in familiar contexts;
- count reliably up to 10 everyday objects;
- recognise numerals 1 to 9;
- use language such as 'more' or 'less, 'greater' or 'smaller', 'heavier' or 'lighter' to compare two numbers or quantities;
- in practical activities and discussion begin to use the vocabulary involved in adding and subtracting;
- find one more or one less than a number from 1 to 10;
- begin to relate addition to combining two groups of objects, and subtraction to 'taking away';
- talk about, recognise and recreate simple patterns;
- use language such as 'circle' or 'bigger' to describe the shape and size of solids and flat shapes;
- use everyday words to describe position;
- use developing mathematical ideas and methods to solve practical problems.'

from QCA (2000)

**Case Study**     *Sean and Callum*

Sean and Callum are playing at the water tray with a range of graded containers. They are filling and pouring from one side of the tray to the other, and also filling up a large bucket.

1 Which Early Learning Goals for mathematical development are supported here?
2 How can an adult enhance the learning still further?
3 What Early Learning Goals for personal, social and emotional development are also supported?

**Professional Practice**     Refer to a copy of the Early Learning Goals in your college library and identify which goals from the other areas of learning were being supported in the case study above.

# Planning, implementing and evaluating curriculum plans

**Activity**

Working with a partner, ask two different settings for samples of their curriculum plans. One should be a Reception class and the other a nursery. Study the plans and answer the following questions.

a) How easy is it to follow the plans?
b) Can you identify the curriculum areas to be covered in the plans?
c) How are the staff planning to identify the learning outcomes?
d) What key concepts can you identify?
e) Where is adult support intended?
f) How do the adults intend to support children's specific needs?
g) How are the content and style of the plans different?
h) How are the content and style of the plans similar?
i) Which style of planning do you feel works best for you?
j) Why is this, do you think?

This activity should help you to start evaluating the clarity of written plans.

**Test Yourself**

1  What are the six areas of learning in the Foundation Stage Curriculum?
2  Give examples of what is considered to be suitable storage for early years resources.
3  What needs to be taken into account when organising the positioning of resources and activities?
4  Give at least three examples of activities to promote personal, social and emotional development.
5  Give at least three examples of activities to promote mathematical development.
6  What is important about written curriculum plans?

## Key terms

You should now understand the following words and phrases. If you do not, read through the chapter again and review them.

| | |
|---|---|
| accommodation | exploratory play |
| assimilation | Foundation Stage Curriculum |
| associative play | freeplay |
| burn-out | Highscope |
| co-operative play | hot-housing |
| cognitive development | iconic thinking |
| empiricists | *laissez-faire* model |
| enactive thinking | Montessori philosophy |

| | |
|---|---|
| National Curriculum | spontaneous play |
| nativists | stages of play |
| nature–nurture debate | Standard Attainment Tasks (SATs) |
| operant conditioning | Steiner philosophy |
| parallel play | structured play |
| plan, do, review | symbolic play |
| scaffolding | symbolic thinking |
| schema | theories |
| social constructivist model | therapeutic play |
| social constructivist play | transmission model |
| solitary play | zone of proximal development (ZPD) |

## Bibliography and suggested further reading

Bruce, T. (1991) *Time to Play in Early Childhood Education*, Hodder & Stoughton, London

Department for Education and Employment (DfEE) (1994) *Code of Practice on the Identification and Assessment of Special Educational Needs*, HMSO, London

DfEE (1995) *Key Stages 1 and 2 of the National Curriculum*, HMSO, London

Duffy, B. (1998) *Supporting Creativity and Imagination in the Early Years*, Open University Press, Milton Keynes

Hobart, C. and Frankel, J. (1999) *A Practical Guide to Activities for Young Children*, 2nd edition, Nelson Thornes, Cheltenham

Hurst, V. and Joseph, J. (1998) *Supporting Early Learning: The Way Forward*, Open University Press, Milton Keynes

Lindon, J. (2001) *Understanding Children's Play*, Nelson Thornes, Cheltenham

Makins, V. (1997) *not ___ just a nursery: Multi-agency Early Years Centres in Action*, National Children's Bureau

Moyles, J. (1989) *Just Playing? The Role and Status of Play in Early Childhood Education*, Open University Press, Milton Keynes

Moyles, J. (ed.) (1994) *The Excellence of Play*, Open University Press, Milton Keynes

Mukherji, P. and O'Dea, T. (2000) *Understanding Children's Language and Literacy*, Nelson Thornes, Cheltenham

Neaum, S. and Tallack, J. (2000) *Good Practice in Implementing the Pre-School Curriculum*, 2nd edition, Nelson Thornes Cheltenham

Pound, L. (1999) *Supporting Mathematical Development in the Early Years*, Open University Press, Milton Keynes

Qualifications and Curriculum Authority (QCA) (2000) *Early Learning Goals*, DfEE, London

Siraj-Blatchford, I. and Clarke, P. (2000) *Supporting Identity, Diversity and Language in Early Years*, Open University Press, Milton Keynes

Siraj-Blatchford, I. and Macleod-Brudenell, L. (1999) *Supporting Science, Design and Technology in the Early Years*, Open University Press, Milton Keynes

Whitehead, M. (1999) *Supporting Language and Literacy in the Early Years*, Open University Press, Milton Keynes

# 9 Human growth and development

## Introduction

The study of growth and development involves looking at the processes and sequences of change within a human life, and the influences upon them.

- **Growth** can be most easily defined by changes in measurement such as height, weight, skeletal frame, or size of feet, all of which can be represented visually, through graphs and tables.

- **Development** is more about increased abilities and the changes that occur within the body's whole structure, for example, the closing of the fontanelles in an infant, or the ossification of the skeleton (how the cartilage in a newborn infant is gradually replaced by bone). Different organs and tissues within the body have their own pattern and rate of development and these processes trigger notable changes throughout the life-span, such as the onset of menstruation in girls, sperm production in boys, the development of secondary sexual characteristics of both girls and boys during puberty and, in later life, physical events such as the menopause in women.

As you read this chapter, you will develop your understanding of what are considered to be the 'normal' expectations of a child's development. This understanding is important as it is a 'bench mark' to guide you when studying children – it will enable you to decide whether an individual child's development is delayed or impaired. The expectations are often referred to as the **developmental norms** or **normative development**. It should be noted, however, that these 'norms' do not accurately reflect all racial and cultural differences. They may also cause concern amongst parents if their child doesn't reach the same milestones as other children of the same age at a similar time. Part of your role as an early years professional will be to reassure concerned parents that 'benchmarks' are simply a guide and that all children develop at their own pace.

An awareness of cultural differences in both upbringing and parental expectations is important. This will add to your overall understanding of the differing aspects of development (social, cognitive, physical, language and emotional) and help you understand how development needs to be considered within context. In working with young children and their families, it is also important that you know how to observe children, evaluate those observations and assess children's development accordingly. This chapter will offer the information and guidance to achieve this.

The field of early years predominantly involves working with children under the age of eight. The long-term impact of experience on a child's development is very relevant, and the adult person is shaped through their childhood experience. It is therefore both interesting and necessary to understand the developmental stages and changes that take place throughout the average human life-span, and also how they are measured. Each of these aspects is discussed in some depth in this chapter.

## Definition of terms

A range of terms are used in the context of development. This chapter will help you understand:
• growth
• development
• rate
• sequence
• delay.

Return to this list once you have finished reading the chapter and note how far your understanding has developed.

## The human life-span

During an average life-span we each move through a range of developmental stages. There are a number of different ways to split the life-span into stages, which you will discover if you read other texts. In this book they are categorised as follows:
• the pre-natal stage – from conception to birth
• the neonatal stage – from birth to one month
• infancy – from one month to one year
• the toddler – from one to two years
• early childhood – from two to five years
• middle childhood – from five to twelve years
• adolescence – from twelve to twenty years (with puberty being a physiological stage that can cross middle childhood and adolescence)
• young adulthood – from twenty to forty years
• middle adulthood – from forty to sixty-five years
• late adulthood – from sixty-five years onwards.

These ten stages of the life-span are summarised in this section. Each stage (except for the pre-natal stage and the neonatal stage) is categorised in terms of physical, cognitive, language, social and emotional development. A summary of the main aspects of the pre-natal stage includes issues of optimum pre-conceptual care and the effects of the environment on both maternal and foetal health. Babies and children are discussed in more detail than the other life-span stages, as these are the main focus of the BTec National in Early Years course.

This section ends with a look at the factors affecting development.

The continuum of life – from infancy to late adulthood

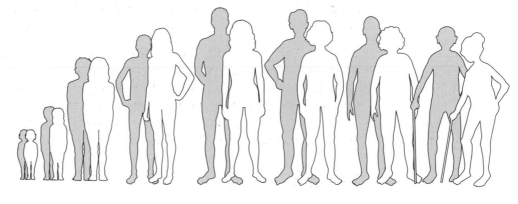

 A useful video to refer to is *The Human Body* (BBC, 1998), which was originally a television series. It offers a very accessible view of development across the whole life-span.

## The pre-natal stage: from conception to birth

### Optimum conditions for pregnancy

A woman planning to have a baby should consider the effects of her current:
* diet
* level of exercise
* smoking habits
* alcohol consumption
* use of drugs (prescribed as well as recreational)
* social life
* relationship
on a potential pregnancy.

Planning ahead can enable a woman to give up smoking or the use of drugs before conceiving, and reduce or eliminate her intake of alcohol. It can give her time to assess whether her relationship is stable, and to begin to eat a healthy diet if this is not currently the case, eliminating foods which are not considered to be completely 'safe'. If she knows she is unprotected against rubella (German measles) it is wise to be vaccinated, but she should then avoid becoming pregnant for at least three months after the vaccination.

Any woman with a long-standing medical condition or disorder should consult her doctor before planning a pregnancy to ensure that any medication she needs to take regularly will be safe for her developing child too. Her doctor may need to change her medication, either because it could harm the foetus or because it could make conception more difficult to achieve.

## Foods to avoid in pregnancy

| Food | Possible outcome |
| --- | --- |
| Soft cheeses | Listeria, which can cause miscarriage |
| Pate | Listeria, which can cause miscarriage |
| Raw eggs | Salmonella, which causes food poisoning |
| Raw meat | Toxoplasmosis, which is a mild infection in adults but can cause serious harm to an unborn child |

In recent years, it has been recommended that women take a supplement of folic acid, starting before concepton up until twelve weeks into the pregnancy, as this contributes to the optimum development of the baby's central nervous system.

## Conception

Conception takes place when the male sperm fertilises the female egg (ovum) and implants itself into the wall of the uterus. The sex cells (the sperm and the egg) have only 23 **chromosomes** each, instead of the full 46 that all other cells contain. This enables the sex of the conceived child to be determined. The male sex chromosome is denoted as Y and the female sex chromosome as X. Therefore:

XY = a boy
XX = a girl.

## Genetic effects on development

The human body is a complex machine built from its basis of 46 chromosomes. Each chromosome is made up of thousands of genes and our genetic inheritance is determined by the influences and combination of the genes present in the chromosomes of our parents. The term **genotype** is used to describe the complete genetic inheritance of one person and the term **phenotype** refers to the visible arrangement of the characteristics that the person has inherited.

Genetically-inherited disorders can be due to either *autosomal recessive*, *autosomal dominant* or *X-linked transference*. There are many other disorders that occur following conception and these are termed *congenital disorders*. Congenital disorders differ from the genetically-inherited disorders in that their origin is not from the gene bank of the parents.

### Autosomal recessive disorder

This type of disorder can occur when both parents are carriers of the defective recessive gene. There is a 1 in 4 chance of offspring being affected, and a 2 in 4 chance of them being carriers. Disorders include Batten's disease, cystic fibrosis, phenylketonuria (PKU), sickle cell anaemia and thalassaemia.

### Autosomal dominant disorder

This disorder occurs when the carrier is also affected by the disorder. If one parent is an affected carrier, there is a 2 in 4 chance of the offspring also being affected. If both parents are affected carriers, the incidence rises to a 3 in 4 chance. Disorders include Huntington's chorea, Marfan's syndrome and osteogenesis imperfecta (brittle bones).

### X-linked disorders

The X-linked disorders are carried on the X chromosomes of the mother. As the mother has two X chromosomes, the defective X acts in a recessive way in female offspring and a dominant way in males, therefore raising a higher likelihood of male offspring being affected than females. X-linked disorders include Duchenne muscular dystrophy, fragile X syndrome, haemophilia and Lowe's syndrome.

For details of each of these and many other disorders, a good source of reference is Gilbert (2000). This is an excellent publication, written in an informative and accessible way. See *Bibliography and suggested further reading*, page 429.

## Screening in pregnancy

Some conditions can be identified during pregnancy and the process for carrying out these tests is known as screening. Screening tests include the following.

### Blood tests

Routine tests on blood can screen for low iron levels, venereal disease and rubella (German measles). Low iron levels may need to be boosted by supplements, and venereal disease will be treated as appropriate. A pregnant woman who is not immune to rubella will be advised to avoid contact with the infection during the early months of her pregnancy as it can cause serious hearing and vision defects in the unborn infant.

### Ultrasound scan

An ultrasound scan is a routine procedure carried out at around 20 weeks gestation to note the development levels and measurements of the foetus. Measurements are taken of main bones such as the femur (thigh bone), the head circumference is noted and the heart chambers carefully examined. Further scans are carried out as necessary by the midwife or obstetrician.

The foetus shown on page 338 is developing within the normal range. The measurements and examinations made included the thigh bone, head circumference, spine, heart chambers, brain and amniotic fluid. The outcome showed that the foetus (now named Jasmine) had bone development and a head circumference that indicated 19+5 weeks of gestation, amniotic fluid associated with 19+1 weeks gestation. These results showed that the foetus was developing well within normal limits, as Jasmine's mother's pregnancy was at 19+3 weeks, according to her dates.

A scan of a 20-week foetus

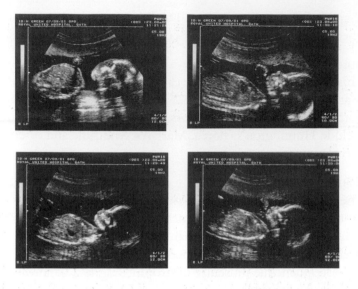

Specific tests are offered to some women depending on their circumstances, for example older women, or women with a family history of certain inherited disorders, will be offered additional screening.

### Serum alpha-fetoprotein (SAFP)

This test is used to identify the possibility of the foetus having spina bifida. It is taken at 16 weeks gestation and is offered to women who are considered to be at risk.

### The triple blood test

The triple blood test takes into consideration the woman's age and measures the levels of human chorionic gonadotrophin (HCG), serum alpha-fetoprotein (SAFP) and the placental hormones (oestriols). The combined outcome gives an assessment of the risk of the foetus having Down's syndrome. Again it is offered to women in the high-risk group, usually those over 35 years.

### Amniocentesis

This test checks for chromosome disorders, such as Down's syndrome. It usually takes place between 16 and 18 weeks gestation and it involves the sampling of the amniotic fluid from the amniotic sac whilst linked up to an ultrasound machine. The link enables the procedure to be carried out with as much visibility as possible, but there is still a slight risk of miscarriage occurring with this procedure.

### Chorionic villi sampling (CVS)

The CVS test involves the removal of a tiny amount of tissue directly from the placenta. It is usually carried out between 8 and 11 weeks gestation and it can help identify a range of inherited disorders but, as with amniocentesis, it carries a risk of miscarriage.

FORWARD to Chapter 10, page 464, for a summary of other screening programmes: neonatal, infant, childhood.

### Environmental effects on foetal development

Even before birth, an infant can be adversely affected by environmental influences, for example the effects of alcohol, smoking and both illegal and (some) prescribed drugs.

### Alcohol

**Foetal alcohol syndrome (FAS)** results from the woman continuing to consume alcohol, usually in considerable amounts, throughout her pregnancy. It was declared as the leading cause of 'mental retardation' in America by researchers in 1991. It affects the development of the infant, causing delay, deformities and learning difficulties. Pregnant women are now advised against drinking alcohol altogether, as even a moderate amount can carry a risk to the infant and judgement can become impaired by alcohol, leading to accidents.

### Smoking

Smoking (tobacco as well as illegal substances) affects birth weight due to the release of nicotine and other substances into the body. It can also lead to learning difficulties in the child. There is a suggestion that infants born to smokers are at a higher risk of being affected by sudden infant death syndrome (also known as SIDS or cot death) and of developing respiratory conditions later. Passive smoking is also thought to contribute to respiratory problems in infants and older children.

### Drugs

Any non-essential drug should be avoided during pregnancy. Illegal drugs, such as crack cocaine, cause low birth-weight and **developmental delay**. Babies who are born addicted to drugs suffer withdrawal symptoms after birth and experience great distress. Many of these babies suffer all-round development problems and some develop epilepsy.

Prescribed drugs are only issued to pregnant women with extreme care, as some have been known to cause deformity and developmental problems. The most well-known example is the effects of the drug thalidomide which was prescribed to women in the 1960s to combat severe vomiting in pregnancy. Their babies were born with severe limb deformities.

It should be remembered that cough and cold remedies are also drugs, and should be treated with the same caution as any other medication. A pregnant woman should always check their suitability with her GP or a pharmacist before taking them.

## Erikson's model of psycho-social development

As you read the following sections, you may find it useful to refer to Erikson's model of psycho-social development, noting the links between age and development stage.

| Stage | Approximate age range | Developmental stages | Personality features | Negative aspects |
|---|---|---|---|---|
| 1 | 0–1½ years | Basic trust versus mistrust | Sense of hope and safety | Insecurity, anxiety |
| 2 | 1½–3 years | Self-control versus shame and doubt | Learning self-control and independence | Dependent and unable to control events |
| 3 | 3–7 years | Initiative versus guilt | Direction and purpose in life | Lack of self-esteem |
| 4 | 6–15 years | Industry versus inferiority | Building skills competence and positive self-esteem | Feels inferior and lacks confidence |
| 5 | 13–21 years | Identity versus role confusion | A developing sense of self confidence and security | No direction in life. Negative self-esteem |
| 6 | 18–30 years | Intimacy versus isolation | Building relationships, loving commitment | Unable to build relationships |
| 7 | 20s–60s | Generativity versus stagnation | Caring for others – reaching out in the community | Introverted – looking inwards – concerned with self |
| 8 | Later life | Ego-integrity versus despair | Sense of meaning to life | Loss of sense of achievement |

## The neonatal stage: from birth to one month

### Birth

Birth is physically very demanding for both mother and child. The type of birth can affect the level of stress experienced by the infant, and therefore how well they appear immediately after delivery. All infants are assessed immediately after birth using a benchmark known as the **Apgar score**. This was devised by Dr Virginia Apgar in 1953 and assesses the vital signs of initial health, indicating whether an infant needs resuscitation or medical treatment. The five features of the assessment are scored at one minute after birth, and then again at five minutes, continuing at five minute intervals as necessary until the infant is responding satisfactorily. The higher the infant scores, the less likely it is that they will need any treatment. Most healthy infants have a score of nine at one minute. They often have discolouration of their hands and feet due to their circulation not yet functioning fully. Infants who are pre-term, of a low birth weight or who have experienced a difficult delivery are more likely to score lower – a score below five indicates a very poorly baby. Infants who fall into this category make up a large percentage of those who do not survive or those who have on-going problems.

## The Apgar score chart

| Sign | Score | | |
|---|---|---|---|
| | 0 | 1 | 2 |
| Heart rate | Absent | <100 beats per minute | >100 beats per minute |
| Respiration | Absent | Slow, irregular | Good, regular |
| Muscle tone | Limp | Some flexion of extremities | Active |
| Response to stimulus (stimulation of foot or nose) | No response | Grimace | Cry, cough |
| Colour | Blue, pale | Body oxygenated, bluish extremities | Well-oxygenated, completely pink |

A premature, difficult or traumatic birth, particularly if either mother or baby are ill and in need of special care, can have an effect on the **bonding** process, due to separation and lack of physical contact. Health professionals work hard to encourage and maintain links between mothers and their babies in these circumstances.

### What to expect to see in a neonate

At delivery babies are wet and covered to some degree in mucus, maternal blood and body fluids. Their skin colour varies due both to ethnic origin and their state of health, with black babies appearing pale at birth, as the skin pigmentation melanin does not reach its full levels until later. Most infants are delivered onto their mother's abdomen and the umbilical cord is clamped and cut shortly after birth. Depending on the type and duration of the delivery, infants vary from being alert and wide awake to drowsy and unresponsive. Medication given to the mother during labour can affect this.

### General appearance of the neonate

- At birth the infant will sleep most of the time, mostly waking for feeds and changing, and often falling asleep during these routines.
- The neonate is unable to control the head and needs to be supported during handling.

- Vernix caseosa may be present. This is a creamy white protective substance which covers the body of an infant during the latter stages of pregnancy. It is usually seen in pre-term infants, and is often present in full-term infants too. It lubricates the skin and should be left to come off on its own, rather than be washed or rubbed.

- A soft downy hair covering the infant during pregnancy may also be present. It is called lanugo and traces are often found on the back, shoulders and ears at birth.

- There are two fontanelles. The posterior fontanelle is a small triangular area near the crown which closes within a few weeks of birth. The anterior fontanelle is near the front of the head and is diamond-shaped. It closes over by eighteen months of age and can often be seen pulsating slightly. A sunken appearance can indicate insufficient fluids, whereas a bulging appearance can indicate an unacceptable level of pressure around the brain or an infection and should always be investigated.

- Newborn infants often have a flattened or misshapened head due to pressure during the passage down the birth canal, or as a result of a forceps or ventouse suction delivery. In a multiple birth, it can occur due to lack of space and it can take some weeks for the natural shape to appear.

- The most usual sign of the neonate is the umbilical 'stump'. The umbilical cord is clamped and cut at birth and the stump will be left to drop off on its own, usually between seven and ten days after birth. The stump needs to be kept dry and clean, although actual cleaning of it is not usually recommended.

- Some infants show signs of swelling or bruising, normally due to a difficult birth. This tends to disappear within a few days.

- Sticky eyes are a common occurrence in the first few days and unco-ordinated eyes are usual. All babies are born with dark eyes and permanent eye colour is not established until later.

- The posture of infants is very flexed and movements tend to be jerky. The extremities (feet and hands) are often bluish in colour due to poor circulation.

- Genitalia appear to be swollen in both boys and girls and blood loss from the vaginal area in girls is quite common. This is caused by the mother's hormones crossing the placenta.

- The breasts of both boys and girls may leak a little milk. Again, this is due to the mother's hormones crossing the placenta.

- The stools (faeces) of the neonate are a dark greenish black. This is due to it containing a tarry substance called meconium, which is very sticky. The colour and consistency change within a few days, as the mother's milk arrives.

- Spots and rashes are very common in the first few days but the infant's skin soon settles down. A particularly common type are 'milia' which are tiny white spots often known as milk spots.

- Peeling skin is quite common on the hands and feet but usually only lasts two or three days.

- Some infants suffer from **neonatal jaundice** where the skin and eyes becomes yellowish due to the infant's immature liver function and a subsequent rise in levels of bilirubin. Bilirubin is formed when red cells break down and the liver is unable to cope with its workload. It usually occurs (if it is going to) on about day three after birth. Jaundice occurring before three days old needs particular investigation as liver disease or sepsis may be present and the infant's life could be in danger. On occasions, jaundice can be a sign of galactosaemia, rubella or cytomegalovirus.

- Birthmarks:
  - Port wine marks are a permanent dark red mark, often on the face or neck. In the past they were often a permanent disfigurement, but many can now be successfully removed or reduced with laser treatment.
  - The strawberry neaveus is quite common. These are raised marks full of blood vessels that are not actually present at birth, but develop in the first few days or weeks. They usually disappear by eight years of age. The full name for this type of neavei is haemangioma.
  - Another common mark is the 'stork bite'. These are tiny red marks found on the eyelids, the top of the nose and on the back of the neck. These gradually disappear and are not usually a problem.
  - Mongolian blue spots are dark marks are found at the base of the spine on non-Caucasian infants. On occasions these marks have been wrongly attributed to physical abuse. They are usually 'mapped' by health professionals in the early weeks. Early years workers need to be aware of these marks.
  - Most people have moles, but some moles can be large and unsightly, for example CMNs (congenital melanocytic naevus). These moles get progressively darker as the infant grows but they can sometimes be successfully removed or reduced with laser treatment or plastic surgery.

### Neonatal reflexes

The primary **reflexes** can be defined as 'automatic body reactions to specific stimulation' (Bee, 1992, page 105). These reflexes include:

- blinking reflex – the neonate reacts to sudden lights, noises or movements in front of the eyes

- rooting reflex – where the neonate turns their face towards their mother to locate the breast

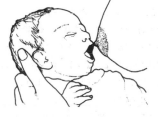

- sucking reflex – infants will usually suck a clean finger, placed gently in the mouth

- palmar grasp – where the infant holds firmly to whatever touches the palm (gently stroking the back of the hand will usually release the grasp)

- plantar reflex – touching the sole of the infant's foot with a finger will result in the flexing of the toes towards your finger
- stepping reflex – the neonate's foot responds to contact with a firm surface, resulting in a small 'step' being taken
- moro reflex – a sudden movement of the neck is interpreted by the infant as falling and they will throw out their arms with open hands and reclasp them over their chest
- startle reflex – the infant throws out their arms at a sudden noise or movement, but the fists remain clenched
- asymmetric tonic neck reflex – when the infant's head is turned to one side, they will respond by straightening the arm and leg on the same side, whilst flexing the limbs opposite.

Some reflexes stay with us for life, for example blinking, but some are lost after the first few weeks (the primitive reflexes). The presence of reflexes are an indicator of an infant's neurological well-being. As the brain gradually takes over the body's responses, these primitive reflexes disappear.

The BBC's *Human Body* video is a good source of reference – the reflexes are clearly demonstrated.

### The senses in a neonate

#### Hearing
- The hearing of infants is acute.
- They blink in response to sound.
- The neonate can discriminate the voice of their main carer almost immediately.
- Noisy objects can only roughly be located.
- Sudden noises distress the infant.
- Infants respond to soothing rhythmic sounds.

#### Vision
- Newborn infants are sensitive to both light and sound.
- Vision is diffused and limited initially to objects within about a 30 cm radius.
- Eyes initially do not work together and they often 'cross' or 'wander'.
- Eye-to-eye contact with the main carer (usually the mother) is an important means of establishing a bonding relationship.
- Infants show a preference for human faces.
- Infants will turn towards a light.

#### Touch
- Skin-to-skin contact is important to the bonding process.
- Most infants are delivered onto their mother's abdomen.
- Contact and handling soothes a distressed infant, but may be contra-indicated in

a premature baby – handling may distress them and they thrive better with minimal handling.
- The temperature control of infants is ineffective.

### Smell
- Infants can identify their mothers by smell.
- Research has shown that infants can distinguish their mother's milk on a breast pad.

### Posture and motor skills

Immediately after birth, many infants naturally curl into the foetal position with their head to one side. Their limbs are kept partly flexed and are hypertonic (have tension) and they tend to display jerking movements. The head and neck are hypotonic (weak) and there is no head control, so full support of the head and neck area is needed whenever the infant is handled.

| **Professional Practice** | Research outcomes recommend that infants are always placed on their back to sleep to minimise the risk of sudden infant death. |
| --- | --- |

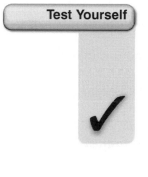

**Test Yourself**

1 Describe at least three primitive reflexes.
2 What is vernix caseosa?
3 What reasons might there be for neonatal jaundice?
4 What does the Apgar score measure?
5 What can be the effects of a mother's hormones crossing the placenta?
6 Which birthmark is only found on dark-skinned infants?
7 Which fontanelle closes by eighteen months of age?
8 Why are black infants usually pale at birth?

## Infancy: one month to one year

### Physical development (gross motor)
- Movements remain jerky.
- Head lag gradually decreases, and head control is usually good by five months.
- Rolling over is first seen between four and six months (from back to side), and then from front to back by about eight months.
- Reaching for objects begins at about four months with the transference of toys from hand to hand from about seven months.
- At four months the infant discovers their own feet and manages to sit with support.
- Sitting alone commences at about seven to eight months, with greater balance gradually developing.
- Crawling can start from six months (commando crawling) and traditional crawling from about eight months. Some infants bear-walk or bottom-shuffle.
- Some infants miss out the crawling stage, and move straight to pulling themselves up on furniture at around eight to ten months.
- Standing alone can occur any time from ten months, but is more usual at around twelve months, when generally balance is more established.
- Walking is normally achieved between twelve and sixteen months.

### Physical development (fine motor)

- Hand and finger movements gradually increase, from the grasping of the adult's fingers in the earliest months, through to playing with own fingers and toes, handling and then holding toys and objects from three to four months.
- Everything is explored through the mouth.
- At about seven months, the infant will try to transfer objects from one hand to the other with some sucess. Pincer grasp is emerging.
- By about ten months, pincer grasp is developed.
- The infant will pick up small objects.
- Toys are pulled towards themselves.
- Pointing and clapping are deliberate actions for most infants by ten to twelve months.
- Controlled efforts when feeding, with some successes.

### Cognitive and language development

- The infant continues to explore orally throughout most of the first year. Piaget called this the sensory motor stage.
- By about four months recognition of an approaching feed is demonstrated by excited actions and squeals.
- Language develops through cooing, gurgling, excited squealing and changing tones of their own voice.
- By five months enjoyment of own voice is obvious. Chuckles and laughs are evident.
- By about eight months the infant babbles continuously and tunefully, for example *mamamama*, *bababab*.
- By nine to ten months the infant achieves what Piaget called object permanence – they know that an object exists even if it has been covered up.
- First 'words' may be apparent by a year, usually *dada*, *mama*, *baba*.
- Understanding of simple instructions or statements begins from about nine months, and are clearly evident by 12 months.

 FORWARD to page 380 for an outline of Piaget's stages of cognitive development.

### Social and emotional development

- The first social smile is usually seen by six weeks.
- Smiling is first confined to main carers, and then in response to most contacts.
- The infant concentrates on faces of carers.
- Pleasure during handling and caring routines is seen by eight weeks.
- Expressions of pleasure are clear when gaining attention from about twelve weeks.
- Social games, involving handling and cuddles gain chuckles from four to five months onwards.
- Infants enjoy watching other infants.
- Sleep patterns begin to emerge from about four months onwards, although these will continue to change.
- From about nine or ten months the infant may become distressed when the main carer leaves them and become wary of strangers.
- Playing contentedly alone increases by one year, but the reassuring presence of an adult is still needed.

## Toddler: one to two years

### Physical development

- Standing alone is achieved but they are unable at first to sit from being in a standing position without help. They begin to let themselves down in a controlled manner from about fifteen months.
- Walking involves hands being held up for balance. The infant uses uneven steps and has difficulty in stopping when they have started.
- They can creep upstairs quite safely (not advisable without an adult supervising).
- They begin to kneel.
- By eighteen months walking should be well established, the arms are no longer needed for balance. The toddler can now back themselves into a small chair, and climb forwards into an adult chair.
- Squatting when playing is now common.
- They can usually walk upstairs holding an adult hand.
- Manipulative skills are developing. Pages of books can usually now be turned quite well, and pencils can be held in a clumsy grasp.
- By two years the child can run safely, starting and stopping at will.
- They are able to pull wheeled toys, with some understanding of direction.
- They are able to control a ball to throw forwards.
- Walking up and (usually) down stairs, holding on, two feet to a stair.
- They cannot yet kick a football without falling into it.
- They cannot usually pedal a tricycle.

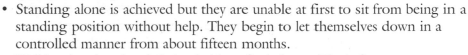

By eighteen months the toddler can climb forwards into an adult chair

The toddler at this age can usually walk upstairs holding an adult hand

### Cognitive and language development

- The toddler is very curious, investigating everything they can.
- They are interested in all that happens around them.
- A precise pincer grasp is displayed.
- They enjoy putting objects into containers.
- They take toys to mouth less often now.
- They enjoy activities that need fitting together.
- The toddler will place an object on another – two object tower.
- They know approximately six words at fifteen months and up to twenty recognisable words by eighteen months.
- By eighteen months they talk continuously as they play (mostly this is unintelligible).
- Brief imitation is seen of everyday activities, for example the feeding of a doll.
- They are contented to play alone.

**347**

- By two years more than fifty words are clearly recognisable.
- They talk to themselves in long monologues, much is incomprehensible to others.
- They can put two or more words together, for example *daddy gone*.
- They refer to themselves by name, for example *Danny shoes*.
- Echolalia is almost constant (repeating the last word they hear).
- They verbalise their needs, for example drinks, toilet, food.
- Simple role play is demonstrated.
- They can build six to eight objects into a tower.
- They can follow simple instructions, for example *Fetch your shoes please*.
- They can succeed with simple jigsaw puzzles.
- Vertical and horizontal lines are drawn.

### Social and emotional development

- By about fifteen months they will indicate a wet or soiled nappy.
- They co-operate (help) with dressing.
- They are dependent on an adult's presence.
- Frustration leads to toys being discarded in anger.
- By eighteen months feeding themselves with a spoon is usually very successful.
- They can handle a cup confidently, but do not put it back down (give it to adult).
- They remove hats, shoes, etc. but can rarely replace them.
- They produce urgent vocalisations when making a demand.
- Bowel control is sometimes attained by eighteen months and is usually attained by two years.
- By two years the child will play parallel alongside others.
- They can be rebellious and resistive and get frustrated when trying to make themselves understood. They can be easily distracted from their tantrums at this age.
- No idea of sharing is normal, and no understanding of the need to defer their wishes.
- They follow adults around. They need reassurance when tired or fearful.
- They can now put on hat and shoes and can reposition a cup on a surface.

**Test Yourself**

1  By what age is the social smile usually seen?
2  What is meant by object permanence?
3  How many words are usual at two years?
4  By what age is bowel control usually achieved?
5  What is echolalia?

## Early childhood: two to five years

### Physical development

- Walking up stairs with alternating feet is usually achieved by three years. Up and down on alternate feet is securely seen by three and a half.
- At two and a half a child can kick a football gently, by three years with force.
- Pushing and pulling of large toys is achieved by two and a half.
- Locomotor skills improve rapidly during this stage of development.

- Use of pedals is often achieved by three years, and a child can steer around corners.
- Balance gradually improves and by four years a child can usually stand, walk and run on tip-toes, and can navigate skilfully when active.
- From three years ball skills increase – catching, throwing, bouncing and kicking.
- Manipulative skills improve.
- Scissor control is developing and greater pencil control is achieved by three years.
- By four years threading small beads and early sewing is achieved.
- Adult pencil control is usually present by four years.

From three years ball skills increase

### Cognitive and language development
- At three years a large vocabulary is understood by all, but still includes unconventional grammar and infantilisms (the child's personal 'baby talk').
- They still talk to themselves at play in long monologues.
- By four years speech is usually grammatically correct.
- They can usually draw a person with main details.
- Role play is frequent and detailed by five years
- Floorplay is very complex.
- Understanding of time, linked to routine, is emerging.

### Social and emotional development
- At two and half tantrums are common when needs are thwarted. A child is less easily distracted from them now.
- They are very resistive of restraint.
- They mostly still watch others or play parallel, occasionally joining in briefly.
- By four years a child can eat skilfully and can dress, wash and clean their teeth (with supervision).
- This is a generally more independent age.
- They co-operate with others but can also be unco-operative if wishes are refused.
- They can be very strong-willed.
- At five years behaviour is noticeably more sensible and controlled.
- They understand sharing and turn-taking and the need for fair play.
- Co-operative play is constant at five years.
- They choose own friends and play well, and are very protective towards younger children, pets and distressed playmates.

**Case Study**

*Maya, Toby and Max*

Maya, Toby and Max are looked after by the same childminder, Kahira. Maya is in Kahira's care every day and either Toby or Max are usually present too. Maya is crawling and pulling herself up on the furniture. Max can walk now, but is still unsteady, using his hands held high to balance himself. Toby can walk well, and loves to play in the garden with a football. He can sometimes kick it without falling forward and is becoming steadier when climbing stairs, still needing to hold an adult's hand.

Toby talks to himself in long monologues as he plays, and adults nearby are able to identify some of his words, linked to his play. Max also talks to himself in play but little of his 'speech' is recognisable. Maya babbles and chuckles to herself as she roams around the floor exploring all that she can find. She appears to get enjoyment from watching Max and Toby, but none of the children attempt to play with each other.

1 What ages would you assume Maya, Toby and Max to be?
2 What else would you expect them to be doing?
3 Which of them would you expect to be able to feed themselves?
4 Would you expect any of the children to have gained bowel or bladder control?

## Middle childhood: five to twelve years

### Physical development

Physically the body's emphasis is now on practice and further development of the skills already gained. Large motor skills will be increased, for example, in how fast a child can run, their stamina when playing group games, and their ability to climb and manoeuvre more difficult objects and in more challenging circumstances. The ever-increasing ability for balance is seen at this stage too.

Hand–eye co-ordination develops allowing a more adult level of control when writing, drawing, sewing, and so on, and greater skill during ball games and activities involving manual dexterity is seen.

For girls, the pre-pubescent stage can begin from nine years onwards. Height develops rapidly here with the thigh bone growing at a faster rate than the rest of the body.

Hand–eye co-ordination develops in middle childhood

### Cognitive and language development

Children between these ages develop from Piaget's pre-operational stage to the concrete operational concept of thinking. They develop the ability to perform and achieve in their minds, for example, adding up, subtracting, reading and ordering.

By the age of eleven, an average child has a vocabulary of 11,000–12,000 words. They are usually fluent readers with substantial reading stamina. Girls have a tendency to read more than boys. Co-operative play from age five onwards becomes very involved, with considerable role play, requiring accuracy and detail.

FORWARD to page 380 for Piaget's stages of cognitive development.

### Social and emotional development
- Co-operative play is frequent and sustained.
- Gender awareness is strong.
- Co-operative play is mostly with same sex peers.
- Individual friendships are very important.
- Children make definite decisions about their friends.
- Parents are less openly important, but their continued support is needed.

**Test Yourself**

1 By what age is language usually grammatically correct?
2 At what age are tantrums common?
3 Give an example of hand–eye co-ordination.
4 When do children understand the need for fair play?
5 What is the difference between gross and fine motor skills?

## Adolescence: twelve to twenty years

### Puberty

This stage includes puberty, a physiological stage that can cross middle childhood and adolescence.

Early adolescence is marked by a variety of changes, including the adolescent growth spurt, maturation of the reproductive system, and the development of secondary sexual characteristics. These changes are collectively known as puberty.

For girls the most important change is the onset of menstruation (periods). It can start from as early as ten years onwards, but ages vary considerably, with some girls still awaiting this physical change at fifteen or sixteen. Ethnic group, heredity, exercise levels and health can all influence individual biological timings. Breast development starts with the budding of the breasts, followed by enlargement, until full breast maturity is reached with the formation of the areola. Once menstruation has begun it usually continues for approximately thirty-five years, only being interrupted by pregnancy.

### Sexual characteristics: girls

| Primary sexual characteristics (formed before birth) | Secondary sexual characteristics (develop during puberty) |
| --- | --- |
| Vagina<br>Uterus<br>Ovaries<br>Fallopian tubes | Breast budding preceding full breast maturity<br>Pelvis widens (in preparation for childbirth)<br>Pubic hair develops<br>Axillary (underarm) hair develops<br>Ovaries start to produce eggs<br>Onset of menstruation |

In boys, puberty starts a little later, with girls being on average two years ahead of boys in their development during this stage of life. The first signs of puberty in boys are usually pubic hair growth, followed by a slight increase in size of the scrotum and testes. The texture of the scrotum changes and when the penis develops it firstly increases in length and then in breadth. The deepening of the voice also occurs during this phase of development.

Both boys and girls have a tendency for oily skin throughout adolescence, leading to skin problems such as acne.

### Sexual characteristics: boys

| Primary sexual characteristics (formed before birth) | Secondary sexual characteristics (develop during puberty) |
| --- | --- |
| Penis<br>Testes<br>Scrotum<br>Seminal vesicles<br>Vas deferens<br>Epididymis | Pubic hair develops<br>Axillary hair develops<br>Chest hair develops<br>Facial hair develops<br>Deepening of the voice (voice 'breaks')<br>Penis increases in size and length<br>Testes grow and begin to produce sperm<br>Ability to ejaculate |

### Physical development
- By 18 years of age puberty is usually passed and the genitalia and reproductive ability of both boys and girls are fully mature.
- Overall physical strength and stamina is increased.
- Shoulders broaden and full height is reached.
- Body image is important.
- Eating disorders are not uncommon, with severe disorders such as anorexia nervosa causing secondary amenorrhea (the absence of menstruation).

- Secondary amenorrhea can also be linked to high levels of exercise, and is quite often noted in athletes, gymnasts and dancers.

### Cognitive and language development
- Emphasis is on learning and developing career options for the future.
- Understanding of abstract concepts has developed.
- Colloquialisms and 'peer talk' is frequently displayed.
- Conflicts arise, particularly with parents and figures of authority.
- Family values are frequently challenged.
- Moral reasoning becomes important.
- There is a need to develop problem-solving skills as greater independence is attained.

### Social and emotional development
- Forming relationships becomes of great importance.
- Interest in the opposite sex develops.
- Sexual identity becomes an important focus.
- Confusion regarding sexuality is common.
- Forming own self identity can at times be difficult.
- Mood swings and hormone imbalance can cause emotional upheaval.
- Peer pressure is intense and can cause difficulties in maintaining beliefs.
- Depression is common at this stage.

In adolescence, forming relationships is important

**Case Study**

*Justin*

Justin is fifteen. He is of slight build and as yet shows little sign of the onset of puberty. His best friends, Steve and Callum, are now both taller and broader than he is, and Steve is already shaving. Justin would like a new jacket as he feels out of place in his old school coat, when his friends are wearing more up-to-date styles. Justin's parents refuse to buy him anything new as they know he is likely to have a growth spurt very soon. Justin starts turning down opportunities to go out in the evenings and at weekends, spending more and more time on his own.

1  What are the main issues here?
2  How might this be affecting Justin's self-confidence?
3  How might this affect Justin in his relationship with his current friends?

4 How might this affect Justin in his relationship with his parents?
5 Is this likely to affect Justin in forming new friendships or relationships?
6 How could the situation for Justin be helped?

## Peer pressure

During adolescence, peer pressure becomes an increasingly important factor. No one likes to be different, or outside of the main crowd, and it can be hard for individuals to maintain their moral thinking and beliefs in the face of pressure to conform to the activities of a social group.

Peer pressure can lead individuals into situations they know are wrong, causing conflict within themselves. This in turn can affect their feelings of self-esteem and personal value.

Peer groups are important in that they can have a significant effect on attitudes as well as actions. This can be both positive and negative. Dealing with negative peer pressure becomes easier as the individual gains in self-confidence and develops a clear sense of right and wrong.

## Moral development

Moral development is about learning what is right or wrong, good or bad. Each person develops their own moral code, which they strive to live by. Young children's moral reasoning is initially defined by obedience in order to avoid punishment, whereas later on it becomes important to them to uphold certain rules, because they feel it is expected of them (conventional morality). The final stage of moral reasoning is only reached when the individual understands that at times rules need to be broken in order to achieve justice and develops a respect for the 'universal value and dignity of human life' (Cullis, Dolan and Groves, 1999).

---

**Kohlberg's six-stage theory of moral development**

*Level 1:*   *Pre-conventional morality (based on external authority)*

    *Stage 1:*   Child acts to avoid unpleasant consequences (punishment)

    *Stage 2:*   Child acts to gain rewards. You should behave fairly and honour deals

*Level 2:*   *Conventional morality (based on judgements about the expectations of others)*

    *Stage 3:*   Child wishes to please others and be thought of as 'nice' – a 'good boy' or 'good girl'

    *Stage 4:*   Child respects social rules. It is good to uphold the law and do one's duty

*Level 3:*   *Post-conventional morality (based on self-chosen ethical principles)*

    *Stage 5:*   Involves recognising rules or laws may be unjust, and so can sometimes be broken

    *Stage 6:*   Reasoning is based on universal principles which show profound respect for life

from Cullis, Dolan and Groves (1999), page 118

Cullis, Dolan and Groves go on to explain that:
- Level 1 reasoning is common until the age of eleven years
- Level 2 reasoning is often seen between the ages of twelve and fifteen years
- Level 3 reasoning develops from fifteen years onwards.

But many people do not reach the higher levels of reasoning, with the majority of adults remaining at Stage 4, only 10 per cent reaching Stage 5, and very few individuals reaching Stage 6.

**Test Yourself**

1 What is puberty and when does it usually occur?
2 What is the difference between primary and secondary sexual characteristics?
3 Name the female secondary sexual characteristics.
4 Name the male secondary sexual characteristics.
5 What is menstruation commonly called?
6 What is secondary amenorrhea?
7 What emotional changes occur during puberty and adolescence?
8 What is meant by the term 'peer pressure'?
9 What is moral reasoning?

## Young adulthood: twenty to forty years

### Physical development
- Maximum physical function is reached at this stage in life.
- Energy levels are high.
- This is the main time of reproduction, with family rearing often a prime focus.
- Bone continues to replace itself until approximately thirty-five years of age when bone density begins to gradually be lost by 1 per cent each year.
- Any weight gained becomes more difficult to lose.
- From their late thirties onwards women can begin the menopause (the cessation of menstruation and their reproductive years).

### Cognitive and language development
- Career paths become important for many people.
- Employment usually becomes established and positions developed.
- For most people studying to any length is over, but the life-long learning ethos is being actively promoted and many adults are learning new skills, particularly in information technology.
- The focus at this stage of life is on using the skills and knowledge that have already been gained.
- This is a stage of great reward (financial and lifestyle) for most people.

### Social and emotional development
- Leaving the family home is usual, if this did not occur during adolescence.
- Responsibilities regarding home-making and financial provision become more likely.
- The trauma of setting up on their own is off-set by the excitement and pleasure of the freedom it brings.
- This is the most frequent stage of life for marriage and parenthood.
- Sexual identity is usually established.

- The general character of the adult is formed, but their identity may still be forming.

 BACK to Erikson's stages of development on page 340.

**Case Study**

*Shirley*

Shirley is thirty-two and the mother of two young children at primary school. She is a full-time college lecturer, teaching hairdressing and beauty therapy. Her mother has looked after her children since they were toddlers, and takes and collects them from school. She also looks after Shirley's disabled father, who the children adore. He rarely goes out and has very little interest in anything but the children.

Shirley's mother has a heart attack, and dies suddenly.

1 What emotions and difficulties might Shirley now be facing?
2 What help and support will she need in the short term?
3 What help and support might she need in the longer term?
4 What impact might this bereavement have on the whole family?
5 How would you define Shirley's father in Erikson's model of psycho-social development?
6 How would you have defined Shirley's mother?

## Middle adulthood: forty to sixty-five years

### Physical development
- Grey hair begins to develop in both sexes.
- Skin may start to lose its elasticity.
- Stress can take its toll on stomach and heart.
- For women, hormonal changes are usual, with the onset of the menopause and the end of reproductive life.

### Cognitive and language development
- By middle age, people have generally acquired a wider range of experience and knowledge.
- Family members look for (and often need) guidance and support.
- There is often some re-evaluation of life, with thoughts of what aims are still unfulfilled.
- Height of work potential is often reached, involving salary peak, management positions and a more affluent lifestyle.
- Redundancy situations can result in unemployment and re-employment difficulties.
- Problems within work and family can also reach a peak at this time.

### Social and emotional development
- Re-evaluation of life and personal situation may raise discontent within relationships.
- Relationships may alter – separation, divorce, step-parenting.
- Demands of family members may occur, causing concern and trauma.

- This stage brings the pleasures of children and grandchildren for many people.
- Mid-life crisis may take place during this stage.

**Case Study**

*Russell*

Russell is forty-eight and a middle manager in a large company. He has always considered himself to be happily married. He has a pleasant wife June, who has a busy social and working life, three children, all now living away from home, who are managing well, and his parents live locally and remain busy and in good health.

Russell has always played golf and enjoys sport on the television and a good read. He is suddenly finding himself dissatisfied and bored with his life. He thinks about the plans he and June had in their younger days and wonders why some of them were never achieved. He begins to feel old and unvalued and starts trying to make himself look younger by wearing brighter colours and more casual style suits. This is bringing a few smiles from the younger staff in his office. Russell is taking the smiles as compliments.

1  What is happening to Russell do you think?
2  Why is Russell feeling unvalued?

## Late adulthood: sixty-five years onwards

### Physical development
- This is a phase of gradual slowing down of all of the body's faculties and systems.
- Physically, life may proceed at a slower pace, but this is often down to personal choice.
- Health problems become more common and more varied.
- Joints gradually stiffen and may become weak.
- Height may be lost due to the thinning of the intervertebral discs.
- Muscles gradually lose power.
- The body begins to lose suppleness, strength and stamina.
- Hearing and eyesight begin to decline.
- Sense of smell may also weaken.

 BACK to Erikson's psycho-social stages (page 340) – stagnation *v.* generativity.

### Cognitive development
- Retirement can be difficult to adjust to.
- A general decline in mental activity is seen in some people, for example, memory may be less acute.
- Many people in late adulthood are respected by younger generations for their wisdom, experience and awareness.

### Social and emotional development
- Retirement age is reached and time is now available to pursue hobbies and pastimes.
- Opportunities for leisure activities are almost endless.

- Time is more readily available for family and friends.
- Finance can become a worry as salaries are exchanged for pensions.
- Bereavement becomes more common.
- Family and friends start to be lost more frequently.
- Socially many people reduce their activities and contacts.
- The need to be cared for becomes common towards the end of an individual's life.

*Remember !* The major events occurring across the life-span involve education, employment, reproduction, retirement and bereavement of close family and friends. Physical health, economic well-being and culture will impact on each stage of life. Rites of passage, such as weddings, baby naming, commitments and funerals will vary from culture to culture.

### Activity

a) What aspects of each of the life stages do you consider to be the most stressful? Why is this do you think?
b) How could individuals best be supported during stressful times?
c) Where might your professional role as an early years worker help families?

**Professional Practice**
- The summaries above set out the developmental expectations of *average* human development within Western culture.
- You should always be aware that cultural differences may have an effect on an individual's response to a situation, or the way in which they handle it. This can apply to the level of information given to children and expectations of them in times of sadness or stress, such as following a death in the family.

## Factors affecting development

Development is known to be influenced by:
- genetic factors
- environmental factors
- social factors
- cultural factors
- economic factors
- nutritional factors.

Genetic factors and the effects of substances crossing the placenta during pregnancy were discussed earlier in the chapter, and this should have helped you understand how additional difficulties can be faced by some children and families.

◀◀ BACK to page 336 to recap on these factors.

An understanding of other influences that can impact on development will enable you to put any concerns and problems you identify in a child into context, noting how some aspects of their lives may have been less privileged and at times seriously disadvantaged compared to other children.

### Poverty and economics

A child raised in poverty is less likely to thrive than a child who enjoys an economically stable life – it is unlikely that a family on a low income will be able to have a diet that is varied, which provides all the nutrients needed for optimum growth and healthy development. Inadequate or barely adequate household equipment, particularly regarding safety features, can raise the possibility of accidents. Limited funds to pay for heating can result in children who are persistently unwell, particularly in winter.

### Poor nutrition and ill-health

A lack of sufficient nutrients impacts on all-round health, resulting long-term in a child who is unlikely to reach their potential. Food is fuel for the heating system of our bodies, and without it we do not function fully.

### Social and cultural factors

Cramped living conditions are stressful to most people. The opportunities for cross-infection are greater because of the close proximity of family members.

Temporary accommodation such as bed and breakfast facilities affect families in that they have no secure base, and the impact of this on the parents is stressful, which has a subsequent impact on children, with older children often worrying about their parents and feeling powerless to help to them.

By contrast, children who live in privileged circumstances and have parents and extended family who are able to give them time in a stress-free environment often feel more settled and have fewer worries. They are more able to enjoy childhood.

Family and cultural practices also affect the development of a child. Some cultures place great emphasis on the importance of older generations and members of the extended family share in the upbringing of the children.

### Stimulation

If a child is brought up in a stimulating environment, this facilitates greater opportunities for learning, helping the child to reach their potential. Stimulation has been shown to start in the womb and some women choose to maximise this by playing music and reading to their unborn child. However, at times parents over-stimulate their children (known as hot-housing). This can be counter-productive in that it often results in tired and irritable children who may eventually become uninterested in learning.

 Walsh *et al.* (2000) offers a useful source of further information on the affects of poverty – see *Bibliography and suggested further reading*, page 429.

1 What is the difference between genotype and phenotype?
2 Explain the difference between a genetically inherited disorder and a congenital disorder.
3 Which of the following disorders are X-linked disorders?
   a) cystic fibrosis
   b) Batten's disease
   c) Duchenne muscular dystrophy
   d) Huntington's chorea
   e) haemophilia
4 How does foetal alcohol syndrome affect an infant?
5 What are the most common affects of smoking in pregnancy?
6 How can poverty have an impact on development?

# Physical development of children

Having read through the summaries of development linked to the life stages, the following sections will enable you to develop your understanding of child development further.

## Motor development

Motor skills can be gross (large) or fine. They include movement and balance, and can be either precise or carefree. Movement can involve the whole body or just one part of it.

The **maturational** changes in physical development can be summarised as follows. It can be said that physical development moves:
- *from the simple to the complex:* This means that a child learns simple actions, such as learning to walk, before they learn the more complex action of being able to hop.
- *from cephalo to caudal:* This can be defined as physical control starting at the head and gradually developing down through the body. For example, head control is attained before the spine is strong enough for an infant to sit unsupported, and sitting unsupported is attained before the child is able to stand.

- *from proximal to distal:* These terms refer to how a child develops actions near to the body before they develop control of outer reaches of the body. For example, a child can hug and carry a large teddy bear before they can fasten its clothing.
- *from general to specific:* The more generalised responses of an infant showing excitement when recognising a favourite carer gradually moves through to the facial smile of an older child on greeting the same person.

The table on page 361 shows how motor skills can be categorised as:
- *locomotor*, which involves the body moving forward in some way, for example walking, running

- *non-locomotor*, which describes large physical movements which take place whilst stationary, for example bending, pulling
- *manipulation*, which involves dexterous actions such as throwing and catching a ball.

The table places these three physical areas sequentially according to the developmental norms.

**The sequence of motor skills** (from Helen Bee, *The Developing Child, 6th edition*, © Allyn & Bacon, reprinted by permission

| Age | Locomotor skills | Non-locomotor skills | Manipulative skills |
|---|---|---|---|
| 1 month | Stepping reflex | Lifts head; visually follows slowly moving objects | Holds object if placed in hand |
| 2–3 months | | Briefly keeps head up if held in a sitting position | Begins to swipe at objects within visual range |
| 4–6 months | Sits up with some support | Holds head erect in sitting position | Reaches for and grasps objects |
| 7–9 months | Sits without support; rolls over in prone; crawls | | Transfers objects from one hand to the other |
| 10–12 months | Crawls; walks grasping furniture, then without help | Squats and stoops | Some sign of hand preference; grasps a spoon across palm but poor aim of food to mouth |
| 13–18 months | Walks backwards and sideways | Rolls ball to adult | Stacks two blocks; puts objects into small containers and dumps them |
| 18-24 months | Runs (20); walks well; climbs stairs – both feet to a step | Pushes and pulls boxes or wheeled toys; unscrews lid on a jar | Shows clear hand preference. Stacks four to six blocks. Turns pages one at a time. Picks things up, keeping balance |
| 2-3 years | Runs easily; climbs up and down from furniture unaided | Hauls and shoves big toys around obstacles | Picks up small objects; throws small ball forward while standing |

| Age | Locomotor skills | Non-locomotor skills | Manipulative skills |
|---|---|---|---|
| 3–4 years | Walks upstairs one foot per step; skips on both feet; walks on tiptoe | Pedals and steers a tricycle; walks in any direction pulling a big toy | Catches large ball between outstretched arms; cuts paper with scissors; holds pencil between thumb and first two fingers |
| 4–5 years | Walks up and down stairs, one foot per stair. Stands, runs and walks well on tip-toes | | Strikes ball with bat; kicks and catches ball; threads bead, but not needle. Grasps pencil maturely |
| 5–6 years | Skips on alternate feet; walks a thin line; slides and swings | | Plays ball games quite well. Threads needles; can sew a stitch |
| 7–8 years | Skips 12 times or more | Rides two-wheeler bike, short distances | Writes individual letters |
| 8 years+ | Skips freely | Rides bike easily | |

Activity

Sarah has been asked to write about the opportunities for enhancing physical development in a range of popular activities. She is using a table like the one below. She intends to include the following activities:

jigsaw puzzles    sponge printing    sports day races
picture books    hopscotch games    using woodwork tools.
farmer's in the den    musical statues
threading cotton reels    Lego

Under which column should Sarah place each activity?

| Locomotion | Non-locomotion | Manipulation |
|---|---|---|
| | | |

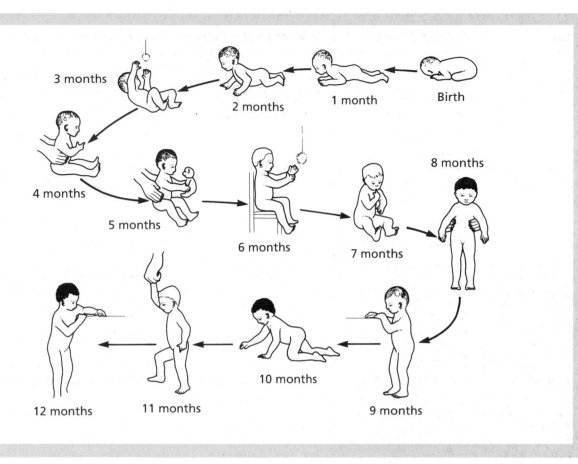

from Dare and O'Donovan (1998), page 126

The development of locomotion

# Health screening

Health screening of children takes place at specified ages, across the whole population. It enables parents and health professionals to identify problems sooner rather than later, giving the opportunity for early intervention and treatment.

Screening is carried out during pregnancy, at birth and throughout schooling. It mostly focuses on the general physical development of individual children, with specific attention being given to hearing and vision.

### Centile charts

The physical development of babies and young children is screened by health visitors and paediatricians using **centile charts** to measure and monitor growth.

An infant grows rapidly during the first year and then at a more steady rate from the toddler stage onwards. As puberty arrives the growth rate rapidly increases once again, easing in the latter years of adolescence. Full height is usually acquired by 18 years, whereas bone density continually develops, and old bone is replaced with new until around age 35, when the body ceases to continue replacing bone at the same rate.

Different centile charts are used for boys and girls because there are slight differences in growth expectations of girl infants and boy infants – boys, on average, are slightly heavier than girls at birth. The 50th centile line is the central line on the centile charts. It indicates what is average at each age. The upper and lower lines represent the boundary within which 80 per cent of children will fall. A child who falls outside these boundaries will be monitored closely and may need further investigation into their development at some stage. The pattern (or line) formed as a child's measurements are plotted on the centile chart is known as a *growth curve*.

Example **How centile charts are used**

The centile charts opposite show Jasmine's measurements at birth and the first nine months measurements of her weight. We can see from these that, as a full-term baby, she was 'small for dates' at birth, weighing 2.780 kg (6 lb 2 oz), and was placed just below the 9th centile. Her length at 54 cm was considered to be long and reached the 98th centile and her head circumference, at 34 cm, was placed just above the 25th centile. Jasmine's weight progressed very slowly, and she remained below the 'norms' of development for an infant of her age and birthweight.

Any infant who falls below the 0.4th centile is closely monitored by health professionals, and an infant who moves downwards across two centile lines is referred to their GP or a paediatrician for close monitoring. At four months old, there was concern that Jasmine would need to be referred, although she was both healthy and alert. By five months, however, her weight began to increase more steadily and she moved above the 2nd centile for the first time at seven months. Jasmine is a very active baby, of petite build, like her mother, and therefore there is no serious concern about her. She has always been healthy and alert and by eight months was walking around the furniture, crawling very fast and rarely still. Her weight gain trailed off again at this stage, but this was attributed to her high level of activity.

**Test Yourself**

1. Which aspects of physical development can be described as developing from proximal to distal?
2. Explain the difference between locomotor and non-locomotor skills.
3. Name three activities to support the development of manipulative skills.
4. What is the main focus of health screening programmes?
5. What are centile charts used to measure?
6. What is the difference between amniocentesis and chorionic villi sampling tests carried out during pregnancy?

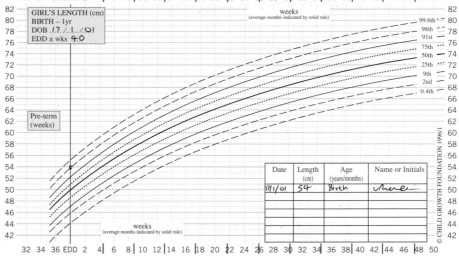

**GIRL'S LENGTH (cm)**
BIRTH – 1yr
DOB .17. /.1. /.01.
EDD ± wks  40

Pre-term
(weeks)

weeks
(average months indicated by solid rule)

99.6th
98th
91st
75th
50th
25th
9th
2nd
0.4th

| Date | Length (cm) | Age (years/months) | Name or Initials |
|------|------|------|------|
| 17/1/01 | 54 | Birth | *Marie* |
| | | | |
| | | | |
| | | | |

© CHILD GROWTH FOUNDATION 1996/1

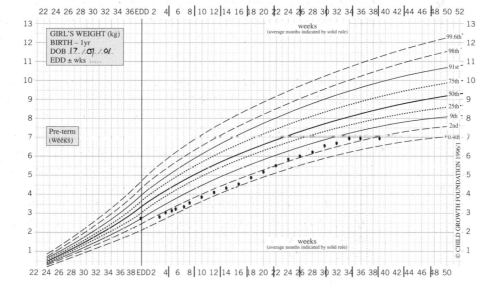

**GIRL'S WEIGHT (kg)**
BIRTH – 1yr
DOB .17. /.01. /.01.
EDD ± wks  .....

weeks
(average months indicated by solid rule)

Pre-term
(weeks)

99.6th
98th
91st
75th
50th
25th
9th
2nd
0.4th

weeks
(average months indicated by solid rule)

© CHILD GROWTH FOUNDATION 1996/1

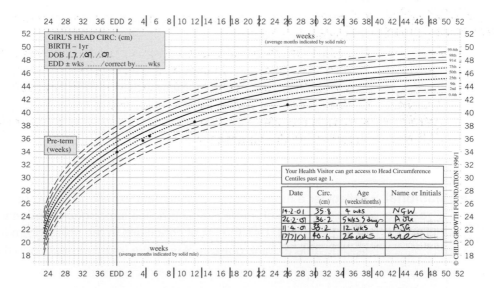

**GIRL'S HEAD CIRC: (cm)**
BIRTH – 1yr
DOB .17. /.01. /.01.
EDD ± wks  ..... /correct by.....wks

weeks
(average months indicated by solid rule)

Pre-term
(weeks)

99.6th
98th
91st
75th
50th
25th
9th
2nd
0.4th

Your Health Visitor can get access to Head Circumference
Centiles past age 1.

| Date | Circ. (cm) | Age (weeks/months) | Name or Initials |
|------|------|------|------|
| 14.2.01 | 35.8 | 4 wks | NGW |
| 26.2.01 | 36.2 | 5 wks 5 days | A Jla |
| 11.4.01 | 38.2 | 12 wks | AJG |
| 17/7/01 | 40.6 | 26 wks | *Mren* |

weeks
(average months indicated by solid rule)

© CHILD GROWTH FOUNDATION 1996/1

**365**

# Emotional development of children

Emotional development involves the child's development of self-awareness, sense of security and personal identity, and learning to understand and express feelings towards other people. Emotions can be both positive and negative; they are our inner feelings which we often find difficult to explain. Children can usually describe how they are feeling physically, although in very young children this may only be in a generalised way, for example a 'tummy ache' may refer to a range of pain experiences, but it is far harder for them to explain how they are feeling emotionally. As adults, we need to allow children the opportunities to express their emotions and reassure them that it is OK to have strong feelings, explaining that adults have them too.

## Conditions for secure emotional development

Emotional development is not simply a maturational process, it needs the appropriate conditions to nurture it in the way that a flower needs sun, soil and water.

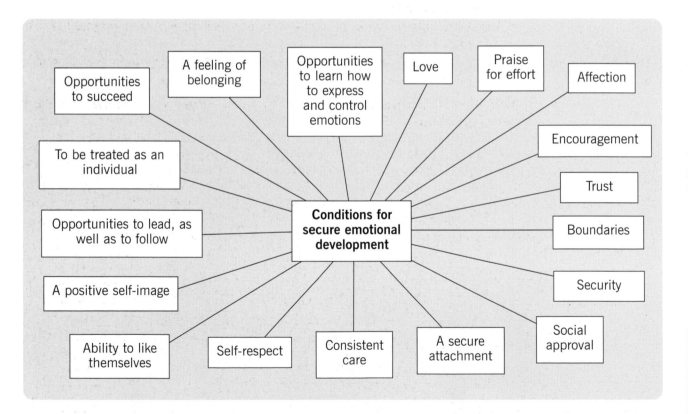

**Professional Practice** Reflect for a moment on the placement experiences you have had. Think of situations in which professional practice supported emotional development particularly well. Use the list of conditions in the spidergram above. You may also be able to think of examples where improvements could be made.

# Emotional disturbance

Many children go through a phase of **emotional disturbance**. It is not usually serious, and with sensitive handling by parents and carers is usually overcome quite quickly.

Emotional disturbance does not refer to the extremes of behaviour found in some developmental phases, such as temper tantrums in toddlers or mood swings in adolescence. It is about the more unusual and worrying behaviours that occur from time to time and which sometimes need professional referral to support and help the child through.

Emotional disturbance can manifest itself in many ways:

- A child may become withdrawn and insecure, clinging to a familiar adult and lacking confidence.
- Anti-social behaviour may be displayed by children who are trying to draw attention to themselves.
- Phobias may occur when a child is anxious about another situation, the child may display a pseudo (artificial) fear to gain attention to the real problem.
- Lonely or neglected children may develop physical habits such as hair-chewing or excessive nail-biting.
- Emotional distress can cause physical symptoms such as tummy upsets, tics and skin irritations.
- Severe emotional disturbance can result in regressed or impeded development, both physical and cognitive.

Emotional disturbance can be triggered by many situations as summarised in the spidergram below.

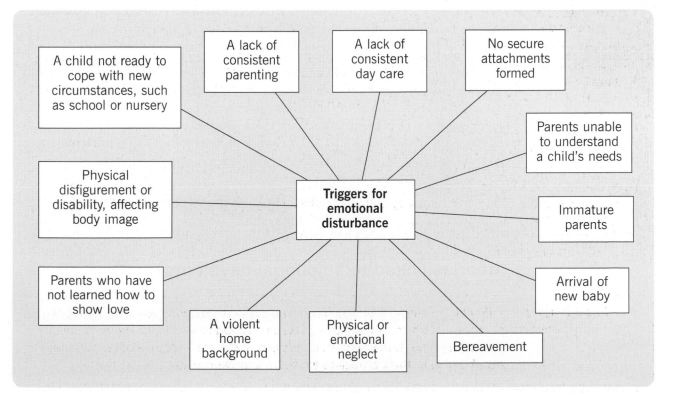

**Activity**

Look at the examples of emotionally disturbed behaviour listed on page 367. Which of them have you experienced during your time in placement? Think about how each situation was resolved and what had triggered it, if you knew (this information may not have been known generally).

## Patterns of emotional development

It is usual for young babies to show a distress response at sudden noises, as these disturb their sense of security. The passive acceptance of the caring routines that is established by a few weeks of age shows how their sense of security is well established, as does the way in which they cease to cry when they are picked up. With older babies the soothing effect of the voice of their main carer and the contented patting of the breast or bottle again demonstrates emotional security.

At around the age of nine months, babies begin to show a fear of strangers and become fretful when separated from their parent or main carer. This is a classical milestone of development, but it is also linked to the quality of the attachment bond that has been established between the parent/carer and the child. The behaviours that accompany separation anxiety may include increased crying and the infant visually searching for the 'missing' adult.

As the infant approaches the toddler stage, this emotional response is often shown in more negative behaviours such as the onset of tantrums at around two years, due to their **egocentric** (self-centred) view of the world. This stage can last until the more socially aware and emotionally mature age of three years, when they begin to develop an understanding of how to defer their needs and share.

The early building-blocks of emotional security have been established by the time a child enters day care or a pre-school setting. These new experiences should enable a child to continue to value themselves as an individual through the images they see and the opportunities they are given. Both experience and opportunity will impact further on a child's perception of themselves, affecting their self-esteem and personal image.

BACK to Chapter 7, page 277, for issues of children's behaviour and how to manage some of the difficulties that may arise.

## Theories linked to emotional development

A number of theories deal with aspects of emotional development. These include theories on bonding and attachment, separation, **self-concept**, personal identity and temperament. A brief summary of each of these is given below, but for detailed information, read Jarvis (2001) – see *Bibliography and suggested further reading*, page 429.

## Bonding, attachment and separation

John Bowlby (1907–90) is one of the most well-known theorists in this field. He first put forward his views on the importance of a secure relationship between the infant and their main carer following research carried out in the 1950s. In 1953 he published his classic book *Child Care and the Growth of Love*. This text influenced many childcare practices but, although the basis of attachment theory is still upheld, his theories have since been challenged and modified.

Bowlby considered that all infants needed one main care giver (usually the mother) to ensure a secure attachment. This attachment he called **monotropism**. Bowlby considered that any separation from this person would have a serious emotional affect on the infant.

> What is believed to be essential for mental health is that an infant and young child should experience a warm, intimate, and continuous relationship with his mother (or permanent mother substitute – one person who steadily "mothers" him) in which both find satisfaction and enjoyment.'
>
> Bowlby (1953) page 13

Modern-day theorists are certain that the role of the mother figure as the essential (monotropic) carer put forward by Bowlby was incorrect, and many subsequent studies (for example, Mary Ainsworth and Michael Rutter) have identified that successful, secure relationships between infants and a range of other care-givers are possible and that the carer's ability to respond to the infant's needs is the greatest influencing factor in the attachment process.

A useful text to refer to for further examples is Barnes (1998) – see *Bibliography and suggested further reading*, page 429.

## Self-concept and personal identity

A child begins to recognise that they are an individual quite early on. From the age of about eighteen months, the growing toddler establishes that the person they see reflected in the mirror is actually them.

Dowling (2000, page 2) suggests that even babies build a picture of themselves, based on the way their care is given and the manner in which their carers respond to them. It is generally accepted that close members of the family, particularly the mother, are instrumental in this process as the baby sees the loving acceptance that the mother gives them as the first signal that they are an individual who is loved and who matters.

Once a child understands that they are an individual, and what they, as that individual, are like, they move on to understand how they are perceived by others.

Developing personal identity: 'I'm good at making models. My friends say I'm good at making models.'

## Temperament

Every individual has their own character, disposition and tendencies, and children are no exception to this. A child is sometimes referred to as being an 'easy' child or a 'difficult' child, but these terms are not helpful – they become labels which can lead to the prejudging of an individual and eventually become a 'self-fulfilling prophecy'.

Children can also be balanced, impulsive or reserved in their actions, which can lead to a greater level of accidents or 'near-misses' in the impulsive child and can limit experience for the reserved child. Temperament is seen even in very young babies, it is part of their natural personality make-up. When you lift up some babies they mould towards you in a pleasurable cuddle, whereas others will remain tense and wary. The same applies to adults. You can probably think of individuals who these descriptions apply to.

Bruce and Meggitt (1996) state that:

> 'A child's temperament is about:
> **emotionality:** the child's feelings – fearful, anxious, enthusiastic
> **activity:** whether the child does things impulsively or slowly
> **sociability:** whether the child likes company or not.'

Again, this applies to adults too.

---

**Professional Practice**

Think about the people you know.
- Who are easy-going and spontaneous?
- Who are approachable and flexible, but carefully weigh up situations?
- Who are at times difficult to work with/live with/socialise with?
- How would you sum each of them up?
- Are they miserable, happy, calm, competitive, hostile?
- How else would you describe them?

**Case Study**

*Stanislas and Pradeep*

Stanislas is an outgoing boy who is always eager to try out new activities and experiences. He is always on the go at nursery and flits from one activity to another, rarely spending long in one place. By contrast, Pradeep likes to spend time on everything he does, making sure he has all that he thinks he will need (various colour pens and so on) before he starts. Pradeep rarely hurries to see anything new, but will eventually try it out or join in when the rush is over. In this way he often has the opportunity to spend more time enjoying the new experience than Stanislas.

1 How do you think the differing temperaments of Stanislas and Pradeep might affect their learning?
2 What long-term issues do you see for each of them if they continue in the same way?

Each of us can be placed into a personality type, but we also display various personality traits. These predispositions towards certain behaviours are part of us as a general type of person, but some of us have a greater amount of some traits than of others. Psychologists who study trait theory can be divided into:
- idiographic theorists, such as Allport (1897–1967) who focused on individual personality traits
- nomothetic theorists, such as Cattell (1905–) and Eysenck (1916–98) who studied the more general laws of personality.

You can find out more about personality trait theory by referring to Cullis *et al.* (1999) – see *Bibliography and suggested further reading*, page 429.

**Professional Practice**

It is easier for most of us to interact with others who are happy and easy-going. They give us a positive extension of themselves that we can link on to. This is often referred to as having 'goodness of fit'.

As early years workers, it is important that the smiling happy child is not given more of your attention than the reserved quiet child. Similarly, the tearful, discontented child should not be dismissed as miserable and be left to their misery. You need to understand that temperament is part of the personality we are born with and to accept the need for differing approaches to the children in your care. You cannot treat all children in the same way – you would not be meeting their individual needs. Childcare workers need to find a way to attain the state of 'goodness of fit' with every child they are in contact with.

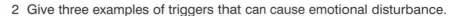

BACK to Chapter 7, page 277, for suggestions on managing personality clashes and encouraging co-operation within settings.

**Test Yourself**

1 List the conditions needed for secure emotional development.
2 Give three examples of triggers that can cause emotional disturbance.
3 What does the term 'monotropism' mean?
4 Which theory is usually associated with John Bowlby?
5 What is meant by the term 'goodness of fit'?

# Social development of children

Babies appear to have an instinctive capacity to relate to other humans. This is referred to as **pro-social behaviour** and opportunities to meet with and relate to other humans, both babies and older age groups, is important to develop socialisation further. Social skills start to be developed through the earliest interactions with the mother or other primary carers following birth, and these turn-taking experiences, in which the mother and infant learn to 'mesh' with each other, form the basis of building later relationships. Infants can be seen imitating certain adult actions, such as tongue poking, mouth shaping and hand movements from shortly after birth.

Infants can be seen to imitate adult actions, such as mouth shaping, from shortly after birth

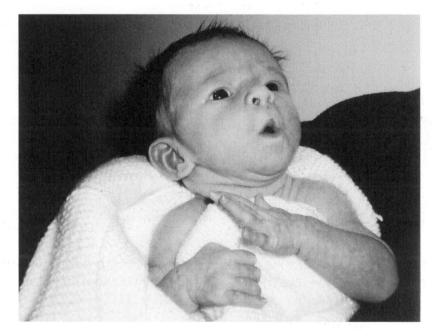

As the mother–infant relationship develops (sometimes referred to as a *dyadic relationship*), the mother tends to anticipate the responses of her infant, and react accordingly. This precipitating response is known as *a priori imitation*, and plays an important part in the development of early relationships of young infants. It relates to Jerome Bruner's theory of scaffolding.

FORWARD to page 385 for more about Bruner.

## Stages of socialisation

Social development can be clearly seen in the way in which children play, as demonstrated in the diagram opposite.

BACK You may find it helpful to refer back to the summaries of development earlier in the chapter (page 334), noting how children develop socially. You may also find it helpful to revisit Chapter 8, page 321.

The development of play shows clearly how
children develop socially

**Co-operative play, over 3 years**
Shared enjoyment, making
joint decisions about play

**Associative play, from 3 years**
Watch other children
May copy their actions

**Parallel play, 2–3 years**
Play alongside another child
Aware of other games, but does not
co-operate

**Solitary play 0–2 years**
Play alone
Need adult reassurance

### Social play stages

As you can see from the diagram above, socialisation develops as a child's play
moves from the solitary actions of the toddler absorbed in their own world
through to the complex games involving rules seen in the infant school
playground. The ability to co-operate with others moves through stages, which
are dependent on both the maturational stage of development of the individual
child and the opportunities and experiences that have been made available to
them.

### Solitary play

The first stage of play is referred to as solitary play. The child plays contentedly
on their own, still needing the reassurance of the adult. This play is typical up to
two years of age. It is frequently imitative, demonstrating a basic understanding
of the actions of others within a child's social world. An example of solitary
imitative play is the child pretending to brush the hair of a doll or teddy, usually
very briefly.

### Parallel play

The next stage in play is parallel play in which a child finds enjoyment playing
alongside, but not with, another child. The children do not necessarily even
acknowledge that the other exists, and make no reference to what the other is
doing. This is true parallel play, one child playing parallel to the other. It usually
begins to emerge between two and three years of age.

### Associative (looking on) play

At this stage in social play the child begins to watch the actions of others,
enjoying their play from a distance. They are not as yet ready to play with others,
but learn a great deal from their observations. This stage of play is typically seen
between three and four years of age.

### Joining in play (simple co-operative)

By four years old, most children are ready to play co-operatively with others. This simple co-operative play begins in an uncomplicated manner, involving the shared enjoyment of a similar activity. A good example of this is a group of children all dressing dolls together. There are no rules and no restrictions. It is simply a pleasurable play experience with others.

### Co-operative play (complex co-operative)

This last and most developed stage in the process of children's play involves them interacting as a group. This can involve the physical co-operation needed to complete a joint task, or play which includes complex rules, involving the taking on of agreed (but 'evolving as they go') roles.

## Effects of stereotyping on development

Social development and play are affected by various experiences and this section focuses on the effects of stereotyping. To stereotype an individual is to mentally place them into a specific compartment according to a preconceived idea. It ignores the person's individual character, their predisposition and temperament and simply includes them as part of a collective group. In generalising in this way, we are likely to make serious errors of judgement about the world we live in and the people we interact with.

### Social stereotyping

Children learn about social behaviour from watching and imitating other people. This is known as social learning. They are particularly influenced by the adults they admire. As an adult working with young children, you are a role model, and you should be aware of how your actions and words can affect them.

#### Social learning theory

Possibly the most well-known example of **social learning theory** was the research carried out by Albert Bandura in 1965. He used a film with three different endings to see how children could be affected by what they had seen. Three groups of children were each shown a different version of the film, which involved an adult hitting and shouting at a Bobo doll (a large inflatable toy weighted at the bottom that always rights itself – you cannot knock it over):

- Group 1: The first film ending showed the adult being rewarded for hitting the doll.
- Group 2: The second film ending showed the adult being punished for hitting the doll.
- Group 3: In the third film, nothing happened to the adult.

After they had watched their particular version of the film, the children in all three groups were given Bobo dolls to play with and were observed by the researchers. The children who had seen the adult rewarded for hitting the doll also showed a higher tendency to hit it.

This study could not claim evidence of a direct cause and effect, but it could certainly suggest that children were most likely influenced by the rewarding of negative behaviour.

*Remember!*
- As an adult working with children, you need to think about the messages you are giving them. These messages have a direct impact on the social learning of the children in your care.
- Messages can be portrayed by actions, words, attitudes and non-verbal behaviour. They can be both positive or negative.

Example    In the playground one dinner time, Jake was playing with a tennis ball, kicking it at the wall. His aim was taking the ball closer and closer to the windows, so Mrs Baker, the school meals supervisory assistant who was on playground duty, explained that he would need to keep away from the windows or he would not be allowed to continue playing ball. Jake took no notice of Mrs Baker, and eventually he had his ball taken away from him. Jake felt very cross with Mrs Baker at the time.

The next day, Jake again played ball, but this time he played over by the fence. He did not want to lose his ball again.

### Socialisation theory
Socialisation theory involves looking at a child's social influences in two ways:
- as **primary socialisation**, which is established as a child understands and develops the customs and practices of their family
- as **secondary socialisation**, which involves the wider influences of other adults and social groups in the community with whom the child has regular contact.

**Activity**

a) Consider this list of examples of primary and secondary socialisation:
Religion
Attitude to other religions
Diet
Social behaviour
Moral behaviour
Attitude shown to elders
Attitude shown to family members
Attitude shown to others

Make a copy of the table and place the examples under the relevent heading.

| Primary socialisation | Secondary socialisation |
|---|---|
|  |  |

b) Which examples could be placed under both headings?
c) What other examples can you add to the table?

### Gender stereotyping

In the earliest years children learn which sex they belong to. This is known as *sex identity* and it refers to body shape and biological make-up. They also learn to behave in certain ways according to their sex identity. This is known as the *gender role*, which leads onto the development of *gender identity*. Generally, when girls know they are girls, they tend to play with other girls and the same applies to boys. When children fully understand that their sex is set for life, they have reached the state of *gender stability*.

In the same way that socialisation affects children's behaviour, it also affects their perceptions of gender. When adults interact with babies, it has been shown that they handle babies in different ways according to their sex. This also applies to the language and tone of voice that they use towards them. For example, most people have heard comments such as 'What a beautiful girl she is' or 'He's a real bruiser isn't he?' These are classic comments, which are used widely and are very gender specific.

Research has shown that gender roles are influenced by the parents and carers of children. Goldberg and Lewis in a study of thirty-two boy babies and thirty-two girl babies, each aged around six months, found that girl babies are held for longer, spoken to in a softer tone and cradled gently, whereas boy babies are approached in a more 'robust' manner. Goldberg and Lewis observed the same infants again at thirteen months in a laboratory setting, with a limited selection of toys available to them. The girls were observed to choose the quieter toys and to stay near to their mothers, whereas the boys chose the more active toys and appeared to be more independent. Goldberg and Lewis drew the conclusion that the earlier experiences had impacted on the later actions of these babies.

Interactions with older children have also been seen to influence gender. Beverley Fagot carried out observations in the homes of many families with children approaching two years. She particularly noted which behaviours were encouraged and discouraged by the parents and found that, on the whole, girls were encouraged to stay near to the parents, to ask for help and to take an interest in stereotypical 'girls' activities (dolls, clothes, dancing). They tended to be discouraged from active play (jumping, running around, rough and tumble games and in being aggressive). Boys, on the other hand, were encouraged to actively explore construction toys, to play with cars and to use their bodies actively. They were discouraged from playing with dolls, and any other stereotypically 'girls' activities. They were also discouraged from asking for help. The boys who tended towards 'girls' activities were more strongly criticised by the parents than the girls who tended towards 'boys' activities.

**Activity**

Make a copy of the table and note in the relevant columns the behaviours that were encouraged and discouraged in the Beverly Fagot research. Discuss the comparison within your group.

|  | Encouraged behaviours | Discouraged behaviours |
|---|---|---|
| Girls |  |  |
| Boys |  |  |

**Case Study**

*Paul and Patrick*

Paul and Patrick were playing outside with balls and hoops, when Rachel, an early years worker called out for 'a big strong boy' to help her get the mats out. Paul and Patrick both ran to help her, but Patrick got his foot caught in one of the hoops and fell heavily. He began to cry. Paul helped him up saying 'Come on Patrick, big boys don't cry. Quick, let's help Rachel.'

1  What messages were being given here?
2  How could Rachel have made both situations more positive?
3  What could be the long-term implications for social learning for Paul and Patrick?

**Professional Practice**
• What personal learning can you take from this case study?
• How might it affect your practice in the future?

Working with children requires a clear understanding of the importance of equality and how all children should be encouraged to use all of the available activities and experience all situations in the setting.

**Activity**

You have been set an assignment asking you to explore children's perceptions of gender within your current nursery placement. It has been suggested that you carry out a small survey of their views of a range of about ten toys/activities.

You need to consider:
• Which toys you would include?
• What has influenced your choices?
• How you will set out your mini survey?

As you make your choices of toys, ask yourself:

- Do I think of certain toys as being 'boys' toys or 'girls' toys?
- Why is this?
- What affect would it have on development if children were limited in their use of toys and equipment?
- Which areas of development would be affected?

Discuss your views with a partner and share the outcomes of your survey too. How do your outcomes compare to the outcomes of others?

**Professional Practice**  What other ideas, apart from toys and activities, could you have used to explore children's perceptions of gender?

### Cultural and racial stereotyping

A child should be accepted for themselves first and foremost. Their background, ethnicity and religion are simply part of what makes them who they are. The individual child's personality is what you should focus upon as you build up a relationship with them. The influences of primary and secondary socialisation will have given them a sense of belonging within their own culture, and this is an important part of their family's way of life, and of their parents' parenting of them. This should be acknowledged and valued by all early years workers.

We live in a pluralist society (one which is made up of a variety of groups who each have their own distinctive ethnic origin, culture or religion) and it is important to have an understanding of a broad range of cultures, religions and beliefs, and be willing to both value and explore differences with the children in your care.

*Remember!*  As with both gender stereotyping and social learning theory, the impact of adult actions and words can have long-term effects.

 BACK to Chapter 2 for a more detailed discussion of equality, diversity and rights.

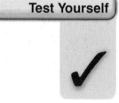 **Test Yourself**

1  What is pro-social behaviour?
2  In what order do the play stages develop?
3  What is the difference between simple and complex co-operative play?
4  Give an example of social learning theory.
5  How does primary socialisation differ from secondary socialisation?
6  What does the term 'gender stability' mean?

# Cognitive development of children

Humans are able to think, reason, plan ahead and manipulate ideas, but whether these abilities are already in place when we are born or whether we are moulded by the experiences we have as individuals has been much debated. This has become known as the nature–nurture debate (nativists *v.* empiricists). Nativists support the idea of the human infant having innate abilities that predispose them towards developing in certain ways, whereas empiricists believe firmly that we are simply moulded by experience. Most modern-day theorists take a combined approach, accepting that we are each born with some genetic influences that are further enhanced by our early experiences.

Family, friends, teachers, pets – do you think you have been moulded by experience?

 **Case Study**

*Lucy*

Simon and Nina sat down to clarify the plans for next week's activities in their nursery class. 'I don't know what to do with Lucy' said Nina. 'She just wants to talk non-stop, she rarely lets anyone else get a word in, and some of her language is pretty awful too. What with her tearing around all the time, it is difficult to get her to listen as she is hardly ever still for more than a few seconds.'

'She probably inherited it from her mother,' said Simon. 'Whenever I speak to her, I hardly manage to complete a sentence without her interrupting me. I've noticed she is the same when she speaks to other parents too.'

'I'm not sure I agree with you about Lucy inheriting her behaviour,' replied Nina. 'I think children are more likely to learn by the way they are brought up, but as Lucy lives in such a noisy and lively household, what else can we expect?'

Consider the conversation.

1 Who was taking a nativist view?
2 Who took a more empiricist view?

A useful publication to help you explore the nature–nurture debate further is Oates (1999) – see *Bibliography and suggested further reading*, page 429.

Cognitive development involves the development of concepts, including thinking, problem-solving and memory. This section discusses in some detail the theories of three influential theorists of cognitive development: Jean Piaget, Lev Vygotsky and Jerome Bruner, and also looks at the theories of Ivan Pavlov and B.F. Skinner.

### The main theorists in cognitive development

| Jean Piaget | Lev Vygotsky | Jerome Bruner |
| --- | --- | --- |
| Particularly associated with:<br>• constructivist theory<br>• stages of cognitive development<br>• schemas<br>• assimilation and accommodation<br>• conservation<br>• discovery learning. | Particularly associated with:<br>• zone of proximal development (ZPD)<br>• social constructivist theory. | Particularly associated with:<br>• the three modes of representation:<br> – enactive<br> – iconic<br> – symbolic<br>• discovery learning<br>• scaffolding. |

## Jean Piaget

### Piaget's stages of cognitive development

Piaget believed that a child's way of thinking changes as they get older. He believed that all children pass through the four stages of cognitive development in the same order, although the age at which they enter and leave each stage may vary considerably. The four stages are:

1 Sensori-motor stage, 0–2 years
2 Pre-operational stage, 2–7 years:
   Pre-conceptual stage, 2–4 years
   Intuitive stage, 4–7 years
3 Concrete-operations stage, 7–11 years
4 Formal operations stage, 11 years onwards.

BACK to Chapter 8, page 299.

### Schemas

Piaget believed that children develop knowledge concepts by using and building on previous experiences. He considered that they gradually adapt these concepts, which he called **schemas**, to establish new understanding. For example, a child recognises a dog as something which is 'larger than themselves and has four legs' – this is a schema.

### Assimilation

The child uses the previously learned schema to fit a new situation. For example, the child uses the schema 'a dog is larger than themselves and has four legs' to refer to a goat as 'dog'. Piaget called this process **assimilation**.

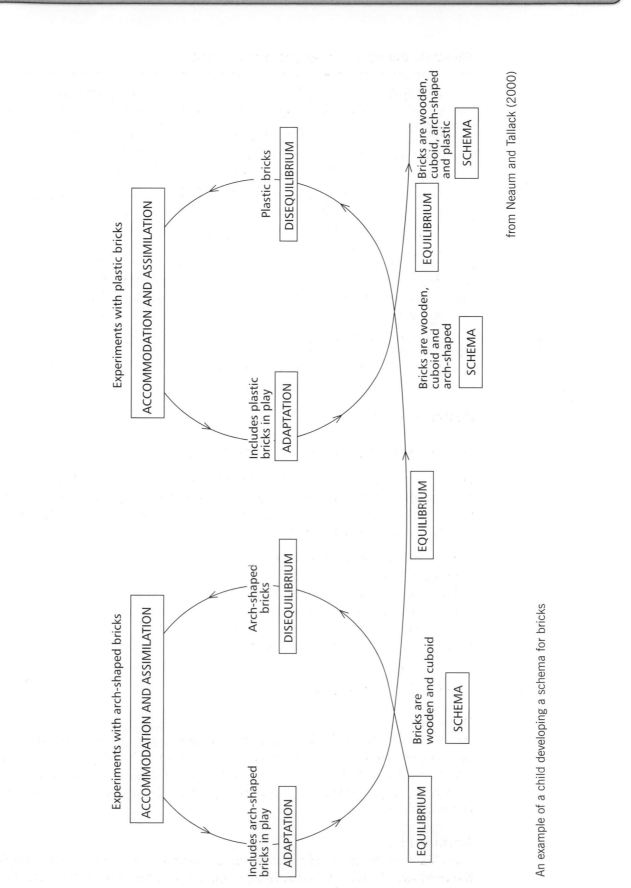

Experiments with arch-shaped bricks

ACCOMMODATION AND ASSIMILATION

Arch-shaped bricks

DISEQUILIBRIUM

Includes arch-shaped bricks in play

ADAPTATION

Bricks are wooden and cuboid

SCHEMA

EQUILIBRIUM

EQUILIBRIUM

Experiments with plastic bricks

ACCOMMODATION AND ASSIMILATION

Plastic bricks

DISEQUILIBRIUM

Includes plastic bricks in play

ADAPTATION

Bricks are wooden, cuboid and arch-shaped

SCHEMA

Bricks are wooden, cuboid, arch-shaped and plastic

SCHEMA

EQUILIBRIUM

from Neaum and Tallack (2000)

An example of a child developing a schema for bricks

### Accommodation

When this misunderstanding is corrected by an adult – the white goat is large, but it is a goat, not a dog – the child will be moved towards a new schema – goats and dogs can be large and either brown or white. Piaget called this process **accommodation**.

### The ongoing development of schemas

As the child comes into contact with different animals, they will continue to learn new schemas, for example, that a dog can be large or small, black, white or brown. They will also eventually have schemas that tell them that other animals can be large or small, and can also be black, white or brown.

### Disequilibrium

When a child is unable to make sense of new information (unable to assimilate) they are considered to be in an unbalanced state which Piaget called **disequilibrium**.

### Equilibrium

As the child accommodates new concepts, they reach a point of **equilibrium** where they are able to understand the new information.

Assimilation → Disequilibrium → Accommodation → Equilibrium → Assimilation

### Conservation

Piaget is also renowned for his views and experiments on **conservation**. He believed that children under the age of six would not be able to conserve (i.e. understand changes in quantity, size and number). He used a variety of tests to explore this. Below are examples of his three most well-known tests.

Examples    **Example A**

The child was shown two identical rows of pennies and was asked if they were the same. The pennies in the second row were then spaced apart and the child was asked if there were still the same number of pennies.
If the child was able to conserve, they would answer that there were the same number. If the child could not conserve, they would answer that there were more pennies in the longer row.

Children at the pre-operational stage say that the two rows contain the same number of pennies …

… but also that there are more pennies in the more spread-out, second row.

**Example B**

The child was shown two identical beakers of water and asked if they contained the same amount. After watching the adult pour the water from one beaker into a taller beaker, the child was asked if the amount of water in the beakers was still the same. If they could conserve, they would answer that the amount of water remained the same. If they could not conserve, they would state that the amount of water was different – that there was more water in the taller beaker.

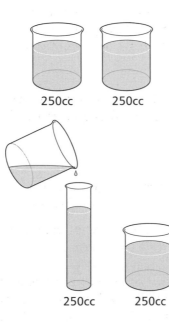

250cc  250cc

Children at the pre-operational stage believe that the volume of water is greater after it has been transferred to the taller glass.

250cc  250cc

**Example C**

The child was shown two identical balls of playdough and asked if they were the same amount. Having seen the adult roll one ball into a sausage shape, the child was asked if the amount of playdough was still the same. If the child could conserve, they would answer that the balls of playdough were still both the same size. If they could not conserve, they would think that the sausage shape was made from a greater amount of playdough.

Piaget's findings have been challenged by many theorists. In 1974, Donaldson and McGarrigle proved that a higher number of pre-operational stage children were able to conserve than had been found by Piaget, by the use of a character called 'naughty teddy'. Naughty teddy was used to 'accidentally' mess up the conservation experiments, for example, the row of pennies. The researchers felt that the way in which the questions had been phrased by Piaget had led children to assume that the adult was indicating that a change had occurred in the number of counters, amount of water, and so on. Using teddy, the children were able to see that it was simply teddy being 'naughty', and that no alteration had been made.

In your placement, try one of Piaget's experiments with children within the pre-operational stage.

- Firstly, ask the questions as Piaget would have done, and record your results.
- Next, introduce a 'helper', which could be a glove puppet, or you could make a paperbag puppet, as a 'naughty teddy' substitute. See if your results are any different. Record the results and compare them with your first results.

What have you learned from this activity?

### Discovery learning

Children learn best by being given opportunities to find out for themselves. Piaget's constructivist theory of play considered children to be active learners in which they enjoy using a range of materials, objects and situations from their everyday life to help them develop their play.

*Cerys*

Cerys was being 'mummy' in the role-play house. She was getting her baby ready to go shopping. She put on a pair of play shoes and picked up a shopping bag. When she was half way across the room, she shouted 'My baby, I've forgotten my baby', and rushed back to collect the pram. Cerys was learning about responsibility through her play.

*Claudia*

Claudia was playing with the magnetic train set. She was trying to link up each of the carriages to the engines, but one carriage would not stay linked up. Cerys tried it at the end of each train she had made, but to no avail (the magnets at one end attract and at the other repel). Eventually she turned the carriage around and this time it linked up successfully. Claudia was very pleased with herself and continued with her game happily.

1 Which of the above case studies gives the best example of discovery learning, do you think?
2 What examples of discovery learning have you seen in your current placement?
3 Does your current placement allow opportunities for discovery learning, or do staff step in to help out whenever a child is seen to be having difficulties?

## Lev Vygotsky

### Vygotsky's social constructivist view of play

Vygotsky believed in the need for children to be able to access a range of objects, materials and situations to develop their play, in much the same way as Piaget did. However, Vygotsky differed in his thinking from Piaget in that he placed considerable emphasis on the child's need for adult input into their play in order for the child to realise their potential through play situations.

### Zone of proximal development (ZPD)

Vygotsky developed his theory of ZPD by studying what a child can achieve playing alone, and what they can achieve with some sensitive input from an adult.

FORWARD to pages 419–21. The observations shown there illustrate Vygotsky's ZPD theory – they show how an adult can enhance the development of a child's understanding, affecting their subsequent thinking and actions.

| **Professional Practice** | • This theory is particularly relevant to any child who is attempting to achieve a new aim, perhaps using a new piece of equipment or a more complex jigsaw puzzle.<br>• Think about where you have observed an adult helping a child in this way. |
| --- | --- |

## Jerome Bruner

### Discovery learning

Bruner believed that children enjoy finding out new things for themselves, and like Piaget he felt that children learn through the use of materials that are freely available to them.

### The three modes of thinking

#### Enactive mode

Bruner emphasised the importance of first-hand experiences and how they enable children to develop their own ideas. He referred to this as the enactive mode of thinking. It links with discovery learning.

#### Iconic mode

This mode of thinking involves the child's development of mental images, such as remembering what somebody or something looks like.

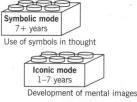

Iconic representation shows that the child is extending their memory, and not purely relying on active learning (enactive mode). A photograph, for example, will remind a child of someone they have met, and enable them to think about the person further. Similarly, the smell of onions may remind them of cooking a barbecue with granny and grandad.

Bruner's three modes of thinking

#### Symbolic mode

The involvement of symbolism, including music, art and language, is what Bruner called the symbolic mode of thinking. It enables older children to extend their thinking and be able to express themselves through a variety of mediums.

BACK to Chapter 8, page 302, for information on Bruner's theory of scaffolding.

## Ivan Pavlov

### Classic conditioning

Pavlov (1849–1936) carried out experiments on responses to stimulus. His famous experiment with dogs involved the use of a bell (the neutral stimulus) and food (response stimulus). When the bell rang, the dogs were fed, and the response stimulus of salivating occurred. After a time, the sound of a bell ringing would elicit the response stimulus (the saliva) without the production of food.

Initially: Neutral stimulus (bell) + Response stimulus (food) = Outcome (saliva)

Eventually: Neutral stimulus (bell) = Outcome (saliva)

---

**Professional Practice**

Classic conditioning theory can also be applied to working with children, encouraging them to act within the structure and boundaries of the setting. Can you think of an example?
Using the model above as a guide, set out your example:

Initially: _____ + _____ = _____

Eventually: _____ = _____

---

## B.F. Skinner

### Operant conditioning

This theory is based on the positive reinforcement of behaviour.

◁◁ BACK to Chapter 7, page 277, for a discussion of strategies to positively reinforce children's behaviour.

B.F. Skinner (1904–90) rewarded rats if they behaved as he wanted them to. In his experiment he set up a box with a lever and the rats only received food if they pressed down on the lever in the box. This form of stimulus response moulds behaviour and Skinner put forward the idea that children learn this way too, for example, language develops by operant conditioning, due to parents and carers giving praise for 'correct' speech and pronunciation.

▷▷ FORWARD to page 391 to behaviourist theory in language development.

**Test Yourself**

1 Explain the difference between constructivist and social constructivist theory.
2 What is a schema?
3 How does a child reach the state of equilibrium?
4 What is the main challenge to Piaget's theory of conservation in pre-operational stage children?
5 Which theorist is associated with the ZPD theory?
6 Which of Bruner's modes of thinking involves the development of mental images?

# Sensory development of children

At birth, the nervous system is still far from complete and it is not easy to understand the level of sensory awareness that an infant has. Theorists are aware that the visual system is not strong initially and that it develops considerably in the first few months, whereas hearing is quite well developed right from birth. The main areas studied are vision, hearing and perception.

## Vision

From birth, infants turn to look at sources of light. They show interest in the human face, and researchers (for example, Robert Fantz in the 1950s) have repeatedly shown that the human face invokes a greater level of response than a range of other similar options.

An ideal source of further reading on this area of development is Oates (1999) – see *Bibliography and suggested further reading*, page 429.

Spontaneous and imitative facial expressions are seen within a few days of birth and the eyes of the newborn infant may be seen to move in the direction of sounds. The early visual interaction between infant and carer strengthens the process of bonding and therefore enhances emotional security in the long term.

### Stages of visual development

| Birth | Infant turns to the source of light. |
|---|---|
| | Imitative facial expressions are seen. |
| | The human face evokes greatest level of attention. |
| | Eyes do not at first move co-operatively. |
| One month | Turns to light sources. |
| | Stares at face of adult carer. |
| | Eyes now usually working in co-operation. |
| | Vision is held by bright mobile or similar object. |
| | Infant can visually track mother's face briefly. |
| Three months | Infant is now visually alert. |
| | Eyes move in co-operation. |
| | Defensive blink has been present for some time. |
| | Infant follows the movement of main carer. |
| | More sustained visual tracking of face or similar. |
| | May now be demonstrating visual awareness of own hands. |
| | Anticipation of feeding is demonstrated from visual clues. |

| Six months | Visually very alert.<br>Infants appear visually insatiable.<br>Eyes and head move to track objects of interest. |
|---|---|
| Twelve months | Hand–eye co-ordination is seen as small objects are picked up using pincer grasp (index finger and thumb).<br>Eyes follow correct direction of fallen or dropped objects. |

based on Sheridan (1991)

**Checklist**

Concerns regarding vision include:
- ✔ lack of eye contact with main carer
- ✔ no social smile by six weeks
- ✔ lack of visual tracking of carer's face or bright mobile by two months
- ✔ lack of visual response to impending breast or bottle feed
- ✔ lack of co-operative eye movement after three months
- ✔ lack of signs that infant reaches out for toys in response to visual stimulus
- ✔ lack of mobility or directed attention by twelve months.

## Hearing

At birth, the hearing of infants is acute as their auditory perception is as yet uncluttered by the sounds of everyday living. They can be seen to respond to sound by blinking and through startled movements (startle reflex). Newborn infants respond to the sound of their mother or main carer. They also show signs of auditory awareness by turning towards other sounds. Many infants are settled by calming or familiar music, often first heard within the safety of the womb.

### Stages of auditory development

| Birth | Startle reactions to sound.<br>Blinking is common in response to sounds.<br>Infant may 'still' to on-going gentle sounds.<br>Infant turns to sounds, including mother's voice. |
|---|---|
| One month | Still startled by sudden noises.<br>Stiffens in alarm, extending limbs.<br>Usually turns to sound of familiar voice.<br>Is usually calmed by the sound of a familiar voice. |

| Three months | Turns head or eyes towards the source of sounds. |
| | Often appears to search for location of sounds. |
| | Listens to musical mobiles and similar sounds. |
| Six months | Shows considerable interest in familiar sounds. |
| | Turns to locate even very gentle sounds. |
| | Vocalises deliberately, listening to self. |
| | Vocalises to get attention, listens and then vocalises again. |
| | Can usually imitate sounds in response to carers. |
| Twelve months | Responds to own name. |
| | Behaviour indicates hearing, by appropriate responses to carers. |

based on Sheridan (1991)

**Checklist**

Concerns regarding hearing include:
✔ lack of response to sudden or loud noises in first few months
✔ lack of response to familiar sounds, either by listening or by being calmed
✔ no tracking of gentle sounds by nine months
✔ no indication of turning to the sound of familiar voice
✔ limited changes in vocalising from about six months
✔ no obvious response to carer's simple instructions at a year.

From one year onwards the development of speech is the greatest indication of a child's hearing levels, although health issues can impact on hearing, for example repeated ear infections or glue-ear.

## Infant perception

Perception is the feedback of information via the body's senses. These senses help in the understanding of all that is happening both *to* us and *around* us. Visual perception (sight) and auditory perception (hearing) are two early indicators (both physical and perceptual) that development is progressing as expected. Vision and hearing link directly with language and cognitive development, and are both assessed at regular intervals during infancy and early childhood.

FORWARD to Chapter 10, page 464, *Screening techniques*.

### The visual cliff investigation: depth perception
Studies carried out on infant perception include the work of Gibson and Walk who, in 1960, devised a visual cliff to investigate depth perception in infants.

The infants were first placed on the 'visually safe' (chequered floor) side of the table and were encouraged to crawl across the surface above the 'visually unsafe' (clear) cliff space towards their mothers. Out of twenty-seven infants aged six to twelve months (who had gained a degree of mobility), only three crawled across the surface. The remaining twenty-four showed a marked reservation regarding crossing from the 'safe' to the 'unsafe' area of the visual cliff surface, even though they would be moving towards their mothers, who would normally be a safe haven for them.

Under the age of six months it is clearly not possible to investigate depth perception in the same way, due to infants' lack of mobility. However, other studies, for example Campos *et al.* in 1970, monitored the heart rates of infants when placed first on one side, and then on the other. At just fifty-five days (approximately eight weeks) the heart rates were perceived to be different, indicating that even at this young age a degree of depth perception is present. Under eight weeks depth perception did not appear to have developed.

The 'visual cliff' experiment by Gibson and Walk

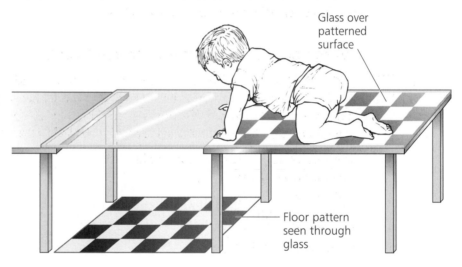

Glass over patterned surface

Floor pattern seen through glass

**Test Yourself**

1 What signs would give you concern regarding an infant's visual development?
2 What would raise your concern regarding their auditory development?
3 What does the term 'perception' mean?
4 How might a lack of sensory awareness affect other areas of development?
5 At what age did psychologists establish that depth perception is developed?

# Language development of children

Language is the main way in which humans communicate with one another. It involves facial expressions, tone of voice, body posture and expression of meaning through the use of words or symbols.

Language is:
- rule-governed – grammatical rules are present in each language (syntax)
- structured – the sound system that makes up the speech sounds (phonology)
- symbolic – words have meanings, building into phrases, and so on (semantics)
- generative – it is the basis of the sharing of knowledge (pragmatics).

## Pre-requisites for language

The normal, unimpeded development of language is affected by other areas of development. For example, socially and cognitively an awareness of the need to interact as means of communication is imperative, as are the physical abilities of vision, hearing and speech. Children learn the basis of their culture through communication (socialisation theory), and develop understanding of themselves and how they fit within their peer and social groups (goodness of fit).

Psychologists believe that language plays an important part in all aspects of human development, with some theorists arguing that language is the basis of learning. An important debate involves the questions: Is language dependent on thought? or Is thought dependent on language?

What are your first thoughts on this language *v.* thought debate? Do you think understanding is needed in order to develop linguistically? Or do you think that language enables understanding to develop? Come back to these questions when you have read the theories outlined below.

## Theories of language development

The theories described below offer some very different ideas about how language develops. As you read them, consider which you could accept and which do not seem possible. A detailed discussion of the theories of language can be found in Cullis *et al.* (1999) – see *Bibliography and suggested further reading*, page 429.

Theories of language development include:
- association theory
- behaviourist theory
- language acquisition device theory
- maturational theory
- interactionist theory.

### Association theory

This theory proposes that a child gradually builds their language by associating words with what they see. This theory works well up to a point, but does not take into account all aspects of language, for example those used to describe feelings or emotions.

### Behaviourist theory

Theorists such as B.F. Skinner proposed that a child's development of language is shaped by the responses given to them by their parents or main carers (operant conditioning), the positive reinforcement of vocalisations encouraging the child to repeat a specific sound over and over again.

Example    Daniel is an infant of six months whose babbling sounds have become *dadadada*. Daniel's mother greets this with delight and encouragement, stating that 'Dada' will be home soon. Skinner believed that the continuous positive reinforcement of 'correct' speech sounds, and the lack of positive response to sounds or (eventually) sentence structure that is not correct, will mould a child's language formation. This theory is based on the same principles as social learning theory, i.e. that humans repeat behaviour that is rewarded positively (remember the Bobo dolls).

Skinner's theory would indicate that children have to carry out a trial-and-error process for every aspect of speech, but this is clearly not the case, although it is accepted that infants are encouraged by the positive reactions of adults. Skinner's theory was challenged by many psychologists and consequently the nativist theories set out below became an inviting alternative.

### Language acquisition device (LAD) theory

Noam Chomsky (a nativist) believed in the biological theory that infants are born with a predisposition for language. He called this the infant's **language acquisition device (LAD)**. He considered that this LAD enabled children to absorb the language that they heard, to decode it and then develop an understanding of its rules and grammatical structure. It has been shown that children of all cultures develop language at much the same time and this gave support to the theories of Chomsky and others like him.

### Maturational theory

Lennenberg believed in a theory similar to Chomsky. He considered that as long as children were exposed to language, they would simply pick it up as their development progressed in other ways too. This should not be confused with the maturational theory of Arnold Gasell who studies biological maturation.

### Interactionist theory

The basis of the interactionist theory is that the schemas that children develop subsequently impact on language development by children first experiencing, and then talking about their experiences. Therefore, this theory sees language as a reflection of cognitive development. Piaget, Vygotsky and Bruner took this interactionist approach to their thinking on language development.

### Activity

Make a copy of the table below and note on it which theories of language fit in with the nature theory and which fit in with the nurture theory.

| Language theory | Nature | Nurture |
|---|---|---|
| Association theory | | |
| Behaviourist theory | | |
| Language acquisition device theory | | |
| Maturational theory | | |
| Interactionist theory | | |

It is interesting that research carried out with hearing children born to deaf parents has noted that, while a child may learn words from what they hear around them (radio, television, videos, and so on), they need to be actively involved in conversation in order to develop their understanding and use of grammar. For some children, speech therapy resulted in a sudden improvement in their language structure which soon brought them up to the expected level of language development for their age. This indicated that they had previously been ready to learn the grammatical rules associated with their culture, but needed the active involvement with others in order to facilitate it.

## Stages of language development

As with every aspect of development, children develop language at differing rates within what is considered to be the 'normal' range. This process of language development can be divided into ten basic stages:

1  Non-verbal communication/expression
2  Speech-like noises
3  Controlling sounds, using mouth and tongue
4  Imitating sounds
5  First words
6  Development of vocabulary (50 words is usual at two years)
7  Putting words together to form simple phrases and sentences
8  Use of grammar
9  Use of meaning
10  Using language to develop other skills, for example early literacy.

These ten stages can be linked to approximate ages as shown in the table on page 394.

| Professional Practice | As you move through the various placements that will make up your professional practice experience, observe and note the differences in speech intonation, questioning and grammar of children at different ages and stages. |
|---|---|

## The development of speech sounds in the English language

Speech sounds are made up of consonants, vowels, syllables and words.

### Consonants
Consonants are 'closed' sounds. This means that for a consonant sound to be produced, there is an obstruction to the airflow, by parts of the mouth coming into contact with each other or almost contacting.

Example
- Try saying the word *book*. To pronounce the *b* in book, the lips need to come into contact.
- To pronounce the *s* in the word *sand*, the tip of the tongue touches the ridge just behind the top front teeth.

These are examples of how the obstructions are made.

The stages of language development

| Age | Understanding | No. of words | Type of words | Average length of sentence |
|---|---|---|---|---|
| 3 months | Soothed by sound | 0 | Cooing and gurgling | 0 |
| 6 months | Responds to voice tones | 0 | Babble | 0 |
| 1 year | Knows own name and a few others | 1 | Noun (naming word) | 1 word |
| 18 months | Understands simple commands | 6–20 | Nouns + | 1 word |
| 2 years | Understands much more than they can say | 50+ | Verbs and pronouns (action + name) | 1–2 word phrases |
| 2½ years | Enjoys simple and familiar stories | 200+ | Pronouns I, me, you; Questions what, where | 2–3 word phrases |
| 3 years | Carries out complex commands | 500–1,000 | Plurals; Verbs in present tense; Questions who | 3–4 word phrases |
| 4 years | Listens to long stories | 1,000–1,500 | Verbs in past tense; Questions why, where, how | 4–5 word phrases |
| 5 years | Developing the ability to reason | 1,500–2,000 | Complex sentences with adult forms of grammar | 5–6 word phrases |

> **The approximate sequential development of consonants in the English language**
>
> | | |
> |---|---|
> | At 2 years | *m, n, p, b, t, d, w* |
> | At 2½ years | *k, g, ng* (as in *sing*), *h* |
> | 2½–3 years | *f, s, l, y* |
> | 3½–4 years | *v, z, ch, j, sh* |
> | 4½ years onwards | *th* (as in *thin*), <u>*th*</u> (as in *the*), *r* |
>
> Double consonants such as *sp*, *tr* and *fl*, and also the sounds *r* and *th*, can develop as late at 6½ years in some children.

There are five main types of consonants:
- plosives
- nasals
- fricatives
- affricates
- approximants.

## English consonant sounds 'at a glance'

| | Bilabial | Labio-dental | Dental | Alveolar | Post-alveolar | Palatal | Velar | Glottal |
|---|---|---|---|---|---|---|---|---|
| Plosive | p, b | | | t, d | | | c/k, g | |
| Nasal | m | | | n | | | ng | |
| Fricative | | f, v | th, <u>th</u> | s, z | sh, zh | | | h |
| Affricate | | | | | ch, j | | | |
| Approximant | w | | | l | r | y | | |

> **Professional Practice**
>
> How we pronounce sounds is quite complex. It is, however, a useful exercise for early years workers to explore their own pronunciation to gain a better understanding of how the parts of the mouth work together and how each sound is subsequently produced. This helps with understanding the difficulties faced by some children in developing their speech sounds.

### Plosives

Plosives are produced by a complete obstruction of the airflow at some position in the mouth, for example, the lips coming together. Air builds up behind the temporary obstruction and when the obstruction is removed (for example, the lips part) the air rushes out (a plosive).

Plosives can be voiceless (produced without the involvement of the vocal chords) or voiced (involving the vibration of the vocal chords). They occur in pairs:

- first pair: *p*, *b*
  The two lips come together to form a complete obstruction. These are known as bilabial plosives (two lips). Try pronouncing them.
- second pair: *t*, *d*
  These involve the tip of the tongue contacting the gum ridge (alveolar ridge) just behind the top front teeth. (Run your tongue over your alveolar ridge to identify where it is). These are known as alveolar plosives. Try pronouncing them.
- third pair: *c/k*, *g* (as in *goat*)
  The back of the roof of the mouth is known as the soft palate (velum). Velar plosives are sounded when the tongue is in contact with the soft palate.

Try pronouncing these three consonant sounds.

## Nasals

When a plosive sound is made, the soft palate is raised so that it touches the back of the throat and stops air from escaping through the nose. Nasals are similar in that there is a complete obstruction of air flow in the mouth, but the air pressure does not build up. It is allowed to escape through the nose by lowering the soft palate. There are three nasals:

- *m* is a bilabial nasal where the sound is formed at the front of the mouth, with the lips coming together
- *n* is an alveolar nasal, where the obstruction is between the back of the tongue and the soft palate
- *ng* (as in *sing*) is a velar nasal. This sound never appears at the beginning of a word in English.

Try pronouncing these nasal consonants.

## Fricatives

These sounds are formed by the narrowing of the mouth passage by any two of the articulators (lips, teeth, tongue, roof of mouth) coming into near contact. The air is forced through a narrow gap creating a friction sound, hence the name, fricative consonant. Each of these sounds can be prolonged by first taking a deep breath.

There are four pairs of fricatives:

- first pair: *f*, *v*
  These are articulated with slight contact between the bottom lip and the top front teeth. They are known as labio-dental fricatives.
- second pair: *th* (as in *thin*), *th* (as in *that*)
  These fricatives involve the tongue nearly contacting the top front teeth. The sounds are quite hard for young children to pronounce and they often use alternatives, for example: *f* instead of *th* and/or *v* instead of *th*.
- third pair: *s*, *z*
  These are formed when the tongue is almost in contact with the alveolar ridge. They are known as alveolar fricatives.
- fourth pair: *sh*, *zh* (as 'sounded' in the middle of the word *measure*)
  These post-alveolar fricatives are formed further back in the mouth when the

middle of the tongue comes into contact with the roof of the mouth, just behind the alveolar ridge. The *zh* sound is never found at the beginning of a word in English.

The final fricative is *h*. It is a glottal fricative. It is made deep down in the throat (the glottis). This sound is never found at the end of a word in English.

Try pronouncing these fricative consonants.

### Affricates

The affricates are the sounds that combine both a complete obstruction with a partial obstruction. They start with a complete obstruction formed by the tip of the tongue contacting the alveolar ridge, but then the air is released slowly with friction, behind the alveolar ridge. No air is released in an explosive way. These sounds are *j* and *ch*. They are post-alveolar affricates. Try pronouncing them.

### Approximants

The term 'approximant' is used when the mouth passage is not completely obstructed, as it is with the plosives and the nasals, nor is it restricted so that friction is developed. Two articulators (tongue, teeth, etc.) approximate closely together.

The approximants are:
* *w*, formed by the two lips approximating closely (bi-labial approximant)
* *l*, made by the tongue approximating to the alveolar ridge (alveolar approximant)
* *r*, sounded by the tongue being behind the alveolar ridge (post-alveolar approximant)
* *y*, articulated with the middle of the tongue approximating closely to the palate (palatal approximant).

Try pronouncing these approximants.

 BACK to the 'at a glance' table on page 395 to help consolidate your understanding.

### Vowels

The basic vowel sounds are *a*, *e*, *i*, *o* and *u*, but there are other vowel sounds too. These include the double sounds such as *ee*, *oo*, and so on. Vowels are 'open' sounds. There is no obstruction to the airflow during pronunciation and each sound differs according to the position of the mouth. For example:
* If the lips are spread widely, the sound *ee* is produced.
* If the lips are rounded, the sound *oo* is produced.
* Vowels can be long sounds as in the word *more*. They can also be short sounds as in the word *pack*.
* There are simple vowels such as *o* as in *pot*, *u* as in *put*, *a* as in *pat*. They are simple because once the mouth is set in position it does not need to alter in order to produce the sound.
* There are also more complex vowel sounds such as *oy* as in *boy* and *ow* as in *cow*. With these sounds, you need to change the mouth and/or tongue position for the full sound to be made.

- All vowels in English are 'voiced'. This means that they involve the vibration of the vocal chords.

### Syllables

Speech sounds combine together to form syllables. A syllable is made up of a combination of consonants (c) and at least one vowel (v). There can be up to three consonants before a vowel and up to four consonants after a vowel in the English language.

Examples of syllables:

*be* = cv (1 consonant and 1 vowel)
*and* = vcc (1 vowel and 2 consonants), and so on
*plot* = ccvc
*strip* = cccvc
*tempts* = cvcccc

The more consonants in a syllable, the harder it will be for a child to pronounce, because it requires a greater ability to co-ordinate the articulators.

### Words

Syllables, in turn, combine together to form words. Some words have just one syllable, for example *cat*, *dog* and *hen*. These are called *monosyllabic words*. All other words have more than one syllable and are known as *polysyllabic words*.

Even in adulthood, some people have difficulty in pronouncing some polysyllabic words. For example, common difficulties are found in pronouncing:

*laboratory* (often mispronounced as *labroratrory*)
*certificates* (often mispronounced as *certsificates*).

### Activity

a) Which words do you find difficult, or stumble over on occasions?
b) Which words have you noticed other adults having difficulty with?
c) How complex are the syllable combinations of these words?

## Disordered or delayed speech

Many children have phases of unclear speech, but they do not all need to be seen by a speech therapist.

### Dysfluency

Many temporary disorders are due to the child hastening to say something and stumbling over it in their eagerness and excitement. This common occurrence is known as **dysfluency**.

Hesitation occurs as a child tries to express themselves. The dysfluency is often associated with them attempting to use more complex language structure. Speech therapists refer to this as *normal developmental dysfluency* as it does not usually need professional intervention.

When conversing with a dysfluent child, it is important to give them time and attention to minimise the affect of the dysfluency.

| **Professional Practice** | The following checklist should be helpful. |
|---|---|

Checklist

✔ Do speak steadily and clearly yourself.
✔ Do give the dysfluent child your full attention.
✔ Do avoid interrupting the child whenever possible.
✔ Do focus on *what* they are saying, and try to ignore the dysfluency.
✗ Do not ask the child to repeat it or to start again.
✗ Do not tell the child to 'take a deep breath' before they speak.
✗ Do not tell the child to slow down.
✗ Do not ask the child to 'think it through' before they speak.
✗ Do not allow discussion of their dysfluency in their presence.

If a child's dysfluency continues for more than a short period of time, or if the parents or the child appear to be worried by the dysfluency, a referral to a speech therapist will usually be made. The British Stammering Association has drawn up the following guidelines to help with decision-making regarding referrals. A referral is made if:

'the child has dysfluent speech and one or more of the following factors are present:
- a family history of stammering or speech or language problems
- the child is finding learning to talk difficult in any way
- the child shows signs of frustration or is upset by his speaking
- the child is struggling when talking
- the child is in a dual language situation and is stammering in her first language
- there is parental concern or uneasiness
- the child's general behaviour is causing concern.'

Mukherji and O'Dea (2000)

### Elision

The term 'elision' refers to when a child regularly misses out part of a speech sound altogether. It is a common occurrence, particularly with the second consonant of a cluster of two, for example:
- the *st* in the word *postman* would become *pos'man*
- the *pt* in the word *slept* would become *slep'*.

In young children this is part of the maturational development of speech patterns. In older children and adults it is usually more likely to be habit!

## Language disorders and speech therapy

Concerns regarding language development include:

- lack of communication with parents and carers in early weeks
- significant feeding difficulties (speech therapists are often involved at this early stage)
- lack of vocalisation from three months onwards
- no babbling from eight to nine months onwards
- lack of verbal responses to play
- vocalisation completely out of line with the developmental 'norms'.

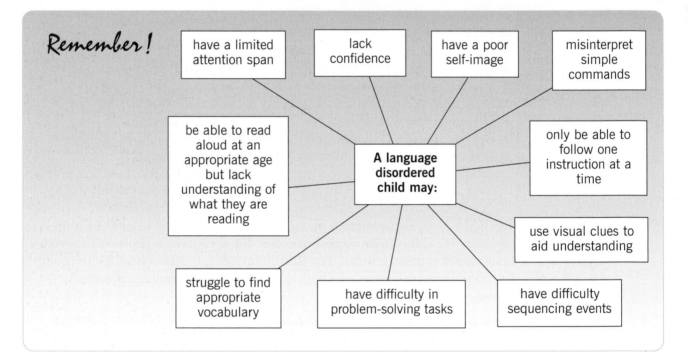

When expressing themselves, language disordered children may:

- have difficulty in finding appropriate words
- display word-order confusion
- have difficulty in giving explanations
- use confused grammar
- omit grammatical word endings
- use confused sounds within individual words.

Language disorder can therefore affect other aspects of a child's learning and development. Additional factors that can affect language include medical problems such as glue-ear. This is a condition of the middle ear in which a sticky mucus is formed which is unable to drain away through the eustachian tubes in the normal way. If severe and left untreated, it can lead to permanent hearing loss.

A cleft lip and palate is another medical and physical problem that can affect speech. A child born with one or both of these physical conditions will automatically be referred to a speech therapist, to ensure that the most appropriate feeding positions are established from birth.

A useful source of further reading to extend your understanding of language development is Mukherji and O'Dea (2000) – see *Bibliography and suggested further reading*, page 429.

## Language delay

As with language disorder, any significant delay in language developing along the expected 'norms' is monitored, and a referral made to a speech therapist as appropriate. There are environmental, medical, social, cultural and genetic factors that can impact on language development, as summarised in the spidergram below.

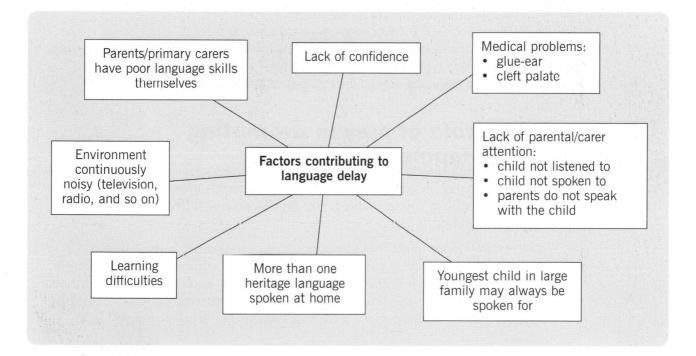

Activity

Television has often been cited negatively as a passive activity for children, but it can also be a good source of learning. How do you think television might affect language development? Make a copy of the table and note your ideas under the headings. Discuss your ideas with a partner.

**The effects of television on language development**

| Positive effects | Negative effects |
|---|---|
|  |  |

## Language as a means of communication

Language is essential to humans in order to communicate our needs, express our feelings and extend our experiences beyond our own environment by interacting with others. These interactions enable us to enhance our thinking and learn new skills. Spoken language is our most important means of communication. It is enhanced by facial expression, tone of voice and body language. Communication is an important aspect of early years professionalism.

 BACK to Chapter 3, *Communication and Supportive Skills*.

**Test Yourself**

1 What is syntax?
2 Name two prerequisites for language.
3 Who proposed the language acquisition device theory?
4 Which theorists supported the interactionist theory of language development?
5 How many types of consonants are there?
6 What is meant by normal developmental dysfluency?

# The role of play in promoting development

In developing an understanding of play and how it can enhance the development of young children, you need to analyse different aspects of each activity offered.

Learning opportunities can sometimes be easy to identify in the activities commonly provided in early years settings, but sometimes they are less obvious. Within the confines of this section it is not possible to cover every form of activity and so the section will simply focus on one that is extremely popular – role play – analysing the learning opportunities for each area of development within it.

Role play is one of the most popular activities in all early years settings

# Role play

One of the most popular activities in any nursery, pre-school or classroom is the role-play area. It is often referred to as the home corner, and it is a flexible activity which can be transformed into many other role-play situations. Popular alternatives to the home would be a hospital, a post office, a hairdressers, a cafe or a railway station. These alternative settings can be set up purely for fun and experience, to help children to explore a current topic, or for the (indirect) benefit of a particular child shortly to face a new event in their life, perhaps something that may be worrying them, such as a stay in hospital.

Role play is usually viewed as being non-directed (free-flow) play. It allows children to use their imagination and be whoever they want to be, without any real restrictions. The area is usually set aside from the main throughway of the nursery or classroom, offering a degree of privacy and ideally it is sufficiently spacious to accommodate a small group of children, and has appropriate equipment, domestic or otherwise, to meet the needs of the children at their current levels of development. Role play should also offer opportunities for children to further their development through exploration and interaction, with attention being given to gender and culture, ensuring that the facilities offered both reflect and promote positive images, therefore giving value to individual children and raising their self-esteem.

The attitudes of the early years staff will have an impact on the way in which a role-play area is equipped, as much of what will be needed is regularly found amongst the surplus of the average home. The involvement of parents, particularly those of other cultures, is invaluable in contributing items to the role-play corner and ensures that a range of cultures are represented sufficiently and appropriately.

BACK to Chapter 2, pages 71–82, for further ideas.

As children involve themselves in role-play situations, they enhance and consolidate aspects of each area of development. For example, socially the child who plays alone or parallel to others will initially be observed to imitate what they have previously seen or experienced, for example making tea, feeding the baby, and so on. As onlookers to the co-operative play of others, these children begin to learn by observation and gradually develop the skills of how to interact with others verbally and how to become involved within a group or paired play setting.

The children who are already playing co-operatively with each other, in the early stages of this type of play, will probably have their own agenda which they will bring to the play. This eventually develops into joint ideas which evolve continuously and spontaneously as they go along. They may take on individual roles, possibly with simple rules for their character, for example 'only mummy wears the high shoes' or 'the baby takes a teddy with them'. These opportunities to be another person enable them to experience an alternative position and viewpoint, and together with a range of culturally appropriate artefacts and a gender-free environment are useful in learning about the values of individuals and the importance of equality. Self-advocacy (being able to put forward their own ideas or opinions) is also enhanced in this way.

Opportunities to care and to share usually arise in role play, with one child looking after the others in some way, although roles may on occasions become confused, perhaps by the 'doctor' getting into bed with the 'patient' or the 'shopkeeper' going home on the bus with the 'shoppers'. This is a natural part of the development of understanding of life situations and the boundaries of various roles. As children apportion roles and tasks, the early stages of fairness and moral reasoning are being developed.

For the quiet, shy child in the group, the role play setting offers a non-threatening opportunity to communicate and interact, helping them to grow in confidence. They can usually be as little or as greatly involved as they want to be and may alternate between parallel and co-operative play.

For the child whose language is delayed or disordered, the non-threatening situation of role play offers the chance to communicate without pressure. The repetitive nature of many role-play games can help a child by consolidating the use of words and their meanings, and also by developing and exploring the use of different objects and articles which help to enhance the learning of new vocabulary.

Many role-play situations offer children the opportunity to explore their concerns and act out their emotions. Situations from their home life may be displayed within their play and at times early years staff may become acquainted with personal family issues that they would not normally be made aware of. If this expression through play is not leading to any distress of either the child concerned or the other children in the setting, it can usually be left to run its course. On occasions, however, a child's anger (or distress) may need sensitive intervention by an adult to help them sort through their feelings.

Physically, role play involves both gross and fine movements with the putting on and taking off of dressing-up clothes. Dressing-up games offer opportunities for tackling zips and buttons, hats and jewellery, gloves and scarfs, on themselves, on each other and on the dolls and teddies they use as additional people or props. The manoeuvring of chairs into buses or trains, and the steering of prams and buggies helps develop muscles as well as spatial awareness and sense of direction.

Cognitively, as children carry out tasks such as setting the table for tea, or sorting out tickets for train journeys they will be using early number skills, matching cups to saucers, placing knives with forks and counting items to match the numbers of children involved in the current game. Literacy skills are developed as the 'ticket office' staff issue tickets, make notes, 'read' timetables, and so on. In the cafe, the orders for food and drinks are taken, notices are put up, menus are written and cheques made out as payment. In the hospital, the nurses will take temperatures, and note them on a chart, doctors will make notes, patients will read books in bed. The opportunities for introducing numeracy and literacy are almost endless – if you supply children with the basic materials, they will explore their own ideas, and experiences and interpret them accordingly.

**Professional Practice** Manufactured artefacts are not essential to the presentation of good role play. Children can be very inventive with quite simple items, and the use of playdough or similar materials to represent food in the home, the cafe or the hospital is a good example of how a child moves gradually towards abstract thought.

**Activity**

The text above gives a range of ideas for role play, but clearly there are many more. Choose one of the following role-play situations:
- doctor's surgery
- pet shop
- railway station.
a) Plan how you would offer it to the children in your current setting. Remember that you will need to take into account the ages and stages of development of the children you are working with.
b) Note how your chosen option can enhance each area of development.

**Professional Practice** Having explored the learning opportunities within role play, you should now be ready to identify opportunities in other areas of play too. Take time to think through the range of activities offered in your current early years placement.

BACK to Chapter 8, page 320, for a list of everyday activities and further discussion on early learning.

# Observational techniques

Observation and recording children's development is an important aspect of the role of an early years worker. Learning the techniques of observation will enable you to understand your future role as a professional and give you a grounding in the skills you will need. Observation forms part of the assessment process within early years courses and is therefore a requirement in order to obtain your qualification.

It is important to understand:
- why observations are carried out
- how observations are carried out
- when and where you will observe
- what you will observe
- a range of techniques for observing children
- how you can record your observations
- how to put an observation portfolio together.

# Why observations are carried out

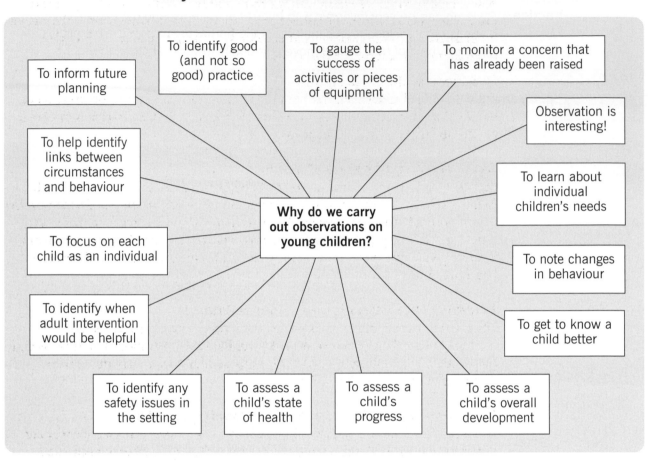

### To learn about individual children's needs
Through observation, you may identify that a particular child is reluctant to socialise with others, or is not accepted by the group and is consequentially on their own for much of the time. Developing strategies with the child, to encourage them to play initially alongside others and then more co-operatively, gradually helps to involve them in interactive play without adult intevention.

### To note changes in behaviour
Observation is a useful means of identifying any significant change in how a child is behaving. For example, a previously happy and bright child who is suddenly very quiet and withdrawn, or possibly aggressive, should raise your concern. Taking time to see if the behaviour is generalised or if it only occurs in isolated situations helps you develop a strategy to help the child back to their former self.

### To get to know a child better
Particularly with a child new to the setting, an outline assessment of their stage of development helps staff understand their needs and enables them to offer an appropriate programme of care and education.

### To assess a child's overall development

Assessment is routine in most settings and an initial assessment is likely to take place when a child moves from one setting to another. It helps identify the rate of progress that a child is making and enables the setting to plan an appropriate programme to meet the child's needs.

### To assess a child's progress

Once an overall assessment has been made of a child, subsequent observation can be useful in identifying whether they are progressing. Areas of concern can be picked up and used as a future focus.

### To assess a child's state of health

In a busy early years setting, a tired child will struggle to achieve and enjoy the facilities offered. Observation can help you monitor a situation and decide whether a child is simply tired or whether they have a medical need. Young children are usually full of energy, particularly at the start of the day, but those who have only recently given up a daytime sleep may need times for rest built into their daily programme.

### To identify any safety issues in the setting

Observation can highlight areas within the setting where supervision is insufficient, or where potential hazards could arise. Observation should be used, in conjunction with reflection of past accidents or incidents, to inform decisions regarding changes in safety policy.

### To identify when adult intervention would be helpful

Some children benefit from sensitive adult input into their activities (remember Vygotsky and Bruner). Observing adults in the nursery or classroom can be a good grounding for you as a student to know when to intervene and when to hold back. As a student you should feel able to ask (at a suitable time) why a decision was made either to intervene or to leave a child to their own devices. This will develop your understanding of observation skills.

### To focus on each child as an individual

Most settings have quite high numbers of children and to observe them as a group would usually mean that the louder and more active child will focus far more centrally in the observation than the quiet child who has been unobtrusively engaged throughout the session. It is quite likely that even with a series of such observations, the same children will be prominent and the same children will be 'missed'. This is why focusing on a child individually ensures that each child is assessed developmentally and that staff can see if they are happy within the setting.

 A useful source of further reading on the importance of observation is Miller (1997). This book sets out exemplary observations with critical discussion as an accompaniment – see *Bibliography and suggested further reading,* page 429.

### To help identify links between circumstances and behaviour

A good example of a link between circumstance and behaviour would be to observe what triggers a regular tantrum in a child. It is also the main focus of event sampling, see page 414.

BACK to Chapter 7, page 286, for the antecedent behaviour in the ABC behaviour management strategy.

### To inform future planning

Observation can identify aspects of developmental need that can be incorporated into future plans. For example, a child who is unable to hold a pencil satisfactorily (to meet their needs) may be disadvantaged as they move into a more formal education setting which requires regular use of pencil skills. Activities to encourage development of the finer skills in general would help such a child develop a more useful level of pencil control. Similarly, a child who has not as yet developed an understanding of the need to share can be encouraged to do so by being involved in a range of adult-supervised 'shared' activities.

### To identify good (and not so good) practice

Observation can reveal examples of excellence, but it can also raise concerns regarding the practice in a setting. A manager or supervisor may use observation as part of a staff appraisal scheme.

BACK to Chapter 3 for pointers on the importance of interactions with children.

What might the observer gain from studying this group of children?

### To gauge the sucess of activities or pieces of equipment

At times certain activities may not seem to be as popular and well-used as expected. This can be for many reasons: for example, the farm set may be too near to a doorway, so the animals regularly get knocked over. This might discourage children from playing with it. A simple solution could be to move the farm to a less busy area of the setting, where the children can enjoy the activity once again.

### To monitor a concern that has already been raised

When a child has been identified as having a particular need, it is likely that their progress will continue to be monitored. This may be by the early years staff within the setting, or it may be by a professional from outside of the setting who visits specifically for the purpose of observation and assessment of the child in a 'natural' environment.

### Observation is interesting!

It is to be hoped that the majority of early years workers and students are developing a career in the field of early years because of their interest in, and love of, children. Observation, although quite time-consuming, offers a fascinating insight into their world. If for no other reason, you should observe the children in your care for the pure pleasure that it will bring you.

| | |
|---|---|
| **Professional Practice** | Most early years workers would claim that they use their observation skills all the time. This is probably true to an extent, but like listening, many people do not give observation their full attention.<br><br>Close your eyes and think about the last person you spoke to before reading this. What were they wearing? What were they saying? How much detail can you remember? How much attention did you give to them? Were you fully attentive to what they were saying, or only half listening? It is likely that you were also focusing on something else at the same time.<br><br>Translate this situation into an early years setting and think about how much you may have missed if it was a child that had only received part of your attention. How might this feel for the child? How professional would this feel to you? |

## How observations are carried out

Observation is only valuable if it is carried out appropriately. It is not something that can be done half-heartedly. When planning to observe, there are certain practical issues that need to be taken into account. Observation can be carried out whilst being involved in an activity with children (this is called *participant observation*), but this is not ideal. It is far better to observe children from a short distance (*non-participant observation*), as you can focus completely on what you are observing and are not distracted by your own involvement.

In college, your tutors will introduce observation techniques to you and will most likely suggest that you have a practice before you start your portfolio. Many tutors will assess your first observations and offer feedback on their strengths and guidance on how they can be improved for the future.

**Checklist for observing children**

✔ Always gain permission to carry out observations of a specific child.

✔ Agree a convenient time for observing with your supervisor.

✔ Be unobtrusive, avoid eye-contact with the child you are observing, but remain within a range that enables you to hear their language use.

✔ Try not to catch the attention of the children in the setting.

✔ Be prepared – have, pen, paper, charts, and so on, to hand.

✔ Know what you are aiming to achieve, set objectives – spontaneous activity, planned activity, and so on.

✔ Try not to be drawn into a child's activity during the observation as this will be likely to hinder your outcomes.

✔ Start with children who appear within the normal developmental ranges. It will be easier for you to evaluate.

✔ Observe for short periods initially and gradually build up the time length.

✔ Try out a variety of observation styles in different situations.

✔ Keep pen and paper handy for those 'spur of the moment' observation opportunities.

✔ If using a timed technique, ensure you have easy access to a clock.

✔ In the event of an emergency, you will have to abandon your observation until another time.

*Remember!* Observations should only be carried out if there are sufficient other adult present to safely meet the required adult:child ratio of the setting. Students are officially exempt from these ratios, but at times they are relied upon to be an additional adult in the supervision of a complex activity.

## When and where to observe

During your training you will visit a range of settings, and each of these will offer opportunities for observation. Diploma students are required to undertake a minimum of 800 hours assessed placement experience involving at least 100 hours in each of the following age ranges:

- 0–1 year
- 1–2 years
- 2–4 years
- 4–8 years.

In special needs settings, placement experience can include older age children too.

It is accepted that at times the age ranges within some settings will differ, and the above guidelines can occasionally be adjusted slightly. You will therefore be able to have placement experience in at least four of the following settings:

- private day nursery
- local authority day nursery
- nursery class or nursery school
- primary school Reception class

- primary school Year 1 or Year 2
- voluntary pre-school
- special needs setting
- hospital
- private home
- registered childminder.

## What to observe

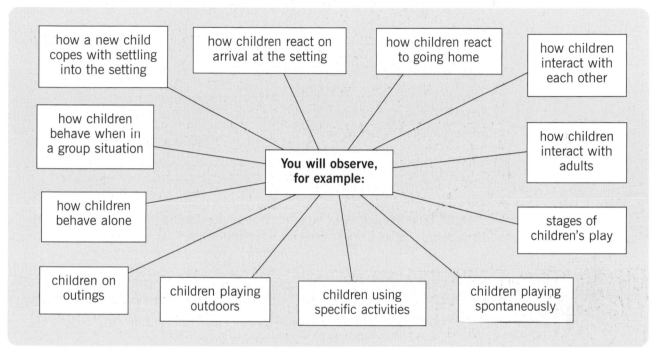

how a new child copes with settling into the setting

how children react on arrival at the setting

how children react to going home

how children interact with each other

how children behave when in a group situation

You will observe, for example:

how children interact with adults

how children behave alone

stages of children's play

children on outings

children playing outdoors

children using specific activities

children playing spontaneously

## Effects of observation on adults and children

Unobtrusive observation will give a truer picture of what is really happening as both adults and children react differently if they know they are being observed. Some adults are uncomfortable being observed by students and some parents are unhappy with their child being focused upon. This is why permission to observe is needed in advance.

*Remember!* You do not usually need to observe children interacting with an adult, unless for a specific purpose.

## Techniques for observing children

There are many different methods of observing children, some enabling you to record detailed information and some being more generalised.

An excellent source of further reading, with examples and discussion of each of the methods mentioned below, is Hobart and Frankel (1999) – see *Bibliography and suggested further reading*, page 429.

### Naturalistic observation (written record)

This is likely to be one of the first methods of observation that you use. It is useful as it needs no specific preparation, you simply need to be able to write down as clearly (and concisely) as you can what you are observing. It can, however, be repetitive and long-winded to write out neatly afterwards – as children are so active, you may find that with this method you miss out on recording some of what they are doing.

### Movement and flow chart

The use of movement and flow chart observations enables you to monitor the movements of a particular child. The simplest way to do this is to produce a rough sketch of the setting, noting where each activity is positioned and then track the child's movements, adding in the times and duration of use at each activity.

Example    The movement and flow chart below tracks Jenny's movements.

### Summary of Jenny's movements:

Jenny arrives at Little Lambs Nursery at 8.30 a.m.

|       |                                                                      |
|-------|----------------------------------------------------------------------|
| 8.30  | She moves straight to the drawing and writing table (8.30–8.40)      |
| 8.40  | Jenny moves to the dressing up clothes (8.40–8.55)                   |
| 8.55  | Jenny plays outside (8.55–9.15)                                      |
| 9.15  | She returns to the dressing up clothes to change her outfit (9.15–9.20) |
| 9.20  | Jenny enters the role-play corner (9.20–9.40)                        |
| 9.40  | Jenny returns the dressing-up clothes to the box (9.40–9.45)         |
| 9.45  | Jenny now moves to the jigsaw puzzle area (9.45–10.10)               |
| 10.10 | From the puzzles Jenny moves to the book corner (10.10–10.30)        |
| 10.30 | She goes outside to play again (10.30–10.50)                         |
| 10.50 | Jenny now returns to the jigsaw puzzles (10.50–11.00)                |
| 11.00 | Jenny plays a board game (11.00–11.15)                               |
| 11.15 | Jenny goes to do some drawing (11.15–11.30)                          |
| 11.30 | Jenny joins the whole group for a story and singing (11.30–11.50)    |
| 11.50 | Jenny is collected by her dad.                                       |

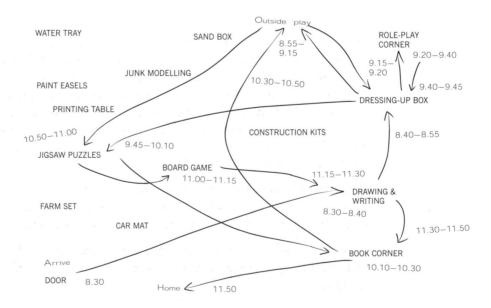

**Activity**

Study the information in the example on page 412. What does it tell you?

**Professional Practice**

The example observation on page 412 would be of limited use to you without further details. To be able to see if Jenny was interacting and playing as usually expected for her age group, you would need to know:

- Jenny's age
- for how much of the morning Jenny was playing alone
- whether she interacted as a pair
- whether there were times when Jenny was playing in a small group
- whether there were times when she was playing in a large group
- whether Jenny interacted with adults during the morning.

Without this information, it is hard to know whether Jenny was having as positive experience as she could have had. She clearly kept herself fully occupied, but did you notice anything about her choice of activities?

At no time did Jenny involve herself in any 'messy' activities. This may not be an issue, as she may simply not have wanted to take up those opportunities on that particular day, but if this was one of a range of similar observations it would be considered unusual. It would also have been useful to include details of how long Jenny has been at the setting. This too could be relevant regarding how well she interacts with others and her confidence in involving herself in some activities.

The main benefit of movement and flow chart observations is to monitor a child's particular choices of activities and in reviewing the layout of activities to maximise use.

### Time sampling

The time sampling method is used to observe a particular child at regular intervals throughout a planned period of time, which would usually be on more than one day. This method can be especially useful if there is some concern about the child, perhaps they have suddenly become withdrawn and no longer seem to interact with other children. Your observation can help identify whether there is a major cause for concern, or whether the child's behaviour simply needs monitoring for a short while. As you time sample, you will need to be as unobtrusive as possible to ensure you obtain a true record.

Time sampling observations can also help to identify whether activities or equipment are being under-used or inappropriately used, by observing the activity at regular intervals, rather than focusing on a specific child.

Time sampling can give accurate information which is easily understood, but it is a time-consuming method and takes a member of staff out of the adult:child ratio equation.

Example: time-sampling record sheet

| Child's initials _____ Date _____ The concern you have: | | | |
|---|---|---|---|
| **Time of observation** | **Social interactions** | **Activity involved with during the observation** | **Emotions/behaviour displayed** |
| 8.30 | | | |
| 8.45 | | | |
| 9.00 | | | |
| 9.15 | | | |
| 9.30 | | | |
| 9.45 | | | |
| 10.00 | | | |
| 10.15 | | | |
| 10.30 | | | |
| 10.45 | | | |
| 11.00 | | | |
| 11.15 | | | |
| 11.30 | | | |
| 11.45 | | | |
| 12.00 | | | |
| 12.15 | | | |
| 12.30 | | | |

## Event sampling

As with time sampling, event sampling necessitates observations being carried out over several days or even longer. This method is useful when a child is displaying worrying and/or aggressive behaviour, which is having an impact on their own and others' daily experience within the setting. It is a useful means of identifying whether there are trigger factors involved in initiating the unwanted behaviours in the child being observed. You record each time the behaviour occurs, how long it continues and whether the behaviour had been triggered by anyone or any specific situation. The advantage of this method is that it is clearly timed and recorded and is easily understood but, as with time sampling, it is also time-consuming.  It may also involve all staff in the recording of events.

In particularly serious cases, the event sample observations may need to be shown to other professionals who become involved with the child's welfare. They may also visit the setting in these instances in order to observe and assess the child for themselves.

Example: event sampling record sheet

| Child's initials _____ | | The concern you have: | | | |
|---|---|---|---|---|---|
| **Date** | **Time** | **Was reaction provoked?** | **Duration of 'incident'** | **Emotions/behaviour displayed** | **Staff observing** |
| | | | | | |
| | | | | | |
| | | | | | |
| | | | | | |
| | | | | | |
| | | | | | |
| | | | | | |
| | | | | | |
| | | | | | |
| | | | | | |
| | | | | | |
| | | | | | |
| | | | | | |
| | | | | | |
| | | | | | |
| | | | | | |
| | | | | | |

### Target child

The target child method is one of the most widely used methods of observation. It was first developed by the Oxford Pre-school Research Project, led by Kathy Sylva, and was originally aimed at identifying which activities and situations helped children to develop their concentration. It is also useful in identifying socialisation in children, and gives opportunities for noting their language, in particular when they initiate conversation.

The target child method involves the remembering, understanding and recording pre-coded information. These codes are recorded in a table under the following headings:

| Min | Activity record | Language record | Task code | Social code |
|-----|-----------------|-----------------|-----------|-------------|
|     |                 |                 |           |             |

The coding is set out minute-by-minute, usually for up to ten minutes at a time. The minutes are recorded in the first column of the table.

### Activity record

The activity record column is a brief comment on what is happening with the activity being used by the target child. The codes used are:

TC = target child (the child's name or initials are not used)
C = child
A = adult

Example

| Min | Activity record | Language record | Task code | Social code |
|-----|-----------------|-----------------|-----------|-------------|
| 1   | TC & C on car mat pushing cars on road |  |  |  |

### Social code

The codes in the social code column (who the child is with) are:

SOL = the target child is playing on their own (solitary)
PAIR = the child is with one other person, child or adult
SG = the target child is within a small group (three to five children)
LG = the target child is within a large group (six or more children).

If the target child is playing with the same activity as others, but not interacting with them in any way (parallel play) you would write one of the following codes:

PAIR/P = the target child is playing parallel to one other child

SG/P = the target child is playing parallel to a small group

LG/P = the target child is playing parallel to a large group.

If there is an adult interacting with an activity, there would be a circle drawn around the social code, for example:

Example

| Min | Activity record | Language record | Task code | Social code |
|-----|-----------------|-----------------|-----------|-------------|
| 1 | TC & C on car mat pushing cars on road | | | PAIR |

### Task code

The entries in the task code column (what the child is doing) include the following codes:

LMM = large muscle movement

LSC = large-scale construction

SSC = small-scale construction

MAN = manipulation

SM = structured materials

PS = problem-solving

SVT = scale version toys

IG = informal games

SINP = social interaction, non-play

DB = distress behaviour.

There are many more task codes covering the complete range of actions displayed and activities enjoyed by children. Most colleges have complete lists.

Example

| Min | Activity record | Language record | Task code | Social code |
|-----|-----------------|-----------------|-----------|-------------|
| 1 | TC & C on car mat pushing cars on road | | SVT | PAIR |

### Language record

To record language (what the child is saying), you would simply write: TC>C if the target child was speaking to another child, or TC>A if they were speaking to an adult.

Example

| Min | Activity record | Language record | Task code | Social code |
|-----|-----------------|-----------------|-----------|-------------|
| 1 | TC & C on car mat pushing cars on road | TC>C 'That my car' TC> 'brmm brmm' TC>C 'Mine!' | SVT | PAIR |
| 2 | 3 Cs now playing | All Cs > 'brmm brmm' | SVT | SG |
| 3 | A joins them on mat | A> 'What a lot of cars' TC>A 'Mine a red car' | SVT | (SG) |

The target child method can be useful as an 'at a glance' monitoring of a child's social development, as a quick glance at the social codes will indicate whether the child is mostly playing with others or alone. This information, together with the child's age, indicates whether they are following the social 'norms'.

**Professional Practice**

The two target child observations A and B, which follow, are good examples of how the intervention of an adult has enabled a child to develop their understanding of the activity they are using further. The sensitive input from the adult in the first example has raised the achievement of the child from what they could achieve alone, to what had been their potential to achieve. This fits in with Vygotsky's ZPD theory.

**Target child observation A**

| Min | Activity record | Language record | Task code | Social code |
|-----|-----------------|-----------------|-----------|-------------|
| 1 | Dries hands & cooks tea | TC> 'All dry. Nice & dry; | DA PRE | SOL |
| 2 | Lays table, matching coloured cups, saucers etc. C arrives & sits at table. TC serves tea | TC> 'Blue... & a blue. Green... & a green', etc. | PRE PRE | SOL PAIR/P |
| 3 | Eats tea | TC> 'Yummy, Nice tea – Sausage' | PRE | PAIR/P |
| 4 | Crying child arrives C stops crying | TC>C 'Don't cry Why you cry? I'm a mummy. Don't cry. Want a sausage?' TC> 'Eat your sausage' | SINP PRE " " | PAIR " " " |
| 5 | TC washes up TC leaves home C & goes to construction table Tries to build tower (Duplo) – It is top heavy! | | PRE SSC | SOL SOL |
| 6 | "       "       " | | " | " |

▶

**Target child observation A** *continued*

| Min | Activity record | Language record | Task code | Social code |
|-----|-----------------|-----------------|-----------|-------------|
| 7 | "    "    " <br><br>Tower won't stand A joins her <br><br><br><br><br><br><br><br><br><br><br>TC leans tower against box & grins | A>TC 'That's a tall tower' <br> TC>A 'It falling down. It keep falling down' <br> TC>A 'How can you stop it falling?' <br> TC>A 'Don't know' <br> TC>A 'You hold it' <br> A>TC 'I could but how will you manage when I go to get the milk?' | " <br><br><br> SSC | " <br><br><br> (PAIR) |
| 8 | TC picks up a brick & considers | A>TC 'Could you use any of these larger bricks to help you?' | SSC | (PAIR) |
| 9 | Adds 2 bricks to bottom of tower <br><br><br><br><br> TC went on to make two more towers | TC>A 'I can stand it. I can stand it.' <br> A>TC 'Well done. That was a really good idea.' | SSC | (PAIR) |

### Checklists

Assessments of children are a routine part of most early years settings and involve the regular observing and assessing of children to ascertain what they are currently able to achieve. An example of these assessment programmes is the

**Target child observation B**

| Min | Activity record | Language record | Task code | Social code |
|-----|-----------------|-----------------|-----------|-------------|
| 1 | Duplo – clipping yellow bricks together, then green, etc. | TC> naming the colours | SSC | SG/P |
| 2 | "          "          " | | " | " |
| 3 | Lines bricks up in rows of 6 | TC> 1 2 3 4 5 6 | SSC | SG/P |
| 4 | "          "          " | | " | " |
| 5/6 | Builds tower of single bricks, It does not balance. TC adds a larger base to tower | | SSC | SG/P |
| 7 | TC builds another tower & stands the 2 towers next to each other. | TC> 'My tower won't fall' | SSC | SG/P |
| 8 | Added large bricks to the tops of towers. They remained standing  TC very proud of her achievement | | SSC | SG/P |

Sound Learning Pre-school Record System. It includes assessment records for all ages of pre-school children and it suggests that the assessments can be completed on a monthly, three monthly or termly basis.

For babies the assessment record requires the use of the codes:

R = rarely
S = sometimes
U = usually.

Example

| 3–36 MONTH DEVELOPMENT RECORDS | Date of assessment | | | | | | |
|---|---|---|---|---|---|---|---|
| Name _____ | Colour code | | | | | | |

| PHYSICAL DEVELOPMENT (1) | R | S | U |
|---|---|---|---|
| Can lift head and shoulders when lying on front.    Waves arms and kicks legs vigorously | | | |
| Has little or no head lag when pulled to sit | | | |
| Can lift head and shoulders when lying on front | | | |
| Sits with firm back when supported | | | |
| Can hold head steady when supported | | | |
| Can hold head steady when upright | | | |
| When held standing, takes weight on feet and bounces up and down | | | |
| Can roll from front to back | | | |
| Can roll from back to front | | | |
| Can sit without support | | | |
| While sitting can reach forward for a toy without falling over | | | |
| Moves around slowly by crawling or bottom shuffling | | | |
| Moves around rapidly by crawling or bottom shuffling | | | |
| Can pull self to standing position using furniture | | | |
| Can get from a lying down to a sitting position | | | |
| Walks around room holding onto furniture | | | |
| Stands alone | | | |
| Walks with adult help | | | |
| Crawls up stairs | | | |
| Walks a few steps alone | | | |
| Walks across room when held by one hand | | | |
| Without help gets up off floor and stands alone | | | |
| Walks pushing large wheeled toys | | | |
| Can climb onto a low chair or step and sit down | | | |
| Walks well alone    Walks well alone | | | |

COMMENTS

Key to code:
R – Rarely
S – Sometimes
U – Usually

For older children within the Foundation Stage it requires the use of:

E = emerging        C = consolidating
W = working on      A = achieved.

Example

| LEARNING AREA RECORD | Communication, Language and Literacy (1) | | | | |
|---|---|---|---|---|---|

| | | | E | W | C | A |
|---|---|---|---|---|---|---|
| Enjoys listening to stories, songs, rhymes and conversation between others | | | | | | |
| Incorporates elements of what he/she has seen and heard into her/his everyday play and learning experiences | | | | | | |
| Enjoys participating in conversations, sharing experience and ideas with others | | | | | | |
| 'Talks' to self during play and during imaginative play with figures or puppets | | | | | | |
| 'Talks' to miniature figures, or puppets, recreating conversations and experiences | | | | | | |
| Recreates conversations and recounts experiences during imaginative and role play | | | | | | |
| Experiments with mark making equipment such as pens, pencils, crayons, brushes, sponges, fingers, sticks | | | | | | |
| Incorporates shapes, symbols and letters in his/her free writing | | | | | | |
| | | | | | | |
| | | | | | | |
| ELG: is able to enjoy listening to and using spoken and written language, and readily turns to it in play and learning | | | | | | |
| Explores sounds in a variety of ways such as: | sounds in the environment | | | | | |
| | sounds made by everyday objects | | | | | |
| | sounds and words made by voices | | | | | |
| Responds to a range of sounds by: | imitating | | | | | |
| | identifying their source | | | | | |
| | linking to make sound patterns | | | | | |
| Recreates words she/he hears and incorporates in own language usage | | | | | | |
| Makes up new nonsense words e.g. rhyming nonsense words 'cap, hap, dap, zap' | | | | | | |
| Makes observations such as 'that sounds like', 'that sounds the same as' | | | | | | |
| Sounds out familiar letters in a simple text | | | | | | |
| Sounds out familiar words in simple text | | | | | | |
| | | | | | | |
| | | | | | | |
| ELG: Explores and experiments with sounds, words, text | | | | | | |

**COMMENTS**

*Key to code:*
E – Emergency
W – Working on
C – Consolidating
A – Achieved

Reproduced by permission of *Sound Learning*

Many early years settings, and some local authorities, have developed their own style of recording sheets. Ask your current setting what they use.

### Sociograms

A sociogram gives an 'at a glance' record of the socialising of a group of children. It can be used to identify friendship groups, secure pair-relationships and also for establishing when a child lacks friends within the setting. The observers should always be aware how quickly friendship groups change, particularly with children under age five, and so it has limited use. The benefit of identifying a relationship concern for a particular child is that strategies can be established to help them to integrate further.

BACK to Chapter 4, page 142 for an example of a sociogram.

### Longitudinal studies

A longitudinal study is a process of observation carried out over a considerable length of time. You will most likely use this method when you carry out a baby or child study. Such studies need written parental permission and involve regular visiting and observing of the child's development and progress over a pre-set period. A baby study may, for example, involve weekly visits for three months whereas a child study is likely to require fortnightly visits for six months or more. Longitudinal studies need to be approached in an objective manner, ensuring the confidentiality of the family, and this needs to be agreed with the parents at the start of the study.

The longitudinal approach will enable you to:
- get to know the child and the impact of their family life on their development
- understand the needs of the child more fully
- identify and record changes in the child's development
- comment on each area of development and how the rates of development vary
- chart the child's development according to a chosen screening process.

The drawbacks of longitudinal studies can be that:
- visits to a child's home can sometimes feel intrusive
- family holidays, illness and visitors can sometimes impact on your planning
- objective observations are not always welcomed by the parents
- a house move by the family may end your study prematurely.

A longitudinal study of a child will benefit from the inclusion of other observation methods too.

Example

> **A visit to a child as part of an on-going child study**
>
> **Date** _____     **Type of visit:** General visit to observe spontaneous play
>
> On my arrival, JM was having her lunch. She ate an egg sandwich, followed by a banana and a small yoghurt. She also had a drink of diluted fruit juice.
>
> She was very pleased to see me and wanted to play straightaway, but was persuaded by her mum and me that she needed to finish her lunch first.

After washing her hands (which she can now do quite well by herself) JM played with her doll's house. She busied herself putting the people to bed, and then getting them up again to have their breakfast. She talked to herself all the time in a monologue; most I could understand, but at other times she was not coherent. JM showed understanding of the roles of family members and where domestic events occur, e.g. washing up in the kitchen, getting dressed in the bedroom, adults dressing the children, etc. She played like this for almost 20 minutes.

Next JM asked me to read her a story. She chose 'We're Going on a Bear Hunt', which she clearly knew very well. First of all we did all the actions together and JM got very excited as we tried to run back home very fast. Next we sat and read the book again, snuggled together on the sofa. She is able to handle the book well, turning the pages carefully and pointing to all the main parts of the story.

JM's speech is now becoming clearer, and I was able to understand most of what she was saying to me

As we came to the end of the story, JM's grandparents arrived unexpectedly and she ran to see them.

I felt that it was appropriate for me to leave at this point, and JM gave me a hug and then waved me goodbye.

Depending on the age of the child being studied, you would be able to comment on how well they are developing according to the developmental 'norms', making specific comments regarding manual dexterity in handling the book, language use in her small world play and when reading the story, and in her memory recall.

## Recording observations and preparing a portfolio

This section describes how you may be asked to set out your observation portfolio, helping you plan how you will summarise and interpret your observations. It is likely that you will be asked to make comparisons between the observations you make, noting similarities and differences between the ages of the children in similar situations. This should consolidate your understanding of how children develop at different rates across all the areas of development, while still remaining within 'normal' boundaries. It will also help you see the benefits of the developmental norm charts, and how at times they can appear misleading, if used simply as a snapshot of an individual child.

Your portfolio will need to include a chart recording the dates, times and outline details of each observation you make, which would usually cross-reference to a matrix. This will enable both you and your tutors to see at a glance that your observations have included children of all age ranges and placement settings experienced during your training.

It is helpful if you give all observations a number. This helps with cross-referencing and ensures that you and your tutors are referring to the same observation during any discussion.

### An 'at a glance' matrix

A matrix is often used to give an 'at a glance' reference to your observations. This helps to ensure that you do not inadvertently miss out any one age range or placement setting, causing you difficulty in completing your portfolio at the end of your course.

Example

| | Home setting | Childminder | Voluntary pre-school | Statutory pre-school | Private nursery setting | Nursery school/class | Primary school | Hospital | Special needs setting |
|---|---|---|---|---|---|---|---|---|---|
| 0–1 year | | | | | | | | | |
| 1–2 years | | | | | | | | | |
| 2–4 years | | | | | | | | | |
| 4–8 years | | | | | | | | | |

**Remember!**

- If you are studying to gain the diploma, you will need to complete 800 assessed hours of placement experience. At least 100 hours of this assessed experience must be in each of your four chosen settings. The additional hours may be gained through additional placements if necessary.
- If you are studying for the certificate, 400 assessed hours of placement experience are required. You are likely to be either employed or committed to a setting as a volunteer. You are therefore asked to complete a minimum of 20 hours experience in two age ranges and three settings in addition to, and different from, the setting in which you work.

### Record of observations

An example of how you could be asked to record your observations in numerical order is shown opposite. It shows the date, age and gender of the child you have observed, together with the setting details (for example, day nursery – painting activity) and the method of observation used. A chart like this can be used to ensure that you have used a range of observation methods and observed a range of different activities and can be used as a contents page for your observation file.

Example

| Observation | Date | Age of child | Gender of child | Setting details | Method of observation |
|---|---|---|---|---|---|
| 1 | 9.10.02 | 3.6 | M | Day nursery – construction | Target child |
| 2 | 16.10.02 | 4.1 | M | Day nursery – painting | Time sampling |
| 3 | 23.10.02 | 3.9 | F | Day nursery – clearing up | Target child |
| 4 | 23.10.02 | 3.7 | F | Day nursery – role-play area | Written record |
| 5 | 6.11.02 | 3.6 | M | Day nursery – painting | Target child |
| 6 | 13.11.02 | 4.2 | F | Day nursery – in general | Movement and flow chart |
| 7 | 20.11.02 | 4.2 | F | Day nursery – water play | Target child |

Other charts that could be requested by your tutors might include a matrix of activities or a matrix showing aspects of development.

Examples

**Matrix of development**

| Area of development observed | Age | | | |
|---|---|---|---|---|
| | 0–1 years | 1–2 years | 2–4 years | 4–8 years |
| Gross motor skills Fine motor skills Spatial awareness Simple co-operative play | | | | |

**Matrix of activities**

| Activity area observed | Age | | | |
|---|---|---|---|---|
| | 0–1 years | 1–2 years | 2–4 years | 4–8 years |
| Threading<br>Pencil skills<br>Shared storytime<br>Small scale construction<br>Emergent writing<br>Role play | | | | |

An accessible text with explanation sof each observation method, and plenty of relevant examples is Hobart and Frankel (1999) – see *Bibliography and suggested further reading*, page 429.

**Test Yourself**

1  What are the benefits of carrying out observations?
2  What is an assessment programme?
3  What is non-participant observation?
4  List as many points as you can from the checklist for observing children.
5  Give five examples of what you could observe.
6  What is naturalistic observation?
7  What is the difference between time sampling and event sampling?
8  When would you use a longitudinal observation method?
9  What are the main factors in interpreting your observations?

# Key terms

**You should now understand the following words and phrases. If you do not, read through the chapter again and review them.**

| | |
|---|---|
| accommodation | development |
| Apgar score | developmental delay |
| assimilation | developmental norms |
| bonding | disequilibrium |
| caudal | distal |
| centile | dysfluency |
| cephalo | ego-centricity |
| chromosome | emotional disturbance |
| classical conditioning | foetal alcohol syndrome (FAS) |
| conservation | genotype |

growth
language acquisition device (LAD) theory
maturational
monotropic
neonatal jaundice
neonate
normative development
operant conditioning
perception
phenotype
primary socialisation

pro-social behaviour
proximal
reflexes
scaffolding
schema
secondary socialisation
self-concept
sequential
social learning theory
stereotyping
zone of proximal development (ZPD)

## Bibliography and suggested further reading

Barnes. P. (1998) *Personal, Social and Emotional Development of Children*, Blackwell, Oxford

Baston, H. and Durward, H. (2001) *Examination of the Newborn: A Practical Guide*, Routledge, London

Beaver, M., Brewster, J., Jones, P., Keene, A., Neaum, S. and Tallack, J. (2001) *Babies and Young Children*, 2nd edition, Nelson Thornes, Cheltenham

Bee, H. (1992) *The Developing Child*, 6th edition, Allyn and Bacon, Boston MA

Bowlby, J. (1953) *Child Care and the Growth of Love*, Penguin, London

Bruce, T. and Meggitt, C. (1996) *Childcare and Education*, Hodder & Stoughton, London

Cullis, T., Dolan, L. and Groves, D. (1999) *Psychology for You*, Nelson Thornes, Cheltenham

Dowling, M. (2000) *Young Children's Personal, Social and Emotional Development*, Paul Chapman, London

Fawcett, M. (1996) *Learning Through Child Observation*, Jessica Kingsley Publishers, London

Gilbert, P. (2000) *A–Z of Syndromes and Inherited Disorders*, 3rd editon, Nelson Thornes, Cheltenham

Hobart, C. and Frankel, J. (1999) *A Practical Guide to Child Observation and Assessment*, 2nd edition, Nelson Thornes, Cheltenham

Jarvis, M. (2001) *Angles on Child Psychology*, Nelson Thornes, Cheltenham

Miller, L. (1997) *Closely Observed Infants*, Duckworth, London

Minett, P., Wayne, D. and Rubenstein, D. (1994) *Human Form and Function*, Collins Educational, London

Mukherji, P. and O'Dea, T. (2000) *Understanding Children's Language and Literacy*, Nelson Thornes, Cheltenham

Neaum, S. and Tallack, J. (2000) *Good Practice in Implementing the Pre-School Curriculum*, 2nd edition, Nelson Thornes Cheltenham

Oates, J. (1999) *The Foundations of Child Development*, Blackwell, Oxford

Mary Sheridan (1991) *from Birth to Five Years: Children's Developmental Progress*, Seventh impression, NFER Nelson

Sheridan, M. (1997) *From Birth to Five Years: Children's Developmental Progress*, Revised edition, Routledge, London

Walsh, M., Stephens, P. and Moore, S. (2000) *Social Policy and Welfare*, Nelson Thornes, Cheltenham

# 10 Child Health

## Introduction

The aim of this chapter is to offer a basis for exploration of a range of **health** issues that affect children and their families. It introduces the roles you may take in the care of children with health problems and explores the promotion of health, both locally and with regard to national targets. It should be remembered that children's understanding of their own health will be linked to their age and stage of development. This needs to be taken into account when introducing health topics in your setting.

Health can be described in terms of three different models.

## The medical model of health

The medical (or biological) model looks at a person's health in terms of the body's natural defences and immunity, genetically-inherited conditions, individual levels of exercise, diet and general healthy (or unhealthy) lifestyles. It sees the body as a machine which can be restored to health by medical intervention. The responsibility for health lies with the medical profession whose role is to understand disease and find cures.

## The social model of health

The social model sees health as being not just about biology and medical intervention, but also as being influenced by the wider natural, social, economic and political environment. This includes, for example, housing, social class, affluence and poverty. This model places emphasis on **health promotion/education**.

## The holistic model of health

The holistic model looks at the individual person as a whole. It can be broadly described as being concerned with 'mind, body and soul'.

The **World Health Organisation (WHO)** is concerned with health in its holistic sense. In 1946 the WHO defined health as being:

> 'a state of complete physical, mental and social well being, not merely the absence of disease and infirmity.'

In 1984 they stated that health is:

> 'a resource for everyday life, not the objective of living; it is a positive concept emphasizing social and personal resources as well as physical capabilities.'

In 1986 they defined health promotion as:

> 'The process of enabling people to increase control over, and improve their health … Health is a positive concept emphasising social and personal resources, as well as physical capacities. Therefore, health promotion is not just the responsibility of the health sector but goes beyond lifestyles to well-being.'

### Activity

Using your college resource centre, find out about the role of the World Health Organisation.

For a detailed discussion of the definitions of health, a useful text is Blaxter (1990) – see *Bibliography and suggested further reading*, page 491.

# Health promotion

There are several approaches to health promotion. These have been summarised by Beattie (1993) as:
- *health persuasion* – to persuade or encourage people to adopt healthier lifestyles
- *legislative action* – to protect the population by making healthier choices more available
- *personal counselling* – to empower individuals to have the skills and confidence to take more control over their health
- *community development* – to enfranchise or emancipate groups so they recognise what they have in common and how social factors influence their lives.

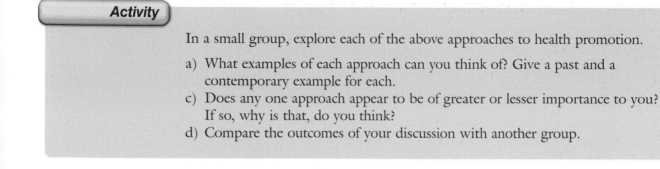

In a small group, explore each of the above approaches to health promotion.

a) What examples of each approach can you think of? Give a past and a contemporary example for each.

c) Does any one approach appear to be of greater or lesser importance to you? If so, why is that, do you think?

d) Compare the outcomes of your discussion with another group.

## Government-led health promotion

Current national targets to improve the health of the UK population have been set out by the government. The white paper *Our Healthier Nation* (Department of Health, 1998) cites the two main aims of the government as being to improve the health of:

- the population as a whole by increasing the length of people's lives and the number of years people spend free from illness
- the worst off in society and to narrow the health divide.

### Factors affecting health

Lalonde (1974), who is considered to be the founder of modern health practice, identified four 'fields' of health as shown in the diagram below.

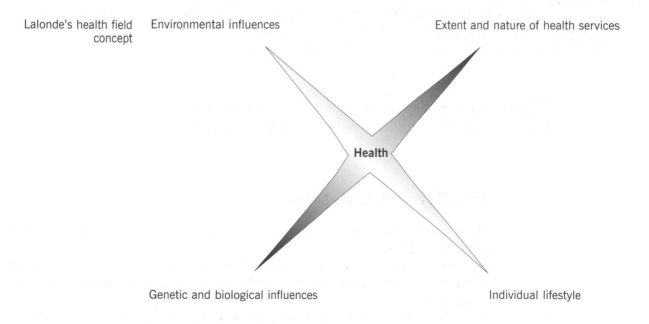

The UK government recognises that many factors affect health and has categorised these factors as shown in the table on page 434, based on Lalonde's health field concept.

## Factors affecting health

| Fixed | Social and economic | Environmental | Lifestyle | Access to services |
|---|---|---|---|---|
| Genes<br>Sex<br>Ageing | Poverty<br>Employment<br>Social exclusion | Air quality<br>Housing<br>Water quality<br>Social environment | Diet<br>Physical activity<br>Smoking<br>Alcohol<br>Sexual behaviour<br>Drugs | Education<br>NHS<br>Social services<br>Transport<br>Leisure |

from Department of Health (1998)

The following summaries are based on *Our Healthier Nation* (Department of Health, 1998).

### Fixed factors affecting health

Genetic and maturational factors influence our health, but we can have only a limited influence over them by modifying some of the known outcomes. Identification of the specific genes responsible for some conditions include the identification of Down's syndrome as a trisomy of chromosome 21 and, more recently, the advances in identifying ovarian cancer as C125.

Clearly, early identification through gene technology can be extremely helpful in alleviating some of the long-term problems of various conditions, but the manipulation of genes also raises a range of ethical issues.

### Activity

What ethical issues can you think of linked to gene technology? Discuss these issues with a partner, or in a small group.

### Social and economic factors affecting health

The impact of poverty, unemployment and social exclusion can make it hard for some people to focus on their health, for example by giving up smoking, because this may be one of the factors that they feel gives them pleasure and keeps them going. Having limited access to shops often means buying from smaller (more expensive) local stores. It is recognised that, although people often acknowledge what steps they need to take to improve their health, the level of hardship and social exclusion they face makes it difficult for them to act upon it. Common conditions prevalent in the lower social classes include a higher rate of infection, respiratory disease and depression.

In 1980, the Black Report noted the significance of social, economic and environmental influences on health. It referred to the issues that were at the heart of the welfare state:

- health care
- social care
- welfare benefits

and how they had been seen as a means to reduce the differences between the social classes. However, as the Report pointed out, even after 40 years of the NHS, appropriate provision was still not being made.

### Environmental factors affecting health

Living in an atmosphere of fear or mistrust can affect health, as can pollution, lack of sufficient heating, lighting or housing. Crime and racial tension in communities has a direct impact on health and mental well-being, and workplace stress also takes its toll on many people in the employment sector due to heavier workloads, increased targets and greater pressures to meet deadlines.

**Activity**

Consider these health issues:
- use of recreational/illegal drugs
- melanomas
- poor health
- poor hygiene practice
- mental health problems.

a) Which do you consider to be more likely to affect the less well-off in society, and which the wealthier section of the population?
b) On what have you based your decisions?

### Lifestyle factors affecting health

Levels of physical activity have decreased for many people, due to the increase in other forms of activity in their lives, for example longer working days and accompanying mental exhaustion. Longer working hours lead to many people relying on fast foods and freezer meals, moving away from the home cooking of past generations. Dependence on smoking, alcohol and recreational drugs has increased, particularly in young people.

> 'In 1996 28% of boys aged 15 and 33% of girls aged 15 smoked regularly and these figures are rising.'
>
> Department of Health (1998), 2.21

Lopez *et al.* (1994) estimate that:

> 'for every 1,000 young smokers, one will be murdered, six will be killed in a road accident and 250 will die before their time because they smoke.'
>
> cited in Department of Health (1998)

Dependence on smoking, alcohol and recreational drugs has increased, particularly in young people

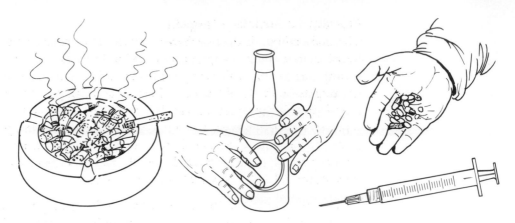

Teenage pregnancy rates continue to rise, reducing the opportunities for education, training and employment for these young people, and continuing the cycle of disadvantage.

BACK to Chapter 2, page 64.

Teenage pregnancy rates continue to rise

### Access to services

The government summarises the impact of having access to high quality services with the following statements:

'1  A decent education gives children the confidence and capacity to make healthier choices.
2  Leisure services have a real influence on health.
3  Ill health is not spread evenly across our society.
4  The link between poverty and ill health is clear. In nearly every case the highest incidence of illness is experienced by the worst off social classes.'

Department of Health (1998)

**Activity**

Explain to a partner what is meant by each of the points above.

If you are able to explain their meaning to another person, it is likely that you have a clear understanding of them yourself.

### Current government targets

The main ethos (distinctive feature) of the government's plans for improving health is to work in co-operation with local health authorities. This involves setting out overall health targets for the nation, but encouraging interpretation of the targets by the local health authorities according to the needs of the local population, in consultation with health professionals and community representatives. These are known as **health improvement plans (HImPs)** and are three-year programmes. The development of this government-led approach fits in with the recommendations of the World Health Organisation's programme 'Health for All 2000' in which they state that:

> 'The focus of the health care system should be on primary health care – meeting the basic needs of each community through services provided as close as possible to where people live and work, readily accessible to all, and based on full participation.'

WHO (1985), page 5

There are currently four priority health areas cited in the government's targets covering:

- heart disease and stroke
- accidents
- cancer
- mental health.

The government targets for each priority health area are set out below and on pages 438–44 together with a table indicating the proposed contract for how the targets can be met, nationally, locally and individually. Each table includes social and economic, environmental, lifestyle and service issues that can be addressed.

### Heart disease and stroke

By 2010 the government target is 'to reduce the death rate from heart disease and stroke and related illnesses amongst people under 65 years by at least a further third'.

## A National Contract on Heart Disease and Stroke

| | Government and national players can: | Local players and communities can: | People can: |
|---|---|---|---|
| Social and economic | Continue to make smoking cost more through taxation<br><br>Tackle joblessness, social exclusion, low educational standards and other factors which make it harder to live a healthier life. | Tackle social exclusion in the community which makes it harder to have a healthy lifestyle.<br><br>Provide incentives to employees to cycle or walk to work, or leave their cars at home. | Take opportunities to better their lives and their families lives, through education, training and employment. |

| | Government and national players can: | Local players and communities can: | People can: |
| --- | --- | --- | --- |
| Environmental | Encourage employers and others to provide a smoke-free environment for non-smokers | Through local employers and others, provide a smoke-free environment for non-smokers.<br><br>Through employers and staff, work in partnership to reduce stress at work.<br><br>Provide safe cycling and walking routes. | Protect others from second-hand smoke. |
| Lifestyle | End advertising and promotion of cigarettes.<br><br>Enforce prohibition of sale of cigarettes to youngsters.<br><br>Develop Healthy Living Centres.<br><br>Ensure access to, and availability of, a wide range of foods for a healthy diet.<br><br>Provide sound information on the health risks of smoking, poor diet and lack of exercise. | Encourage the development of healthy schools and healthy workplaces.<br><br>Implement an integrated Transport Policy, including a national cycling strategy and measures to make walking more of an option.<br><br>Target information about a healthy life on groups and areas where people are most at risk | Stop smoking or cut down, watch what they eat and take regular exercise. |

| Services | Encourage doctors and nurses and other health professionals to give advice on healthier living. Ensure catering and leisure professionals are trained in healthy eating and physical activity. | Provide help to people who want to stop smoking. Improve access to a variety of affordable food in deprived areas. Provide facilities for physical activity and relaxation and decent transport to help people get to them. Identify those at high risk of heart disease and stroke and provide high quality services. | Learn how to recognise a heart attack and what to do, including resuscitation skills. Have their blood pressure checked regularly. Take medicine as it is prescribed. |

from Department of Health (1998), page 64

### Accidents

The government target for accidents is 'to reduce accidents by at least a fifth'.

## A National Contract on Accidents

| | Government and national players can: | Local players and communities can: | People can: |
|---|---|---|---|
| Social and economic | Improve areas of deprivation through urban regeneration. Tackle social exclusion and joblessness. | Tackle social exclusion and joblessness in the community. | Take opportunities to combat proverty through education, training and employment. |

| | Government and national players can: | Local players and communities can: | People can: |
|---|---|---|---|
| Environmental | Improve safety of roads.<br><br>Ensure compliance with seatbelt requirements and other road traffic laws.<br><br>Help set standards for products and appliances.<br><br>Promote higher standards of safety management. | Improve facilities for pedestrians and cycle paths.<br><br>Develop safer routes for schools.<br><br>Adopt traffic calming and other engineering measures and make roads safer.<br><br>Work for healthier and safe workplaces.<br><br>Make playgrounds safe. | Check the safety of appliances and use them correctly.<br><br>Install smoke alarms.<br><br>Drive safely.<br><br>Take part in safety management in the workplace. |
| Lifestyle | Provide information on how to avoid osteoporosis so that accidents don't lead to broken bones.<br><br>Run public safety campaigns.<br><br>Ensure strategies are coordinated across Government Departments and Agencies.<br><br>Provide information on ways to avoid accidents. | Ensure those in need have aids to prevent accidents, like car seats for babies.<br><br>Work for whole school approaches to health and safety.<br><br>Target accident prevention at those most at risk. | Adopt safe behaviour for themselves and their children.<br><br>Wear cycle helmets.<br><br>Wear a seatbelt.<br><br>Not drink and drive.<br><br>Keep physically fit.<br><br>Eat a balanced diet which contains enough calcium and vitamin D, take regular exercise and stop smoking to protect themselves from osteoporosis. |

| Services | Encourage health professionals to give appropriate advice. Ensure professionals are trained in accident prevention. | Provide appropriate treatment to high-risk groups to prevent osteoporosis. Provide child pedestrian and cycling training. | Have regular eye-tests. Know emergency routine. |

### Cancer
The government target for cancer is 'to reduce the death rate from cancer amongst people under 65 years by at least a further fifth'.

## A National Contract on Cancer

| | Government and national players can: | Local players and communities can: | People can: |
|---|---|---|---|
| Social and economic | Continue to make smoking more costly through taxation. Tackle joblessness, social exclusion, low educational standards and other factors which make it harder to live a healthier life. | Tackle social exclusion in the community to make it easier for people to make healthy choices. Work with deprived communities and with businesses to ensure a more varied and affordable choice of food. | Take opportunities to better their lives and their families' lives through education, training and employment. |
| Environmental | Encourage employers and others to provide a smoke-free environment for non-smokers. Encourage local action to tackle radon in the home. Continue to press for international action to restore the ozone layer. | Through local employers and others, provide a smoke-free environment for non-smokers. Tackle radon in the home. | Protect others from second-hand smoke. Cover up in the sun. |

|  | Government and National players can: | Local Players and Communities can: | People can: |
|---|---|---|---|
| Lifestyle | End advertising and promotion of cigarettes.<br><br>Prohibit sale of cigarettes to youngsters and ensure enforcement.<br><br>Support Healthy Living Centres.<br><br>Provide reliable and objective information on the health risks of smoking, poor diet and too much sun. | Encourage the development of healthy workplaces and healthy schools.<br><br>Target health information on groups and areas where people are most at risk. | Stop or cut down smoking and watch what they eat.<br><br>Be careful when they are in the sun and ensure that young children are not exposed to too much sun.<br><br>Follow sensible drinking advice. |
| Services | Encourage doctors and nurses and other health professionals to give advice on prevention.<br><br>Ensure that healthy schools work with pupils and parents to improve health.<br><br>Implement effective and high-quality cancer screening programmes.<br><br>Ensure equal access to high-quality treatment and care. | Provide help in stopping smoking to people who want to stop.<br><br>Improve access and availability to a variety of affordable food in deprived areas.<br><br>Ensure hard-to-reach groups come forward for cancer screening services.<br><br>Ensure rapid treatment for cancers when they are diagnosed. | Attend cancer screenings when invited.<br><br>Seek medical advice promptly if they are worried. |

from Department of Health (1998), page 75

### Mental health

The government target regarding mental health is 'to reduce the death rate from suicide and undetermined injury by at least a further sixth'.

## A National Contract on Mental Health

| | Government and National players can: | Local Players and Communities can: | People can: |
|---|---|---|---|
| Social and economic | Tackle joblessness, social exclusion and other factors which make it harder to have a healthier lifestyle.<br><br>Tackle alcohol and drug misuse. | Develop local support networks, eg for recently widowed/bereaved, lone parents, unemployed people and single people.<br><br>Develop court diversion schemes.<br><br>Develop job opportunities for people with mental illness.<br><br>Develop local strategies to support the needs of mentally ill people from black and minority ethnic groups. | Develop parenting skills.<br><br>Support friends at times of stress – be a good listener.<br><br>Participate in support networks.<br><br>Take opportunities to better their lives and their families' lives through education, training and employment. |
| Environmental | Continue to invest in housing and reduce homelessness.<br><br>Encourage employers to address workplace stress.<br><br>Reduce isolation through transport policy.<br><br>Promote healthy schools.<br><br>Address levels of mental illness amongst prisoners. | Develop effective housing strategies.<br><br>Reduce stress in workplace.<br><br>Improve community safety. | Improve workload management. |

| | Government and national players can: | Local players and communities can: | People can: |
|---|---|---|---|
| Lifestyle | Increase public awareness and understanding of mental health.<br><br>Reduce access to means of suicide.<br><br>Support Healthy Living Centres. | Focus on particular high-risk groups, eg young men, people in isolated rural communities.<br><br>Encourage positive local media reporting.<br><br>Develop and encourage use of range of leisure facilities | Use opportunities for relaxation and physical exercise and try to avoid using alcohol/smoking to reduce stress.<br><br>Increase understanding of what good mental health is. |
| Services | Develop standards and training for primary care and specialist mental health services.<br><br>Improve recruitment/retention of mental health professionals.<br><br>Identify/advise on effective treatment and care.<br><br>Develop protocols to guide best practice. | Promote high-quality pre-school education and good mental health in schools and promote educational achievement.<br><br>Ensure mental health professionals are well trained and supported.<br><br>Develop a range of comprehensive mental health services for all age groups and alcohol and drug services for young people and adults.<br><br>Support carers of people with long-term disability and chronic illness.<br><br>Provide advice on financial problems.<br><br>Develop culturally sensitive services. | Contribute information to service planners and get involved.<br><br>Contact services quickly when difficulties start.<br><br>Increase knowledge about self-help. |

from Department of Health (1998), page 79

**Activity**

Make a copy of the table below and list on it the ways in which you think each of these priority health areas could have an impact on the health and well-being of children. Consider both the short-term and long-term impacts.

| Heart disease and stroke | | Accidents | |
|---|---|---|---|
| Short-term impact | Long-term impact | Short-term impact | Long-term impact |
| | | | |
| **Heart disease and stroke** | | **Accidents** | |
| Short-term impact | Long-term impact | Short-term impact | Long-term impact |
| | | | |

## Different approaches to health education/promotion

Primary health care teams are made up of a range of health professionals. These include those who focus on health care and health education at each of the three different levels of health care:

- **primary health care** – health care in the community, involving GP practices, dentists, opticians, and so on
- **secondary health care** – all referrals for health care, for example, to hospital departments for further treatment or investigation
- **tertiary health care** – on-going care for chronic conditions such as cystic fibrosis. It also includes the involvement of individual health professionals such as the community diabetic nurse.

Health education is about providing well-rounded information that enables individuals to make informed choices regarding their health.

### Primary health education/promotion

The aim of primary health education/promotion is to prevent ill health by eliminating the likelihood of contracting a disease in the first place. An example of this is the childhood immunisation programme. Nationwide immunisation can have a significant impact on the incidence of some illnesses, such as the immunisations programmes for haemophilus influenzae type B (HiB) and measles, mumps and rubella (MMR) in the UK which have dramatically reduced the incidence to these childhood diseases in the UK. Worldwide, eradication of smallpox was due to immunisation.

With the MMR vaccination in the UK, parents are presented with an explanation of its merits and are actively encouraged to have their children vaccinated. In developing countries, however, vaccination decisions are largely made on behalf of the population, and parents are simply told that their child 'needs' whatever vaccination is being given.

FORWARD to page 461 for the current guidelines on immunisation.

### Secondary health education/promotion

Secondary approaches to health education/promotion include **screening** procedures. Examples are the PKU (phenylketonuria) test taken from seven-day-old infants via a heel prick blood test (the Guthrie test) and cervical screening in women, where a pre-symptomatic change may be detected, allowing early intervention.

### Tertiary health education/promotion

The tertiary approach to health education/promotion is aimed at the control and reduction of illness and is about helping individuals to achieve their full health potential. An example of this is supporting the control of chronic asthma and diabetes. Tertiary health education/promotion often involves the use of leaflets and other printed resources. It also includes the involvement of support groups.

You may find it helpful to refer to Naidoo and Wills (2000) for further reading on the different levels of health care, education and promotion – see *Bibliography and suggested further reading*, page 491.

---

**Activity**

Make a copy of the table below. Working with a partner, research a range of additional health issues and add them to the most appropriate column of the table. Examples have been given to get you started.

| Primary health education/promotion | Secondary health education/promotion | Tertiary health education/promotion |
|---|---|---|
| Child immunisation | PKU screening<br>Cervical screening | Supporting chronic:<br>asthma<br>diabetes |

**Case Studies**

### Klaus

Klaus is six years old. He has recently been diagnosed as having type 1 diabetes (insulin-dependent), as opposed to type 2 which is non-insulin dependent. He spent three days in hospital while his condition was stabilised and he and his parents acclimatised to planning for his diabetic dietary needs. Klaus and his parents are now being supported by the primary health care team through the diabetic specialist nurse, who oversees most of his care. The diabetic nurse supervises the administration of his injections and checking his blood sugar levels. This responsibility will soon transfer to Klaus' parents, who will be able to get support via a telephone support link. Klaus is also having regular appointments with a dietician at the local hospital to monitor his food intake and balance.

1  Which members of the primary health care team have been involved in the care of Klaus to date?
2  Who would be involved in his long-term care?
3  Why is this important?

### Mollie

Mollie is two years old and has cystic fibrosis (CF). She is the first member of her generation in her family to have the condition, although it has occurred twice before in her family (an uncle and an aunt are currently affected). Mollie's mother had been (positively) carrier-tested prior to her pregnancy and, although foetal screening for the condition is now available, she opted not to have her unborn infant screened, due to the risk of miscarriage. As there was a definite possibility of Mollie having CF, health professionals were able to monitor her from birth, watching for the earliest signs and offering appropriate advice regarding specialised dietary needs.

1  Which members of the health care profession have been involved to date?
2  What role did the primary health care professionals play in the pregnancy?
3  Will any other form of health care be needed for the future?

## The role of health educators

Health education is about educating individuals about issues that affect their health and well-being and changing their beliefs and behaviour (links to empowerment). In early years settings, it should aim to involve both children and their families.

Historically, improvements to health have been based on improvements to public health measures rather than to improvements in medicines and clinical practice. In the nineteenth century, the first health visitors (1852) had a duty to:
• carry and distribute carbolic powder
• direct home owners to the attention of bad smells.

Health education materials were specifically targeted at the working classes with publications such as *Dirty Dustbins and Sloppy Streets* (Buenois, 1881) and *A Practical Dietary for Families, Schools and the Working Class* (Smith, 1864).

Why would these book titles be inappropriate in contemporary society?

Naidoo and Wills (2000) usefully summarise 'The Old Public Health' and 'The New Public Health' (see below), showing how health promotion has moved from being the remit of local government through to the government working in partnership with local authorities.

**The old public health**

| | |
|---|---|
| **1842** | Edwin Chadwick's *Report on the sanitary condition of the labouring population of England* is published. |
| **1843** | The Royal Commission on the Health of Towns is established. |
| **1844** | The Health of Towns Association is founded. |
| **1845** | Final report from the Royal Commission on the Health of Towns is published |
| **1848** | Public Health Act for England and Wales requires local authorities to provide clean water supplies and hygienic sewage disposal systems, and introduces the appointment of medical officers of health for towns. |
| **1854** | John Snow controls a cholera outbreak in London by removing a contaminated local water supply. |
| **1866** | Sanitary Act – local authorities had to inspect their district. |
| **1868** | Housing Act – local authorities could ensure owners kept their properties in good repair. |
| **1871** | Local Government Board (which became the Ministry of Health in 1919) was established. |
| **1872** | Public Health Act makes medical officers of health for each district mandatory. |
| **1875** | Public Health Act consolidates earlier legislation and the tone changes from *allowing* to *requiring* local authorities to take public health measures. |
| **1906** | Education Act established the provision of school dinners. |
| **1907** | Eduction Act establishes the school medical service. Notification of Births Act and the development of health visiting is encouraged. |

**The new public health**

| | |
|---|---|
| **1974** | Lalonde Report 'A new perspective on the health of Canadians' identifies the environment as crucial for health. |
| **1985** | The World Health Organisation launches its 'Health for All' programme. |
| **1986** | The World Health Organisation publishes the Ottawa Charter for health promotion. |
| **1987** | The Public Health Alliances is created. |

| 1988 | Acheson Report establishes the post of Director of Public Health within the NHS. |
|---|---|
| 1992 | The Association for Public Health, a multidisciplinary organisation to promote public health policy, is created. |
| 1992 | Rio Earth Summit and Agenda 21. |
| 1995 | The Standing Nursing and Midwifery Advisory Committee (SNMAC) reports to Ministers on the contribution of nurses, midwives and health visitors to public health. |
| 1997 | Creation of a Minister of Public Health. White Paper: 'The New NHS – Modern, Dependable'. 3-year local health improvement programmes introduced. |
| 1998 | Green Papers: 'Our Healthier Nation' health strategy for England; 'Working together for a Healthier Scotland'; 'Better Health, Better Wales'; 'Fit for the Future' (Northern Ireland). Chief Medical Officer's project to strengthen the public health function. Health Action Zones (HAZs) – 11 pilot projects announced. |
| 1999 | Launch of the UK Public Health Association, incorporating the Public Health Alliance and the Association for Public Health. |

Reprinted from Naidoo and Wills, *Health Promotion: Foundations for Practice, 2nd Edition*, pages 184 and 190 (2000) by permission of Baillière Tindall

A range of Acts, reports and papers are quoted by Naidoo and Wills in the texts above. You may find it useful to research more about each of them.

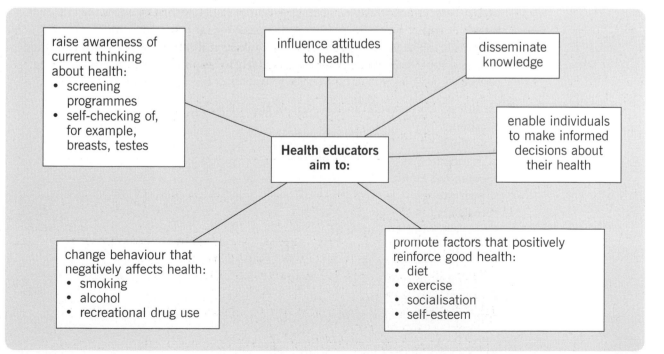

The aims of the health educator

**Activity**

Choose a health issue that particularly interests you. Design a leaflet for young children to educate them about the issue. Your leaflet will benefit from being as visual as possible. Remember to consider a range of languages and ethnic groups.

There are many leaflets available on a wide range of health issues

## Who are the health educators?

A health educator is anyone who has influence over someone else regarding their health choices and lifestyle. Their role can be either formal or informal and their influence can at times be clearly promoted, while at others it is more covert (disguised). The high levels of peer pressure seen in modern-day society increase the need for a sensitive approach particularly in improving the health of young people.

Health educators could include any of the following:
- parents
- siblings
- grandparents
- extended family
- peer group
- teachers
- pre-school/playgroup staff
- nursery staff
- childminders/nannies
- after-school staff
- playscheme staff
- primary health care team:
  - GP
  - practice nurse
  - community nurse

- health visitor
- health promotion nurse
- midwife
- dentist
- orthodontist
- dental hygienist
- pharmacist
- optician
- chiropodist
- counsellor
- media:
  - television
  - newspapers
  - journals
  - magazines
  - radio.

## Activity

a) Identify ways in which you have been influenced by health educators/promoters.

b) How important has peer pressure been in influencing your health choices?

c) Through which mediums have you received information, and which have you found to be most influential?

d) What positive and negative health education/promotion programmes can you think of?

e) Who would you turn to for advice on health issues?

f) Educators can be good or bad. What do you consider to be the characteristics that make them so. Copy the table and list your ideas under the headings.

| Good health educators | Bad health educators |
|---|---|
|  |  |

Health education is about giving people informed choice. Society cannot dictate, only advise. Health promotion campaigns are about raising understanding of the consequences of the choices each individual makes for themselves and, if parents, for their children. The 'herd' vaccination programmes carried out in the developing world are clearly well-meaning and contribute to the health and well-being of many children and their families. They do not, however, allow for informed choice, as those of us living in the western culture have come to expect.

Effective health
education is rooted in
information

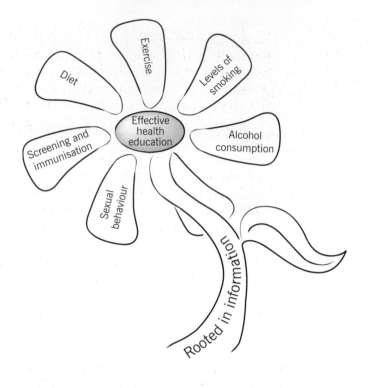

# Health promotion programmes

## Planning a health promotion campaign

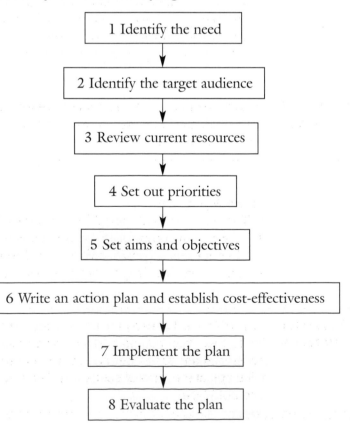

| |
|---|
| 1 Identify the need |
| 2 Identify the target audience |
| 3 Review current resources |
| 4 Set out priorities |
| 5 Set aims and objectives |
| 6 Write an action plan and establish cost-effectiveness |
| 7 Implement the plan |
| 8 Evaluate the plan |

**Remember!**

- Most local health authorities have a health promotion office, often situated in a main hospital. This is an excellent source of information. Often there is a facility to research and read through current literature, with options for ordering a vast array of resources, including printed literature, videos and 3D aids. Many resources are available in alternative forms, such as audio tapes, Braille and translated into a range of languages.

- Health promotion staff are often willing to attend functions and provide display materials. Sometimes these are free of charge and sometimes there is a small charge made to cover administration costs. Before developing a new health promotion resource, it is worth finding out if there is already a sufficient amount of material on the market. There is no point in re-inventing the wheel – your efforts would be better placed in developing something that is really needed.

- The Health Education Authority publishes health promotion materials. It has a useful website for further information on health education: www.hea.org.uk

- Health-related charities produce their own health education materials.

Any campaign to pass on information needs to be accessible to its target audience and therefore it needs to appeal, be visually interesting, and the information needs to be readily available and free from patronising or moralistic tones.

### Visual presentation
- Visual presentation is important to gain initial attention.
- Photographs, cartoons and illustrations can all be used successfully.
- The visual approach selected needs to be relevant to the main target group, without excluding others who may also find it useful.

**Professional Practice**

Illustrations need to be bolder and clearer in information aimed at young children than in information aimed at teenagers, where a cartoon or graphic design would be more likely to appeal.

### Language style
- The language used should be relevant to the targeted group.
- Teenagers will appreciate a more contemporary use of language.
- Children need a greater ratio of visual to written information.
- Translations into languages other than English should be made where possible.

**Professional Practice**

Any written text aimed at young children should be presented using upper and lower case lettering and punctuation correctly, i.e. use capitals only at the start of sentences and for proper names, write in short sentences, do not forget to use full stops at the ends of sentences. The text should be easy to read, set in large and bold type.

### Promotional content

- The content should start with the main emphasis of the health promotion programme.
- Positive messages should be made very clear.
- Judgement statements that could annoy or alienate the reader should be avoided. For example, avoid statements such as 'Only a fool continues to…'.
- Getting the balance of information right is crucial to ensure that the message is taken in.
- Too much information can put people off reading any further.
- Too little information can leave the reader both unimpressed and uninformed.

### Activity

In a group, find out what current government health promotion campaigns there are in your area.

a) Research and gather information on each campaign for different target groups. Ensure that you include young children in this.
b) Consider what elements of each campaign appeal to you personally. Use the points raised above as a guideline to get you started.
c) Select three pieces of promotional material and ask a range of people questions about them. For example:
   - What they think of them?
   - Would they be likely to pick them up?
   - Would they be likely to read them?
d) Collate the outcomes of your group.
e) What conclusions have you come to about the potential success of the promotional materials you selected?
f) What have you learned from this about preparing information materials for other people?

### Professional Practice

- It is important to consider how you will put over your message to people who have limited vision or literacy.
- How accessible would the resources you found in the above activity have been for people in these situations?
- How could they have been made more accessible to them?

### Activity

Having evaluated a range of health promotion materials, return to the leaflet you designed for the activity on page 450. Reflect on and evaluate your leaflet in the light of what you have read about presentation.

Health promotion was incorporated into the Education Reform Act 1988 with health education being included as a cross-curricular subject within the National Curriculum. In the Education Act 1993, sex education became mandatory in secondary schools, with a 'right to withdraw' clause for parents.

---

**Activity**

Imagine that you are developing a health promotion campaign to either:

a)  promote sex education in secondary schools, or to
b)  tackle cross-infection in schools ('tummy bugs', threadworms, and so on).

Using the flow chart on page 452 as guide, plan your campaign with a partner.

---

**Test Yourself**

1  What is the medical model of health?
2  What is the social model of health?
3  Which model of health is the World Health Organisation particularly concerned with?
4  Give an example of a fixed factor influencing the health of an individual.
5  What three issues are at the heart of the welfare state?
6  a)  What does the abbreviation HImP stand for?
    b)  What are HImPs?
7  What are the four priority health areas being targeted by the UK government?
8  Which level of health care looks after the long-term care of chronic conditions?
9  Which type of diabetes is insulin-dependent?
10  Give at least five aims of health educators.
11  List at least ten people who could be considered to be health educators.

# Causes of ill health

The human body's natural state is to be healthy and be able to fight off illness. What we put into our bodies and what our bodies are exposed to have an impact on how well our bodies manage to maintain their healthy states, illustrating how important health education programmes can be. It is worth revisiting the definitions of health to consolidate your understanding of what 'health' actually is. Think also about how the body automatically defends itself, through:

- *the eyes*
  - The blinking mechanism helps prevent particles entering the eyes.
  - Tears contain a mild antiseptic which cleanse the eyes.
- *the blood* – Leucocytes (white blood cells) fight infected tissue and destroy germs.
- *the skin* – Sebum is an oily substance that is secreted through the surface of the skin and acts as a protective layer.
- *mucus*
  - Each opening into the body (for example, the nose) has a lining of mucus membrane at the entrance to help prevent infections from entering.
  - Ciliated epithelium (small hairs) trap and collect foreign bodies, such as earwax and mucus from the nose.

- *the spleen* – This is a vascular organ with a large number of blood vessels, which filters out foreign bodies from the blood and produces antibodies.
- *the gut* – Good bacteria in the gut kills both good and bad bacteria when fighting infection, causing diarrhoea.

 BACK to page 432 for the definitions of health.

## The causes of illness

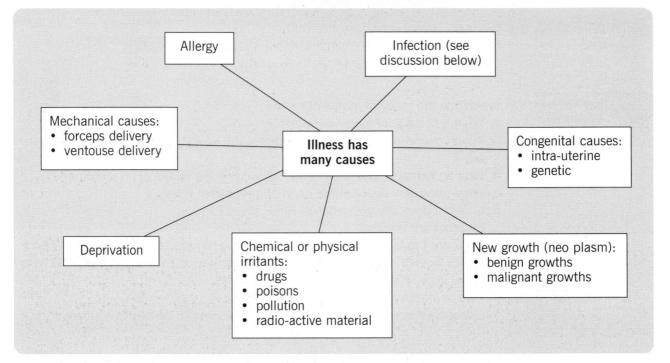

 BACK to Chapter 9, page 336, for genetic factors resulting in a congenital or genetically inherited condition.

### Infection

The microbiological (infectious) causes of illness are varied, and this is the area you will most often deal with as an early years worker. These germs (**pathogens**) can be roughly divided into five groups:

- *bacteria* – tough cells which rapidly multiply and thrive in the body's warm, moist conditions; treatable with antibiotics; for example ear infections and conjunctivitis
- *viruses* – parasites which invade other cells and then reproduce themselves; cannot be treated with antibiotics; can be relatively harmless or significantly serious; for example, the common cold, influenza and chickenpox
- *fungi* – spread by contact with fungi spores; do no serious harm to humans but cause much irritation and discomfort; some harmless fungi are permanently

with us; treatment with an anti-fungal product as necessary; for example, athlete's foot
- *parasites* – organisms spread by cross-infection; can be seen with the naked eye; many different varieties and difficult to eradicate once they have taken hold in a nursery or school class, due to cases of reinfection; for example scabies, headlice and threadworms
- *protozoa* – single-cell 'organisms'; many cause human distress through illnesses such as severe stomach upsets, toxoplasmosis (often caught through handling cats or cat litter) and amoebiasis (causing diarrhoea).

Pathogens can enter the body in different ways. They can be:
- ingested – taken in through the mouth
- inhaled – breathed in through either the mouth or the nose
- inoculated – taken in through a break in the surface of the skin.

They can be spread by:
- **direct contact** – germs transmitted by touch, for example broken skin contacts, kissing and sexual activity
- **indirect contact** – germs left on surfaces subsequently in contact with another person
- **droplet infection** – air-borne germs spread through sneezing, coughing, and so on, as microscopic droplets are released into the atmosphere.

### Activity

Make a copy of the table below. Check your understanding of common childhood illnesses by placing as many conditions as you can under one or more headings. You may find it helpful to return to this activity once you have read the rest of this chapter.

|  | Bacteria | Virus | Fungi | Parasite | Protozoa |
|---|---|---|---|---|---|
| Ingested |  |  |  |  |  |
| Inhaled |  |  |  |  |  |
| Inoculated |  |  |  |  |  |
| Direct contact |  |  |  |  |  |
| Indirect contact |  |  |  |  |  |
| Droplet infection |  |  |  |  |  |

### The impact of socio-economic factors on health
The on page 458 below summarises the main effects on health of the three socio-economic categories: poverty, housing and unemployment. Use the case studies that follow it to explore socio-economic issues further.

## Socio-economic factors affecting health

| Poverty | Housing | Unemployment |
|---|---|---|
| Money problems | High-rise flats/isolation | Lowest income group |
| Unpaid bills | Lack of stimulus | Low self-esteem |
| Debts | Insufficient heat | Stigma |
| Lack of leisure activities | Overcrowding | Social exclusion |
| Poor diet | Lack of labour-saving equipment | Boredom |
| | Disordered communities | Depression |
| | Communities in fear | |

**Case Studies**

### Wilson, Marlow and Maisie

The Johnston family live in a two-bedroomed flat on the sixth floor of a high-rise flat in north London. Mr Johnston is a builder who is currently unemployed and Mrs Johnston was a cashier in a supermarket, but has not worked since her children were born. Wilson is ten, Marlow is eight and Maisie is two.

The family have been asking to be rehoused since before Maisie was born as they have very limited space, and Maisie still shares a bedroom with her parents out of necessity, not choice.

Mr Johnston takes the boys to school each morning, but then returns to the flat. He spends long hours staring out of the window. His (initially) weekly visits to the Job Centre have ceased, as he has lost faith that he will regain employment. Mrs Johnston rarely goes out as the lift in the block of flats is unreliable and Maisie is only just walking. Maisie is quite a sickly child and she sleeps a great deal during the day, but is unsettled at night. The estate is a place of tension and the boys do not play out after school. None of the family goes out after dark and friends are not encouraged to visit.

1 What socio-economic issues can you identify?
2 What do you consider will be the likely impact on the health of the children?
3 What do you consider will be the likely impact on the health of the parents?
4 Is there likely to be any long-term impact on Maisie's development if the family's situation does not change?
5 Could the Johnston family do anything else to improve their situation, do you think?

### Arabella, Chloe and Josh

The Stenner family live in a four-bedroomed house in north London. Mr Stenner was an office manager in a company which has just gone into liquidation. He is now unemployed. Mrs Stenner is a qualified book-keeper, but has not worked since her children were born. Arabella is ten, Chloe is eight and Josh is two.

Mr and Mrs Stenner have owned their home for twelve years and each child has their own bedroom.

Mrs Stenner and Josh take the girls to school each morning, returning home after coffee with friends. Mr Stenner spends long hours in the garden. He surfs the Internet to see what employment opportunities are available locally, and is grateful that he does not have to stand and read the noticeboard at the local Job Centre. He is unsure whether he will find similar employment. Mrs Johnston is enjoying having her husband around more and Josh, who is an active little boy, loves helping him in the garden. The children have had to give up some of their out-of-school activities due to reduced finances, but are able to have friends to play instead.

1  What socio-economic issues can you identify for this family?
2  Do you consider there will be any likely impact on the health of the children?
3  Do you consider there will be any likely impact on the health of the parents?
4  Is there likely to be any long-term impact on Josh's development if the situation for the family does not change?
5  Could the Stenner family do anything else to improve their situation, do you think?

What effect does housing have on the lifestyle of the people in it?

**Activity**

In many ways the situations for the Johnstons and the Stenners are similar, but how do the two case studies compare in real terms? Refer back to the socio-economic issues listed in the table on page 458.

## Methods of preventing illness

A range of approaches exist to prevent illness:
- environmental approaches
- public health approaches
- dietary approaches
- educational approaches.

These are summarised below. What else can you add to each of them?

### Environmental approaches

Globally, environmentalists strive to improve both health and the quality of the planet by highlighting the effects of:

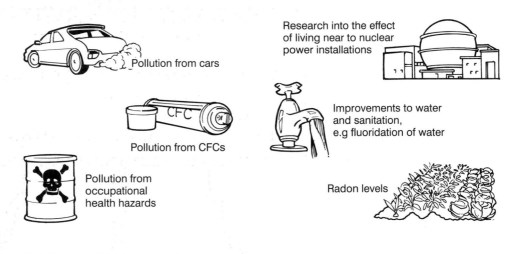

Pollution from cars

Research into the effect of living near to nuclear power installations

Pollution from CFCs

Improvements to water and sanitation, e.g fluoridation of water

Pollution from occupational health hazards

Radon levels

### Public health approaches

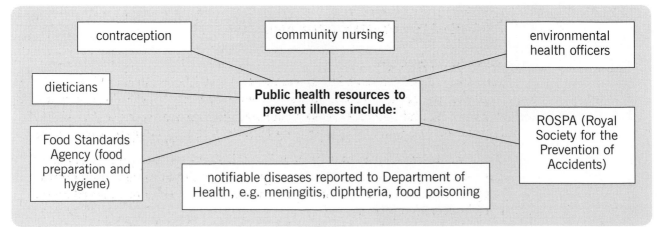

contraception

community nursing

environmental health officers

dieticians

**Public health resources to prevent illness include:**

Food Standards Agency (food preparation and hygiene)

ROSPA (Royal Society for the Prevention of Accidents)

notifiable diseases reported to Department of Health, e.g. meningitis, diphtheria, food poisoning

### Dietary approaches

Dietary aspects of campaigns to help prevent and reduce ill health include:

Promotion of healthy eating plans

Reducing obesity

Impact of fruit and vegetables on cancer

Monitoring of individuals' weight/height via tables

Folic acid given in early pregnancy

Cultural issues, such as lack of vitamin D in Asian children due to prolonged (exclusive) breast-feeding

Preventing dental caries

### Educational approaches

Educational approaches include:

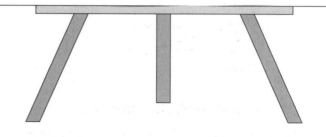

**Health promotion programmes**

Personal, Social and Health Education (PSHE) in schools

Government-led health campaigns

Local health campaigns

Charity-led campaigns (for example, by the Meningitis Trust)

## Immunisation programmes

### What is immunity?

Immunity is the body's ability to resist disease. Each individual builds up an immunity to various illnesses during life. As infants, we are each born with a degree of natural immunity to some illnesses and diseases, based on the immunity of our mothers. Immunity is extended by breast-feeding for up to four months.

There are different types of immunity. The table on page 462 gives examples of how immunity can occur either naturally or be acquired through **immunisation programmes**, and also how immunity can be active, passive or achieved by the **herd immunity** process.

## Types of immunity

| Type of immunity | Description | Example |
|---|---|---|
| Active natural immunity | An immune response to a naturally occurring infection that the child has contracted | Antibodies formed following chickenpox or rubella |
| Active acquired immunity | An immune response to an antigen (a toxin produced by bacteria to make antibodies) | Via the (live) polio vaccine which is given as part of the childhood immunisation programme |
| Passive natural immunity | Naturally occurring immunity passed across the placenta, and in breast milk | Infants are born with a degree of natural immunity based on their mothers' immunity |
| Passive acquired immunity | Antibodies are transferred via an injection (immunisation programme) | Ready-made antibodies, such as diphtheria and tetanus given as part of the immunisation programme |
| Herd immunity | If a high enough proportion of the whole population is immunised it will keep the rest free from the disease (usually needs 90 + per cent) | The HiB vaccine campaign has successfully reduced the incidence of HiB |

based on Keene (1990), page 75

### Immunisation of children

Vaccines can be **live** (active) or **non-live** (passive). As children are particularly vulnerable to contracting disease, a programme of immunisation is recommended by health experts. Immunisation not only protects the immunised child from falling ill, it also helps to protect children with suppressed immune systems who may not be able to have all vaccinations in the programme.

Immunisation is only given with parental consent, and although technically there is no contra-indication for a child with a minor cough or cold receiving an immunisation, most people prefer their children to be free from illness at the time of the immunisation being administered. The recommended programme is set out in the table below.

## The immunisation programme

| Age | Immunisation | Method |
|---|---|---|
| 2 months | HiB and meningitis C<br>Diphtheria, whooping cough and tetanus<br>Polio | 1 injection<br>1 injection<br>By mouth |
| 3 months | HiB and meningitis C<br>Diphtheria, whooping cough and tetanus<br>Polio | 1 injection<br>1 injection<br>By mouth |
| 4 months | HiB and meningitis C<br>Diphtheria, whooping cough and tetanus<br>Polio | 1 injection<br>1 injection<br>By mouth |
| 12–15 months | Measles, mumps and rubella (MMR) | 1 injection |
| 3–5 years: pre-school booster<br>MMR booster | Diphtheria and tetanus<br>Polio<br>Measles, mumps and rubella | 1 injection<br>By mouth<br>1 injection |
| 11–14 years | BCG (Bacillus Calmette-Guerin) vaccine to protect against TB (tuberculosis). All children are Heaf-tested first to check their immunity. | 1 injection |
| 15–18 years: leaving school booster | Diphtheria and tetanus<br>Polio | 1 injection<br>By mouth |

| Professional Practice | • Children sometimes have a slight reaction to immunisations, such as a raised temperature and feeling miserable.<br>• Plenty of fluids should be given, along with paracetamol if this occurs.<br>• A careful eye should be kept on the child, particularly a young baby.<br>• If a raised temperature does not come down within 24 hours, or it continues to rise, medical advice should be sought.<br>• Some health professionals recommend that paracetamol is automatically given after an immunisation. |
|---|---|

- Some health professionals support the idea of giving it just beforehand, to minimise the risk of a rise in temperature.
- Paracetamol is not registered to be given to babies under the age of three months.
- Infant ibubrofen suspension is as effective as paracetamol and is an alternative, but should not be given to children with moderate or severe asthma.
- Children under twelve should *never* be given aspirin, due to a slight risk of it causing Reye's syndrome.

As with all medication, paracetamol and infant ibubrofen suspension should be given in the doses appropriate for the age of the child.

### Children with suppressed immunity

Children with certain illnesses or conditions may have a **suppressed immunity**, for example leukaemia, HIV and AIDS. For these children it is not appropriate to give live vaccines, as a live vaccine is a weakened version of the condition itself. Artificial vaccines can sometimes be offered to these children and to those in close contact with them, such as siblings. An example is the polio vaccine, which is given orally.

It should be noted that children who are HIV positive will not necessarily develop AIDS.

### Homoeopathic immunisations

Some parents choose not to have their children immunised through the mainstream programme, but may choose to use homoeopathic alternatives instead. There is little evidence to support the efficacy of the homoeopathic alternatives, but they do offer a degree of protection for some children. Although immunisation is recommended for most healthy children, as an early years professional you should respect parents' right to choose not to have their child immunised and make no value judgements about them.

## Screening techniques

Screening is the process of examining a whole population to determine who is showing signs of having a particular condition or disease and who may develop or be predisposed to a condition or disease. Screening in the UK is available for every child, with the consent of their parents.

Screening is important because it:
- enables early intervention where a problem is confirmed
- keeps parents informed about their child's progress or likely progress
- highlights the need for specific areas of stimulation for a child to meet their potential
- raises awareness for the future and allows informed decisions to be made, with or without genetic counselling.

## Foetal screening

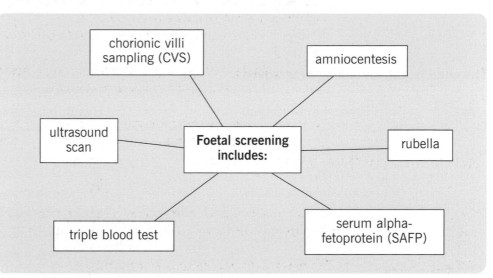

BACK to Chapter 9, page 337, for a description of how each of these tests are made and why they are offered.

## Neonatal screening

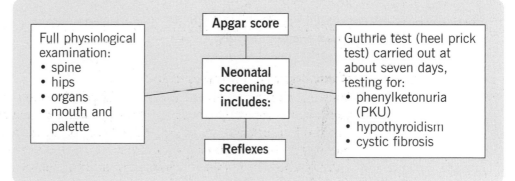

BACK to Chapter 9, pages 341 and 343, for further information on the Apgar score and the primitive reflexes present at birth.

## Infant screening

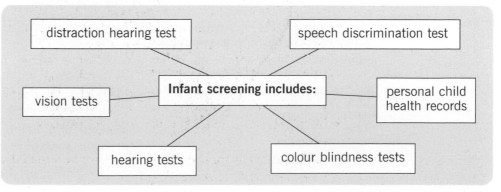

The table below describes a general screening programme following a child through the earliest years.

## The child health screening programme

| Age | Screening procedure | Health promotion |
|---|---|---|
| | These procedures are performed by midwives, doctors and health visitors throughout childhood. | Health visitors discuss the following issues with parents and carers to heighten their awareness of important issues affecting their child at critical ages. Health education is offered appropriately and tactfully. |
| Birth | FULL PHYSICAL EXAMINATION<br>**Usually performed by a hospital paediatrician before the mother and baby are discharged home. If the baby is born at home the general practitioner will conduct the examination:**<br>■ weight<br>■ heart and pulses<br>■ hips<br>■ testes<br>■ head circumference<br>■ eyes<br>■ Guthrie test (after 6 days of milk feeding) to test for phenylketonuria (PKU), hypothyroidism and cystic fibrosis<br>■ sickle cell and thalassaemia test if suspected | Cot death (SIDS) prevention<br>Feeding techniques<br>Nutrition<br>Baby care<br>Crying<br>Sleep<br>Car safety<br>Family planning<br>Passive smoking<br>Dangers of shaking baby<br>Sibling management |
| 10–14 days | **Health visitors perform these checks, usually at the birth visit in the home.**<br><br>Review of birth check<br>Assess levels of parental support | Nutrition<br>Breast-feeding<br>Cot death (SIDS) prevention<br>Passive smoking<br>Accident prevention: bathing, scalding and fires<br>Explanation of tests and results |

| 6–8 weeks | **All babies receive this check performed by the GP and health visitor.**<br>REVIEW:<br>Parental concerns, e.g. vision, hearing, activity<br>Risk factors, including family history of abnormalities<br>FULL EXAMINATION INCLUDING:<br>■ weight<br>■ head circumference<br>■ length<br>■ hip check<br>■ testes<br>■ eyes: squint, movement,<br>■ tone and general development<br>■ heart and pulses<br>■ Guthrie test result given to parents | Immunisation<br>Nutrition and dangers of early weaning<br>Accidents: falls, fires, over-heating, scalds<br>Hearing<br>Recognition of illness in babies and what action to take, e.g. fever management<br>Crying<br>Sleeping position<br>Cot death (SIDS) prevention<br>Passive smoking<br>Review of car safety |
| 2– 4 months | **Health visitor check.**<br>Parental concerns<br>Hip check | Weighing as appropriate<br>Maintain previous health promotion<br>Promotion of language and social development<br>Hearing<br>Discourage future use of baby walkers |
| 6–9 months | **Health visitor check.**<br>Hip check<br>Distraction hearing test<br>Discussion of developmental progress asking about vision, hearing and language development<br>Check weight and head circumference<br>Observe behaviour and look for squints | Parental concerns<br>Nutrition<br>Hearing<br>Accident prevention: fires, choking, scalding, burns, stair and door gates, fire guards, etc.<br>Review of car transport<br>Dental care<br>Play and development needs |

| Age | Screening procedure | Health promotion |
|---|---|---|
| 18–24 months | **Health visitor check.**<br>Parental concerns – behaviour, vision and hearing.<br>Observation of gait (walking posture)<br>Emphasis on value of comprehension and understanding of spoken and non-verbal communication in relation to speech development<br>Height measured and plotted | SAFETY:<br>Accident prevention, falls from heights, drowning, poisoning, road safety<br>DEVELOPMENT<br>■ language and play<br>■ management and behavioural issues<br>■ promotion of positive parenting<br>■ toilet training<br>■ diet, nutrition and prevention of iron deficiency |
| 3 years 3 months to 3 years 6 months | **Health visitor check.**<br>Enquiry and discussion of vision, squint hearing, behaviour, language development and referral to other professionals as necessary<br>Discussion of education needs and choices<br>Notification of any special educational needs<br>Height measured<br>Testes checked if necessary<br>Hearing test if hearing impairment suspected | SAFETY:<br>Accident prevention, burns, falls from heights, drowning, poisoning, road safety<br>DEVELOPMENT:<br>■ language and play, socialisation<br>■ management of behaviour<br>■ issues<br>■ school readiness<br>■ toilet training<br>■ dental care<br>■ diet, nutrition and prevention of iron deficiency |
| 5 years school entrant | **School nurse check. School health doctor if necessary.**<br>SCHOOL ENTRANT REVIEW:<br>Review of pre-school record<br>Discuss parents and teachers concerns<br>Height – compared with previous measurements<br>Weight<br>Hearing sweep audiometry test<br>Snellen vision test<br>Observation of gross and fine motor skills | Consent for planned programme of health checks<br>Access to school health service surveillance programme<br>Sleep<br>Friendships/settling in at school<br>Accident prevention, road safety, stranger danger<br>Dentist<br>Dietician<br>Management of medicines at school<br>Care in the sun |

| Year 3: 7–8 years | **School nurse check.** Teacher concerns Review of records Height, weight, vision General health check Issues raised by the child | Accident prevention, road safety, safety at play, stranger danger Friendships Exercise, nutrition and dental care Care in the sun |
| --- | --- | --- |

from Keene (1999), pages 90–1

## Common childhood illnesses

There are many illnesses that are common in childhood. Most last only a short period of time, but can be very unpleasant during the process. Long-term consequences can result from some conditions and the severity of conditions such as measles, particularly in children who have not been immunised, should never be under-estimated. This section describes some common childhood conditions and some chronic long-term conditions found in children.

The common childhood conditions described in this section are:
• chickenpox
• rubella
• measles
• hand, foot and mouth disease
• coughs and colds
• gastro-intestinal problems.

The chronic long-term conditions described in this section are not infectious. Some are conditions that children are born with, and others can develop at a later stage. They are:
• asthma
• cystic fibrosis
• diabetes
• coeliac disease
• skin conditions – eczema and psoriasis.

 Some of the information on the following conditions is based on Keene (1999) This is an excellent source of further reading on a variety of health care issues – see *Bibliography and suggested further reading,* page 491.

### Chickenpox

#### What is chickenpox?
Chickenpox is an itchy and highly contagious condition, which causes spots which blister, weep and subsequently crust over.

#### What causes chickenpox and how is it spread?
• It is a viral infection called herpes zoster, spread by droplet infection.
• The same virus can cause shingles in adults who have previously had chickenpox, if exposed to the virus a second time.

### Recognising chickenpox
- Spots appear in groups, initially on the torso and then more 'groups' of spots appear anywhere on the body over several days.
- The spots turn into fluid-filled blisters which weep and then dry after about three days.
- As the spots appear in successive groups, they will also dry up in successive groups.

See Keene (1999), Plate 1.

### Initial actions
- Comfort and reassurance are needed.
- If initial spots appear in a day-care setting, parents need to be contacted. Paracetamol is usually given to reduce the discomfort.
- Antihistamines can be useful to reduce the irritation.
- Calamine (or similar) lotion can be applied to the spots to soothe them.
- Using bicarbonate of soda in a cool bath can also help reduce the itching.

### On-going care
- Paracetamol is usually given as needed.
- Use of calamine and bicarbonate of soda over a few days.
- Ensure the child has plenty of fluids and is kept comfortable.
- Cut finger nails short to avoid scratching.
- In young babies cotton mittens can be useful.

### Possible complications
- Some children have internal spots: nostrils, throat, vagina, anus.
- Secondary infections can occur through scratching.
- Encephalitis: inflammation of the brain.
- Pneumonia: inflammation of the lungs.

### Immunisation?
- None available at present.
- It is important that pregnant women and immuno-compromised children and adults are not exposed to the chickenpox virus.

### Incubation period and potential to infect others?
- The incubation period for chickenpox can be up to twenty-one days.
- Children are infectious for about three days prior to the first spots appearing, and remain infectious until all the scabs have dried over.

## Rubella (German measles)

### What is rubella?
Rubella is usually only a mild condition in children. It involves a high temperature and an all-over rash.

### What causes rubella and how is it spread?
Rubella is a virus spread by droplet infection.

### Recognising rubella
- The appearance of the rash is usually preceded by a raised temperature.
- The all-over pale rash, which usually starts on the face, does not itch.
- Glands are often swollen behind the ears and in the neck.

See Keene (1999), Plate 1.

### Initial actions
- Paracetamol to reduce the temperature.
- Drinking plenty of fluids should be encouraged.

### On-going care
- Avoid contact with women who are, or could be, pregnant as contact during the first twelve weeks can affect the foetus.
- No other special care is needed, and children usually recover quickly.

### Possible complications
To an infected foetus:
- loss of hearing or vision
- impaired hearing or vision
- heart deformities
- learning difficulties.

### Immunisation?
Rubella vaccine is given as part of the MMR triple vaccine at aged fifteen months and four years.

### Incubation period and potential to infect others?
- The incubation period for rubella is fourteen to twenty-one days.
- Children are infectious from about seven days prior to the rash appearing and until four or five days afterwards.

## Measles

### What is measles?
Measles is a highly contagious virus with a distinctive rash. It can be a very serious condition.

### What causes measles and how is it spread?
It is caused by RNA-containing paramyxovirus, spread by droplet infection.

### Recognising measles
- Children usually appear unwell for three or four days before the rash appears.
- Runny nose and general cold symptoms are common.
- The rash is dense, blotchy and red, usually starting on the neck and face before spreading down over the whole body.
- White spots form inside the mouth and on the cheeks (Koplik's spots).
- Eyes become sore and an avoidance of bright lights is common.

See Keene (1999), Plate 1.

### Initial actions
- Paracetamol should be given to reduce the raised temperature.
- Plenty of fluids should be encouraged.
- Children would only be visited by a GP in exceptional circumstances, but will usually be seen by a health visitor to confirm diagnosis, and referred to the GP if necessary.
- Children will normally be most comfortable resting with curtains closed to reduce the light.

### On-going care

- Paracetamol as necessary.
- Continue with a high fluid intake.

### Possible complications

- Eye infections may need antibiotics.
- Ear infections may need antibiotics.
- Hearing needs to be checked within a few weeks of illness if ears were affected.
- Inflammation of the brain can occur (encephalitis).

### Immunisation?

The measles vaccine is given as part of the MMR triple vaccine at aged fifteen months and four years.

### Incubation period and potential to infect others?

- The incubation period for measles is eight to fourteen days.
- Children are infectious from the day before the symptoms appear until four or five days afterwards.

## Hand, foot and mouth disease

### What is hand, foot and mouth disease?

This is a mild, but highly infectious condition which is common in children of pre-school age. It is in no way connected to foot and mouth disease found in cattle and other hoofed animals.

### What causes hand, foot and mouth disease and how is it spread?

It is a virus is called coxsackie, spread by droplet infection.

### Recognising hand, foot and mouth disease

- The child's temperature may be raised slightly.
- Very small blisters are often found inside the cheeks, which may ulcerate.
- Blistery spots with a red surrounding edge appear about two days after the mouth blisters on hands and fingers, and tops of feet.

### Initial actions

- Paracetamol to reduce the raised temperature.
- Plenty of fluids – avoid anything that might irritate the sore mouth.
- Foods suitable for a slightly sore mouth should be offered.

### On-going care

Prolonged mouth blisters may require treatment by the GP.

### Possible complications

No real complications noted.

Immunisation?
There is no immunisation available for hand, foot and mouth disease.

Incubation period and potential to infect others?
There is no known incubation period.

## Coughs and colds

### What are coughs and colds?
Coughs and colds can vary from the very mild to quite severe. They can be highly contagious.

### What causes coughs and colds and how are they spread?
- Coughs and colds are caused by viral infections and are spread by droplet infection
- Coughs can also be part of another condition, such as bronchitis or pneumonia.

### Recognising coughs and colds
- Colds usually start with a raised temperature and runny nose and eyes.
- Accompanying coughs can be dry and ticklish, or deep and chesty.

### Initial actions
- Paracetamol to reduce the raised temperature.
- Plenty of fluids should be offered.

### On-going care
Continued paracetamol as necessary.

### Possible complications
- Ear infections may require antibiotics.
- Chest infections may require antibiotics.

### Immunisation?
There is no immunisation for the common cold.

### Incubation period and potential to infect others?
Each cold virus is unique and so there is no known incubation period.

## Gastro-enteritis

### What is gastro-enteritis
Gastro-enteritis is the most common irritant of the stomach and intestinal lining.

### What causes gastro-enteritis and how is it spread?
- It is caused by bacteria and viruses.
- It can be spread in food due to poor hygiene during food handling.
- It can be spread by direct or indirect contact.

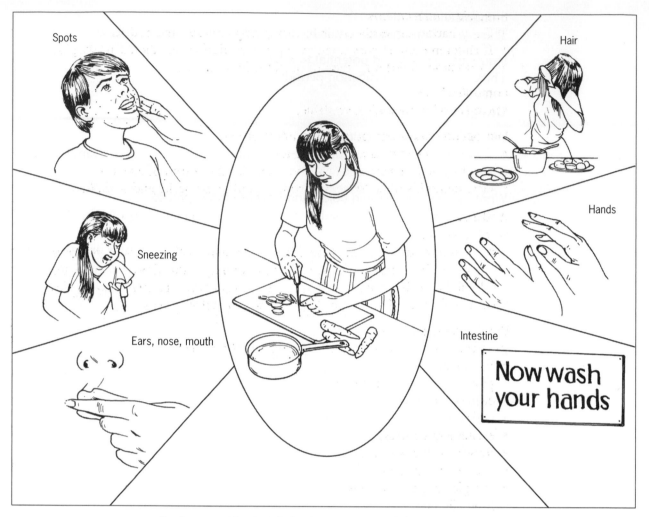

Spots

Hair

Sneezing

Hands

Ears, nose, mouth

Intestine

Now wash your hands

Good personal hygiene helps to prevent cross-infection

### Recognising gastro-enteritis

Children appear unwell, lethargic and miserable before the onset of the main symptoms, which include:

- vomiting
- diarrhoea
- raised temperature
- loss of appetite.

### Initial actions

- Only clear fluids (cooled boiled water) should be given for twenty-four hours.
- Rehydration drinks may be used for children over the age of one year, particularly if symptoms are severe.

### On-going care

- Breast-fed babies should continue to breast feed as usual.
- If there is no improvement after twenty-four hours, medical advice should be sought, particularly in very young children.
- Continue with clear fluids, together with 'ice-pops' to give the child some sugar.
- Light foods should be offered when appetite returns.
- Diet drinks are not considered to be suitable.

### Possible complications
- Dehydration can easily occur in very young children and babies.
- If children cease to pass urine frequently medical advice should be sought.
- Intravenous fluids may need to be given in severe cases.

### Immunisation?
There is no immunisation available.

### Incubation period and potential to infect others?
- There is no known incubation period.
- Strict hygiene is needed to try and minimise the spread of infection.
- Gastroenteritis often 'sweeps' through families, nurseries and schools.

## Asthma
### What is asthma?
Asthma is a condition of the lungs. It is a narrowing of the airways, which is reversible with the right treatment. The narrowing of the airways reduces the child's ability to breathe freely. The walls of the airways (bronchioles) swell and become inflamed. The inflamed airways secrete a sticky mass.

### What causes asthma?
An asthma attack can be caused by a variety of 'triggers':
- infections
- going out into the cold air
- cigarette smoke
- exercise
- excitement or stress
- fumes (such as from cars)
- allergies to animals
- allergies to pollen or dust
- food allergies.

Many children with asthma belong to families where allergies are common.

The causes of asthma

### Recognising an asthma attack

- Coughing
- Shortness of breath
- Wheezing
- A tightness in the chest area

### Initial actions

- You will need to keep calm in order to encourage calm in the child.
- If this is a child's first attack, seek medical help.

| **Professional Practice** | Each setting should have a written plan for each known asthmatic child, issued by the asthma nurse at the child's GP practice. |
|---|---|

Keene (1999) sets out a ten-point plan for managing an asthma attack:

1. Reassure the child.
2. Encourage relaxed breathing – slowly and deeply.
3. Loosen tight clothing around the neck.
4. Sit the child upright and leaning forward, supporting themselves with their hands in any comfortable position.
5. Stay with the child.
6. Give the child their brochodilator to inhale if they are known asthmatics – dosage according to the GP's instructions.
7. Offer a warm drink to relieve dryness of the mouth.
8. Continue to comfort and reassure. *Do not panic* as this will increase the child's anxiety which will impair their breathing.
9. When the child has recovered from a minor attack they can resume quiet activities.
10. Report the attack to the parents when the child is collected. If the child is upset by the episode the parents should be contacted immediately.

An ambulance should be called if:

- it is the child's first known attack
- after 5–10 minutes there is no improvement in the child
- the child becomes increasingly distressed and exhausted
- blueness of lips, mouth or face begins to occur.

### On-going care

There are two different types of inhalers:

- preventers, which contain medicines to reduce the swelling and mucus in the airways. They are usually in brown/orange inhalers and are used on a regular basis to prevent asthma attacks
- relievers, which contain medication that dilates the airways. They are usually in blue inhalers and are used to relieve symptoms of wheezing and coughing when an attack occurs or are used prior to exercise to prevent an attack.

### Possible complications

Each year a small number of children die during an asthma attack.

Spacers are used to enable very young children to inhale their medication more easily

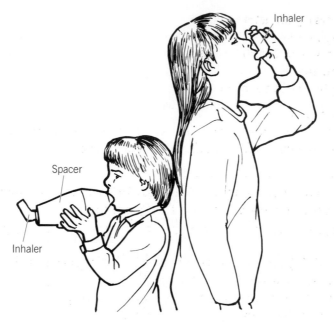

Inhaler

Spacer

Inhaler

### Cystic fibrosis (CF)

#### What is CF?
- Cystic fibrosis is a serious condition of the respiratory and digestive systems.
- It is a life-limiting condition in which the secretions produced by the lungs are not able to flow away in the normal way. The secretions build-up in the airways which subsequently restricts breathing.
- Risk of infection of the airways is high.
- The digestive tract is affected due to the pancreas not being able to produce the appropriate enzymes needed to break down the food and absorb it into the body's system.

#### What causes CF?
- Cystic fibrosis is inherited as an autosomal recessive condition.
- Approximately 1 in 2,000 children has CF.
- It is more prevalent in some ethnic groups than others. The highest incidence is seen in Caucasians (light-skinned people of European, North African, SW Asian and Indian origin). It is rare in families of African-Caribbean origin and almost non-existent in people of Far Eastern origin.

#### Recognising CF
- CF is present in some infants from birth. It is detected by the presence of a blockage (called meconium ileus) at the opening of the intestine.
- The Guthrie test at seven days after birth includes a test for CF.
- For infants not diagnosed at birth, the first few months of life may see them failing to thrive due to malabsorption of food.
- Chest infections and coughs can indicate CF chest problems.
- Diarrhoea and fatty offensive stools can indicate CF digestive problems.

### Initial actions

- Any suspicion of CF must be referred immediately to the GP.
- A 'sweat' test is occasionally the initial action, if parents have noticed a salty taste to their child's skin, but this form of testing can be quite distressing for a child.
- Genetic testing will confirm whether the suspected diagnosis is correct.

### On-going care

The on-going care of a child with cystic fibrosis involves:

- physiotherapy of the chest at regular intervals throughout the day to loosen secretions (known as percussion physiotherapy)
- regular exercise to help expand the lungs regularly
- antibiotics to prevent chest infections
- pancreatic enzyme supplements, taken at each meal time to help absorb food
- a diet that is low in fat, but high in protein and carbohydrates.

Children with CF will have continuous care and support from a dietician, a community children's nurse and/or a CF specialist.

### Possible complications

- During periods of exacerbation or infection the physiotherapy sessions may need to be more intensive.
- Infections will often result in admission to hospital.
- Many children also develop diabetes (the only type in which a high carbohydrate/sugar intake is given).
- Cystic fibrosis has no cure.
- A high carbohydrate diet usually allows a longer and better quality of life.
- Some children benefit from heart–lung transplants.
- Individuals with CF do not usually live into old age.

## Diabetes mellitus (type 1 diabetes)

### What is diabetes mellitus?

Diabetes mellitus is an endocrine disorder in which the pancreas does not make enough insulin. Insulin helps the body to use and store sugar. When it is not used efficiently the sugar overflows into the urine.

### What causes diabetes mellitus?

- It is often triggered following a severe viral infection.
- It is not an inherited condition, but there is a familial trait to diabetes.

### Recognising diabetes mellitus

Most children are diagnosed following a sudden onset of the two most common symptoms:

- extreme thirst
- frequently passing urine.

Also the breath may smell of pear drops.

Less obvious onset includes:

- tiredness
- constantly lethargic
- weight loss

- loss of appetite
- urinary tract infection due to excessive sugar in the urine.

### Initial actions

- Medical diagnosis involving the testing of urine and blood for excessive sugar levels.
- A short stay in hospital is usual in order for the child's blood sugar levels to be stabilised and their dietary needs agreed and understood by parents.

### On-going care

- Insulin injections and a carefully controlled diet will be necessary for life.
- Checks on blood sugar levels are taken (at least) daily.
- Diet will be monitored by a dietician.
- A generally 'healthy heart' diet is needed (high fibre, low sugar, low fat).
- A return to hospital is unlikely, unless illness causes dehydration.

### Possible complications

- Dehydration due to illness.
- An imbalance of blood sugar levels can lead to either *hypoglycaemia* (sweating and clammy skin – needs to be given extra sugar or a boost of sugar) or *hyperglycaemia* (sugar levels are too high, so extra insulin is needed).
- Signs of a hypoglycaemic attack include sweating, dizziness, confusion and rapid breathing. A snack or a glucose drink or similar should be given to the child. It is important that someone remains with the child until they have stabilised.
- Illness, under-dosing on insulin and sudden growth spurts can all affect the blood sugar level balance.

Keene (1999), page 259

Blood glucose is kept steady by a balance between exercise and insulin on one side and carbohydrate, excitement and infection on the other.

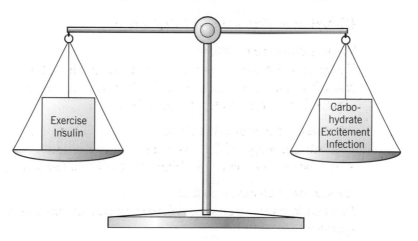

Common reasons for hypoglycaemia are:
- Unusual exercise, e.g. extra games
- Not enough carbohydrate, e.g. missed snack
- Too much insulin, e.g. mistaken dose

Common reasons for hyperglycaemia are:
- Less exercise than usual, e.g. missed games
- Not enough insulin, e.g. growing out of dose
- Too much carbohydrate, e.g. extra snacks
- Sudden excitement or strain, e.g. exams
- Infection, e.g. cold

**Professional Practice**

- Supplies of glucose tablets should be taken with you when you accompany a child with diabetes on any outing.
- Supplies should be readily available in the school or early years setting.
- Children with diabetes should be closely observed during exercise, particularly if they are trying something new.
- Contact numbers for parents should always be readily available.
- Staff working with a child with diabetes should be taught how to cope with their needs and any attacks.
- Privacy should be allowed when children need to test their blood sugar levels during the day.
- Catering staff need to be informed and be able to deal with special dietary needs.
- Good long-term dietary care will help prevent other ill health, such as heart, liver and vascular disease and eye disease.

**Case Study**

*William*

William is five years old and is diabetic. He is on his first school trip to the zoo. He is very excited and has rushed around from enclosure to enclosure during the morning. At lunch time William was too busy talking to his friends about their favourite animals that he did not each very much of his packed lunch. As the afternoon wore on William became lethargic and by the time he got onto the coach he was sweating a great deal and stumbled getting into his seat. Other children were also tired and stumbling.

1 Would you be concerned about William?
2 What signs of hypoglycaemia is William possibly displaying?
3 What would you do initially?
4 With hindsight, what else should staff have done?
5 What have you learned from this case study?

## Coeliac disease

### What is coeliac disease?
- Coeliac disease is a condition affecting the lining of the small intestine. It is an immunological reaction to gluten, a protein found in wheat, rye, barley and, in some people, oats too.
- Children are usually diagnosed when they start to have solid food from about four months onwards.
- In adults coeliac disease can occur at any time, often triggered by an unknown cause.

### What causes coeliac disease?
The reaction to gluten causes the villi protrusions along the intestine to become flattened and therefore reduces the surface for absorption of food.

### Recognising coeliac disease
- Babies fail to thrive in the usual way, not putting on weight and being low on the centile charts.
- Young children become very unwell, lethargic and miserable, with abdominal bloating.

- Stools are pale, fatty, smell unpleasant and are difficult to flush away.

### Initial actions
- There has usually been some concern shown for the child (or adult) prior to diagnosis.
- Blood tests and faecal samples are taken initially.
- A biopsy of the jejunum usually follows if concerns are raised from blood and faeces results.
- A dietary 'challenge' would be carried out in early puberty.

### On-going care
- A gluten-free diet is necessary throughout life.
- Gluten is found in many everyday foods and it takes time to identify all foods that need to be avoided.
- Guidance is given from a dietician to help establish a balanced diet.
- Coeliac UK gives helpful advice and a regularly updated food list.
- Many supermarkets now display a gluten-free symbol on suitable foods.

### Possible complications
- Iron deficiency anaemia is a possibility due to malabsorption of food.
- Calcium deficiency can also be present, again due to malabsorption.
- In the long term, there is a higher incidence of intestinal cancer in people with coeliac disease if it remains untreated.
- For individuals diagnosed at later ages, further problems can occur:
  - osteoporosis, which is a calcium deficient condition resulting in repeated fractures
  - osteopaenia, which indicates borderline osteoporosis, and is often picked up during bone density scanning for osteoporosis

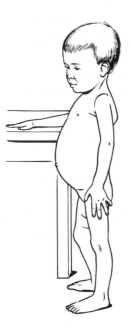

The gluten-free symbol

Bone density scans are offered for individuals where either condition is suspected and calcium supplements (with vitamin D) are then recommended for life.

### Familial?
There is a familial tendency regarding coeliac disease, but it is not termed as hereditary. Babies born into a family where coeliac disease has previously been diagnosed should be observed closely for early signs and gluten should ideally be withheld from their diet until their first birthday. In some cases, early exposure to gluten has triggered the condition.

## Eczema

### What is eczema?
Eczema is due to an allergic reaction and is common amongst young children. It dries the skin, forming itchy inflamed areas which crack open and often weep. It is extremely unpleasant and causes great misery to many children. Fortunately the majority of children cease to be affected by eczema by the time they reach puberty. Some, however, continue to suffer from eczema, along with asthma (another allergic reaction).

### What causes eczema?
Eczema is a reaction to a 'trigger factor'. These triggers vary between individuals, with common causes being dairy produce, washing powders and soaps. It can also be triggered or exacerbated by stress or excitement.

### Recognising eczema

The initial signs of eczema usually appear between three and eighteen months. It occurs initially on the face and scalp, the shins and forearms, and later it affects the backs of knees, inside of the elbow joints and at the ankles. Symptoms include:
- dry scaly skin which cracks and itches
- the itchy rash often weeps
- the sore areas crust over
- in the long term, the skin becomes thickened and leathery.

Young children find it difficult to sleep due to the itching.

### Initial actions

- If a child develops itchy or sore areas of skin, they should be seen by a health professional to confirm or discount a diagnosis of eczema.
- Childcare staff need to be aware that a child's condition may become more acute in extremes of weather. They become very sensitive to changes in temperature.

### On-going care

- It is important to keep the skin softened, using an emollient cream.
- Emollients should be applied regularly throughout the day, and this is particularly important after a bath. It can often be helpful to cover the affected area with cotton tubular sleeves (bandages).
- Special bath oils can be used to help remoisten the skin, which naturally loses its oils through bathing.
- Affected children should not use normal soaps; there are special preparations available.
- Children should be taught to avoid any known trigger factors.
- Keeping fingernails cut short helps minimise scratching.
- Very young children may benefit from wearing cotton mittens at night.
- Loose cotton clothing helps the skin breathe and reduces chaffing of the skin.
- Some children need prescribed products to help control the effects of eczema.
  - Cortico-steroids can be prescribed as creams or ointments for very intense phases.
  - Antihistamines are also used to reduce the itching, helping children to sleep better.
  - For some children, forms of Chinese medicine have been helpful in treating both eczema and psoriasis (under the guidance of a recognised and qualified practitioner).
- Any referral to an 'alternative' practitioner should always be with the full knowledge of the child's GP, as there could be contra-indicative effects if used in conjunction with their current medication.

### Possible complications

- Antibiotics, taken orally or as creams, may become necessary to counter the effects of secondary infections, caused by excessive scratching.
- Children with severe eczema can become the victims of teasing. Early years staff need to be ready to deal with this.

### Familial?

- Many children with eczema are born into families where there are others with a range of allergic conditions.

- Many will have parents or older siblings who have had eczema as a child themselves.

---

**Professional Practice**

- Consideration is needed to ensure that children with eczema are not excluded from activities because of their condition.
- Applying creams to the affected areas during the day should be done without fuss and with some privacy.
- It is important to wear disposable gloves when applying the creams, to avoid any risk of introducing infection to the child, and to prevent the absorption of corticosteroids into your own skin.

---

**Case Study**

*Christopher*

Christopher is four years old and is severely affected by eczema. His hands are leathery and regularly encrusted with scabs from the weeping sores. He is pale and lethargic most of the time due to lack of sleep and constant discomfort.

1 The other children in the nursery are reluctant to hold Christopher's hands as they feel strange and rather unpleasant. How will you deal with this during circle games such as 'Farmer's in the den', without making Christopher feel isolated or different?
2 Christopher loves finger-painting and playing in the sand and water. How will you ensure that his skin is protected while he plays? What precautions should you take?

## Psoriasis

### What is psoriasis?

Psoriasis is a severe skin condition which most commonly appears from the age if ten onwards, but is occasionally seen in younger children where there is a strong family history of the condition.

### What causes psoriasis?

- It is considered to be an inherited condition, but its cause is unknown.
- The first incidence of psoriasis often follows a period of stress or an infection involving damage to the skin.
- The most common form of psoriasis in young children is guttate psoriasis which causes small patches of the skin rash, often as a result of a severe sore throat.
- The skin cells form at a rate ten times faster than the body discards cells, resulting in the thickened patches that appear on the skin.

### Recognising psoriasis

- A thickened red rash appears on the scalp, arms, legs and body, often covered with silvery scales.
- The rash is not usually itchy but may irritate through a tightening of the skin and general feeling of discomfort.

### Initial actions

Referral is needed to a dermatologist (skin specialist) who will consider the severity of the condition and treat as appropriate, usually with similar medications to eczema.

### On-going care

- Treatment with emollient creams, coal tar products and corticosteroids, both through direct application and as a bath oil.
- As with eczema, some people will benefit from Chinese medicines in the treatment of psoriasis.

### Possible complications

- Secondary infections can occur.
- Social isolation is possible if the condition is very noticeable.

### Familial?

- Psoriasis is considered to be an inherited condition.
- It is also a condition for life, although for many people it can be managed quite well with medication.

**Test Yourself**

1 What are the body's natural defences?
2 What is a leucocyte, and what does it do?
3 What are ciliated epithelium, and what is their role in defending the body?
4 What are the five groups of pathogens (germs) called?
5 Which type of pathogen is a single-celled organism?
6 Define the terms 'ingested', 'inhaled' and 'inoculated'.
7 Give at least three examples of socio-economic factors that affect health, linked to poverty.
8 Give at least three examples of socio-economic factors that affect health, linked to housing.
9 Give at least three examples of socio-economic factors that affect health, linked to unemployment.
10 What is the difference between active natural immunity and active acquired immunity?
11 What is meant by the term 'herd immunity'?
12 What does HiB stand for and which other vaccination is it offered with?
13 From what age is paracetamol registered as suitable to treat pyrexia (high temperature)?
14 What are the benefits of screening?
15 Give three examples of conditions common in childhood.
16 Give three examples of chronic conditions that can affect children.
17 Which condition can result in shingles in an adult who has previously had the virus in its common childhood form?
18 Which condition is associated with Koplik's spots?
19 Which condition is caused by the virus coxsackie?
20 Which condition is associated with percussion physiotherapy?

# The impact of ill health on children and families

The medical needs of a child clearly take precedence when they are ill, but their social, emotional and cognitive needs also need to be taken into account. Illness can affect children in a number of ways, particularly emotionally, as they may feel confused or scared about what is happening to them. During periods of short-term illness a slight change in routine or diet does not normally have any significant impact, but with long-term conditions there can be considerable changes in behaviour, diet and habit that can be difficult to cope with. Children's reaction to illness and its subsequent impact on them is directly linked to their age and stage of development. They need to have their questions answered honestly, and be kept informed as to what will happen next, without alarming them unduly. As with adults, children are more likely to be able to cope with whatever treatment or investigation they need if they have some idea of what to expect.

It is important that children are not told that 'it won't hurt', if it clearly will, as this will be likely to affect their security even further, and may cause them to lose the trust they have in the adults caring for them. In recent years, parents have been able to stay with their child in hospital for much of the time. This is partly due to the work of the organisation Action for Sick Children.

## Activity

Research the history, aims and work of the organisation Action for Sick Children.
a) What was it originally called?
b) When was it first set up?
c) What was its original aim?
d) How has the work of the organisation changed?
e) What research can you find that supports the aims of the organisation?

## The impact of ill health on children

Factors to consider regarding a child who is ill may include some or all of the following, shown in the chart on the next page.

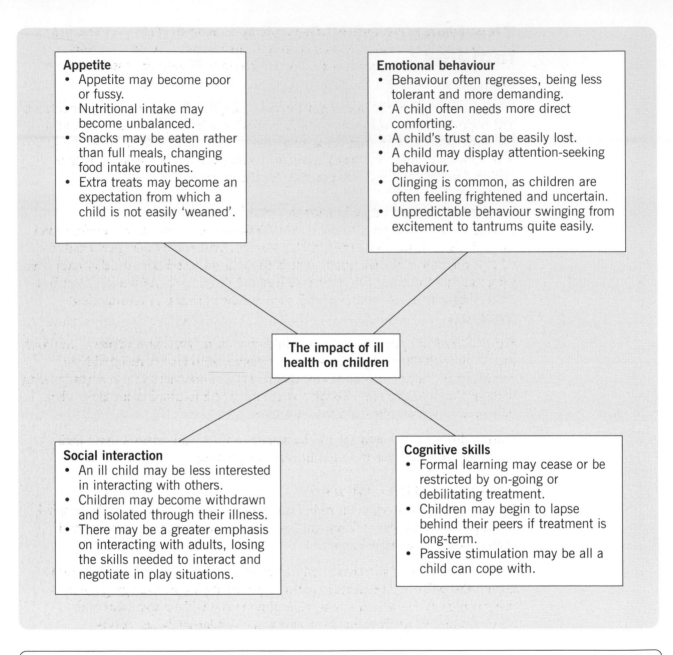

**Appetite**
- Appetite may become poor or fussy.
- Nutritional intake may become unbalanced.
- Snacks may be eaten rather than full meals, changing food intake routines.
- Extra treats may become an expectation from which a child is not easily 'weaned'.

**Emotional behaviour**
- Behaviour often regresses, being less tolerant and more demanding.
- A child often needs more direct comforting.
- A child's trust can be easily lost.
- A child may display attention-seeking behaviour.
- Clinging is common, as children are often feeling frightened and uncertain.
- Unpredictable behaviour swinging from excitement to tantrums quite easily.

**The impact of ill health on children**

**Social interaction**
- An ill child may be less interested in interacting with others.
- Children may become withdrawn and isolated through their illness.
- There may be a greater emphasis on interacting with adults, losing the skills needed to interact and negotiate in play situations.

**Cognitive skills**
- Formal learning may cease or be restricted by on-going or debilitating treatment.
- Children may begin to lapse behind their peers if treatment is long-term.
- Passive stimulation may be all a child can cope with.

**Professional Practice**
- Children need a great deal of emotional support during periods of illness.
- Patience and understanding are vital.
- Children need clear explanations as to what will be happening to them, including routine procedures such as temperature taking and blood pressure checks.
- All explanations need to be appropriate for the child's age and level of understanding.

## Preparing a child for hospital

Clearly it is easier to prepare a child for a planned admission to hospital, as there is time to talk about it in advance at a pace suitable to the child's age and understanding, whereas when a child is admitted as an emergency there is little time to talk about what they will see, hear or experience. Children are only admitted to hospital when it is absolutely necessary. Whenever possible they are treated at home.

A week or so before the due admission date, hospital discussion can be introduced and opportunities to role-play hospital 'scenes' may be very helpful to a child. If the hospital offers a pre-admission tour of the ward, this can be very helpful in acclimatising a child to what to expect when they arrive. This helps to reduce anxiety for the child, and consequently for their parents too.

### Preparation a few days before the child is admitted

During the few days prior to the child's admission to the ward, it is useful to talk through the information sent from the hospital. This will usually give details of what is on offer in the playroom, details of the hospital school, together with what the child needs to take with them into hospital. It can be helpful to let them buy something new to take into hospital, such as new pyjamas, or a flannel and toothbrush.

Hospital staff recognise the need for children to take with them whatever comforts them. Older children may at times feel embarrassed to take in their teddy or comforter (in case their friends visit them). Parents may need to take a teddy along without the child knowing. Teddy will then be there to comfort the child when they need it without the child feeling foolish.

During this time, children need to be reassured if they are anxious, have their questions answered clearly and as honestly as possible.

### Once the child is on the ward

It is important for all children to become familiar with the layout of the hospital ward, particularly older children, as this will allow them more autonomy and enable them to feel more in control.

Children will need to be introduced to the hospital play staff, usually a nursery nurse, who will often be further trained in hospital play. Encouraging them to select play materials as soon as possible after arrival will occupy them both physically and mentally and help to ease some (understandable) nerves.

## The needs of parents and siblings

Families face difficulties too when a child is ill, and experience changes to the usual routine, particularly if the child is in hospital or a **hospice**. There will be times when family members feel isolated because they are unable to leave the family home, or because they need to stay with their child in hospital for prolonged periods.

Meeting other families in similar circumstances is important to them, linking up via condition-led support groups or parent networks locally or within the hospital itself. These groups enable parents to share experiences and discuss and explore issues that concern them. They are able to meet others whose child is further along the road to recovery, or who have reached a different stage in their condition. Families need support from many different people, for many different reasons, for example:

- from health professionals to:
  - reassure parents that they are experienced and knowledgeable about their child's condition
  - reassure parents about their child's condition and any prognosis
  - keep parents informed about day-to-day changes in their child's condition and what procedures are planned or being considered
  - provide information about the treatment options about which they may need to make decisions
  - link parents with support groups for families with a child with the same condition
  - occupy siblings while parents speak with specialists, enabling them to concentrate on the information they are being given without distraction
- from employers, schools and others to:
  - support the parents' need to be with their ill child
  - support the daily running of households when a child is in hospital
  - offer educational support if home tutoring is needed
  - support families on low incomes to help finance hospital visits
  - support siblings by understanding that they too have needs and feelings during the illness or hospitalisation of another child in the family
  - give appropriate levels of information to siblings in accordance with parents' wishes.

### Financial implications for families

Extra financial needs can be incurred when a child is ill. One parent may need to give up working temporarily to take on the caring role. Additional resources may be needed, for example increased heating costs, additional wash loads, and so on.

Support can often be obtained from a medical social worker, who can help with the issues such as the cost of transport or childcare facilities. They may also be involved in arranging for interpreters or an advocate for families for whom English is not the first language or who have difficulty in understanding or expressing information.

 BACK to Chapter 3, page 100, for information on advocates.

**Professional Practice**  Parents in financial difficulties can apply for support to organisations such as the Benefits Agency, the Citizens Advice Bureau and other groups dealing with welfare issues. They provide both financial and practical help.

## Treatment for children with health problems

Treatment for children can take place in the home or in hospital and, for children who are terminally ill, it may also be in a hospice. The need for medical treatment or intervention is of course a priority, but it should not overshadow the needs of a child for play. Play is invaluable in reducing stress and uncertainty and can offer a positive focus for the whole family. As mentioned earlier, the age and stage of a child's development and understanding will determine how much they are told about their illness and treatment and which approaches are taken.

# Treatment in the home

Common childhood illnesses will always be treated at home, unless there are complications. The parents' role will expand to include nursing skills and play provision, taking into account the child's age and general interests. Children may have less energy than usual and they may spend much of the day resting, therefore activities will need to be easily managed, offering satisfying play without too much effort.

Suitable activities include colouring and drawing, dot-to-dot books and simple puzzles. Construction materials that are easily handled and not too fiddly are better than those which are very precise and need a great deal of concentration. Activities involving small pieces need to be placed on deep-sided trays if the child is in bed, to avoid knocking off vital parts which may affect the satisfaction of the activity as a whole.

Children like to read and hear familiar books and stories, often having them repeated many times – a common practice with young children generally. In slightly older children, the familiarity and reassurance of reverting to this phase is often helpful to them emotionally.

**Case Study**

*Lucy*

Lucy is 3½ years old and currently has chickenpox. She is absolutely covered in spots, and has them internally too. She has been in great discomfort and very distressed at times, but is beginning to feel a little better. Lucy's mother has asked you for advice regarding how best to occupy Lucy.

1  What toys and activities would you suggest for Lucy, bearing in mind how she is feeling?
2  Would you recommend her mother playing with Lucy, or for Lucy to play alone?
3  What would you have suggested for an older child to do in similar circumstances?
4  How would you occupy a young toddler in this situation?

# Treatment in hospital

On hospital wards there is a range of staff especially trained to work with children. These include:
- *play specialists*, who are often nursery nurses who have qualified initially through level 3 courses and then taken a specialist course in hospital play
- *teachers*, who work with the children who are well enough, linking activities to the appropriate stage of the National Curriculum, or with younger children, the Foundation Stage Curriculum.
- *nursery nurses*, who support the work of the teachers and play specialists. They are often on duty outside of 'school hours' and encourage and arrange a variety of play activities for children of all ages. They are often happy to involve the siblings of the children who are currently having treatment too.

Play on the ward often includes medical props to help familiarise children with what they may see. This could include medical kits, involving stethoscope, eye patch, and so on. It may also include syringe painting (without the needles, of course) or making plaster casts of children's hands. A range of books giving positive images of hospital routines and treatments are usually to be found on hospital wards. Teddies and dolls can be bandaged, injected or given other treatments that it is felt appropriate to simulate.

## Treatment in hospices

Many terminally ill children are cared for in hospitals or at home. Others are able to benefit from time in a children's hospice. Although there are not a huge number of hospices for children, they play an important role.

A hospice is a place of care and treatment specifically for terminally ill children. Some hospices have a community team who will help to care for the child in the family home. Hospices offer support for parents and families, as well as the ill child, and they discuss with the family what will meet the needs of the child and the whole family and do what they can to meet those needs.

Hospices also offer training in bereavement skills to other professionals who may become involved with families who have lost a child, or will shortly face such a loss.

The support offered to families of a terminally ill child involves:
• respite care
• care of siblings
• emotional support
• practical help and advice
• opportunities to grieve
• opportunities to share experiences with others.

In supporting the child, they offer:
• 'normal' routines whenever possible
• opportunities to discuss their futures
• opportunities to talk about their families and what will happen when they die (where this is applicable).

Staff who work in terminal care need to be sensitive to the parents' emotionally fragile state. They try where they can to build up a rapport with them, which can help them to support them after they have been bereaved. Becoming aware of a family's cultural practice is important, to ensure that cultural traditions are both valued and maintained.

Families will go through different stages of grieving. This will usually be shock, even if the death was known to be imminent, followed by confusion, fear, anger and guilt. Parents may feel they will never be able to cope again, and that they no longer have a role in life. This can be particular acute if they have cared for their child intensively over a long period of time. Anger and guilt arise, as the unfairness of the situation takes hold. Why their child? What had the child done to deserve such a death? They may also start to question whether they did all they could have done for the child.

This is a difficult time for families and also for those who work to support them.

**Professional Practice**

- Sensitivity is needed at all times when supporting terminally ill children and their families.
- Parents will often forget, or not take in, what they have heard, because they are distressed at the time.
- Siblings need support too.

**Test Yourself**

1. List at least ten of the effects that ill health can have on a child.
2. Why is it important for children to be familiar with hospital routines and procedures?
3. What support needs might parents of ill children have?
4. Who are the non-medical children's professionals usually found on children's wards?
5. What role does a hospice play in supporting children and their families?

# Key terms

**You should now understand the following words and phrases. If you do not, read through the chapter again and review them.**

causes of ill health
direct contact
droplet infection
environmental factors affecting health
health
health education
health promotion
health promotion campaigns
herd immunity
HImPs
holistic model
hospices
immunisation programmes
indirect contact
lifestyle factors affecting health

live vaccines
medical model
non-live vaccines
pathogens
preparing children for hospital
primary health care
role of health educators
screening
secondary health care
social and economic factors affecting health
social model
suppressed immunity
tertiary health care
the impact of ill health
World Health Organisation (WHO)

## Bibliography and suggested further reading

Beattie, A. (1993) 'The changing boundaries of health', in Beattie, A., Gott, M., Jones, L. and Sidell, M. (eds) *Health and Well-being: A Reader*, Macmillan/Open University, Basingstoke

Blaxter, M. (1990) *Health and Lifestyles*, Tavistock/Routledge, London

Department of Health (1998) *Our Healthier Nation*, HMSO, London

Keene, A. (1999) *Child Health: Care of the Child in Health and Illness*, Nelson Thornes, Cheltenham

Lalonde, M. (1974) *A New Perspective on the Health of Canadians*, Ministry of Supply and Services, Ottowa

Naidoo, J. and Wills, J. (2000) *Health Promotion: Foundations for Practice*, 2nd edition, Baillière Tindall, London

# Glossary of terms

| | |
|---|---|
| **ABC procedures** | A sequential emergency first aid process |
| **ABC behaviour strategy** | Considering the antecendant, the behaviour and the consequence of situations |
| **Accommodation** | Piaget's term for a child understanding a new concept |
| **Accurate records** | Factual records kept by the setting following an accident or concern |
| **Active listening** | Ensuring that you are focusing on what you are listening to |
| **Advocacy** | Representing another individual or speaking on their behalf |
| **Aggressive** | Taking a forceful approach |
| **Alternative forms of care** | The range of care options available to children |
| **Anonymity** | Ensuring that an individual's identity remains unknown |
| **Apgar score chart** | The chart noting the health score given to a baby at birth |
| **Aphasia** | When a child is unable to express their thoughts in words |
| **Area Child Protection Committee (ACPC)** | A group of professionals who meet to discuss individual child abuse or protection cases |
| **Artificial ventilation** | Breathing for another person, when they are unable to do so for themselves |
| **Assertive** | Being able to put your ideas or viewpoint across without aggression |
| **Assimilation** | Piaget's theory of a child trying to understand a new concept |
| **Associative play** | Children playing with the same activity, but who are not yet playing co-operatively |
| **Aural stimulation** | Stimulation through sound |
| **Baby massage** | A pleasurable form of physical contact which aids relaxation, and can help the bonding of parent and child |
| **Baby signing** | A scheme to enable hearing babies to make their needs known prior to gaining speech |
| **Bar chart** | A method of presenting data, often used in research, particularly useful for showing descriptive categories |
| **Barriers to communication** | Any obstruction to understanding between more than one individual |
| **Behaviour management** | Strategies for setting children boundaries |
| **Behaviour policies** | Written agreements setting out the behaviour management (of an early years setting) |

| | |
|---|---|
| **Body language** | The non-verbal signals given out by our bodies |
| **Bonding** | The close relationship formed between a child and one or more of their main carers |
| **Burn-out** | Becoming exhausted or over stimulated |
| **Care of the environment** | Considering the safety needs of the early years setting |
| **Care order** | A legal order in which a child is placed in the care of the local authority |
| **Caudal** | Referring to the lower parts of the body |
| **Causes of ill health** | The range of reasons why individuals become ill |
| **Centile chart** | A chart used to record the growth in infants and young children |
| **Cephalo** | Referring to the head |
| **Changing face of the family** | How family life continually changes within society |
| **Chest compressions** | An emergency first aid procedure |
| **Child Assessment Order** | A legal order applied for in court when a child is considered to be at risk or already suffering significant harm |
| **Child Protection Register** | A computerised list, kept by the local authority of children who are considered to be 'at-risk' |
| **Chromosome** | Part of the human genetic make-up |
| **Classical conditioning** | A conditioned response theory often associated with Ivan Pavlov |
| **Closed questions** | Questions which place a limit on the answers |
| **Cognitive development** | The development of learning through thinking and problem-solving |
| **Colic** | Acute spasmodic abdominal pain common in young babies |
| **Communication** | The means of passing and receiving information |
| **Communication cycle** | A reciprocal form of passing and receiving information |
| **Confidentiality** | Keeping information to yourself; not passing on information inappropriately |
| **Conservation** | Being able to understand change in quantity, size and number. A term often associated with Jean Piaget |
| **Containment** | Helping a child to express their emotions safely |
| **Continuity of care** | Routine and familiarity which helps children feel secure |
| **Cooled boiled water** | Used to prepare formula feeds and to clean the eyes of newborn babies |
| **Co-operative play** | The stage of play when children play with each other, sometimes taking on simple roles or making simple rules for their games |
| **COSHH** | Control of Substances Hazardous to Health |

| | |
|---|---|
| **Cross-infection** | The passing of infection from one person to another |
| **Cycle of disadvantage** | The process whereby the experiences of one generation of a family have an impact on the next, continuing some or all of the problems they face |
| **Development** | The changes that take place as an individual grows |
| **Developmental delay** | The term often used when a child's development is not following the pattern of averages (or 'norms') |
| **Developmentally appropriate** | What is expected of a child at a given stage of development |
| **Direct contact** | Cross-infection through contact with an infected individual |
| **Discrimination** | The unfair treatment of an individual, group or minority, based on prejudice |
| **Disclosure** | Telling someone about the abuse suffered, either currently or in the past |
| **Disequilibrium** | Linked to Jean Piaget's theory, where a child is at a stage of not fully understanding the new concepts they are faced with |
| **Distal** | A distance away from the central point (of the body) |
| **Diversity** | Being different or varied |
| **Droplet infection** | A common cause of cross-infection |
| **Dysfluency** | Being unable to speak words fluently, stammering; a common (temporary) occurrence in young children |
| **Dysphasia** | When a child has difficulty in expressing their thoughts into words |
| **Ego-centricity** | Placing self at the centre of everything. A natural stage of development in young children in which they do not understand the necessity for their needs to be deferred, or for anyone else's needs to be considered |
| **Emergency Protection Order** | An order of law, applied for through the courts to help protect children from harm |
| **Empiricists** | Those who uphold the theory that knowledge is gained form experience (nurture theory) |
| **Emotional abuse** | The continual rejection, terrorising or criticism of an individual |
| **Emotional disturbance** | Evidenced by behaviour which causes concern and needs professional intervention (when serious or long-term) or sensitive handling by parents and carers (for temporary or common problems such as tantrums) |
| **Enactive thinking** | Thinking based on memory, on what has already been experienced |
| **Environmental factors** | Any influences from around an individual that could have an impact on them in any way |
| **EPOCH** | The organisation End Physical Punishment of Children |
| **Equality** | The state of being equal, of having an equal opportunity |
| **Equity** | Fairness combined with equal opportunity |
| **Evacuation procedures** | The planned process of removing children from an unsafe situation to a safe environment |

| | |
|---|---|
| **Evaluation** | Reflecting on and giving consideration to a past event, action or project |
| **Evidence** | Supportive material or information |
| **Exploratory play** | Play in which a child is able to find out by experimentation and discovery |
| **Eye-contact** | Looking directly at an individual when conversing or explaining something to them |
| **Feminist model** | An approach taken (specifically) from a women's perspective |
| **First aid** | The emergency actions taken following an accident or sudden illness |
| **Foetal alcohol syndrome (FAS)** | Physical and cognitive abnormalities often found in children born to alcoholic mothers |
| **Food-related customs** | Acceptable and unacceptable foods linked to culture |
| **Foundation Stage Curriculum** | A government-led curriculum for children from age three years |
| **Freeplay** | Play which is undirected |
| **Genotype** | The complete genetic inheritance of an individual |
| **Good-enough parenting** | A term used to refer to parenting that is adequate, although may not be considered to be ideal by many people |
| **Growth** | Increasing in size, height, weight and so on |
| **HASAWA** | The Health And Safety at Work Act (1974) |
| **Health** | The state of well-being |
| **Health education** | Learning about health, either formally or informally |
| **Health promotion** | Pro-active encouragement on health issues |
| **Health promotion campaigns** | Information on specific health issues being actively distributed or advertised through the media, or others |
| **Herd immunity** | Vaccination programmes which work by immunising a high enough proportion of society, therefore dramatically reducing the likelihood of becoming infected with the condition. |
| **Highscope** | A specific programme of learning |
| **HImPs** | Health Improvement Programmes, initiated by the government |
| **Historical perspective** | Considering what has happened in the past and its relevance to the present |
| **Holistic model** | Taking an all-round consideration |
| **Hospices** | A care setting for individuals who are terminally ill |
| **Hot-housing** | Over-stimulating (in children) to achieve more at an early age |
| **Human resources** | The personnel (staff, parents, professionals, and so on) involved |
| **Iconic thinking** | The development of mental images |
| **Identifying needs** | Being able to recognise a need using professional judgement, knowledge and understanding |

| | |
|---|---|
| **Immunisation programmes** | A process of vaccinations for children to prevent illness and to help eradicate certain conditions from society |
| **Impact of ill health** | Any outcome that occurs due to the ill health of an individual or their family |
| **Incest** | Sexual intercourse between two relatives who are too closely linked to legally be able to marry |
| **Indicators of abuse** | Signs and symptoms that may be seen in children which could suggest that abuse has taken place |
| **Indirect contact** | Cross-infection where there is no specific contact with an infected individual |
| **Institutional discrimination** | The policies or practice of an organisation which systematically discriminate against a minority group or groups |
| **Interpersonal skills** | Communicating with others in a positive (good skills) or negative (bad skills) manner |
| ***Laissez-faire* model** | Taking an approach involving unrestricted freedom or indifference |
| **Language acquisition device** | A theory of language development associated with Noam Chomsky, referring to children's predisposition to acquire language |
| **Lifestyle factors affecting health** | The impact of lifestyle choices such as smoking that have an impact on health |
| **Line graph** | A method of presenting data, particularly useful for showing trends or changes in quantity |
| **Live vaccines** | A vaccine which uses a small amount of the 'live' condition. Live vaccines are not given to individuals with suppressed immunity |
| **Long-term effects of abuse** | The on-going affects suffered by an individual following abuse |
| **Managing unwanted behaviour** | Methods to lesson undesirable behaviour in children |
| **Marginalise** | Treating someone or something as insignificant or unimportant; to place at the edge (of importance) |
| **Maturational** | To do with maturity |
| **Mean** | The average most widely understood. It is calculated by adding together sets of scores, and dividing by the total number of scores involved |
| **Media** | Different methods of giving information, such as television, radio, newspapers |
| **Medical model** | An approach taken (specifically) from a medical perspective |
| **Mode** | A 'score' that is the most common in a set of numerical data |
| **Monotropic** | A term associated with John Bowlby referring to maternal deprivation and the attachment of an infant to only one carer |
| **Montessori philosophy** | A specific programme of learning, with its own range or resources |
| **National Curriculum** | The curriculum followed by children in all state schools |

| | |
|---|---|
| **Nativists** | Those who uphold the theory that knowledge is innate (nature theory) |
| **Natural immunity** | A degree of immunity present in the body without the use of vaccination |
| **Nature–nurture debate** | The question of whether individuals acquire knowledge through their genetic inheritance or through their experiences from birth onwards |
| **Negative images** | Illustrations or descriptions that portray limitations or negativity regarding individuals |
| **Neglect** | A form of abuse where the care of a child is insufficient or inappropriate |
| **Neonatal jaundice** | A problem with the function of the liver during the first weeks of life |
| **Neonate** | The first month of life |
| **Non-live vaccines** | Artificially-made vaccinations, often given to individuals with suppressed immune systems, due to conditions such as leukaemia, HIV or AIDS |
| **Non-verbal communication** | The messages that are given through body language and facial expression |
| **Normative development** | The expected rate of development, according to averages |
| **Objectivity** | Without bias |
| **Observation skills** | The ability to carry out appropriate methods of observation, knowing when to use them and how |
| **Open adoption** | Adoption where there is an element of contact remaining between the child and their birth mother/family |
| **Open questions** | Questions which encourage a detailed answer |
| **Operant conditioning** | A theory about positive reinforcement of behaviour, often associated with B.F. Skinner |
| **Paedophile** | An individual who is sexually interested in children. The term is commonly used to describe anyone who sexually molests children |
| **Paramountcy principle** | A main principle of the Children Act 1989 where the welfare of the child must be the paramount consideration. |
| **Paraphrasing** | To restate what you have heard; used to clarify understanding |
| **Parents' expectations** | What parents expect (of an early years setting) when they leave their child in their care |
| **Perception** | Gaining insight or awareness |
| **Personal safety** | Being responsible for own safe working practice |
| **Phenotype** | The visible arrangement of characteristics inherited by an individual from their parents |
| **Physical environment** | The surroundings (building, room layout, lighting, ventilation, and so on) |
| **Physical resources** | The range of equipment available |
| **Pictograph** | A method of presenting data using a pictorial or symbolic form. It has similar uses to a bar chart |

| | |
|---|---|
| **Pie chart** | A method of presenting data using a circular chart, which resembles a pie. The 'pie' can be 'sliced' into portions to represent quantities or categories |
| **Plan, do and review** | A process of planning and evaluation associated with the Highscope programme of learning |
| **Placement log** | An on-going record charting students' experience in a range of placements |
| **Play therapy** | The use of play to help alleviate some of the effects of abuse or other traumas experienced in childhood |
| **Police protection** | Legal protection of a child from harm |
| **Positive images** | Illustrations or descriptions that positively portray all the individuals included within it |
| **Positive reinforcement** | Rewarding good (behaviour), rather than responding to undesirable (behaviour) in children |
| **Potential hazard** | Any situation which has the potential to cause harm. |
| **Predisposing factors** | Any known information that could indicate a specific outcome |
| **Prejudice** | An opinion formed in advance, a pre-judgement |
| **Preparing children for hospital** | Considering children's physical, emotional and cognitve needs prior to planned hospitalisation |
| **Primary health care** | The care of health within the community, includes doctors, nurses, dentists, opticians and so on |
| **Primary research** | Research you have carried out yourself |
| **Primary socialisation** | The impact of immediate family and social groups on a child |
| **Principles of diet and nutrition** | The basis of healthy eating |
| **Professional** | A person who is qualified, competent and experienced at what they do |
| **Pro-social** | An innate predisposition to relate to other people |
| **Proximal** | Close to the central point (of the body) |
| **Psychological model** | An approach taken (specifically) from a psychological perspective |
| **Pyrexia** | A high temperature, fever |
| **Quality assurance** | A set standard, achieved when specified criteria have been met |
| **Qualitative research** | Research which obtains the viewpoints and personal feelings of individual participants |
| **Quantitative research** | Research which produces results that can be expressed numerically, using charts, tables and so on |
| **Racism** | The belief that some races have cultural characteristics that make them superior (or inferior) to others |
| **Range** | In research, the difference between the lowest and highest result found in numerical data |

| | |
|---|---|
| **Raw data** | The information gathered during the research process before it has been collated, for example, information taken from questionnaires |
| **Recovery Order** | A legal order enabling the police to take into their possession a child who is the subject of police protection or an Emergency Protection Order, if they are missing, have run away, or been abducted from the person responsible for their care |
| **Recovery position** | The position individuals are placed in following an accident or sudden illness, after their situation has been stabilised, whilst they await further medical treatment (for example, following an accident), or rest (for example, following an epileptic fit) |
| **Referral procedures** | The process of reporting concerns about a child's safety |
| **Reflective listening** | Where the listener echos the last (or most significant) words spoken by the speaker |
| **Reflexes** | An involuntary response to a stimulus, for example blinking |
| **Reliability** | In research terms the use of an appropriate research method for the subject being studied which ensures validity to the outcomes |
| **Replication** | Being able to repeat something and get the same outcomes. In research, replication will ensure reliability |
| **RIDDOR** | Reporting of Injuries, Diseases and Dangerous Occurrences Regulations (1995) |
| **Rights** | Our entitlements as individuals |
| **Role of health educators** | To raise awareness of health issues relevant to the target audience |
| **Routines** | A set procedure that should meet the needs of all concerned |
| **Safety marks** | National standards regarding safety, printed on the packaging of objects, to guide consumers as to their suitability for the intended use or recipient, for example, on toys, baby equipment, electrical appliances |
| **Scaffolding** | A term usually associated with Jerome Bruner in which the adult supports and extends a child's learning |
| **Schema** | A body of understanding and interest which is continuously built on, developing further schemas |
| **Screening** | The process of examining a whole population to identify who is showing signs of a disease, or may be predisposed to develop it |
| **Secondary health care** | Involves early intervention of health issues, often linked to the outcomes of screening |
| **Secondary research** | Use of material from research which has not been directly carried out by yourself |
| **Secondary socialisation** | The impact of social contacts on a child, outside their immediate family and social group. This would include teachers, early years professionals, and so on |
| **Self-awareness** | Being able to understand how you are perceived by others, and the impact you have on other individuals |
| **Self-concept** | An understanding of our own identity as seen by others |

| | |
|---|---|
| **Self-protection strategies** | Ways in which to keep ourselves safe and to be able to reject involvement in situations or unwanted advances |
| **Sequential** | Occurring in a sequence |
| **Setting boundaries** | Stating acceptable limitations |
| **Short-term effects of abuse** | Effects that take place immediately, for example physical pain, injuries or infection |
| **Signed language** | Communication without the necessity of speech |
| **Skin care** | Appropriate care of different types of skin |
| **Social and economic factors affecting health** | Health problems linked to issues such as poverty |
| **Social constructivist theory** | Learning by exploring a range of experiences and objects from everyday life |
| **Social learning theory** | Learning by observing and copying others. A theory often associated with Albert Bandura and the Bobo dolls |
| **Social model** | An approach taken (specifically) from the perspective of society |
| **Solitary play** | Playing alone, a normal stage of development in young children |
| **Spontaneous play** | Play that is unplanned, undirected and allows freedom |
| **Stages of play** | The changes in how children's play develops, usually linked to age |
| **Standard Attainment Tasks (SATs)** | Tests carried out at regular intervals during formal schooling |
| **Standard deviation** | A curved illustration of all the numerical 'scores' gathered from research data, as taken from a specific point |
| **Steiner philosophy** | A specific learning process with its own ethos |
| **Stereotyping** | Categorising, taking away individuality |
| **Sterilising techniques** | Methods of ensuring that utensils (bottles, teats and so on) used for babies are free from bacteria |
| **Stimulate** | To arouse curiosity, interest and development |
| **Stimulating play** | Activities or objects which stimulate |
| **Structured play** | Play which is predetermined or has specific constraints |
| **Subjectivity** | Open to the influence of bias |
| **Submissive** | Avoiding conflict or confrontation |
| **Supervision Order** | A legal order in which a child is under the supervision of the local authority, but where the authority does not have parental responsibility |
| **Suppressed immunity** | Where the immune system is impaired in some way, leaving an individual susceptable to infection |

| | |
|---|---|
| **Symbolic play** | The use of objects to represent other objects in play |
| **Symbolic thinking** | Being able to use representation in thought |
| **Table** | The most basic method of presenting numerical or written information |
| **Teamwork** | Working co-operatively with a group of colleagues |
| **Tertiary health care** | On-going care of chronic conditions, often by specialist community-based health professionals |
| **Theories** | Ideas, philosophies |
| **Therapeutic play** | Play which is provided in order to alleviate, restore or heal |
| **Topping and tailing** | The washing of the facial area of a baby, together with a nappy change |
| **Tokenism** | Making only a small effort, or providing no more than the minimum, in order to comply with criteria or guidelines |
| **Transmission model** | An approach in which the adult controls the learning process, often suppressing the child's own initiative |
| **Treasure basket** | A small basket of natural objects ideal for babies from about six months of age to enable exploration of a range of natural materials, smells and shapes |
| **Turn-taking** | Responses made by young babies to adults when they make 'conversation' with them. This can be an expression, a movement, a smile or a sound |
| **UN Convention on the Rights of the Child** | This international constitution was adopted by the United Nations Assembly in 1989 to uphold agreed rights for children whenever possible |
| **Underpin** | To support and strengthen (knowledge and understanding) |
| **Validity** | In research terms validity is described as something that gives a true representation of what was being researched |
| **Visual stimulation** | Stimulation through sight |
| **Vocational** | Learning through practical experience as well as theory |
| **Weaning** | The introduction of solid food to young babies |
| **WHO** | World Health Organisation |
| **Zone of proximal development (ZPD)** | A theory in which the child is lifted to a level of achievement they would be unlikely to reach without additional support from the adult. The theory was initiated by Lev Vygotsky |

# Index